SECURITIES MARKETS
AND CORPORATE GOVERNANCE

To the memory of my father, Wei Zhanyang

Securities Markets and Corporate Governance

A Chinese Experience

YUWA WEI
Soochow University, China

Routledge
Taylor & Francis Group

LONDON AND NEW YORK

First published 2009 by Ashgate Publishing

2 Park Square, Milton Park, Abingdon, Oxfordshire OX14 4RN
52 Vanderbilt Avenue, New York, NY 10017

Routledge is an imprint of the Taylor & Francis Group, an informa business

First issued in paperback 2020

British Library Cataloguing in Publication Data
Wei, Yuwa.
  Securities markets and corporate governance : a Chinese
  experience.
  1. Securities--China. 2. Corporate governance--China.
  3. Investments, Foreign--China.
  I. Title
  332.6'42'51-dc22

Library of Congress Cataloging-in-Publication Data
Wei, Yuwa.
  Securities markets and corporate governance : a Chinese experience / by Yuwa Wei.
    p. cm.
  Includes bibliographical references and index.
  ISBN 978-0-7546-7177-0 (hardback) -- ISBN 978-0-7546-9130-3(ebook)
  1. Securities--China. 2. Corporate governance--Law and legislation--China. I. Title.

  KNQ962.W45 2009
  346.51'0922--dc22

                                                                  2009022606

ISBN 13: 978-0-7546-7177-0 (hbk)
ISBN 13: 978-0-367-60299-4 (pbk)

Contents

**PART IV   CHINA'S CAPITAL MARKET IN AN ERA OF
GLOBALIZATION**

List of Cases

Preface

In 2003, I published the book *Comparative Corporate Governance: A Chinese Perspective* (Kluwer Law International), which, from a comparative perspective, discussed the development of corporate governance in China in the historical, cultural, legal and economic contexts. The focus of the book was on the internal corporate governance in China's corporate system, emphasis on the external mechanism of corporate governance was however limited. Since then, I have longed to tell readers the other half of the story, that is, the development of the securities market in China – governing through the capital market. By publishing this work, I am now very pleased to say that I have done it. I am grateful to Ashgate Publishing Limited and publisher Alison Kirk for offering me an opportunity to achieve this goal.

This book focuses on the role of the securities market in corporate governance. It reveals the monitoring function of the securities market over companies and how China has exerted this function. The discussions proceed from a comparative perspective and in the context of China's history, politics, and economic reforms. In doing so, I hope that I have provided to readers the panorama of the law and practice concerning corporate governance in China.

I wish to thank Mr Wang Shuai, Mr Peng Qingyi, and Mr Huang Wei for supporting my empirical research in China.

I dedicate this book to my husband Kewu Li, my son Kuo Li, my mother and my sisters for their unfailing support.

Professor Yuwa Wei
Suzhou, China, 2009

Acknowledgements

I wish to acknowledge the following organizations and journals:

Currents: International Trade Law Journal for permitting me to include the contents of my article "Speculation and Regulation: A Story of China's Securities Market" (Volume xvi) in the book;

Macquarie Journal of Business Law for permitting me to include the contents of my article "China's Capital Market and Corporate Governance: The Promotion of the External Governance Mechanism" (Volume 4) in the book;

Suffolk Transnational Law Review for permitting me to include the contents of my article "Volatility of China's Securities Market and Corporate Governance" (Volume 29, No. 2) in the book;

Loyola of Los Angeles International and Comparative Law Review for permitting me to include the contents of article "Development of the Securities Market and Regulation in China" (Volume 27, No. 3) in the book;

International Company and Commercial Law Review (Sweet & Maxwell) for permitting me to include the contents of my article "Maximising the External Governance Function of the Securities Market: A Chinese Experience" in (Volume 3, 2008) in the book; and

Socio-Legal Research Centre, Griffith University, Australia: for the financial support to the research project "Securities Market and its Regulation in China: New Investment Opportunities for Australian Investors". The research outcomes are included in the book.

Introduction

Companies are fundamental cells of modern commercial society. Although people generally regard the rise and fall of companies as part of the natural circle of corporate development, the collapse of large corporations and the consequentially profound social and economic impact have caused great concern in the community, particularly when corporate failure has resulted from mismanagement. For this reason, issues of corporate governance have attracted enormous attention since the 1980s.

Securities markets and takeover activities are important mechanisms of corporate governance.[1] The law and economics tradition recognizes that the hostile takeover performs a desirable disciplinary function by placing management under the market's judgment.[2] According to the law and economics literature, the pressure of takeovers and the advantages of being listed on a stock exchange are effective stimuli of promoting good corporate governance. Furthermore, by having a wide and varied scope of owners, listed companies generally tend to improve on their management standards and efficiency in order to satisfy the demands of their shareholders.

In the past two decades, interesting developments have occurred in this area, particularly in some emerging economies such as China. In China, the securities market and its regulation play essential roles in encouraging and advocating sound corporate governance practices.[3] It is widely recognized for a while that the securities market is not only a place where companies raise funds, but also a means of assisting China's enterprise reforms and promoting good corporate governance.[4]

---

1   *See* Yuwa Wei, *Maximising the External Governance Function of the Securities Market: A Chinese Experience*, 3 International Company and Commercial Law Review 111 (Sweet & Maxwell, 2008).

2   *See* Frank H. Easterbrook and Daniel R. Fischel, *The Proper Role of a Target's Management in Responding to a Tender Offer*, 94 Harvard Law Review 1161 (1981); Frank H. Easterbrook and Daniel R. Fischel, *Corporate Control Transactions*, 91 Yale Law Journal 698 (1982); Daniel R. Fischel, *Efficient Capital Market Theory, the Market for Corporate Control, and the Regulation of Cash Tender Offers*, 57 Texas Law Review 1 (1978); and John C. Coffee, Jr, *Regulating the Market For Corporate Control: A Critical Assessment of the Tender Offer's Role in Corporate Governance*, 84 Columbia Law Review 1148 (1984).

3   *See generally* Daniel M. Anderson, *Taking Stock in China: Company Disclosure and Information in China's Stock Markets*, 88 Georgetown Law Journal 1919 (June 2000).

4   *See* Yuwa Wei, *The Development of the Securities Market and Regulation in China*, 27.3 Loyola of Los Angeles International and Comparative Law Review 480 (2005).

However, structural defects, corporate misconduct, and legal violations in the securities business, have undermined the efforts to reform China's financial sector and enterprise system.[5] These problems have not only jeopardized the efforts to promote good corporate governance in state-owned listed enterprises, but also encumbered the development of the securities market.

The Chinese experience has once again proven that a well-functioning securities market and a sound system of corporate governance are mutually dependent: The development of the securities market provides an external monitoring mechanism of corporate governance, and good practice of corporate governance, in turn, ensures the orderly operation of the securities market.[6]

This book examines the functions of the securities market and the rationalities behind takeover activities. It analyzes the relationship between securities regulation and corporate governance, and investigates the Chinese experience in fully exploiting the monitoring function of the capital market over listed companies. The legal regimes governing securities markets and takeovers in some leading corporate economies including the US, Germany, Japan and the UK will also be examined. In doing so, this book demonstrates that in a world of commercialization and globalization, securities markets and speculative activities have played an increasingly important role in disciplining listed companies. The examination and analyses are to be developed in four parts as set out below:

Part I provides an overview of the historical development of the securities market and a review of literature on the economic functions of securities markets. It investigates the role of human and social cognitive and emotional biases in economic decision-making and how they affect market prices and resources allocation. In doing so, it explains the function of speculation in the financial market, its economic benefit, and its undesirable effects on the market. Part I will ultimately establish that there is a need for regulatory intervention in order to restrain the undesirable consequences of speculative behavior.

Part II seeks to measure the potential disciplinary capacity of capital markets as an instrument of corporate accountability. It attempts to ascertain a balanced approach that recognizes the social utility of the securities market for corporate control on the one hand, and appreciates the possibility of market failure and the need for limited regulatory intervention on the other.

Part III focuses on the Chinese experience of utilizing the securities market as an effective mechanism of corporate control. The Chinese government anticipates that the securities market will play an important role in promoting good corporate governance in China's listed companies. However, there is a danger that China's endeavors to reform its financial sector and enterprise system may be thwarted by the problems inherent in its corporate system. The Chinese experience suggests

---

5   *See* Yuwa Wei, *Volatility of China's Securities Market and Corporate Governance*, 29.2 Suffolk Transnational Law Review 236 (2006).

6   *See* Wei, *supra* note 1, at 111.

that there is a close relationship between the maturity of a country's capital market and the perfection of its legal system.

Part IV analyzes the future development of China's financial market in the current environment of economic globalization. It discusses China's current and future financial sector reforms, and the development of the capital market and corporate governance in post-WTO entry China.

Any discussion on China's securities market without taking the factors of globalization into account will be incomplete. The economic climate of the world has been undergoing changes, with the forward moving force of economic globalization steered by international organizations such as the WTO and economic powers. In this new environment, China faces a series of economic and political challenges. Although it is expected that economic globalization will bring China more business opportunities and widen the country's access to advanced technologies and much needed investment capital, the path towards success is overgrown with brambles. Before enjoying the fruits of globalization, China has to deal with a number of issues concerning environmental deterioration, financial stability and economic safety. At the economic aspect, China's capital market is on the front line. An orderly and effective capital market is essential in assisting China to undertake its financial reforms and ensuring its economic success. How successful the Chinese will be in tackling the problems on the capital market in the context of globalization is a touchstone testing China's capacity to survive and strive in an era of globalization.

After decades of economic growth, the weight of China's economy in the world economy has increased dramatically. Nowadays, China has become one of the top attractions for international investments. By 2006, capital brought into China's capital market by qualified foreign institutional investors (QFIIs) reached nearly US$60 billion. Today, China's industries can no longer satisfy the appetite of foreign investment. More and more international investors are targeting China's financial market. The inflow of international hot money, the removal of trade barriers under the WTO rules, the fever of investing in China, and revaluation of Chinese currency have all been contributing factors responsible for the frequent turbulences on China's capital market since 2006. Combating irregularities on the securities market in order to enhance China's ability to resist financial depression and crises has been a priority of the Chinese government.

Part IV of this book provides a detailed account of China's experiences and efforts in developing a capital market while coping with the challenges of globalization. In the meantime, it looks into the future development of China's capital market in a globalized world.

A Review of the Securities Market

The securities market is part of the financial market which comprises the securities market and other markets for various financial instruments including commodity markets, money markets, derivatives markets, future markets and foreign exchange markets.[7] Most of the above markets and their transactions are concentrated in a few financial centers called stock exchanges.[8] The securities market includes both the stock market and the bond market. It is the place where shares, debentures and bonds are traded.[9] It is also referred to as the capital market. On some occasions, people used the terms "securities market" and "stock market" interchangeably, owing to the important function of the securities market in providing long-term finance to companies.[10] The modern development of the securities market can be better understood if the evolution of the stock market is known.

The stock market evolved from ancient merchants or bankers associations trading with debts and government securities in Europe.[11] It assumed its modern form around the seventeenth century, when shares were invented and sold to the public by Dutch, French and English joint stock companies.[12] Share trading in London gained extraordinary momentum by the eighteenth century due to the flourish of joint stock companies expanding aggressively in overseas and domestic trading.[13] Shares were sold at the Royal Exchange, as well as in taverns and coffeehouses between Cornhill and Threadneedle Street in London.[14] It was at this time that specialized brokers and jobbers emerged.[15] Public investment in company shares soon turned into a speculative mania resulting in the incredible inflation of share prices in the stock market. Eventually, the market crashed spectacularly, following the burst of the South Sea Bubble.[16] It was not until 1844, when the

---

7   *See* the Editor, Wikipedia, available at <http://en.wikipedia.org/wiki/Financial_markets#Definition>.

8   *See* Kenneth Midgley and Ronald Burns, The Capital Market: Its Nature and Significance 1 (London: The Machillian Press Ltd, 1977).

9   *See* the Editor, Wikipedia, available at <http://en.wikipedia.org/wiki/Securities_market>.

10   *See* Zhijun Li, Government Regulation of the Securities Market 11 (Changchun: Jilin People's Press, 2005).

11   *See* the Editor, Wikipedia, available at <http://en.wikipedia.org/wiki/Stock_market#History>.

12   *See* K.G. Davies, *Joint-Stock Investment in the Later Seventeenth Century*, 4 The Economic History Review 288, 291–2 (1951–52). *See* also Josette Peyrard, La Bourse 1 (Paris: Librairie Vuibert, 1998).

13   *See* Alan Jenkins, The Stock Exchange Story (London: Heinemann, 1973) 11.

14   *See* E. Victor Morgan and W.A. Thomas, The Stock Exchange: Its History and Functions 20, 36–7 (London: Elek Books Limited, 1969).

15   *Ibid*, at 14–17.

16   In 1711 the South Sea Company was established. The new company offered to buy the government's war debts, in return for a monopoly on English trade with the Spanish colonies of South America. Thus, the outstanding short-term war debts, not funded by a specific tax, were converted into equity of the proposed joint-stock company. The company's share price inflated from 120 to 950 before its collapse in 1720. *See* Morgan and Thomas, *supra* note 13, at 29–40.

Limited Liability Act was passed by Parliament, that the UK securities market was able to recover from the South Sea crisis.[17]

Since then, the securities business in the UK grew steadfastly. Industrial expansion encouraged the continued formation of joint stock companies and the further development of the stock market. In the years following the industrial expansion, the London Stock Exchange evolved into the largest stock exchange in the world, lasting until the end of World War II.[18]

The history of stock markets in the US dates back to 1792 on Wall Street, New York.[19] In 1817, the New York Stock Exchange (NYSE) was formally established.[20] The NYSE only admitted large and well established companies, whilst smaller companies had to trade outside it. This fueled the formal establishment of the American Stock Exchange (AMEX).[21] The US capital market developed rapidly by the mid-1800s due to the fast growth of industrial firms, which required large amounts of capital input.[22] Because European economic powers went up in smoke during World War II, the US replaced the UK in becoming the leading economy in the world.[23] The NYSE has also replaced the London Stock Exchange and become the largest stock exchange in the world.

The history of the stock market shows that shares facilitate the expansion of companies, and also demonstrates the fact that the stock market is one of the most important devices by which companies can raise capital. It is therefore necessary to regulate the stock market to ensure its prosperity and efficiency.

The securities market is also known as the speculators' market, and speculation often causes the market to behave irrationally.[24] Investors in the secondary market mainly trade with the goal of making short-term profits by reselling shares to others. The prices of shares are exposed to subjective speculation of investors and the market can therefore becomes volatile.[25] Individual investors' speculation can result in waves of manias and panics in the market. The common scenario is that

---

17 *See* R.J, Briston, The Stock Exchange and Investment Analysis 23–4 (London: George Allen & Unwin Ltd, 1973).

18 *See* Baisan Xie, Xuelai Dai and Lan Xu, *A Comparative Study of US and Chinese Securities Markets*, in Baisan Xie (*ed.*), International Comparison of Securities Markets 6 (Volume 1, Beijing: Qinghua University Press, 2003).

19 *See* the Editor, *The History of the Stock Market*, The New Enlightenment, available at <http://www.hermes-press.com/wshist1.htm>. *See* also LI, *supra* note 10, at 21.

20 *Ibid.*

21 The market started at the curbstone on Broad Street near Exchange Place and was moved indoors in 1921. *See* the Editor, Wikipedia, available at <http://en.wikipedia.org/wiki/American_Stock_Exchange>.

22 *See* the Editor, Wikipedia, at <http://www.stockmarketinvestinginfo.com/smi_history.html>.

23 *See* the Editor, Encyclopaedia of American History, available at <http://www.answers.com/topic/market-1>.

24 *See*, *supra* note 18, at 8–11.

25 *Ibid.*

share prices are pushed unreasonably high before plummeting. This is evidenced by the South Sea Bubble event in the London stock market and the disastrous market crashes that occurred on the NYSE in 1929 and 1987. The securities market crash in 1929 instigated a long term economic depression in the US, which haunted the country until World War II. The market crash in 1987, though less disastrous compared with the 1929 crash, once again depressed the country's economy.

Facts and empirical studies suggest that irrational volatilities in the securities market do not necessarily have a definite cause, and sometimes are primarily related to investors' psychology.[26] Classical economics investigated the relationship between economics and psychology. Regrettably, psychology faded away in the mainstream neoclassical economics by the 1920s.[27] The dominant view of the neoclassical economics is that individuals/investors in the market are rational agents acting according to rational principles. Although they are subject to errors and inconsistencies, they generally make rational decisions and choices, since an individual who systematically makes mistakes would eventually be ousted from the market.[28] It was not until the 1970s that the concepts of Behavioral Finance and behavioral economics were revisited by some economists.[29] Behavioral Finance and behavioral economics are two related scientific fields studying the role of human cognitive and emotional biases in economic decision-making and how they affect market prices, returns and the allocation of resources.[30] The aim of these two scientific fields is to combine psychological and neoclassical economic theories to explain economic choices where there is uncertainty.[31]

Behavioral finance/economics does provide explanations for volatilities such as bubbles and crashes in the securities market when the orthodox doctrines including the rational choice model and the efficient market hypothesis in neo-classical economic theory do not satisfactorily rationalize the market behavior. Behavioral finance/economics acknowledges that individual biases do not impact

---

26   *See generally* David Cohen, Fear, Greed and Panic: The Psychology of the Stock Market (New York: John Wiley & Sons, 2001).

27   *See* the Editor, Wikipedia, available at <http://en.wikipedia.org/wiki/Behavioral_ Finance>.

28   *See* Robin M. Hogarth and Melvin W. Reder (*eds*), Rational Choice: The Contrast Between Economics and Psychology 6 (Chicago: The University of Chicago Press, 1987).

29   *See* representative works including Daniel Kahneman and Amos Tversky, *Prospect Theory: An Analysis of Decision under Risk*, XLVII Econometrica 263–91 (1979); Andrei Shleifer, Inefficient Markets: An Introduction to Behavioral Finance (New York: Oxford University Press, 1999); Matthew Rabin, *Psychology and Economics*, Journal of Economic Literature, or 36(1) American Economic Association 11–46 (1998); Hersh Shefrin, Beyond Greed and Fear: Understanding Behavioral Finance and the Psychology of Investing (New York: Oxford University Press, 2002); and Colin F. Camerer, George Loewenstein and Matthew Rabin (*eds*), Advances in Behavioral Economics (Princeton: Princeton University Press, 2003).

30   *See supra* note 27.

31   *Ibid.*

the securities market.[32] It is only when individual biases evolve into social or cognitive biases that the market may be affected.[33] Notions such as herd behavior, group thinking, and mass panic are all used to illustrate this point of view.

The highly speculative nature of the securities market makes it vulnerable to manipulative conduct, which under certain conditions will result in social psychological phenomenon such as herd behavior or mass panics, which may upset the market order. It is therefore important to bring speculation under control. In most jurisdictions, regulation is regarded as an efficient mechanism for controlling the manipulative behavior in the securities market.[34]

Furthermore, the functions of the securities market and its significant role in the economy, particularly in developed markets, also justify regulation of the market in a pervasive fashion.[35] The securities market primarily has the following functions: (1) raising capital for companies; (2) mobilizing savings for investment, facilitating company growth, and redistributing wealth; (3) creating investment opportunities for investors; (4) raising capital for governments to develop projects; and (5) through corporate control, allowing managerial failure to be corrected through its markets.[36] Because of the above utilities, no government can overlook the inefficiency of the securities market, and the securities market is usually closely monitored.

Securities Markets and Corporate Governance

The securities market has been viewed as a mechanism of corporate governance. The law and economics literature acknowledges the contribution of securities markets in promoting good corporate governance. The main argument of the law and economics tradition is that stock exchanges facilitate takeovers and dispersed ownership, and produce listing rules for listed companies. These functions of

---

32 *Ibid.*

33 *Ibid.*

34 *See* Li, *supra* note 10, at 21–49. *See* also Shujiang Xie, China's Capital Market: An Analysis Based on the Theory of Competition 43 (Beijing: China Finance and Economy Press, 2004).

35 When the NYSE sneezes, the whole of America feels sick. *See* Thomas Lee Hazen, The Law of Securities Regulation 8 (St. Paul, Minnesota: West Group, 1996). *See* also John Coffee and Joel Seligman, Securities Regulation: Cases and Materials 2–7 (New York: Foundation Press, 2003).

36 *See* Colin Mayer, *Stock-markets, Financial Institutions, and Corporate Performance*, in Nicholas Dimsdale and Martha Prevezer (*eds*), Capital Markets and Corporate Governance 179 (Oxford: Clarendon Press, 1994) and Paul Marsh, *Market Assessment of Company Performance*, in Nicholas Dimsdale and Martha Prevezer (*eds*), Capital Markets and Corporate Governance 66, 67 (Oxford: Clarendon Press, 1994).

the securities market provoke listed companies to improve on their management standards and efficiency.[37]

According to the literature, hostile takeovers perform a unique disciplinary function by placing management under the market's scrutiny.[38] This is because the managerial efficiency of a listed company is closely reflected in the share price of the company.[39] The shares of a poorly managed company are unattractive to investors. Investors may be willing to invest in the company if the company is willing to reduce investors' investment risks by selling its shares at a discount price. In doing so, the company becomes vulnerable to takeover predators. If the company is taken over by a bidder, the bidder usually dismisses the current board and appoints new directors. Takeovers thus pose a threat to the management of a listed company. To avoid becoming a takeover target, one of the predominant aims of management is to improve the managerial efficiency and the economic performance of their companies.[40]

As mentioned above, when a company's shareholdings become dispersed, the chances of the company being taken over increase. This is because small and dispersed shareholders are more likely to sell their shares in the stock market.[41] The securities market makes public investment possible and therefore facilitates scattered shareholdings. This further enhances the threat of takeovers.

Nevertheless, some reports have found that takeovers, as a mechanism of accountability, are imperfect.[42] Some point out that takeovers do not always push corporations to improve management.[43] It could encourage corporate managers to focus on short-term performance, because managers may make business decisions just to frustrate potential takeovers.[44] For example, company managers may try to make themselves indispensable, and therefore, costly to replace.[45] In addition, studies have shown that the shareholders of the bidder company may be worse off after the takeover.[46]

---

37   *See* Wei, *supra* note 4, at 485.
38   *See* Coffee, *supra* note 2.
39   *See* Wei, *supra* note 4, at 483.
40   *See* Daniel R. Fischel, *Efficient Capital Market Theory, the Market for Corporate Control, and the Regulation of Cash Tender Offers*, 57 Texas Law Review 1 and 9 (1980).
41   *Ibid.*
42   *See* Thomas Lee Hazen, *The Short-Term/Long-Term Dichotomy and Investment Theory: Implications for Securities Market Regulation and for Corporate Law*, 70 North Carolina Law Review 182–3 (1991).
43   *Ibid.*
44   *See* Pauline O'Sullivan, *Governance by Exit: An Analysis of the Market for Corporate Control*, in Kevin Keasey, Steve Thompson and Mike Wright (*eds*), Corporate Governance: Economic and Financial Issues 125 (London: Oxford University Press, 1997).
45   *Ibid.*
46   *See* Hazen, *supra* note 42, at 191.

Given that the threat of takeover does not always effectively influence the management of some listed companies, share prices can still act as motivation for management to work towards greater efficiency. It is especially relevant for managers that are only motivated to work for security and personal gain. This is because such goals are likely to be best achieved by expanding their businesses into bigger organizations and therefore creating themselves better paid positions.[47] Business expansion requires finance. Poorly performing companies are likely to have difficulties in attracting investors, and thus fail to raise sufficient funds. Hence, it may be costly for managers to ignore investors' interest and the reputation of their company on the securities market.

Research also shows that price movements often provide incentives or penalties on a personal basis for managers who have shareholdings in their companies.[48] When directors hold significant shares in their companies, they have a personal incentive to improve the economic performance of their companies. This is because the poor performance of a company will result in a downgrade of its share price and eventually cause personal losses to the directors, whereas advancement of the company's share price brings personal gain to the directors.

In addition, a company's share price can have some secondary disciplinary influence over the management. Since depressed share prices indicate ineffective and incompetent management, those managers who do mind their image and reputation in the industry and the labor market will be motivated to promote economic efficiency within their companies.[49]

Apart from consciousness of share price movements, listed companies are subject to the scrutiny of the stock exchanges. Stock exchanges produce their own rules regulating the participants and transactions. These rules are known as listing rules. Listing rules provide conditions for companies to be admitted to the stock exchanges and regulate the conduct of listed companies.[50] To be admitted into a stock exchange, a company must meet the listing requirements of the specific stock exchange and comply with the rules of conduct. Non-compliance with the rules of conduct may result in the company being de-listed. Stock exchanges either incorporate codes of corporate governance in their listing rules or publish codes of corporate governance as a separate regulatory document.[51] Consequently, higher standards of corporate governance apply to listed companies.

47　*See generally* Robin Marris, The Economic Theory of "Managerial Capitalism' (London: Macmillan, 1964).

48　*See* Midgley and Burns, *supra* note 8, at 16.

49　*Ibid*, at 18.

50　*See* Jinqing Zhu, Securities Law 54 (Beijing: Peking University Press, 2007).

51　For example, the UK Combined Code contains Code of Best Corporate Governance Practice, while China Securities Regulatory Committee (CSRC) and the State Economic and Trade Commission (SETC) jointly published "Code of Corporate Governance for Listed Companies in China" in 2001.

    In a market where there is a lack of transparency, business order and effective regulation, share prices are usually distorted and thus do not truly reflect their companies' managerial and economic efficiency.[52] In such a market, market misconduct may have little consequence. Poorly performed companies are likely to conceal their economic failure by misleading or manipulating investors. In such an environment, the market is somewhat handicapped in identifying well managed companies from poorly managed companies. Thus, the function of takeovers as a corporate control mechanism is substantially lessened. Furthermore, since directors can avoid personal penalties for market misconduct, the incentives for directors holding shares in their companies to promote the companies' economic performance diminish. For example, the directors can pass the losses caused by low share prices onto other investors through inside trading.

    When a person trades securities based on the information intended to be available only for a corporate purpose and not for anyone's personal benefit, the person engages in insider trading.[53] Directors and managers of companies have access to the companies' price sensitive information unavailable to the public. In a market where insider trading is not effectively controlled, directors and managers are likely to abuse their positions and trade their shares based on inside information. Sometimes, managers may engage in insider trading in combination with other forms of market misconduct. For example, the directors of an unsuccessful company may disclose misleading information and create false trading impressions on the market, and then sell their own shareholdings before the market receives the correct information.[54]

    The above discussions further demonstrate the need for regulating the securities market. An inadequately regulated securities market cannot function effectively. In a well functioning securities market, there is adequate disclosure to facilitate informed judgments and participants are thus able to act with integrity.[55]

The Chinese Experience

In China, the securities market and its regulation have developed in tandem with its economic reforms.[56] They have been a means of achieving the goals of the country's economic reforms.[57] This is evidenced by the increasing attention paid to the development and regulation of the securities market by the Chinese government

---

    52   *See* Li, *supra* note 10, at 75–97.
    53   *See* Coffee and Seligman, *supra* note 35, at 1071.
    54   The situations happen in notorious cases including Hainan Minyuan case, Yinguangxia case, and Beihai Yinhe case.
    55   *See* Commonwealth of Australia, *Financial System Inquiry Final Report* 16 (1997).
    56   *See* Wei, *supra* note 4, at 1.
    57   *Ibid.*

in the past decade. However, at the beginning of China's economic reforms, the development of the securities market was not a significant concern.

Before the economic reforms, China adopted a planned economy. Under the planned economy, enterprises were wholly state-owned and operated according to state plans. This meant that the state supplied resources and labor for production and was entitled to all the final products. Since there was no connection between production and profitability, the state-owned enterprises had little incentives to promote economic efficiency and technological innovation.[58]

At the initial stage of China's economic reforms, the key concern was the modernization of China's enterprise system by introducing competition and modern managerial mechanisms into the state-owned enterprises. In contrast to Russia's reform strategy, China took a more cautious approach.[59] Reforming a planned economy into a market economy was an unprecedented project. There was no existing reform model to follow.[60] The goal of the economic reforms was to create a market economy. However, no one could be sure of the best method for achieving that goal. This made the reform an arduous task. The Chinese therefore decided to adopt the approach of trial and error, partial reforms and reinforcing reforms.[61] Western economists describe the Chinese reform style as "gradualism". The Chinese themselves described their reform strategy as "crossing the river by feeling stones under feet and stepping on the stones".

In the beginning, the Chinese attempted to introduce incentives and competition into the enterprise system without corporatizing and privatizing the enterprises.[62] However, the strategies used brought new problems, and had only limited success.[63] In the end, corporatization became the only solution for modernizing the organizational structure of China's enterprises and an important step in improving

---

58 *See* Shenshi Mei, Research on the Structure of Modern Corporate Organs' Power: A Legal Analysis of Corporate Governance 3 (Beijing: Publishing House of China University of Political Science and Law, 1996).

59 Peter Nolan and Robert F. Ash in their research into the Chinese reforms concluded that China's success stems primarily from its refusal to implement "transition orthodoxy" (shock therapy) which Russia has whole heartedly embraced. *See* Peter Nolan and Robert F. Ash, *China's Economy on the Eve of Reform*, in Andrew G Walder (*ed.*) China's Transitional Economy, 35 (New York: Oxford University Press, 1996).

60 *See* Wei, *supra* note 1, at 112.

61 *See* Yuwa Wei, Investing in China: Law and Practices of Joint Ventures 8 (Sydney: Federation Press, 2000).

62 *See* Wen Liang, *Some Legal Problems of Reforming the State Owned Enterprises into Limited Companies*, in Hua Chen and Jingwei Jiu (*eds*), Research on the State Owned Enterprise Reform and Corporate Law 29–30 (Xiamen: Publishing House of Xiamen University, 1997).

63 *See* Comments by Guangyuan Li, in Wenmin Zhang et al. (*eds*), The Great Economic Debate in China 14–15 (Beijing: Economic Management Press: 1997). *See* also Nicholas R Lardy, China's Unfinished Economic Revolution 22–3 (Washington D.C.: Brookings Institution Press, 1998).

the economic efficiency of the enterprises.[64] However, the Chinese government made it clear that corporatization should not challenge the dominance of public ownership.[65] Consequently, most state-owned enterprises were converted into state-owned companies. Corporatization commenced in the early 1980s and was mostly completed by the end of the 1990s.[66]

The newly corporatized enterprises were troubled with new problems. The problem that was most difficult to overcome was insider control. Insider control problems existed in state-owned or dominated companies where the state was the sole or dominant shareholder. In such companies, the state as a shareholder did not have a physical appearance and must rely on agents.[67] Furthermore, the state lacked information about managerial efficiency and corporate performance. Consequently, managers of the companies seized the control of the companies. In such a company, the directors on the board of directors and the supervisors on the supervisory board were usually appointed by the same government department, and they were likely to work together to promote their common interests at the expense of the shareholder's (the state's) interest.[68] Mechanisms responding to the insider trading problem were needed. To solve this dilemma, the Chinese policy-makers envisioned that the securities market could bring external control mechanisms into these companies.[69]

When China decided to develop a securities market in the mid-1980s, the policy-makers aimed to achieve three primary goals. Firstly, companies would have new channels to raise funds.[70] With the deepening of the enterprise reforms and reforms in the banking sector, as well as an increase in exposure to international competition, companies required more and more capital for further expansion.[71] The securities market could aid companies in raising capital. Furthermore, the securities market would assist the development of privately owned enterprises by providing them with a means of obtaining outside finance.

Secondly, the securities market would absorb a large amount of bank savings and make the best use of them.[72] From 1978 to 1990, individual savings in China

---

64 *See* Jianmin Dou, Research on the History of Corporate Ideology in China 108 (Shanghai: Publishing House of Shanghai University of Finance and Economics, 1999).

65 *See* Yuwa Wei, Comparative Corporate Governance: A Chinese Perspective 20–21 (London: Kluwer Law International, 2003).

66 *Ibid*, at 103–7.

67 *See* Mei, *supra* note 58, at 34.

68 *See* the World Bank, China's Management of Enterprise Assets: the State as Shareholder 51 (Washington D.C.: The World Bank, 1997). *See also* Wei, *supra* note 65, at 121.

69 *See* Stephen C. Thomas and Chen Ji, *Privatizing China: The Stock Markets and Their Role in Corporate Reform*, 58 China Business Review (1 July 2004).

70 *See* Baisan Xie, China's Securities Market 3 (Guangzhou: Guangdong Economics Press, 2002).

71 *See* Qingquan Ma, The History of China's Securities Business 2–3 (Beijing: CITIC Publishing House, 2003).

72 *Ibid*, at 3.

had increased dramatically from 21,600,000,000 yuan to 703,420,000,000 yuan.[73] Chinese enterprises also had a substantial amount in bank deposits.[74] The existence of a securities market would allow these net savings to flow to well performing enterprises and efficient sectors, exerting their best utility.

Thirdly, the securities market would discipline the listed companies and promote good corporate governance within these companies.[75] To be listed on the stock exchanges, companies needed to satisfy the minimal capital requirement, demonstrate that it made profits over the past three consecutive years, and provide evidence that it had not been involved in serious breaches in the last two years, etc.[76] After being listed on the stock exchanges, the company was subject to continuous disclosure requirements and other behavioral rules specifically targeted at listed companies. It was understood that the incentives of being listed on the stock exchanges and the consequences of de-listing for breaches would act as a disciplinary force stimulating listed companies to embrace good practice of corporate governance. Therefore, except in the core sectors essential to the national economy and people's livelihood, state-owned/dominated companies were encouraged to be listed on domestic and foreign exchanges.

The Chinese government's determination to develop a securities market in China resulted in the establishment of two national stock exchanges in the beginning of the 1990s.[77] The past 15 years have witnessed mixed outcomes. The development of the securities market occurred in three phases. The first phase was the initial stage of development, which started in 1978 and ended in 1990. In this stage, the concepts of bonds and shares were not well understood by most ordinary Chinese. By 1981, China resumed the practice of issuing government bonds (treasury bonds). Very few were interested. The government had to allocate the bonds to government organizations, state institutions and enterprises for further distributing them to individuals. Senior officers and party members were called on to set an example by purchasing possibly more treasury bonds. Ten years later, the wealth of those who purchased the bonds increased several hundreds times, while those who refused to buy maintained the status quo.[78] Gradually, Chinese citizens realized the benefits of subscribing for treasury bonds.

The issuing of shares began in 1984. Pilot projects were extended to some cities, the most notable being Shanghai and Shenzhen. Share issuance was under close government supervision and guidance.[79] Most of the time, the market was quiet. However, this only remained the case until 1990. From March 1990, the

---

73 *Ibid.*

74 *Ibid.*

75 *See* Thomas and Ji, *supra* note 67.

76 *See* the People's Congress, the 1993 *Company Law of the People's Republic of China*, sec. 152.

77 They are Shanghai Stock Exchange and Shenzhen Stock Exchange.

78 *See* Xie, *supra* note 70, at 252.

79 Share issuance at this stage was subject to government approval.

securities business suddenly thrived, mainly because the public discovered that the earlier investors had made a fortune overnight.[80]

After the establishment of the two national stock exchanges in 1990, China's securities market came into its second phase of development, the era of vigorous development. From 1991 to 2000, the securities market soared. The number of new issues was far behind the demand of investments. The government introduced new procedures including application, casting lots and quota allocation methods for distributing newly issued shares. Quota control was an important means of keeping the capital market in check. By having quota control in place, the government firmly took the power of deciding which companies' stocks should be admitted into the market. Theoretically, quota control would ensure the quality of listed companies. However, because of policy preference quota control was, in fact, exercised to safeguard the interests of state-dominated companies. Consequently, state-dominated companies were given priority in obtaining quotas. During this period, various types of shares including A, B, H, and N shares were introduced. A regulatory framework was built up. The market generally boomed, however, it also fluctuated violently.[81]

Since 2001, the securities market has come into the third phase of its development. This is a period of adjustment. From July 2001, the market experienced more than four years of depression.[82] Between June 2001 and June 2005, the index fell from 2245 points to 998 points.[83] The government has been introducing methods to restore investors' confidence. The pace of reducing state shares has been accelerated. Since April 2006, the market has begun to recover. However, this time the market is even more volatile, and manipulation is more acutely felt. The market showed signs of picking up by April 2006, but soon dipped by 4.84 percent on 13 July 2006.[84] From September it became clear that a bull market was coming. The market soared by the end of December 2006 and January 2007, and then plummeted on 31 January 2007. In the following five weeks, the market fluctuated frequently and drastically. The Shanghai index reached its historical high of above 3000 points on 26 February 2007. On the morning of 27 February, the market opened with 3048 points and fell spectacularly five hours later.[85] The index lost 8.84 percent in this single day, the biggest fall in a single trading day within a decade. On 14 and 16 March, the market plunged twice with the Shanghai Composite Index falling more than

---

80   *See* Ma, *supra* note 71, at 60.

81   *See* Wei, *supra* note 5, at 37–8.

82   *Ibid*, at 32.

83   *See* Baisan Xie, *China Needs Not to Go with the Tide on the US Securities Market*, available at <http://cn.biz.yahoo.com/070317/16/l9c6.html>.

84   *See* Xiaobing Wu, Wenjun Liu and Ye Chen, *Who Pulled the Trigger?* available at <http://zhoukan.hexun.com/-Magazine/ShowArticle.aspx?ArticleId=11963>.

85   *Ibid.*

100 points on 14 March, and 21.22 points on 16 March.[86] Volatility continued throughout the year. The market plummeted on 30 May, 11 September and 8 November respectively.[87] Coming into 2008, there has been no sign that the fluctuation may ease. The continual decline of the index has raised the question of how long the bull market could last.

Many factors have contributed to the market depression and volatility. Bubbles existed before 2001. By early 2001, A shares were sold, on average, 70 times above their issuing prices.[88] This was caused by great demand for new issues. Official explanations intimated that the past few years of recession were mainly due to the market's natural adjustment after a decade of substantial market growth.[89] Financial policies including interest rate policies, imperfect regulatory infrastructure, a lack of legal protection for investors, and macro-economic policy adjustment could all have contributed to the market recession.[90]

Some researches tend to attribute the market depression and volatility mainly to the market irregularities and irresponsible conduct of listed companies.[91] Many companies see the securities market as a place where they can raise easy and quick money.[92] Instead of improving the corporate governance and economic efficiency of their companies, directors and managers are more interested in manipulating the market and investors by disclosing misleading information or creating false trading impressions.[93] Some unqualified companies obtained listing by giving false accounting and auditing information in their applications.[94] Consequently, investors' confidence has been hit hard by high profile market misconduct.

Statistics indicate that the objectives behind developing the securities market have not been effectively achieved. The market has not cured the insider trading problems in state-dominated listed companies, and abuse of the market and

---

86   *See* the Commentator, *The Market on the Two Stock Exchanges Continues to Fall, and the Index Dives More Than 21 Points*, available at <http://finance.people.com.cn/GB/67815/68059/5480901.html>.

87   *See* Shaoye Xu, *Farewell 2007: Shanghai and Shenzhen Indices Obtained the Longest Yang Line in China's History*, Shanghai Securities Daily (29 December 2007), available at <http://news.xinhuanet.com/fortune/2007-12/29/content_7333087.htm>.

88   A shares are shares issued to Chinese investors on the domestic securities markets, and should be paid in Renminbi yuan. *See* China Securities Regulatory Committee, Studies of Cutting edge Issues concerning the Development of China's Securities Market 3, 12–13, 41–3 (Beijing: China Finance and Economics Press, 2005).

89   *Ibid.*

90   *See* Qilin Fu, Well-Known Cases relating to China's Securities Market in the Past Ten Years 70 (Beijing: Publishing House of China University of Political Science and Law, 2002). Huang, Z., Civil Liability and Civil Litigation in US Securities Law 7 (Beijing: Law Press, 2003).

91   *See* Xie, Dai and Xu, *supra* note 18, at 1, 3–4; *See* also Wei, *supra* note 5.

92   *See* Xie, *supra* note 70, at 70, 152, 168.

93   *Ibid*, at 80.

94   *Ibid*, at 202. *See* also Xie, *supra* note 34, at 133–4.

misbehavior by listed companies has been widely reported.[95] Today, insider control continues to plague Chinese listed companies in which the state is the dominant shareholder. This problem undermines China's efforts to promote sound corporate governance in listed companies and is responsible for the irregular volatility of the securities market.[96]

Furthermore, in China's capital market, takeovers as an external mechanism of corporate control have contributed little to the improvement of management efficiency in listed companies. Irregularity and widespread breaches have seriously undermined the efficiency of the securities market. Fraudulent conduct such as misleading disclosure and market manipulation by listed companies and market intermediaries confuses the market and thwarts investors in their effort to differentiate well performed companies from poorly performed companies. Consequently, the threat of takeover to inefficient management is significantly compromised.

China's experience illustrates that corporate governance and securities markets are interactive and interdependent. Therefore, the economic efficiency in China's companies must be promoted in conjunction with improving corporate governance practice and advancing a transparent and orderly securities market. To build a modern corporate governance system, China needs to make further efforts to rationalize the shareholding structure in its companies. It also needs to continue to develop its securities regulation and reinforce the monitoring function of the securities market.

The Future

For the purposes of establishing an efficient corporate governance system in China and ensuring the healthy operation of China's securities market, the Chinese will have to shoulder heavy responsibilities in the coming years. The experience of successful corporate economies illustrates that a sound corporate governance system is one that is adapted to its political, economic, cultural and legal environment, and takes maximum advantage of its political, economic, cultural and legal traditions.[97] The corporate governance system must be reinforced by the political, economic, cultural and legal strength of the system. It should promote and enhance certain social, political, economic, cultural and legal values of the society in which it is implemented.[98] This is evidenced by the co-existence of the diversified but equally successful corporate governance practices in the world's leading corporate economies, namely, the US, Germany and Japan.

---

95   *See* Xie, Dai and Xu, *supra* note 18. *See generally* Wei, *supra* note 5.
96   *Ibid.*
97   *See* Wei, *supra* note 65, at 175.
98   *Ibid.*

While the US corporate governance system is characterized by a highly developed capital market and managerial capitalism, German and Japanese corporate governance systems are described as bank-based and co-operative systems where corporate ownership is concentrated, usually in the hands of banks and related companies.[99] In the US, the focus of corporate governance is on reducing agency costs caused by dispersed ownership and control and on management accountability. Takeovers, as a side product of the developed stock market and dispersed ownership, play a significant role in corporate governance. In Germany and Japan, a goal of corporate governance is to increase corporate finance choices, enhance monitoring capacity of the board and other corporate organs, and reduce pressure on banks.[100]

Whilst China is determined to develop a modern corporate economy with its unique characteristics by retaining a significant proportion of state ownership in its industrial and financial sectors, it has endeavored to establish a US-style securities market and regulatory regime. The question is whether China can reconcile the two contradictory systems and create a new method of achieving economic efficiency. From what is occurring in China today, it appears that China has made efforts. One strategy is to divide the shares of a joint stock company into state shares, state-owned legal person shares, and individual shares.[101] While state shares are prohibited from being traded on the stock market, shares of state-owned legal persons can only be transferred among legal persons.[102] Only individual shares are freely transferable on the market. However, they account for only 30 percent of the total shares.[103]

---

99   *See* Alfred D. Chandler, Scale and Scope: The Dynamics of Industrial Capitalism 383–592 (Massachusetts: The Belknap Press of Harvard University Press, 1990). *See* also Johannes Hirschmeieer, *Entrepreneurs and the Social Order: American, Germany and Japan*, 1870–1900, in Keiichiro Nakagawa (*ed.*), Social Order and Entrepreneurship 7–8 (1977). *See generally* Mark J. Roe, *Some Differences in Corporate Structure in Germany, Japan, and the United States*, 102 Yale Law Journal 1927–2003 (1993).

100   *See* Ronal Gilson and Curtis J. Milhaupt, Choices as Regulatory Reform: The Case of Japanese Corporate Governance (Columbia University Law School, Center for Law Economic Studies Working Paper No 251; Stanford Law School, John M. Olin Program in Law and Economics, Working Paper No. 281; and European Corporate Governance Institute, Law Working Paper No. 22/2004), available at <http://ssrn.com/abstract=537843>. *See* also Helmut M. Died, Capital Markets and Corporate Governance in Japan, Germany and the United States: Organizational Response to Market Inefficiencies 120 (London: Routledge, 2005).

101   *See* Chengxi Yao, Stock Market and Futures Market in the People's Republic of China 18 (New York: Oxford University Press, 1998).

102   A legal person is a body that has an independent personality in law. A state-owned legal person is usually a state-owned company.

103   *See* Baisan Xie, *Huge Deficits of Shen Kang Jia Reveal the Serious Problem in the Company's Share Issue*, in Baisan Xie (*ed.*), International Comparison of Securities Markets 170 (Volume 1, Beijing: Qinghua University Press, 2003).

This approach has achieved the purpose of retaining substantial state ownership on the one hand, and introducing market mechanisms on the other. Consequently, wholly state-owned companies continue to be financed by the state via state-owned banks, and state-dominated companies are able to have access to external finance through being listed on stock exchanges. In doing so, such state-dominated companies can prevent losses of state assets, guarantee state domination, and obtain outside investments. In the meantime, it is also expected that these companies will accept market supervision and uphold good corporate governance.

However, as discussed in the beginning of this book and in the previous section, the plan has not worked satisfactorily. Unlisted state-owned companies continue to burden state banks with non-performing loans.[104] The misconduct of listed companies has not been curtailed by the operation of the stock market, and, in some cases, it has even been exacerbated. Enormous opportunities for profits existing in China's securities market have provoked some companies to purposely engage in irresponsible and manipulative conduct. Inevitably, the market has suffered and will continue to suffer the consequences. This illustrates the fact that the existence of a securities market does not automatically guarantee a better regime of corporate governance. On the contrary, poor corporate governance may shake investors' confidence and eventually undermine the market.

There are three alternatives available to China in regulating its capital market and improving corporate governance of its companies. Firstly, if China is to retain substantial state ownership in essential sectors for social and economic reasons, it may need to look at the experiences of the countries successfully running a corporate economy with a high proportion of state ownership.[105] The representatives of such countries include France and Italy. In France and Italy, a large amount of firms are state owned.[106] In these systems, it is believed that the state should play an important role in directing large corporations in order to ensure that companies will serve public interests.[107] In such countries, the government bureaucrats have substantial discretional power in the allocation of credit, foreign exchange and licenses.[108] Since China accumulated a rich experience in state guidance and

---

104   *See* Yanrong Hong, Studies of Legal Issues concerning Asset Backed Securitization 223–4 (2004, Peking University Press); *See* also Baozhong Gao, Institutional Analysis of Asset Securitization in China 155 (Beijing: Social Science Academic Press, 2005).

105   *See generally* Simon Johnson, Peter Boone, Alasdair Breach and Eric Friedman, Corporate governance in the Asian Financial Crisis (Rutgers University Department of Economics, Working Paper No. 279, 1999).

106   *See* Yiwen Deng, Cross Swords: Great Debate on State Ownership Reforms (Beijing: Ocean Press, 2005).

107   *See* Henry Hansmann and Reinier Kraakman, The End of History for Corporate Law 6 (Harvard Law School, John M. Olin Center for Law, Economics, and Business Working Paper No. 280, 2000).

108   *Ibid.*

control over economic activities under the planned economy, the state oriented model of corporate governance may well be a practicable approach.[109]

China may also draw inspiration from the experience of bank-based systems, namely Germany and Japan, to fully exploit state banks' potential in monitoring companies. Since a comprehensive and practical legal infrastructure is a fundamental requirement for building a successful corporate economy (this is evident in all leading corporate economies), China needs to continue to perfect its legal infrastructure. In addition, it is important that China develops a corporate culture that promotes transparency, business efficiency, fair competition and managerial accountability.

Secondly, if China wants to fully exploit the governance function of the securities market and thus enhance the governance practice of listed companies, it needs to take the following steps to improve the market efficiency:

The first step is to strengthen regulation over the securities market and listed companies by enhancing disclosure requirements. Disclosure is the key in ensuring transparent and orderly transactions on the securities market. It is generally recognized that publicity is the best remedy for social and industrial problems.[110] Disclosure is thus the focus of most countries' securities regulation.[111] The fact that many incidents of market misconduct in China involve misleading disclosure or non-disclosure further demonstrates the necessity of improving disclosure requirements.

The second step is to increase the protection of investors and small shareholders' remedies. Research has shown that successful corporate economies all seek to provide sufficient remedies to shareholders, particularly small shareholders in their laws.[112] It is important that investors have the option of pursuing a legal remedy. When investors pursue their legal rights, they bring the management of their companies under further scrutiny. Currently, the Chinese law is silent on what civil remedies share investors may have in the case of market manipulation by corporations.[113] Although amended *Company Law* has made shareholders' derivative actions possible, a lack of detailed policy makes the implementation difficult.[114] In the meantime, shareholders' right to class actions is still unclear.

---

109 *See* Wei, *supra* note 65, at 202.

110 *See* Louis D. Brandeis, Other People's Money and How the Bankers Use it 92 (New York: A.M. Kelley, 1971).

111 *See* Zhu, *supra* note 50, at 92.

112 *See generally* Simon Johnson, Peter Boone, Alasdair Breach and Eric Friedman, Corporate governance in the Asian Financial Crisis (Rutgers University Department of Economics, Working Paper No. 279, 1999).

113 *See* Zhu, *supra* note 50, at 164.

114 *See* the People's Congress, the 1993 Company Law (amended in 2005), sec. 152. The 1993 *Company Law* was amended twice. The first amendment was made in 1999 and the second in 2005. The amendments in 2005 were Substantial, with 137 sections amended, 41 inserted, and 46 repealed.

There is a need to improve Chinese law in order to offer further protection to share investors.

The third step is to gradually reduce state shareholdings and liberalize non-tradable shares. The current price distortion on China's securities market is mainly caused by a lack of transferable shares.[115] Reduction of state shareholdings may ease the pressure, and therefore diminish bubbles in the market.

However, China may wish to go for the third alternative: fully taking the advantage of the securities market, while retaining significant state control in essential sectors. This is the current approach of the Chinese government, and is the optimal, but ambitious, choice. A difficulty of this strategy is making state-owned and state-dominated companies truly competitive. A possible solution is to terminate the traditional relationship between the companies and state banks, and make sure that the banks fully exert their supervisory functions. Currently, China is introducing the practice of securitization. The Chinese government allows state banks to securitize non-performing loans and sell the bonds on the securities market. In doing so, the government hopes that the state banks and state companies will no longer be tied together, and companies will be under greater pressure to pay back the debts.[116] Using securitization to control non-performing loans is a popular practice in many countries that have introduced securitization, particularly within Asia and Latin America.[117] What distinguishes China from other countries is the fact that securitization in China is expected to play an important role in assisting the banking sector reforms. The outcome of the securitization practice will have a far reaching influence on China's economic life in coming years. How far China can go along this path remains to be seen.

The world's financial products and markets are moving towards globalization. China's entry into the WTO has accelerated the integration of its financial sector and securities market into the world economy. China will inevitably achieve greater financial liberalization and develop a more sophisticated capital market. However, the globalization of financial services and the capital market could be a double-edged sword. While capital flows do help China's economic growth and bring in new knowledge and technology, Chinese banks will face fierce competition from international financial institutions. China's capital market will offer attractive opportunities to international investors, which will increase competition and result in a race for opportunities. Both China's financial sector and its listed companies will encounter unprecedented challenges in their quest for survival and expansion. A task faced by Chinese policy-makers and the corporate elite is how to enhance the competitive strength of the country's financial sector and national industries,

---

115   *See* Xie, *supra* note 34, at 114, 116, 122.

116   *See* Baozhong Gao, Institutional Analysis of Asset Securitization in China 161–3 (Beijing: Social Science Academic Press, 2005).

117   Two notable countries are Japan and Korea. *See* Baozhong Gao, Institutional Analysis of Asset Securitization in China 165 (Beijing: Social Science Academic Press, 2005).

while enjoying a high inflow of international capital. Globalization is a challenge as well as an opportunity to the Chinese. China can use the opportunity to speed up the reforms to China's financial sector and to modernize China's capital market and corporate governance system. History once again tests the Chinese on their wisdom and determination.

Conclusions

Large and small investors around the world are hunting for investment opportunities including direct investments, bank deposits, and investing in securities markets or real estate. The development of the securities market in China provides a new channel for capital flow. However, opportunities in securities markets always come with risks. Making informed investment decisions is one way to reduce these risks. It is therefore important to closely watch the investment environment in China's securities market.

Political, social, local, international, economic, and financial pressures all impact on the securities market. The development of China's securities market is part of the economic reform package. The establishment of the market is closely guided and monitored by the Chinese government, and is therefore more responsive to the government's policy changes. However, after the initial stage of development, administrative intervention has become less effective. The problems inherent in China's corporate system and companies have persisted. It is time for the Chinese to respond to these problems and strengthen their regulatory intervention.

Experience indicates that to achieve the goal of the enterprise reforms, China needs to continue to improve its corporate governance practice, and standardize securities activities. The two are interconnected. Good corporate governance facilitates the transparent operation of the securities market, while an orderly performing securities market can greatly promote good corporate practice in listed companies.

PART I
Securities Market and its Regulation

Chapter 1
Speculation and Regulation

This chapter investigates individuals' decision-making behavior on the securities market. It points out that the securities market is susceptible to psychological biases and therefore susceptible to manipulation. Because of this fact, the market is highly speculative and manipulable. This is evidenced by a number of high profile speculative events that have occurred in the capital markets. The second part of this chapter explains that the securities market must be regulated in order to restrain over-speculation in the securities market, and analyzes the methods of regulation. In doing so, it is observed that efficient regulatory mechanisms are crucial to ensuring long-term prosperity and stability of the securities market, and a combination of governmental regulation, market self-regulation and the market's own function of adjustment is the best possible regulatory approach for achieving these goals.

Speculation

As far as the financial market is concerned, the boundary between speculation and investment is often blurring.[1] In finance, investment generally refers to the purchase of a financial product or other item of value with an expectation of favorable future returns.[2] Speculation is also perceived as an action of purchasing investments by taking risks, with respect to trying to predict the future in the hopes of making quick and large gains. The key distinction between the two lies in the degree of risk involved and the amount of profits or gains expected. Speculation involves taking above-average risks to achieve above-average returns, and thus is not based upon thorough analysis of the market, risks and loss. In contrast, investment, by nature, is a financial operation upon thorough analysis, presents sufficiently low risk and "promises safety of principal *and* a satisfactory return".[3] Based on the degree of risk assumed, speculation is placed at a position between investment

---

1   *See* Robert Sobel, The Money Manias: The Eras of Great Speculation in America, 1770–1970 1 (New York: Weybright and Talley, 1974).

2   *See* the definitions for the term of investment provided by Investorwords and Businessdictionary available at <http://www.investorwords.com/2599/investment.html> and <http://www.businessdictionary.com/definition/-investment.html>.

3   *See* Benjamin Graham and David Dodd, Security Analysis 63–4 (New York: McGraw-Hill Book Company, 1940).

and gambling.[4] However, a clear cut line between investment and speculation, or between speculation and gambling may not be drawn easily.

There is a body of literature upholding that speculation is necessary and helpful for the healthy operation of a financial market. Some representative arguments include those in *The Intelligent Investor* by Benjamin Graham and *Practical Speculation* by Victor Niederhoffer and Laurel Kenner.[5] Apart from creating possibilities of gaining huge investment rewards, it is commonly understood that for the sake of the market, speculation adds liquidity to the market, encourages consumption, and reduces surplus.[6] However, unbridled speculation causes mispricing, deviation of prices, and market crashes.[7] Nevertheless, it is clear that financial markets need both investors and speculators. In other words, people who invest in financial markets can be normally classified into investors and speculators, depending on the risks they are willing to assume.

Ever since they first evolved, securities markets have been a utopia and an arena for speculators. However, over-speculation results in bubbles, and the market crashes when bubbles eventually burst. This appears to be the driven force behind the failure of the capital market. Discovering mechanisms of curtailing the bubble effect in order to avoid market crashes or crises is critical to all economies. This objective abundantly justifies regulatory or governmental intervention into the operation of the capital market.

In the process of dealing with the capital market, people, either the market participants or regulators, inevitably contemplate why the securities market behaves in the way it does. On this issue, the mainstream economic theory of finance is insufficient in providing satisfactory explanations. The mainstream finance theory assumes that people are rational beings and they act in their own best economic interests.[8] In other words, a rational economic person is the one who has utility functions and constantly maximizes these functions. Based on this assumption, theories have been developed to assist people in maximizing their financial interests. These theories mainly include arbitrage theory, portfolio theory,

---

4   *See* the definition of speculation in Businessdictionary available at <http://www.businessdictionary.com/-definition/speculation.html>.

5   *See* Benjamin Graham and Jason Zweig, The Intelligent Investor: The Definitive Book on Value Investing 21 (New York: HarperCollins, 2003); *See* also Victor Niederhoffer and Laurel Kenner, Practical Speculation 5–20 (New Jersey: John Wiley & Sons, 2003).

6   *See* Paul Staines, *The Benefits of Speculation: A Bond Market Vigilante Replies to Will Hutton's The State We're in* 1 (Written for Libertarian Alliance, 1996), available at <http://libertarian.co.uk/lapubs/econn/econn069.pdf>.

7   *See* Victor Niederhoffer, *The Speculator as Hero*, The Wall Street Journal (10 February 1989), available at <http://www.dailyspeculations.com/vic/spec_as_hero.html Daily Speculations>.

8   *See* Adam Smith, The Wealth of Nations 452–7 (Oxford: Clarendon Press, 1976).

asset pricing theory and option pricing theory.[9] However, evidence suggests that such theories do not add investors greatly.[10]

Another well respected approach to the mainstream theory in finance – the Efficient Market Hypothesis, also seems unable to convincingly interpret the irrational behavior of the capital market. The concept of the "efficient market" was first introduced by Fama in the late 1960s.[11] According to the Efficient Market Hypothesis, the efficiency of the capital market lies in whether or not the market is able to reflect all relevant information, or whether or not the share prices can reflect all relevant information in the market.[12] The Efficient Market Hypothesis assumes that the market is efficient. In an efficient market, capital and information flow freely. Since participants all act rationally with the goal of maximizing their financial interests, they respond to the information in a similar way, and adopt similar strategies and thus reach similar business decisions.[13] As a result, any unexploited profit opportunities do not remain in the market for long.

The rational person assumption and Efficient Market Hypothesis are contested by the existence of many anomalies. Studies of stock market volatility, over-reaction and loss realization present increasing challenges to the rational person and efficient market assumptions.[14] Indeed, neither the rational person assumption nor the Efficient Market Hypothesis can convincingly explain the causes of investment manias (or the so called speculative booms if the economic terminology is preferred) and market crashes that have taken place on the capital market. For instance, in Holland, in the 1630s, people frantically speculated in tulips. The fanaticism lasted about a year and then suddenly came to a standstill.[15] These phenomena have never been credibly explained.[16] Such a story has been repeated in subsequent events, including the South Sea Bubble in 1720, the great railway boom in the 1940s, and the Florida land boom in the 1920s.[17] In elucidating the reasons of the above market phenomena, orthodox theories, particularly the

---

9   *See* John R. Nofsinger, The Psychology of Investing 6 (New Jersey: Prentice Hall, 2005).

10   *Ibid*, at 1.

11   It was discussed in Eugene Fama, Lawrence Fisher, Michael Jensen and Richard Roll, *The Adjustment of Stock Prices to New Information*, 10 International Economic Review 1–21 (1969).

12   *Ibid*.

13   *See* Eugene F. Fama, *Efficient Capital Markets: A Review of Theory and Empirical Works*, 25 Journal of Finance 383–417 (1970).

14   *See* Hersh Shefrin, Beyond Greed and Fear: Understanding Behavioral Finance and the Psychology of Investing 10 (Boston: Harvard Business School Press, 2000).

15   *See* Charles P. Kindleberger and Robert Z. Aliber, Manias, Panics and Crashes: A History of Financial Crises 99–100 (Basingstoke: Palgrave Macmillan, 2005).

16   *See* David Cohen, Fear, Greed and Panic: The Psychology of the Stock Market 24 (New York: John Wiley & Sons, 2001).

17   *Ibid*, at 25–35.

rational behavior paradigm, seems insufficient. Consequently, in recent decades, these theories have been more frequently challenged.

In the course of challenging the orthodox economic theories, the school of Behavioral Finance leads the debates. Today, economists still cannot fully agree with each other in defining Behavioral Finance. While the defenders of the mainstream theories describe the Behavioral Finance as nothing more than "anomalies dredging",[18] Behavioral Finance scholars define their research as the application of psychology to financial behavior, which comprises three themes: heuristic-driven bias, frame dependence and inefficient markets.[19] Behavioral Finance rejects the argument that market participants are rational beings who constantly and consistently make rational choices, and claims that business decisions are influenced by psychological biases and people often act in an apparently irrational manner.[20] Behavioral Finance also disputes the efficient market claim, and holds that markets are inefficient.

Questions arise: can the difference between the mainstream theories and Behavioral Finance be described as the difference between economists and psychologists? Should we hope that the two disciplines can continue to develop in separate ways, without collaboration? The reality is that more and more efforts have been made by both economists and psychologists to apply both economic and psychological perspectives to the studies of the complex phenomena associated with decision-making, because neither of the disciplines can independently provide a comprehensive account of interpreting choice behavior.[21]

When closely looking at the psychological approach, one can see it does not fundamentally reject the rational choice assumption. It is not trying to say that people make decisions without purposes and thus without reasons. On the contrary, it recognizes that people do have motivations and do use reasons to respond to these motivations.[22] In other words, people do endeavor to be rational. The reason why people make irrational choices lies in that individuals' capacity to process information varies. They are limited by knowledge and means of computation.[23] Moreover, the focus or attention of individuals is susceptible to the influence of irrational factors including emotions, motivations, and sensory stimuli.[24]

---

18   *See* Eugene F. Fama, *Efficiency Survives the Attack of the Anomalies*, GSB Chicago Alumni Magazine 14–16 (1998).

19   *See* Eugene F. Fama, *supra* note 13, at 3, 4.

20   *See* Eugene F. Fama, *supra* note 13, at 1.

21   *See* Robin M. Hogarth and Melvin W. Reder, *Introduction*, in Robin M. Hogarth and Melvin W. Reder (*eds*), Rational Choice: The Contrast between Economics and Psychology 16–17 (Chicago: The University of Chicago Press, 1987).

22   *See* Herbert A. Simon, *Rationality in Psychology and Economics*, in Robin M. Hogarth and Melvin W. Reder (*eds*), Rational Choice: The Contrast between Economics and Psychology 25 (Chicago: The University of Chicago Press, 1986).

23   *Ibid*, at 27.

24   *Ibid*, at 26.

According to the psychological approach, people make reasoning errors. The brain frequently processes information through shortcuts and emotional filters, the so called psychological biases.[25] Decisions made under the influence of these psychological biases are usually different from the decisions that would otherwise be made. The sources of psychological biases can come from a person's mood, self-deception, or even the brain's tendency to make shortcut analyses when limited cognitive resources are available.[26] Taking these psychological and emotional factors into account, it is not so difficult to understand how and why a person makes an irrational decision through a seemingly rational procedure. Furthermore, decision-making is also under the influence of peer effects. When people interact, for example, when they share information and communicate their feelings about the information, they may influence each other's decisions.[27]

Hence, the true difference between the neoclassical economic approach and the cognitive psychological approach lies in that the rational person of neoclassical economics does not recognize the role of emotion in making choices, while psychology attaches great importance to the context of behavior, such as background feelings, and examines how reason operates within the context.[28] In other words, the rational person of neoclassical economics makes decisions that are both objectively and substantively rational, whereas a rational person of cognitive psychology is usually procedurally reasonable but not necessarily substantively rational in making choices.

Psychological analysis assists people in seeking explanations for some phenomena in capital markets. The cognitive psychology approach appreciates that investors are influenced by a range of behavioral biases including the hindsight bias, the availability bias, the optimism bias, the reliance on heuristics, the bounded rationality, the endowment effect, and satisficing. Some behavioral biases do, to various degrees, boost investors' preference for speculation. Interactively, investors' speculative preference makes them prone to certain behavioral biases such as overconfidence that impair their ability to process information and make decisions.[29] Kahneman and Tversky's *Prospect Theory* further reveals the complexity concerning anomalies of human behavior in managing risks and uncertainty. Same people may demonstrate different behavior when facing the same choice in different contexts. For instance, people who have displayed risk-aversion behavior under certain conditions may adopt risk-seeking behavior when the same choice is formulated in a different way.[30]

---

25   *See* Nofsinger, *supra* note 7, at 3.

26   *Ibid*, at 6, 7.

27   *Ibid*, at 7.

28   *See* Cohen, *supra* note 16, at 295. *See* also Simon, *supra* note 16, at 37.

29   *See* Stephen J. Choi and Adam C. Pritchard, *Behavioral Economics and the SEC*, 56 Stanford Law Review 15 (2003).

30   *See* Daniel Kahneman and Amos Tversky, *Prospect Theory: An Analysis of Decision under Risk*, 47(2) Econometrica 164–8 (1979).

The concept of "herd behavior" is also helpful in explaining market bubbles, investment mania and crises. Investors are influenced by their psychological biases, and an investor's decision can be affected by others. When many investors are influenced by their psychological biases in a common way, a herd forms.[31] The most dangerous aspect of herd behavior is that, in a herd, psychological biases can intensify and magnify.[32] When this happens, the market will eventually feel the effect and the prices will deviate from their fundamental values. This analysis logically leads to inefficient market postulation and further challenges the Efficient Market Hypothesis.

After acknowledging the irrational decision-making and inefficient market postulations, one naturally goes to the next issue: are the psychological biases exploitable? The fact that many people seek fortunes through manipulating the market, lawfully or unlawfully, incontrovertibly suggests that people are willing to take opportunities to exploit others' psychological biases in the capital market.[33] This is further evidenced by publications advising investors how to take the advantages of others' reasoning errors when dealing with securities. Nathan Rothschild set one of the earliest classic examples relating to exploiting securities investors' psychology.

On 20 June 1815, Rothschild received the report on the Battle of Waterloo hours before anyone in London. He rushed to the Stock Exchange. Owing to the uncertainty of the battle, the price of the English government stock, Consols, was low. However, the price would rise if people knew that Great Britain had defeated Napoleon. Rothschild decided to manipulate the market. He sold some Consols, and the price fell more. He then sold more. Everyone understood the message: Rothschild, one of the best informed financiers in Europe, was selling his Consols. They followed. When the price fell to the bottom, Rothschild placed one huge purchasing order. A few minutes later, the price of Consols soared since the official news of the Battle was out. Rothschild won his victory through successfully manipulating others' psychology.[34]

There were much worse stories of exploiting and manipulating investors' psychology in the history of the capital market, which involved rampant fraud

---

31   *See* Harrison Hong, Jeffrey D. Kubik and Jeremy C. Stein, *Social Interaction and Stock-Market Participation*, 59(1) The Journal of Finance 152–62 (2004). *See* also Esther Duflo and Emmanuel Saez, *Participation and Investment Decisions in a Retirement Plan: The Influence of Colleagues' Choices*, 85 Journal of Public Economics 121–48 (2002). *See* also Nofsinger, *supra* note 2, at 82.

32   *Ibid.*

33   For example, Humphrey Neill, The Art of Contrary Thinking (Caldwell: Caxton Printers, 1980); Frank J. Williams, If you Must Speculate Learn the Rules (New York: Fraser Publishing Company, 1981); Bradbury K. Thurlow, Rediscovering the Wheel: Contrary Think and Investment Strategy (New York: Fraser Publishing Company, 1981); and Martin J. Pring, Investment Psychology Explained: Classic Strategies to Beat the Markets (New York: John Wiley & Sons, 1992).

34   *See* Cohen, *supra* note 16, at 2.

and swindles. One of them happened in 1910 in Shanghai, China. At that time, shares of the companies producing rubber products were in high demand. Some foreign banks and business people decided to exploit the investors by promoting a number of phony "rubber companies". They forged their companies' rubber businesses, misled investors and manipulated the prices of the companies. The whole of Shanghai, including some influential banks and bankers, were drawn into this rubber mania. The drama ended when McBain, an English merchant and the fiercest shark in the event, fled abroad with huge amount of funds scooped out of the Shanghai stock exchange. The Shanghai financial market then crashed, and several Chinese banks declared bankruptcy within a week.[35]

It is clear that investors' psychology is exploitable, and the capital market manipulable. Issues then arise as to whether speculation on capital markets should be controlled; to what degree it should be controlled; and whether speculation is controllable after all. Speculation should be controllable though it may not be entirely eliminated from the economic world. This works in the same way that we may never eliminate gambling, but playing under the rules of casinos definitely allows the authority to bring gambling activities under a degree of control. The question is what kind of control is rational. It is generally accepted that the object of regulating the capital market is to control excessive speculation, not speculation.[36] Speculation is inherent in capital markets. Nevertheless, the market fails to function if it is overly speculated.[37] Past experience has proven that the consequences of over-speculation on capital markets are catastrophic.

The next question is: Can the market control speculation through its internal correction functions? The traditional economics certainly says yes, because it holds that the market is better off if it is guided by its "invisible hand".[38] Nevertheless, the traditional economics also acknowledges the notion of market failure and therefore recognizes the necessity of limited regulatory or governmental intervention.[39] Since the economic recessions and depressions in the late 1800s and early 1900s, interventionists including Marxists and Keynesianists gained momentum. However, interventionism was subject to increasing scrutiny following a series of governmental failure. Today, a common view is that a balance between market control and regulatory control should be

---

35   *See* Zhong Chen, Wind and Cloud on the Securities Market in China 13–15 (Shanghai: Publishing House of Shanghai University of Transportation, 2000).

36   *See* Zhijun Li, Government Regulation of the Securities Market 82–3 (Changchun: Jilin People's Press, 2005).

37   *See* Jinglian Wu, Where to Seek Great Wisdom 12 (Shanghai: Xuelin Press, 1997).

38   *See* Smith, *supra* note 8, at 456.

39   *See* John Maynard Keynes, The General Theory of Employment, Interest and Money 380 (London: Macmillan Cambridge University Press, 1936). *See* also Dwight Jaffee and Bertrand Renaud, Strategies to Develop Mortgage Markets in Transition Economies 4 (World Bank Policy Research, Working Paper No. 1697, 1996).

achieved.[40] The following section will closely examine the practice of capital market regulation.

Regulation

As Baldwin and Cave summarized, the term "regulation" can be understood in the following senses: a specific set of commands; deliberate state influence; and all forms of social contrail or influence.[41] Regulating the capital market is about intervention into the market by the government, or regulatory agencies.

Regarding whether or not securities markets should be subject to regulatory control and to what degree the markets should be regulated, the debates between liberalism, a modern restatement of the old "free market" orthodox, and interventionism, a philosophy to control or influence capital market activities through governmental powers, have continued for decades. The overwhelming speculative investments on securities markets have inspired scholars and commentators to compare securities markets with casinos.[42] According to them, many investors view the securities market as a casino, and they are influenced by behavioral biases and trade in a manner akin to compulsive gambling. When the law has elected to intervene into compulsive gambling, why not compulsive investing.[43]

Governments customarily justify their regulatory intervention for the reason of protecting public interest. The argument is that uncontrolled markets will result in market failure, and thus "fail to produce behavior or results in accordance with

---

40   *See* Robert L. Heilbroner and Lester C. Thurow, Economics Explained 17–18 (New Jersey: Prentice Hall, 1982); *See* also John C. Coffee Jr., Privatization and Corporate Governance: The Lesson from Securities Market Failure 18–21 (Columbia Law School Center for Law and Economics Studies, Working Paper No. 158, 1999), available at <http://papers.ssvn.com/paper.taf?abstract_id=190568>; *See* also John C. Coffee Jr., *Regulating The Market for Corporate Control: A Critical Assessment of the Tender Offer's Role in Corporate Governance*, 84 Columbia Law Review 1154 (1984). *See* also Hong Wu and Wei Hu, Market Regulation Law – Basic Theory and System of Market Regulation Law 25–6 (Beijing: Peking University Press, 2006).

41   *See* Robert Baldwin and Martin Cave, Understanding Regulation: Theory, Strategy, and Practice 2 (New York: Oxford University Press, 1999).

42   *See* Lynn A. Stout, *Are Stock Markets Costly Casinos? Disagreement, Market Failure and Securities Regulation*, 81 Virginia Law Review 611 (1995); Paul G. Mahoney, *Is There a Cure for "Excessive" Trading?*, 81 Virginia Law Review 713 (1995); and Christine Hurt, *Regulating Public Morals And Private Markets: Online Securities Trading, Internet Gambling, And The Speculation Paradox*, 86 Boston University Law Review 371 (2006).

43   *See* Gauri Manglik, *Countering Over-confidence and Over-optimism by Creating Awareness and Experiential Learning amongst Stock Market Players*, Program for the European Association of Law and Economics 24th Annual Conference 16 (13–15 September 2007).

the public interest".[44] With increasing corporate failures and crashes of securities markets, interventionism has gradually permeated popular thinking about securities investment and securities markets.

A question then arises over whether regulators should have a focus on investors' behavioral biases in making regulatory policies. If the answer is yes, which form of regulatory response is the most appropriate: training, education, institutional rules, or legal intervention? Some securities markets have experimented with the educational approach by requiring investors to demonstrate a minimum level of knowledge or rationality in order to engage in certain types of securities transactions.[45] However, it has been observed that training or education is not a cure for investor biases, since such biases are displayed by all types of investors, unsophisticated and sophisticated, professional and non-professional.[46] Most jurisdictions have resolved to enhance their disclosure regimes in response to investors' irrational behavior, with some disclosure requirements specifically targeting certain behavioral biases. For example, disclosure of the information about the past returns of mutual funds and about the incentives received by analysts in making securities recommendations may substantially mitigate investors' undue emphasis on past returns and reliance on analysts' recommendations.[47] Nevertheless, there is a lack of empirical evidence verifying that disclosure is capable of overcoming investors' behavioral biases effectively.[48]

The issue of regulation targeting investors' behavioral biases becomes further complex when taking regulators' behavioral biases into consideration. Several behavioral biases having impact on securities regulators have been identified, including over-confidence, the confirmation bias, framing effects, and groupthink.[49] Research shows that monopolistic regulators are particularly prone to the above behavioral biases.[50] Currently, such biases have not received sufficient attention in all jurisdictions.

Although theoretical differences between liberalism and interventionism remain, and arguments relating to efficient measures targeting certain behavior biases in the capital markets continue, most countries have adopted regulatory measures monitoring their capital markets.[51] Based on level of regulatory authority, securities regulation is classified into governmental regulation and self-regulation.

---

44 *See* Baldwin and Cave, *supra* note 41, at 9.

45 *See* Jill E. Fisch, *Regulatory Responses to Investor Irrationality: The Case of the Research Analyst*, 10 Lewis and Clark Law Review 75 (2006).

46 *See* Arnold S. Wood, *Behavioral Risk: Anecdotes and Disturbing Evidence*, The Journal of Investing 8 (1997); Arnold S. Wood, *Fatal Attractions for Money Managers*, Financial Analysts Journal 3 (1989).

47 *See* Fisch, *supra* note 45, at 74.

48 *Ibid.*

49 *See* Stephen J. Choi and Adam C. Pritchard, *Behavioral Economics and the SEC*, 56 Stanford Law Review 20–36 (2003).

50 *Ibid.*

51 *See* Li, *supra* note 36, at 6.

The US is a country where both capital markets and regulation are highly developed. The development of the current US securities regulatory regime started in the 1930s, right after the 1929 crash. Before that, the US securities market was mainly self-regulatory. The first document of self-regulation was the Buttonwood Agreement signed on 17 May 1792 by 24 merchants who subsequently became the founders of the New York Exchange. The signers agreed to trade securities only among themselves, to set trading fees, and not to participate in other auctions of securities.[52] It was not until the early 1910s that all stock exchanges in the US stopped operating under their own trading rules.

Since 1911 some US states introduced securities laws to prevent fraudulent share trading.[53] After the 1929 Great Crash, it was believed that, for restoring the public's confidence in the securities market, governmental intervention was necessary. Keynesianism then gained popularity. In the meantime, there was the necessity to bring uniformity to the state regulatory scheme by adopting a uniform securities law.[54] Consequently, Congress passed the *Securities Act of 1933*. In the following year, the *Securities Exchange Act of 1934* was introduced. The two Acts formed the foundation and framework of the US securities regulatory system. The 1934 Act created the Securities and Exchange Commission (SEC) as a regulatory body to supervise the stock market and trading activities on the market.[55] In the meantime, Congress also introduced a series of Acts regulating the capital market and listed companies, including the *Glass-Steagall Act of 1933* and the *Public Utility Holding Company Act of 1935*. Since then the US has established the most developed and powerful securities regulatory regime in the world. Following the occurrence of a series of corporate finance scandals, Congress passed the *Sarbanes-Oxley Act* of 2002, which is announced as the most far-reaching reforms of American business practices since the time of Franklin Delano Roosevelt.[56] The *Sarbanes-Oxley Act* has three focuses: financial disclosures, auditor independence, and corporate responsibility. Its principal aim is to restore the public's faith in the capital markets.[57]

---

52 *See* the Editor, *The History of the Stock Market*, The New Enlightenment, available at <http://www.hermes-press.com/wshist1.htm>.

53 These laws were known as "blue sky" laws. The justification for these securities laws was to prevent the sale of fraudulent securities, because many securities salesmen would sell "building lots in the blue sky". *See* Paul Mahoney, *The Origins of the Blue Sky Laws: A Test of Competing Hypotheses*, available at <http://repositories.cdlib.org/cgi/viewcontent.cgi?article=1016&context=berkeley_law_econ>.

54 *See* the State of Wisconsin Department of Financial Institutions, *A Brief History of Securities Regulation*, available at <http://www.wdfi.org/fi/securities/regexemp/history.htm>.

55 *See* the SEC, *The Investor's Advocate: How the SEC Protects Investors, Maintains Market Integrity, and Facilitates Capital Formation*, available at <http://www.sec.gov/about/whatwedo.shtml>.

56 *Ibid.*

57 *Ibid.*

An advanced legal regime and a powerful regulatory commission are the two cornerstones of the US securities regulation. It is evident that the history of the SEC is about enhancing regulatory intervention and steadily phasing out of the self-regulatory rules of stock exchanges and other organizations in the securities business. In the beginning, the SEC could only alter 13 types of self-regulatory rules. When Congress amended the *Securities and Exchange Act of 1934* in 1975, the SEC's authority was extended to being able to verify all new self-regulatory rules introduced by any organization in the securities business. Today, the SEC can almost terminate, alter, add or remove any effective rule of self-regulation. It can even exempt a market participant from complying with the *Securities and Exchange Act of 1934*.[58]

The US model of securities regulation has significant influence on other countries' law making and practice. For example, Japan's securities legislation mirrors the US securities laws. Securities laws in China and China Hong Kong also closely follow the US model. The introduction of the over-the-counter markets associated with an automated quotation system in many European and Asian countries also demonstrates the US influence.[59] The interventionist approach thus forms the main theme of securities regulation. This theme further develops into a trend of centralization, due to the increasing support for harmonization of securities laws and practices by establishing international securities markets.[60]

However, governmental intervention or regulation has both advantages and disadvantages.[61] Undue or excessive governmental intervention can equally result in market inefficiency.[62] Some describe this as government failure.[63] Moreover, the efficiency of the interventionist approach is further reduced when the costs associated with the application increases. The general trend is that interventionism gains momentum after market scandals, and then liberalism prevails after interventional failures. Eventually, a compromise is found and self-regulation is favored. Compared with governmental regulation, self-regulation of the capital market is perceived to have the following advantages:

---

58 *See* Dale Arthur Oesterle, *Securities Markets Regulation: Time to Move to a Market Based Approach*, available at <http://www.cato.org/publs/pas/pa374.pdf>. *See* also Li, *supra* note 36, at 35.

59 In 1971, the US introduced the National Association f Securities Dealers' Automated Quotation System (NASDAQ). In the following years, Canada, Austria, France, Holland, Germany, Italy, the UK, China, Hong Kong, Japan, Singapore, Thailand, Australia, and New Zealand all introduced the same system. *See* Baisan Xie, China's Securities Markets 85 (Guangzhou: Guangdong Economics Press, 2003).

60 *See* Paul G. Mahoney, *The Exchange as Regulator*, 83 Virginia Law Review 1454 (1997).

61 *See* George J. Stigler, *Public Regulation of the Securities Markets*, 37(2) The Journal of Business 124–26 (1964).

62 *See* Hong Wu and Wei Lu, Market Regulation Law – Basic Theory and System of Market Regulation Law 14 (Beijing: Peking University Press, 2006).

63 *Ibid.*

Firstly, self-regulation of the securities market increases regulatory efficiency. Self-regulating organizations in the securities business, particularly the stock exchanges, are closely involved with the securities market and therefore better understand the needs of investors and broker-dealers.[64] They can better detect any departure from acceptable standards and take appropriate action swiftly. They are also in a better position to adapt to changes in the capital market. Moreover, stock exchanges have incentives to make rules providing for better protection to investors.[65] In addition, these organizations possess more expertise and professional staff, and are thus able to speedily formulate plans and methods to avoid or cope with risks.[66]

Secondly, self-regulation can reduce the costs of regulating the capital market.[67] Comparatively speaking, governmental regulation is a much more expensive practice. It involves, at least, legislative efforts, implementing measures, and enforcement mechanisms. The government has fewer incentives to reduce the regulatory costs.[68] By contrast with governmental intervention, self-regulation offers more flexibility. For example, the stock exchanges can pass the costs of rule-making and dispute settlement to industries. Furthermore, self-regulation organizations are better motivated to efficiently allocate funds due to close supervision from their members.[69]

In addition, it is argued that self-regulation effectively restrains opportunism on the capital market. Over-speculation undermines the orderly operation of the market and will eventually drive the market into crisis. Hence, for the members' interest as a whole, self-regulating organizations usually elect to confine the opportunistic conduct of its individual members.[70]

On the other hand, research and past experience suggest that self-regulation has a number of disadvantages. Firstly, the rules of self-regulation are usually vague and the standards are broadly defined. Secondly, the standards of self-regulation can hardly be enforced against non-members. Thirdly, the regulators are insulated from public opinion. Finally, self-regulation is restrained by the objective of maximizing the interests of the organization itself and its members, and thus naturally condones anti-competitive conduct.[71] All of these disadvantages undermine public confidence in self-regulation.

---

64   *See* Lori Richards, *Self-Regulation in the New Era*, available at <http://www.sec. gov/news/speech/spch398.htm >.

65   *See* Mahoney, *supra* note 60, at 1462.

66   *See* Li, *supra* note 36, at 168.

67   *Ibid.*

68   *See* Fuqian Fang, The Theory of Public Choices 195 (Beijing: People's University of China Press, 2000). *See also* Li, *supra* note 36, at 173.

69   *See* Li, *supra* note 36, at 168.

70   *Ibid*, at 175.

71   *See* Oesterle, *supra* note 58. *See* also Stephen Craig Pirrong, *The Self-Regulation of Commodity Exchanges: The Case of Market Manipulation*, 38 Journal of Law and Economics 141 and 154 (1995). *See also* Mahoney, *supra* note 41, at 1460–61. Mahoney

The UK has made its securities regulation distinctive by allowing self-regulation to dominate the landscape of its regulatory scheme for capital markets. Before 1986, the UK securities business and stock exchanges were entirely subject to rules of self-regulation. However, criticism of and dissatisfaction with the UK practice are widely expressed.[72] In 1986, the UK Parliament passed the *Financial Services Act* (FSA) and created the Securities and Investments Bureau (SIB) as the securities regulatory authority, which has the power to implement the FSA. Since then a new regulatory framework combining governmental regulation and self-regulation has come into existence. Nevertheless, self-regulation is still fundamental to UK securities regulation.

Given the insufficient aspects of both governmental regulation and self-regulation, some suggest adopting a regulatory approach combining the strength of governmental regulation and self-regulation.[73] Countries may, according to the situations of their capital markets and their regulatory traditions, either choose a regulatory system with governmental regulation as the principal regulatory method supplemented by self-regulation, or vice versa. In the past few decades, there has been a tendency to converge the two approaches. Some countries with legal regulatory tradition, including the US and some continental European countries, have gradually attached more importance to the role of self-regulation, while in the UK governmental regulation has steadily been enhanced.[74]

Securities Analysis and Capital Market Forecast

A distinction needs to be drawn between financial speculation and illegal financial speculation. Speculation inherently exists in financial transactions and commercial life. It involves trading commodities, properties and financial instruments including stocks and bonds in order to profit from fluctuations in their prices.[75] Speculation in capital markets is subject to the control or regulation of law, but should not be and has never been a thing to be eliminated, or unduly confined. The law only attempts to restrict undue speculation or speculation through unlawful strategies including insider trading and market manipulation. Lawful speculation is permitted, even

---

used two examples to demonstrate exchanges' rules aiming at reduce competition: fixed commission rates and limits on off-exchange trading.

72 *See* L.C.B. Gower, *Review of Investor Protection: A Discussion Document* (HMSO, January 1982). *See* also L.C.B. Gower, *Review of Investor Protection: Final Report* (Cmnd, 1984); *See* also Richard White, *The Review of Investor Protection – Gower Report*, 47 The Modern Law Review 553–66 (1984), available at <http://www.jstor.org/view/00267961/ap030246/03a00030/0>.

73 *See* Oesterle, *supra* note 58. *See* also Richards, *supra* note 64.

74 *See* Li, *supra* note 36, at 50–51.

75 *See* the Editor, Investopedia, available at <http://www.investopedia.com/terms/s/speculation.asp>. *See* also the Editor, Wikipedia, available at <http://en.wikipedia.org/wiki/Speculation>.

encouraged or blessed. This is evidenced by the emergence of various analytical and forecasting devices and services relating to the securities business and capital market. Today, securities analysis and capital market analysis are important tools assisting securities investors in investment decision-making.

Securities analysis or securities investment analysis is about assessing the assets, debt, equity of companies based on publicly available information.[76] Capital market analysis basically deals with securities market efficiency, valuation of traded securities, risk and return, finance and financing structures, and valuation of companies.[77] Securities analysis focuses on specific securities and issuers, whereas capital market analysis concentrates on the movements of the capital market.

Securities and securities market analysis originated in developed economies, mainly the US and the UK.[78] Nowadays, investment/securities analysts have become a high profile profession in securities businesses. They usually study the records of companies or securities issuers, and provide reports on the companies' investment potential or the securities ratings to their clients.[79] Theories, techniques and tools have been developed to serve the purpose of analyzing securities and the capital market. Based on observation of the capital market over hundreds of years, two distinctive analytical techniques have been developed in the field of investment analysis. They are: fundamental analysis and technical analysis.

Fundamental analysis is currently the dominant approach. It is about determining the intrinsic value of a specific market by examining all related macroeconomic and specific factors affecting the price of the market, including economic conditions, industry conditions, financial conditions, and management of companies.[80] Fundamental analysis studies the cause of market movement. It aims at working out the true value of a specific stock or financial instrument in order to inform investors about the position of the current price, *i.e.*, under-priced or overpriced. Investors are thus able to make right investment decisions – buying when the financial instrument is under priced, and selling if it is overpriced.

Technical analysis is regarded as an analytical approach opposed to fundamental analysis. It does not concern itself with the reasons causing price movement, rather,

---

76   *See* Benjamin Graham and David Dodd, Security Analysis: The Classic 1934 Edition (New York: McGraw-Hill Companies, Inc., 1934).

77   *See* David Blake, Financial Market Analysis (New York: John Wiley & Sons, 2000). *See also* Raymond William Goldsmith, Capital Market Analysis and the Financial Accounts of the Nation (New Jersey: General Learning Press, 1972).

78   *See* China Securities Association, Securities Investment Analysis 11 (Beijing: China Finance and Economy Press, 2004).

79   *See* the Editor, Wikipedia, available at <http://en.wikipedia.org/wiki/Financial_ analyst>.

80   *See* John J. Murphy, Technical Analysis of the Financial Markets: A Comprehensive Guide to Trading Methods and Applications 5 (New York: New York Institute of Finance, 1999). *See* also *ibid.*

it directly examines prices themselves and the patterns in the price information for forecasting future price trends.[81] The primary tools of undertaking technical analysis are charts. Technical analysis is built on the theory that market prices at any given point in time reflect all known and unknown factors affecting the intrinsic value of a market.[82] After all known factors have been discounted, the prices only react to unknown factors.[83] In other words, technical analysis claims that market prices tend to lead the unknown factors. Hence, the primary task of technical analysts is merely reading charts for interpreting the future trends of the market.

Apart from fundamental analysis and technical analysis, recent years have seen rapid development of some other theories of market analysis including psychological analysis and academic analysis.[84] Psychological analysis analyzes individual and group psychology. It attempts to guide investors to observe the capital market from an appropriate perspective.[85] Academic analysis is based on the efficient market theory. Its central argument is that investors should selectively acquire under-valued securities and look for long-term investment return. The most distinctive part of academic analysis lies in that it does not aim at beating the market.[86]

Different investors have different investment needs. It is essential that they adopt investment strategies matching their needs. Financial analysis helps investors to make investment decisions based on scientific investigation in order to increase investment efficiency.

The purpose of investing in the capital market is to gain financial returns. The rate of expected profitability is generally associated with the degree of risk. It is expected that high risk investments usually bring high returns. It is therefore crucial to accurately assess the risk associated with a specific securities investment in order to limit commercial risks. Furthermore, financial analysis is useful in maximizing investment profitability and minimizing investment risk through analyzing all related conditions and forecasting the trend of the market.

In an efficient capital market, information and price distortion is minimized. Investors speculate based on their analysis of securities and the market. The opportunities of making huge, dubious profits are limited. The risk of market crash thus diminishes. Investors are confident in the long-term prosperity of the market and are willing to invest in securities that bring long-term returns. Such a market offers sustainable development.

---

81   *Ibid*, at 1.

82   *See* Michael Covel, *Technical Analysis v. Fundamental Analysis: Difference?* Available at <http://www.turtletrader.com/technical-fundamental.html>.

83   *See* Murphy, *supra* note 80, at 6.

84   *See* China Securities Association, *supra* note 78, at 13.

85   *Ibid. See* George Katona, *Contribution of Psychological Data to Economic Analysis*, 42 (239) Journal of the American Statistical Association 449–59 (September 1947).

86   *Ibid.*

Conclusions

Speculation is inherent in the securities market. The prices of securities are affected by a number of factors including demand and supply, financial policies including taxation and interest policies, investors' psychology, and changes of economic environment. Many investors, particularly short-term investors, trade for profiting from the rise and fall of securities prices. This involves studying and forecasting the price action of the capital market, and making investment decisions. Any specific securities investment decision concerns calculation of profits and risks. This business engagement is characterized as "speculation". Hanry Manne simply described securities investors as gamblers.[87] It appears that speculation is both unavoidable and indispensable to the sustenance of the capital market.

However, excessive speculation is definitely harmful to the healthy growth of the market in the long run. Regulatory intervention hence has a role to play in addressing the delicate issue of facilitating an orderly and liquid securities market on the one hand, and constraining unbridled speculative conduct and eliminating bubbles on the other.

The objectives of regulation have to be ensuring effective operation, development and improvement of the securities market and assuring the transparency of the activities of securities market participants. When considering regulatory strategies, the elements of efficiency and cost have to be taken into account. There have been debates on which regulatory approach – legal intervention or self-regulation, is superior. The US has set up an example of vigorous legislative intervention. The fact that the US has developed the strongest corporate economy and the largest capital market is more or less considered to be a justification for the US style regulatory approach. Recent corporate scandals involving self-regulatory organizations including accounting firms and law firms, such as the Enron case, further shake people's confidence in self-regulation.

Nevertheless, the merit of self-regulation as a low cost and timely regulatory mechanism continues to be appreciated by business people. It is generally perceived that an efficient regulatory regime should be the one that has proficiently combined the strength of both governmental regulation and self-regulation.

---

87   *See* Henry G. Manne, *Our Two Corporation Systems: Law and Economics*, 53 Virginia Law Review 267 (1967).

Chapter 2

A Historical Review of the Securities Market Regulation: Governmental Intervention versus Self-regulation

Chapter 1 defined the meaning of speculation and reviewed the theoretical literature on investor biases. It discussed the connection between investor biases and "speculation". After drawing the relationship between speculation in securities markets and the need for regulation, Chapter 1 focused on the two dominant models of securities regulation in the world: legal intervention and self-regulation by analyzing the strength of them respectively and comparing their features and capabilities. This chapter continues the discussions on the two models through introducing their origins in the US and the UK and how they operate in these two leading corporate economies. The following chapter, Chapter 3, will discuss speculative behavior in China's securities market and introduce China's efforts in controlling excessive speculation in securities dealings. In doing so, Chapter 3 will provide to readers an overview of China's approach of regulating capital markets, so that readers can clearly perceive that the regulatory framework for securities markets in China has much been influenced by the US experience. The unique part of China's securities regulation is that compared with the US and UK experiences, China's regulatory approach has been shaped by the country's political economy to a greater degree. Another message that readers will receive from Chapter 3 is that although Chinese investors in the securities market are often plagued by speculative preference, the regulators have not yet placed the need of producing rules specifically targeting investors' behavioral biases on their regulatory agenda.

Looking back at the development of capital markets, one can see that initially, capital markets were largely unregulated. The so called *Bubble Act* 1720 was one of the earliest regulations aimed at disciplining capital markets.[1] The event of the South Sea Bubble alerted the UK parliament to the destructive consequence of an uncontrolled securities market. The enactment of the *Bubble Act* was an important

---

1   A law was passed by the UK Parliament in 1720, which prohibited an undertaking from acting as a corporate body and from raising transferable stocks and shares unless a Crown Charter or an Act of Parliament was conferred. The difficulty and expense of a Royal Charter and an Act of Parliament were politically designed to curb the expansion of incorporation. *See* L.C.B. Gower, Gower's Principles of Modern Company Law 28–9 (London: Sweet & Maxwell, 1997).

step taken to prevent similar disasters. Since the 1930s serious attempts to regulate securities business were generally made in developed countries. This chapter closely examines two influential securities regulatory systems – the US regulatory regime and the UK practice. By studying their experiences, the chapter intends to reveal the role of regulation in improving the efficiency of capital markets.

The US-style Regulatory Practice

The earliest securities transactions in the US were completed in some coffeehouses. In 1791, the country's first stock exchange was established in Philadelphia. In the following year, 24 merchants and brokers initiated a stock exchange under a buttonwood tree at 68 Wall Street, New York.[2] Gradually, Wall Street became the center of securities businesses. In 1817, the New York Stock and Exchange Board was established and located in Wall Street.[3] In 1863, the New York Stock and Exchange Board was renamed as the New York Stock Exchange (NYSE). Before the 1930s, the NYSE was a paradise for speculators and market manipulators. These speculators and manipulators were basically given a free rein. They sought huge profits through controlling the market and manipulating prices. They were called "Robber Barons" due to their unethical conduct on the capital market.[4]

There were calls for regulating the capital market. Some warned that without regulatory restrains, dishonest securities salesmen would sell building lots in the blue sky.[5] Against this background, following the lead of Texas, many US states introduced laws aimed at curbing fraudulent conduct on the securities market. These laws were also called blue-sky laws for the reason that they were introduced to prevent selling building lots in the blue sky. By 1913, about 23 US states had enacted blue-sky laws. However, these laws imposed limited control on securities business and had thus limited effect in containing securities frauds. An important reason for this is that at that time, the majority of US voters preferred an economic policy that was less interfering to business.[6] In other words, "this is a business country ... and it wants a business government".[7] This *laissez-faire* sentiment dominated the US national policies until the Great Crash in 1929.

---

2 *See* Peter Eisenstadt, *How the Buttonwood Tree Grew: The Making of a New York Stock Exchange Legend*, 19 Prospects: An Annual of American Cultural Studies 75 (1994).

3 *Ibid.*

4 *See* the Editor, Wikipedia, available at <http://en.wikipedia.org/wiki/Robber_baron_(industrialist)>.

5 *See* Paul Mahoney, *The Origins of the Blue Sky Laws: A Test of Competing Hypotheses*, 46 Journal of Law and Economics 229 (2003).

6 *See* Joel Seligman, The Transformation of Wall Street: A History of the Securities and Exchange Commission and Modern Corporate finance 2 (New York: Aspen, 2003).

7 *Ibid.*

Since 28 October 1929, the NYSE suddenly slumped.[8] Between 1 July 1929 and 1 July 1932, the value of all stocks listed on the NYSE shrank from nearly US$90 billion to under US$16 billion – representing a loss of 83 percent.[9] The crash of the securities market triggered the economic crisis known as the Great Depression in the US, which soon swept other industrialized countries. The whole capitalist world sank into economic recession.

The Great Crash urged US policy-makers to rethink the effectiveness and rationality of the *laissez-faire* approach in directing the economy. Investigations suggested that over speculation and bubbles were a cause of the capital market crisis. By the time of the 1920s, about 55 percent of individual bank savings went to the securities market for speculation.[10] A substantial amount of speculative money on the securities market was bank loans.[11] When the securities market plunged, banks demanded payment. This caused further stumble of securities prices. After lengthy debates and investigation, the US government eventually came up with a policy in favor of intervention.[12] The direct result was the enactment of the *Securities Act* of 1933 and the *Securities Exchange Act* of 1934. Since then, the US entered into an era of regulatory intervention.

The Securities Laws

The *Securities Act* of 1933 and *Securities Exchange Act* of 1934 are federal laws. The former mainly concerns the new-issue market, and the latter primarily targets the trading market. The *Securities Act* of 1933 does not directly compel listed companies to avoid illegal conduct by setting up behavioral standard and inserting penalties, instead, it requires listed companies to disclosure all information sensitive to securities prices. The *Securities Act* of 1933 is therefore regarded as a conservative response to the Great Crash and the Great Depression.

Originally, this approach was not favored by some economists including Roosevelt's principal campaign adviser Raymond Moley, University of Wisconsin president Van Hise, Professor Rexford Tugwell, and Professor Adolf Berle. These economists preferred a more rigorous regulatory regime and even claimed that the *Securities Act* of 1933 was a "grave mistake" and only had "a negative effect upon recovery".[13]

---

8   *Ibid*, at 3.

9   *Ibid*, at 1.

10   *See* Jing Wang and Biyan Teng, Comparative Study of Securities Law 24 (Beijing: China University of People's Public Securities Press, 2004).

11   *Ibid*.

12   *See generally* Herbert Hoover, Memoirs: The Cabinet and the Presidency (New York: Macmillan, 1952).

13   *See* Raymond Moley, The First New Deal 306 and 314 (New York: Harcourt, Brace and World, 1966).

However, President Roosevelt firmly preferred a progressive approach and believed that securities misconduct would be curtailed when companies and speculators were fully exposed to public scrutiny. The President's attitude was decisive in shaping the fundamental principles in the *Securities Act* of 1933 and the *Securities Exchange Act* of 1934. After more than half a century's implementation, these principles, particularly the disclosure philosophy, have become well established.

Generally speaking, the US securities regulatory system has the following distinctive features: firstly, it builds up a centralized, uniform regulatory regime. The *Securities Exchange Act* of 1934 provides that the Securities and Exchange Commission (SEC) is the sole government agent responsible for monitoring stock exchanges. All stock exchanges must register with the SEC as national securities exchanges, unless exempted. Furthermore, according to the *Securities Act* of 1933, securities issuers should register issuances with the SEC and provide detailed information relating to the issuances.[14] The issuers will incur criminal and civil responsibilities for fraudulent and misleading disclosure of information.[15] The SEC enjoys a great degree of independency and is not subject to interference from other governmental bodies including the White House. Self-regulatory institutions including stock exchanges are subject to the administrative intervention of the SEC. For instance, the SEC has the authority to modify policies and regulations adopted by stock exchanges for governing their own operations in the public interest.

The second feature of the US securities regulatory system is that it is backed by a powerful legal regime. The law forbids frauds on the securities market and provides for detailed measures of penalizing market misconduct including insider trading and manipulating securities prices. The rights to bring class actions and derivative actions further enhance capacity of securities investors to scrutinize transactions in the securities market.

Thirdly, disclosure forms the cornerstone of the US securities regulation system. The US securities law emphasizes timely, accurate and complete information disclosure. It is believed that disclosure is able to allow the securities market to function effectively at lowest costs. This belief is summarized by Louis Brandeis in his most famous remarks: "Publicity is justly commended as a remedy for social and industrial diseases. Sunlight is said to be the best of disinfectants; electric light the most efficient policeman".[16] This disclosure philosophy has been the spirit of all US securities laws.

Half a century later, the US possessed the most developed and prosperous capital market in the world. The US capital market adopted the most complex market structure and the most advanced technology. The US capital market not

---

14   *See* sec. 6 of the US *Securities Act* of 1933.

15   *Ibid*, secs 11, 12, 20 and 24.

16   *See* Louis Brandeis, Other People's Money and How the Bankers Use It 92 (New York: A.M. Kelley, 1971).

only played an important part in the US economy, but also had significant impact on the global economy. Due to the important status of the US capital market, the US securities regulatory approach was highly admired. It was regarded as a model for other countries to follow, and thus had far-reaching influence on shaping securities regulation world wide.

However, since the beginning of the new millennium, a series of high profile corporate and accounting scandals became known to the public. The publicity of these scandals revealed widespread breaches in corporate finance, accounting and auditing processes. Those involved included large public companies such as Enron, Tyco International, WorldCom, and leading accounting and audit firms such as Arthur Anderson, Deloitte and Touche, Ernst and Young, KPMG and PricewaterhouseCoopers. With the collapse of some large listed companies including Enron and WorldCom, millions of securities investors were affected. The confidence of the general public in the capital market was shaken. People began to doubt the effectiveness of the US securities regulatory system.[17] The US government responded by promulgating the *Sarbanes-Oxley Act* of 2002. The *Sarbanes-Oxley Act* introduced significant changes to corporate governance regulation and financial practice. The SEC also reponded by putting forward a number of reform proposals. Since then, the US securities regulatory regime has started to experience significant reforms.

The Future Development

The *Sarbanes-Oxley Act* of 2002 came into effect on 30 July 2002. It was enacted to protect investors by improving the accuracy of corporate disclosure.[18] Measures of compelling companies to comply with existing and new rules were introduced. The most significant strategies are as follows:

Firstly, the *Sarbanes-Oxley Act* has increased corporate controllers' responsibility in relation to corporate finance. The *Sarbanes-Oxley Act* requires listed companies to include with their annual report to the SEC a separate report by management on the assessment of the adequacy and accuracy of the company's internal control over financial reporting. Section 404 states the company's annual report should contain an internal control report stating the responsibility of management for establishing and maintaining an adequate internal control structure and procedures for financial reporting; and assessing the effectiveness of the internal control structure and procedures of the company for financial reporting.[19] Section 302 and section 906 state that principal executive officer(s) and principal financial

---

17   *See* Andrew Osterland, *Board Games*, CFO Magazine (1 November 2002), available at <http://www.cfo.com/-article.cfm/3007026?f=search>.

18   *See* the Editor, Wikipedia, available at <http://en.wikipedia.org/wiki/Sarbanes-Oxley_Act>.

19   *See* sec. 404 of the *Sarbanes-Oxley Act* of 2002.

officer(s) should certify and approve their periodic financial reports and assume civil and criminal liabilities for any breaches.[20]

Secondly, the *Sarbanes-Oxley Act* attaches importance to the function of the company's internal auditors. Section 301 requires that all listed companies must set up an audit committee and the members of the audit committee should comprise independent directors. The responsibilities of the audit committee are: (1) discussing annual and quarter financial reports; (2) discussing company's risk assessment and management policies; (3) employing registered accounting firms; (4) organizing the operation of internal control organs of the company; and (5) employing independent legal advisers and external auditors.

Thirdly, the *Sarbanes-Oxley Act* enhances financial disclosure. It requires that financial statements published by listed companies must be accurate and presented in a fashion that does not contain incorrect statements. The SEC is required to study and report on the extent of off-balance transactions resulting in transparent reporting.

Finally, the *Sarbanes-Oxley Act* introduces strict rules regulating to external auditors. It intends to ensure the independency of external auditors in order to effectively improve the corporate governance of public companies. Methods are introduced to enhance the independency of external audit functions. The Public Company Accounting Oversight Board's (PCAOB) is established to strengthen controls over the quality of audit work and determine stringent penalties for audit firms that violate audit standards.[21]

In the meantime, the SEC has also adopted a series of reform strategies. Firstly, measures are introduced to promote faster and fuller disclosure. Companies are required to make timely and complete disclosure. The deadline for companies to deliver quarterly reports has been reduced from the previous 45 days to 30 days. The deadline for companies to lodge annual reports has been reduced from the previous 90 days to 60 days. Companies are required to disclose information concerning executive compensation, director compensation and related party transactions.[22] Chief Executive officers are imposed increased personal liability for untrue statements.

Secondly, the SEC has endeavored to enhance corporate governance. An important step is urging the NYSE and the Nasdaq Stock Market, Inc. (NASDAQ) to strengthen their corporate governance listing standards. In 2002 and 2003, the

---

20   *See* secs 302 and 906 of the *Sarbanes-Oxley Act* of 2002.

21   *See* Ethiopis Tafara, *Speech by SEC Staff: U.S. Perspective on Accountancy Regulation and Reforms* 2, available at <http://www.sec.gov/news/speech/spch070803et. htm>.

22   *See* Locke Liddell and Sapp L.L.P., *Corporate Governance Alert: SEC Adopts Reforms to Executive Compensation Disclosure Rules* (3 August 2006), available at <http:// attorneys.lockeliddell.com/files/-Publication/c66a8233-3273-4634-bb65-07e4d7e7d2fc/ Presentation/PublicationAttachment/4c6737a2-4bf4-417a-bc1d-0ad29136324d/-Corporate %20Governance%20Alert%20-%20August%202006.pdf>.

NYSE and the NASDAQ proposed new rules enhancing corporate governance standards. Listed companies on the NYSE and the NASDAQ were required to meet the new requirements relating to the board independence, independent committees, codes of conduct and other corporate governance issues. In 2004, the SEC approved the new rules. These requirements were in compliance with spirit of the *Sarbanes-Oxley Act*, and went beyond the *Sarbanes-Oxley Act*. For instance, according to the new requirements, a majority of board members should be independent; board independence. Today, these new provisions are contained in Corporate Governance Certification Form and Amex Company Guide.

Thirdly, the SEC is determined to carry out a series of accounting reforms. The establishment of the PCAOB was a crucial move of combating financial frauds. The PCAOB is responsible for setting up rules of self-regulation, and has the authority to discipline accounting firms and auditors including disqualifying accountants and auditors. Furthermore, the SEC introduces measures to eliminate conflict of interests by accounting firms in providing consultation services.

In addition, the SEC has also introduced methods to ensure the independency of securities analysts, and required securities analysts to disclose information concerning the relationship between analysts.

The capital market reforms in the US since 2002 are the most comprehensive reforms undertaken by the US government after 1933. The general trend of the reforms is to further strengthen regulation over the securities market. Significant changes are made in the areas of disclosure, corporate governance, accountability, and auditor oversight. It is expected that these new strategies are able to effectively cope with corporate, managerial, accounting, and auditing failures. Given the model effect of the US securities laws, the reforms have had and will have a far-reaching influence to the world.

Securities Regulation in the UK

The UK was the first industrialized country. The securities market has a long history in the UK. The fast development of joint stock companies by the end of the seventeenth century provided sufficient tradable stocks to support a stock market and a trade of professional stock brokers.[23] In the 1760s, 150 brokers founded their private club to buy and sell securities in Jonathan's Coffeehouse, London.[24] Their attempt of expelling non-member stock brokers was frustrated by the government's intervention. This resulted in the establishment of the Stock Exchange. In 1773, the members of the club purchased a new building for brokerage. The new building

23 *See* Alan Jenkins, The Stock Exchange Story 18–20 (London: Heinemann, 1973).

24 *Ibid*, at 20 and 40–41. *See* also E. Victor Morgan and W.A. Thomas, The Stock Exchange: Its History and Functions 68 (London: Elek Books Limited, 1969). *See* also Harold Wincott, The Stock Exchange 7 (London: Sampson Low, Marston & Co., 1946).

was known as the New Jonathan's, and was for the members' exclusive use.[25] The previous club was formally named as the Stock Exchange. In the beginning of 1801, the members of the Stock Exchange decided to have a more exclusive club and consented to close the Stock Exchange and reopen it as a Subscription Room.[26] The Subscription Room was opened on 3 March, and in order to obtain membership, a broker needed to pay a one-time entrance fee and then annual subscription fees.[27] A set of self-policing rules were set up for members to follow and fines would be imposed on a rule breaker.[28] A regulated, modern stock exchange was born. The third of March 1801 was generally regarded as the birthday of the London Stock Exchange.[29]

The London Stock Exchange was a self-policing organization since the very beginning. When the brokers conducted their business at the Jonathan's, they resolved to tackle the problem of defaulting in settlement by reaching the agreement that defaulters would be expelled from the coffeehouse and would have their names be written down on the blackboard at the Jonathan's as a warning to others who might deal with them at a later stage, a punishment severe enough to restrain potential defaulters.[30] Since its establishment in 1801, for promoting its business reputation, the London Stock Exchange constantly introduced and updated its self-regulatory rules.[31]

Throughout the eighteenth century until World War I, there was a strong sentiment for free trade in Britain. The dominant economic ideology, namely the Adam Smith free market argument, endorsed the self-policing practice in the financial market. In his celebrated *The Wealth of Nations*, Adam Smith devoted most of the length to expound and prove the idea of a free market and limited government. His arguments were based on three principles: the rational mind, the rights of the individual and political-economic freedom.[32] He claimed that most forms of government interference in economic activities were costly and would create inefficiency.

It is noteworthy that in 1796, the British government attempted to regulate brokerage practice and enacted the *Act to Restrain the Number and Practice of*

---

25   *See* Jenkins, *supra* note 23, at 45.

26   *See* Morgan and Thomas, *supra* note 24, at 61.

27   *See* Ranald Michie, The London Stock Exchange: A History 35 (Oxford: Oxford University Press, 1999).

28   *See* Morgan and Thomas, *supra* note 24, at 69.

29   *See* London Stock Exchange, Our History (London Stock Exchange webpage), available at <http://www.london-stockexchange.com/en-gb/about/cooverview/history.htm>.

30   *Ibid*, at 69.

31   *See* Edward Stringham, *The Emergence of the London Stock Exchange as a Self-Policing Club*, 17(2) Journal of Private Enterprise 8–12 (2002).

32   *See* James Pyland, *Free-market Activists Distort Original Message of Adam Smith's "invisible hand"*, Online Journal (11 February 2006), available at <http://www.onlinejournal.com/artman/publish/article_499.shtml>.

Brokers and Stock-Jobbers to discipline the conduct of brokers.[33] In an atmosphere of free market ideology domination, the 1697 Act was destined to be short lived and was repealed in 1707. Since then, the UK securities market was mainly under self-regulation through stock exchanges themselves and several self-regulation organizations including the Council of Securities Industry.

Stock exchanges are the foundational self-regulatory organizations. The listing rules and business rules of the stock exchanges are important sources of securities' regulation. Stock exchanges are incorporated. Only members of a stock exchange can be securities dealers on the exchange. Stock exchanges have rules providing requirements of admission or approval of listed companies. Listing companies are required to continually disclose necessary information.[34] A stock exchange has the right to: disapprove the application of a company to be listed on its exchange, and the right to de-list a company. In addition, a stock exchange supervises the conduct of its members in their securities dealing. It may cancel or refuse to renew the license of a securities dealer.

Very few significant legislative initiatives were made in the UK to regulate securities until 1986. In 1986, the UK introduced the *Financial Services Act* 1986. It came into effect in 1988. The *Financial Services Act* 1986 stipulated that all investment businesses must apply for authorization through their self-regulatory organizations, by a recognized professional body unless they were exempt from investment activities. It was a criminal offence to provide investment advice without authorization or exemption. The *Financial Services Act* 1986 created the Securities and Investment Board (SIB) to oversee self-regulatory organizations and produce regulatory policies. Apart from the *Financial Services Act* 1986, provisions regulating securities can also be found in other Acts. For example, the *Companies Act* 1985 provides the requirements of a prospectus.

In October, the authority announced the reform of financial services regulation and the creation of a new regulator on 20 May 1997. Banking supervision and investment services regulation were merged into the SIB. The SIB formally changed its name to the Financial Services Authority, and all the functions of the SIB were transferred to the Financial Services Authority (FSA). In May 2000 the FSA took over the role of the UK listing authority from the London Stock Exchange.[35]

---

33   *See* George Gilligan, *Expecting Too Much? Enforcement Limitations in the Regulation of Financial Markets* 10 (conference paper at Conflicting Interests: Evaluating Regulation, Ethics and Accountability in Capital Markets Governance, Australian National University, Canberra, 14–15 March 2007), available at <http://cbe.anu.edu.au/-capitalmarkets/papers/GILLIGAN-CAPITAL-MARKETS.pdf>.

34   *See* the Editor, *London Stock Exchange Listing Requirements*, Stock Exchange Secrets, available at <http://www.stockexchangesecrets.com/london-stock-exchange-listing-requirements.html>.

35   *See* FSA, History (FSA website), available at <http://www.fsa.gov.uk/Pages/About/Who/History/index.shtml>.

In 2000, the *Financial Services and Markets Act* 2000 was promulgated and replaced the *Financial Services Act* 1986.[36] The *Financial Services and Markets Act* 2000 became effective on 1 December 2001. The primary objects of the Act are to maintain confidence in the financial market, increase public awareness of the financial market, protect investors/consumers, and reduce financial crimes.[37]

The FSA is given statutory powers by the *Financial Services and Markets Act* 2000. Apart from the authorities previous exercised by the SIB, the *Financial Services and Markets Act* 2000 gives the FSA some new responsibilities – in particular, taking action to prevent market abuse.[38] In addition, the *Financial Services and Markets Act* 2000 has transferred to the FSA the responsibilities of several other organizations including Investment Management Regulatory Organization Securities and Futures Authority.[39]

According to the *Financial Services and Markets Act* 2000, the FSA is an independent non-governmental body. It is a company limited by guarantee and financed by the financial services industry. The FSA Board should be appointed by the Treasury.

Since 1986, the UK securities regulatory regime has entered into an era of landmark reforms. The UK securities regulation has since transformed from a fully self-regulative system into a system that combines legislative supervision and self-regulative administration.

The *Financial Services and Markets Act* 2000 provides a set of comprehensive provisions regulating the securities market. This was a major step towards bringing securities markets and activities under legislative control. However, the legislation regulating the UK securities market since 1986 has all been founded on the established self-regulatory framework. The powers of the FSA, as the regulatory authority created by the *Financial Services and Markets Act* 2000, are also inherited from the previous self-regulatory organizations. The laws, in fact, have confirmed the self-regulatory framework from the legislative perspective.

The Trend

To business people, the perfect world is of *laissez-faire* – leave us alone. Regulation should be limited to the extent of being beneficial to businesses. Self-regulation is thus the most preferred disciplinary measure. Business people, either in ancient guilds, present companies or other business associations, have always had their own rules. Rules of self-regulation of ancient guilds were aimed at facilitating fair

---

36   *See the Financial Services and Markets Act* 2000 (Promotion of Collective Investment Schemes) (Exceptions) Order 2001, available at <http://www.hm-treasury.gov.uk/media/A/3/fsma_ria.pdf>.

37   *See* sec. 2, Part I of *the Financial Services and Markets Act.*

38   *See* FAS, *supra* note 35.

39   *Ibid.*

competition among members. This was usually achieved through excluding non-member competitors from the market and monopolizing technology.[40] These rules mainly concerned controlling and managing productive techniques and process, row materials, tools and equipments, quality of products, and apprenticeship.[41]

The securities market at its early stage of development was also largely left to self-regulation. In the UK, the Stock Exchange was brought into being at the New Jonathan's for the purpose of excluding some disreputable securities brokers in order to attract more businesses. Non-member brokers attempted to petition the UK government to force the Stock Exchange to be public accessible. The members of the UK parliament rejected the requisition and declared that the establishment of the Stock Exchange as an exclusive club would be "open to honorable men and closed shut for ever to notorious cheats".[42]

The most noticeable advantage of self-regulating the securities market perceived is that self-regulation allows for gradual progression and experimental changes. Self-regulation gives brokers the opportunity to try different regulations and select the most efficient ones.[43] The following comments of Hayeke give convincing explanations:

> It is this flexibility of voluntary rules which in the field of morals makes gradual evolution and spontaneous growth possible, which allows further experience to lead to modifications and improvements. Such an evolution is only possible with rules which are neither coercive nor deliberately imposed ... Unlike any deliberately imposed coercive rules, which can be changed only discontinuously and for all at the same time, rules of this kind allow for gradual and experimental change. The existence of individuals and groups simultaneously observing partially different rules provide the opportunity for selection of the more effective ones.[44]

There are also other advantages of self-regulation including reducing regulatory cost and minimizing market risk. Nevertheless, the general trend in all jurisdictions has been increase of governmental regulation. Even in the UK, the capital market has been one of the legislative focuses since the 1980s.

History tells that when the size of the market and the complexity of business activities increase, the might of self-regulation diminishes. Self-regulation prevailed when guilds dominated the economic landscape before the industrial revolution. The development of technology has made firms and businesses

---

40   *See* Yiehua Chen, Theories of Securities Self-Regulation and China's Practice 30–31(Beijing: China Financial Press, 2006).

41   *Ibid.*

42   *See* Morgan and Thomas, *supra* note 24, at 72.

43   *See* Stringham, *supra* note 31, at 3.

44   *See* Friedrich A. Hayek, Constitution of Liberty 62–3 (Chicago: University of Chicago, 1960).

compete in ever growing markets while coping with increased managerial and technological complexity. In such an environment, labor movement, material distribution, technological innovation, and market admission are far beyond the control of a guild. Logically, guilds, together with their rules of self-regulation, have faded from modern economic life as a result of technological and economic development. Governmental regulation has replaced self-regulation in most trades and businesses previously regulated by the rules of guilds.

With the increase of the significance of the capital market in today's economy, securities markets and businesses have attracted and will inevitably attract increasing governmental regulation. Nevertheless, government regulation is subject to doubt and challenge in the case of regulatory failure or governmental failure. A task faced by every government is to constructively exert the strength of both government regulation and self-regulation in order to achieve the most desirable regulatory efficiency.

Conclusions

The UK securities market has a long-standing history of self-regulation. The most distinctive feature of the UK's securities regulation is its emphasis on self-regulation. In contrast to the US approach of enacting stringent legislation and establishing a powerful administrative body (the SEC), in the UK, stock exchanges and self-regulatory organizations comprise the main force of securities' regulation.

Like the UK securities market, initially, the US capital market was basically unregulated. The legislative efforts since the 1910s and mainly in the 1930s were essentially propelled by serious market failure or crashes. The securities market definitely played a more important role in the economic life of the US, compared with the UK securities market at the initially stage of development. The trading value of the US capital market was large and the complexity of the business was great. The US could not afford to leave the securities market in a state of *laissez-faire*.

It is generally perceived that the US securities regulatory system has shown considerable capacity in coping with crashes and redressing regulatory faults and defects. Currently, many countries' securities regulation is adapted from the US model.

Nevertheless, it is self-evident that self-regulation has an indispensable role to play, particularly in regulating the internal relationship between stock exchanges and issuers, as well as between stock exchanges and securities dealers.

Chapter 3
Speculation and Regulation: The Story of China's Capital Market

Securities markets and related activities were phased out of China's economy in the era of the planned economy between the 1950s and the 1970s.[1] Since the 1980s, bonds and stocks have again been traded and the securities market has flourished. In the early 1990s, two national stock exchanges were opened in Shanghai and Shenzhen. In the following 15 years, China has evolved into one of the largest capital markets in Asia.[2] However, the development of China's capital market has not been smooth. Over-speculation and price distortion are the most worrying problems jeopardizing the healthy development of China's capital market. The South-East Asian economic recession between 1997 and 1998 is a warning to the Chinese that if these problems in China's financial market persist, the country's economy could well be driven into serious troubles. With increasing exposure to international speculators due to compliance with the WTO rules and China's economic integration into the world economy, time is running out for the Chinese to develop workable strategies addressing these problems.

Speculation in China's Capital Market

China's capital market is far from efficient. Widely reported breaches and irregularities suggest that the market is overly speculated. The breaches take various forms including non-disclosure and misleading disclosure, trading on inside information, swaying stock prices, and other types of securities breaches and crimes. The offenders and wrongdoers are mainly listed companies and their controllers and staff, securities companies and their staff, and officers of securities supervisory and regulatory bodies. Greed and the willingness to take chances in a young and insufficiently regulated market have fueled widespread opportunistic conduct.

---

1   *See* Qingquan Ma, The History of Securities Business in China 3 (Beijing: CITIC Publishing House, 2003).

2   By 2002, the number of listed Chinese companies was 1,224. The value of the two exchanges reached 38 percent of the country's GDP. *See* Zheng Sun, Zhe Juan and Yongqing Hu, Innovations and Regulatory Studies of Emerging Capital Markets 1 (Shanghai: Shanghai Finance and Economy University Press, 2005). *See* also Zhijun Li, Government Regulation of the Securities Market 97 (Changchun: Jilin People's Press, 2005).

At the initial stage of the capital market development, the chief object of the government was to help state-dominated companies to raise funds without excessively burdening the state banks. An important strategy introduced was "quota control".[3] Under this scheme, only a limited number of companies were permitted to be listed on the stock exchanges and share issuance was scrutinized.[4] The number of companies to be listed and the volume of shares to be issued were decided by the relevant governmental authority following certain procedures of examination and approval.[5] At that time, China's economy expanded rapidly and all enterprises sought to raise funds through the capital market. However, a sophisticated legal infrastructure governing the securities business was yet to be established, and laws regulating securities and stock exchanges had not been completed. Moreover, companies and professionals in the securities trade were still in the course of learning the securities business. It was generally understood that the issuance of shares must be closely administrated, since without some degree of control, the market would run into chaos and eventually harm investors.[6] It was believed that quota control would be the best way of keeping the capital market in check. An important reason for this was that by having quota control in place, the government had control over deciding which companies' stocks should be admitted onto the stock exchanges. In doing so, the government could ensure that state-dominated companies took full advantage of public issuance by giving them priority in obtaining quotas.[7] It was also expected that quota control would allow the government to effectively avoid and cope with possible confusion in the market.[8]

However, the quota system exacerbated the imbalance between the demand and supply on China's securities market, and resulted in too many investors eagerly seek to buy a limited number of shares. Corruption cases involving the members of governmental departments and institutions with the authority of allocating the quotas were subsequently reported.[9] The quota control method also motivated companies to engage in dubious conduct in the course of obtaining quotas. Many companies invested significant amounts of energy and finance in acquiring quotas.[10] Some of them resolved to forge their finance and performance records, and some even resorted to bribing officers who could sway the quota allotment.[11]

---

3   *See* Ma, *supra* note 1, at 146.

4   *See* Zheng Sun, Zhe Juan and Yongqing Hu, Innovations and Regulatory Studies of Emerging Capital Markets 5 (Shanghai: Shanghai Finance and Economy University Press: 2005).

5   *Ibid.*

6   *Ibid.*

7   *See* Li, *supra* note 2, at 82–3.

8   *Ibid.*

9   *See* Jinqing Zhu, Securities Law 83 and 285 (Beijing: Peking University Press, 2007).

10   *See* Sun, Juan and Hu, *supra* note 4.

11   *See* Shujiang Xie, China's Capital Market: An Analysis Based on the Theory of Competition 124 (Beijing: China Finance and Economy Press, 2004).

Such companies usually lacked the aspiration and motivation to improve their economic and managerial efficiency.[12] Consequently, the money raised from the securities market by these companies was not spent on technological innovation or business expansion, but on increasing salaries and improving the welfare of the managers and employees. The worst situation was the money raised being deposited in banks or trust funds for interest or investment returns, or even being used to speculate on the stock exchanges.[13]

Local governments, parent companies, and companies offering securities services (securities companies) all consciously or unconsciously encouraged and supported candidate companies engaging in improper conduct in the course of fighting for quotas, and in some cases, even took part in such conduct. Some local governments told their enterprises to work ten times harder to obtain quotas.[14] Securities companies competed to underwrite for quota companies. In order to prevail in the competition, they would turn to all possible means, proper or improper, legal or illegal.[15] Parent companies usually injected funds or provided other forms of assistance to their subsidiaries to help them to obtain quotas. Once the subsidiaries got the quotas, the parent companies would use any means to extract the subsidiaries' funds raised from the capital market, including borrowing, making the subsidiaries guarantee borrowing contracts in favor of the parent or other member companies in the group, and leasing facilities or properties from the subsidiaries.[16] This was referred to as "feeding pigs for pork".[17]

Because the demand for shares was so great, considerable earnings for every purchase of newly issued shares were almost guaranteed.[18] The enormous profit and the enticing opportunities of fortune provoked many to risk breaching the laws. There were notorious cases where companies, including quite a few companies providing securities services, had used clients' funds or public funds to trade shares on the capital market.

One can see that breaches and irregularities in the early stages of capital market development in China were generally associated with misconduct and offenses in share issuance, including embezzlements, briberies, misappropriation of public funds for speculating on the capital market, and misconduct in securities services. The breaches mainly related to accounting and administration offenses.

With the development of China's securities market, misconduct directly linked to securities dealings has increased rapidly.[19] The market is constantly affected by

12 *Ibid.*
13 *Ibid.*
14 *See* Sun, Juan and Hu, *supra* note 4.
15 *Ibid.*
16 *See* Zhu, *supra* note 9, at 68–9.
17 *Ibid.*
18 *See* Lei Gu and Baojie Wang, Crimes and Irregularities on the Securities market and Legal Control 28 (China Prosecution Press, 2004).
19 *Ibid*, at 5–6.

non-disclosure, misleading disclosure, insider trading, market manipulation, and breach of duties by market intermediaries.[20]

Forging companies' accounts has become a common breach by listed companies. Although tough laws regulating company financial reports and accounting practice are in place, fraudulent accounting practices are widespread. According to the Chinese law, a listed company's financial reports and accounts should be scrutinized by qualified, independent accountants and double checked by external auditors.[21] However, it is not uncommon that internal accountants and external accountants and auditors collaborate in making false accounts and financial reports. For instance, in the Gongguang Case, in order to meet the listing requirements, the management of the Gongguang company instructed that the company's accounts should reflect that it had made profits in 1996, knowing that the company made a loss of RMB 53,778,000 yuan. Such instruction was effected by the financial officers of the company with the assistance of external accountants, lawyers, the assets evaluation organization, and the securities company. All the parties involved in making the false accounts received considerable kickbacks from the company.[22]

The purpose of forging company accounts and financial reports is to mislead investors. Surveys show that forging accounts and financial reports is rampant. According to Xinhua News Agency, between March and November 2001 alone, there were 16 listed companies that were penalized by China Securities Regulatory Commission (CSRC) for misleading the market.[23] The impact of misleading disclosure on the securities market is enormous. For example, in the Yin Guang Xia case, after the misleading disclosure in the Yin Guang Xia company's financial statements was reported, the share price of the company plunged, and on average, each shareholder incurred a loss of RMB 500,000 yuan.[24]

Other forms of breaches including insider trading and market manipulation are also widespread.[25] The most disturbing fact is that securities companies, as market intermediaries, have played an active role in market manipulation and speculation.[26] It used to be common for securities companies to use money on

---

20   *See* Yuwa Wei, *Volatility of China's Securities Market and Corporate Governance*, 29.2 Suffolk Transnational Law Review 212–22 (2006).

21   *See* the People's Congress, the 1993 Company Law of the People's Republic of China (amended in 2005), secs 153, 165, 171; and the 1998 Securities Law of the People's Republic of China (amended in 2005), sec. 161.

22   *See* Lei Gu and Baojie Wang, Crimes and Irregularities on the Securities market and Legal Control 21 (China Prosecution Press, 2004).

23   *See* Xinhua News Agency, *The Companies that Received Penalties from CSRC for Making Misleading Disclosure*, in Zhe Jiang Daily (18 January 2002), at 3.

24   *See* Zhu, *supra* note 9, at 162.

25   For a detailed recount on insider trading and market manipulation in China's capital market, *see* Yuwa Wei, *Volatility of China's Securities Market and Corporate Governance*, 29.2 Suffolk Transnational Law Review (2006).

26   *See* Zhu, *supra* note 9, at 71.

clients' accounts to speculate on the market. Some securities companies were allowed to participate in securities investments while providing securities services. Enticed by greed and pressured by increasing competition, many such companies engaged in misappropriating clients' money, bonds and shares to gain profits in their own speculative activities. This has resulted in serious crises and instability in the market.[27]

There are many reasons for the rampant breaches on China's capital market. Firstly, the regulators of the market have attached great importance to ensuring that the state's interest in the securities business is preserved. On many occasions, preferential policies and strategies are introduced to secure the financial benefits of state-dominated listed companies, securities companies, and investment funds at the expense of market discipline. A typical example was the introduction of the quota control system. Another example is the administrative preference conferred on securities companies. For instance, when securities companies faced financial pressure during the market recession, the CSRC allowed these companies to manage their clients' accounts, knowing the likelihood that these companies would misappropriate clients' money and assets placed in their care, and engage in market manipulative activities.[28]

Secondly, the division of the market has fueled opportunistic conduct in China's capital market.[29] China's securities market is divided into A share, B share and H share markets on the one hand, and state share, legal person share and public share markets on the other. This division results in price distortion in the A share market.[30] As a result, there is a significant price gap between the primary market and secondary market for A shares. The share prices on the secondary market can be many times higher than the initial issue prices on the primary market.[31] The result is: investing in any A share on the primary market is profitable.[32] The situation was further worsened when the government restricts initial share prices to below 20 times of their earnings following the recession in 2001.[33] The highly profitable investment opportunities cloud many minds with avarice. It is therefore not a surprise that enterprises would use their development funds, and securities companies would misappropriate their clients' funds in order to speculate on the securities market.

---

27   *See* Jing Chen, Special Research on Securities Law 196 (Beijing: High Education Press).

28   *Ibid*, at 269.

29   *See* Shujiang Xie, China's Capital Market: An analysis based on the theory of competition 116 (Beijing: China Finance and Economy Press, 2004).

30   *Ibid*.

31   See Zhu, *supra* note 9, at 64.

32   *See* Gu and Wang, *supra* note 22, at 28.

33   *See* Yuwa Wei, *The Development of the Securities Market and Regulation in China*, 27.3 Loyola of Los Angeles International and Comparative Law Review 502 (2005).

Thirdly, there are serious problems associated with the management of listed companies. State-dominated companies are still susceptible to excessive administrative intervention and have serious insider control problems. The supervisory board and independent directors in many companies are powerless in dealing with the dominant shareholder – the state.[34] This is usually because the supervisors are insiders and independent directors are not aware of their responsibilities. For instance, in the Zheng Baiwen case, the executive directors of the company engaged in market manipulation activities. The independent directors, however, knew nothing of the breaches. When the court delivered a judgment imposing a fine on ten independent directors for negligence, the independent directors ironically believed that their positions were only honorary and they therefore were not responsible for any breach by the company.[35] Moreover, many listed companies engage in market misconduct including fraudulent disclosure and market manipulation.

Fourthly, corruption in the state assets management system results in China's capital market being vulnerable to manipulation. China has accumulated more than six billion yuan of state assets.[36] Due to the loopholes in state assets administration, a huge amount of state assets, in the form of capital, capable of swaying the market, floods into the capital market to participate in securities speculation.[37] This further upsets the orderly operation of the market.

Another reason why China's capital market is susceptible to manipulation is that Chinese investors are less mature and lack understanding of the nature of securities investments. Many Chinese securities investors have unrealistic expectations in relation to securities investments. They establish the goal of making a fortune overnight. Instead of obtaining and studying price sensitive information about the market and listed companies, investors are more interested in spending time on tracing and investigating the movements of bankers and hope to gain a windfall from the securities market by following big players' moves.[38] Furthermore, Chinese investors also have unrealistic expectations of risk aversion. They believe that they will be able to avoid those business risks naturally associated with securities investments. When the market experiences a downturn, investors tend to call for governmental intervention. They hope that the government can inspire an resurgence in the market by introducing policies and methods to avoid a substantial decline in share prices.[39] The government's intervention on a few

---

34 *See generally* Wei, *supra* note 25.

35 *See* Shiling Ma and Zhongfu Yao, *The Case of Lu Jiahao (Former Independent Director of Zheng Bai Wen) Versus the CSRC Will Be Heard Next Thursday*, in Baisan Xie (ed.), International Comparison of Securities Markets 497–8 (Volume 2, Beijing: Qinghua University Press, 2003).

36 *See* Xie, *supra* note 29, at 179.

37 *Ibid.*

38 *See* Chen, *supra* note 27, at 269.

39 *Ibid*, at 61.

occasions has further misled investors' blind belief that speculation in China's securities market is generally safe.[40] Investors' enthusiasm in PT and ST shares is a typical example. Under-performed listed companies are classified as Particular Transfer (PT) or Special Treatment (ST) companies. These companies will be delisted if they are unable to make improvements within a given time period. The PT and ST labels are intended to serve as a warning to potential investors. To the securities regulator's surprise, following the announcement of STs and PTs, investors' interests in such companies usually increase. This is because the CSRC rarely delists companies and often restructures some delinquent companies in order to allow the investors of such companies to avoid losses.[41] A famous restructuring case of a collapsed company is the Hainan Minyuan case. The Hainan Minyuan company forged its annual report and was subject to delisting. For the purpose of maintaining the stability of the securities market and protecting investors' confidence in the securities market, instead of ordering it to be delisted, the CSRC arranged for the company to be restructured. A new company was established, and the investors of Hainan Minyuan sold their shares to the new company in return for an equal number of shares in the new company. As a result, the investors suffered no loss from the misconduct of the previous company, and in fact, profited from the restructure.[42] Based on such experiences, many investors are keen to invest in PTs and STs in the hope that they may profit from administrative intervention at some later stage.[43] This type of investment psychology tends to drive securities investments into purely speculative games.

In addition, imperfect laws are unable to curtail misconduct and breaches in the capital market effectively.[44] In the area of financial market regulation, legislation generally lags behind practice. China did not have a comprehensive Securities Law until 1998. It was only after 1997 that the *Criminal Law* has begun to deal with securities offences such as insider trading and fraud on securities investors. Furthermore, the penalties for securities offences are inadequate and are thus not effective at deterring breaches. Moreover, on many occasions, securities offenders and wrongdoers are able to escape civil liabilities for losses suffered by investors.[45]

Due to China's increasing integration into the world economy, China's capital market is exposed to more and more international speculators and their speculative money. China's capital market becomes even more vulnerable than ever when

---

40   *See* Li, *supra* note 2, at 204.

41   *See* Minliang Li, Studies of Hotly Debated Legal Issues concerning Securities Market 284 (Beijing: Commerce Press, 2004).

42   *See* Qilin Fu, Well-Known Cases relating to China's Securities Market in the Past Ten Years 70 (Beijing: Publishing House of China University of Political Science and Law, 2002).

43   *See* Li, *supra* note 2, at 204.

44   *See* Xie, *supra* note 29, at 177.

45   *See* Chen, *supra* note 27, at 272.

facing the manipulative capacity of international sharks. If the susceptibility existing in China's capital market, listed companies and regulatory framework persists, China's finance safety will be under unprecedented threat.

The evidence suggests that the Chinese capital market is overly speculated. Over-speculation and unfair competition in the securities market have harmed the order of the market and shaken investors' confidence. If no effective restraint is put in place, the healthy development of the capital market will be hindered, and eventually financial and social instability will be triggered. China must endeavor to introduce effective control mechanisms in order to ensure the market's long term prosperity.

Regulation of China's Capital Market

China's securities market has been marked with strong government intervention since it came into existence. The Chinese government's decision to issue national bonds was made with the purpose of easing the country's budget deficit. At that time, a capital market had not been contemplated by the policy makers. Later, the state banks were under increasing pressure to fund financially stressed enterprises.[46] The government needed to find a new channel for financing the enterprises, and it eventually decided to establish a capital market.[47] The creation of the securities market was therefore a side product of China's economic reforms.[48] The economic reforms in China have been carefully guided by the government. The Chinese government has taken the initiative in every crucial step of the economic reforms. This interventionist approach has been regarded as both necessary and inevitable. It is generally believed that only the government has the power and vision to promote such comprehensive social and economic changes. Consequently, the development of China's capital market has unexceptionally been under the government's close supervision and guidance. However, unrestrained governmental intervention into economic life can be costly and dangerous. The Chinese experience of capital market regulation has proven that the power of the government must be checked.

The history of China's securities market regulation can be divided into three phases. The first phase is the period of dispersed, strategic regulation.[49] In this period, the securities activities and markets were supervised by multiple authorities including the People's Bank of China, the State Council, the Ministry of Finance,

---

46   *See* Yuwa Wei, *Maximising the External Governance Function of the Securities Market: A Chinese Experience*, 3 International Company and Commercial Law Review 111 (London: Sweet & Maxwell, 2008).

47   *Ibid.*

48   *See* Li, *supra* note 2, at 60–61.

49   *See* Chen, *supra* note 27, at 33.

the Securities Regulatory Commission, as well as local governmental bodies.[50] Consequently, the laws governing securities activities were dispersed. The State Council enacted the *State Treasury Bonds Regulations* in 1981, the *Provisional Regulations Administrating Enterprise Securities* in 1987, the *Announcement about Enhancing the Management of Enterprises' Internal Securities* in 1987, and the *Regulations concerning Special State Treasury Bonds* in 1989. The People's Bank of China promulgated the *Provisional Methods of Regulating Securities Companies* in 1990, the *Provisional Methods of Regulating Securities Transactions Cross Administrative Districts* in 1990, and the *Announcement about Strict Control of Share Issuance and Transfer* in 1990. Local legislation included the *Methods of Administrating Over the Counter Transactions in Shanghai City* of 1987, the *Provisional Methods of Managing Shares in Shanghai* of 1987, the *Provisional Methods of Administrating Securities in Shanghai* of 1987, and the *Provisional Methods of Administrating the Securities Transfer Business in Beijing City*, which took effect in 1987.

The regulatory approach during this period was "one law for one matter" or "one law for one type of securities".[51] Securities practice in this phase was a matter of trial and error, and the law was in a constant race to catch up and accommodate new practices and situations. The primary object of the regulation in this period was to bring securities activities under the close administration and supervision of the government. Share issuance was subject to the approval system of "quota control", and the laws only permitted the enterprises with significant state or public ownership to issue securities.[52] Privately owned enterprises were allowed to issue bonds, but prohibited from issuing shares to the public.[53] The People's Bank of China played an important role in making laws during the period, since it was initially given substantial authority to administrate and monitor securities businesses and markets.

The second phase, from the early 1990s to the late 1990s, was the period of local regulation. In this stage, China centralized securities markets by establishing two national stock exchanges in Shanghai and Shenzhen. Nevertheless, the securities business was generally regulated by local laws, mainly by laws enacted by the authorities in Shanghai and Shenzhen. Important legal documents included: the *Administrative Methods of Securities Transactions in Shanghai City* of 1990, the *Provisional Methods of Administrating Share Issuance and Trade in Shenzhen City* of 1991, the *Provisional Methods of Administrating Securities Institutions in Shenzhen City* of 1991, and the *Provisional Methods of Regulating Listed Companies in Shenzhen City* of 1992.

---

50   *See* Hong Wu and Wei Hu, Market Regulation Law – Basic Theory and System of Market Regulation Law 228 (Beijing: Peking University Press, 2006). *See* also Wei, *supra* note 33, at 489.

51   *See* Chen, *supra* note 27, at 33.

52   *See* Xie, *supra* note 29, at 133.

53   *Ibid.*

During this period, the Chinese government realized the necessity of concentrating the regulatory powers to a single authority. This would eliminate confusion and uncertainty in the securities law caused by the division of regulatory powers, and would increase the efficiency of the securities market.[54] An important step was clarifying that the CSRC was the ultimate regulatory body of the securities business, which would directly report to the State Council. The government also encouraged self-regulation of the stock exchanges and securities business. The stock exchanges and the Securities Business Association were the main bodies that advocated self-regulation. A regulatory framework of governmental regulation supplemented by self-regulation was basically completed. Nevertheless, in this stage, the CSRC was working hard to gain a firm foothold and could devote limited energy to establishing a legal infrastructure for the securities business.[55] Consequently, securities law making largely remained in the hands of local authorities.

The third phase, from 1998 to present, is the period of regulatory centralization. With the further development of the securities business, there was a need to establish a centralized regulatory framework. China has endeavored to achieve this goal. In this phrase, national legislation has gradually replaced local laws and a generally complete legislative system has come into existence.[56] Some important legislative efforts included: the *Provisional Methods Prohibiting Securities Fraudulence* of 1993 (the State Council), the *Regulations concerning Enterprise Securities* of 1993 (the State Council), the *Provisional Regulations Concerning Administrating Share Issuance and Trade* 1993 (the State Council), the *Special Provisions concerning Public Companies Being Listed and Issuing Shares on Overseas Stock Exchanges* of 1994 (the State Council), and the *Implementary Regulations concerning Information Disclosure by Companies Issuing Shares to the Public* of 1995 (the CSRC). The landmark legislative effort was the enactment of the *Company Law* in 1993 and the *Securities Law* in 1998 by the People's Congress, and the subsequent amendments to these two laws in 1999 and 2005.

During this phase, the "quota control" was abolished. Applications for listing on a stock exchange no longer undergo the process of examination and approval by the CSRC. Instead, the CSRC only verifies the application according to the requirements in the law.[57] The rules regulating securities issuance and transactions have been improved. The law has enhanced the supervisory function of the CSRC

---

54   *See* Wu and Hu, *supra* note 50, at 229.

55   *See* Carl E. Walter and Fraser J.T. Howie, *Privatizing China: The Stock Markets and Their Role in Corporate Reform* 60–62 (Singapore: John Wiley & Son (Asia) Pte Ltd, 2003).

56   *See* Chen, *supra* note 27, at 34–5.

57   *See* the People's Congress, the 1998 Securities Law of the People's Republic of China, secs 14, 15, 16 and 167.

by broadening its powers of investigation and by allowing the CSRC to freeze and detain assets of listed companies.[58]

China's experience in regulating securities business in the past two decades illustrates the fact that the main challenge for Chinese securities law-makers and policy-makers is how to maintain a balance between governmental intervention (the visible hand) and the self-control function of the market (the invisible hand). Although the market contains a self-correction function, abundant evidence suggests the inevitability of governmental/regulatory intervention in cases of market failure, which appears to be inherent in the market.[59]

Market failure confirms the necessity of regulatory intervention. However, it is not clear how to make regulatory intervention effective. The task faced by the Chinese is to determine a method for achieving efficient regulatory intervention and avoiding regulatory failure. The dismal performance of China's securities market between July 2001 and early 2006 has brought people's attention to the question of whether excessive or inappropriate governmental intervention has added to irregularities on the market, and therefore encumbered the standardization of the securities market.[60]

In China, the primary motivation for developing a securities market has been to find new sources of raising capital for state-dominated enterprises.[61] This paramount objective requires tight government control.[62] The "quota control" method, the examination and approval requirements for companies being listed, and a series of strategies of "rescuing the market" or "lifting the market" have all been part of the control package ensuring state enterprises take full advantage of the securities market. However, it is always important to acknowledge that undue intervention inevitably results in regulatory failure.[63] Excessive regulatory intervention interrupts the natural expectations of the market, adds further instability in the business decision-making process, and misleads investors in perceiving the severity of business risks.[64] Hence, regulatory intervention should be limited to the extent of improving market efficiency.[65]

Since the establishment of the securities market, the Chinese government has endeavored to manipulate the rise and fall of the market within a range that it thinks rational to ensure the long term prosperity of the market and to eliminate

---

58   *Ibid*, s. 168.

59   *See* Robert L. Heilbroner and Lester C. Thurow, Economics Explained 31, 235–6 (New Jersey: Prentice Hall, 1982).

60   *See* Jing Lu, Institutional Defects that Hampering the Development of China's Securities Market, available at <http://www.china-review.com>. *See* also Li, *supra* note 2, at 195.

61   *See* Xie, *supra* note 29, at 149.

62   *Ibid*.

63   *See* Li, *supra* note 2, at 117.

64   *See* Lu, *supra* note 60.

65   *Ibid*.

possible more hidden perils that may cause financial turmoil in the future. The government is cautious about, and has limited tolerance toward, sharp fluctuations in the market. When the market at the Shanghai Stock Exchange fell more than 70 percent in July 1994, the CSRC and the State Council speedily introduced three remedial policies: ceasing the approval of any new issuance, tightening the requirements for companies to be listed, and allowing more investment funds to participate in the securities business.[66] The market reacted immediately. On 10 August 1994 alone, the Shanghai Stock Exchange index jumped 111.72 points.[67] By the beginning of 1996, both the Shanghai and Shenzhen stock exchanges were making significant gains. The State Council, after consulting with the CSRC, believed that it was necessary to put controls on the overheating investment momentum in order to eliminate bubbles and foster a stable environment for the development of the securities market.[68] Warnings first came from the so called "twelve decrees", a series of regulations enacted by the CSRC, including the *Announcement of Standardizing the Conduct of Listed Companies*, the *Methods Regulating Stock Exchanges*, and the *Announcement Firmly Prohibiting Overdraft in Share Issuance*. To further demonstrate the government's determination to settle the overheated market, the *People's Daily* published an editorial entitled "On Correctly Understanding the Current Stock Market", which alerted investors to the highly speculative nature of the stock market.[69] Eventually, investors began a selling frenzy, and the market went down 38 percent within eight trading days.[70] Similar events occurred in 1997 when the government once again influenced the market movement by restricting new issuance, and by disclosing the government's intention to intervene into the market in a *People's Daily* editorial.[71]

Such events have resulted in China's securities market becoming sensitive to government policy changes. On many occasions, volatility has been caused by policy changes. Government policies have also become an object of speculation. Those who have the means of obtaining divulged information concerning imminent policy changes have made significant profits.[72] They are able to act before the official news reaches the market, and take investment opportunities that other investors are unaware of. This is evidenced by the fact the market often fluctuates before a new policy is made public. A typical example is the so called "2.19 incident". In February 2001, the decision of allowing Chinese citizens to purchase B shares in Reminbi was made by the government, and the decision was

---

66   *See* Xie, *supra* note 29, at 150.
67   *Ibid.*
68   *Ibid.*
69   *See* Walter and Howie, *supra* note 55, at 212.
70   *Ibid.*
71   *See* Xie, *supra* note 29, at 151.
72   Such securities investors are usually securities companies, institutional investors, or special individuals that have close relationships with the government or officials in authorized departments.

going to be officially published in the official news report on TV on the evening of 19 February.[73] On the morning of 19 February, B share trading was unusually active at both the Shanghai and Shenzhen Stock Exchanges, and quickly reached a record high at the Shanghai Stock Exchange. The CSRC sensed the possible divulgence of the yet to be announced new policy, and decided to halt all B share transactions.[74] At 1 pm, investors were told that B share transactions would be resumed after the official announcement of the new policy concerning B shares. Many investors were outraged when the news was broadcast on TV that evening. This instigated demands for the investigation of whether the price information had been divulged and if corruption had been involved.[75]

China's past experience demonstrates that stringent regulatory control is not the most appropriate solution to the problems in the securities business. Over-intervention may only escalate the irregular movement of the market and intensify unfair competitive conduct in the securities business. China's experience also establishes the necessity of embracing the idea of fully exploiting the market's self-regulation function.[76] Although self-regulation has its limits, to a certain extent, it is able to play a positive role in restraining governmental interference and maintaining a free market. Moreover, it provides a means for the government to withdraw from intense engagement in market regulation. An efficient regulatory system should be one that combines the strength of governmental regulation, self-regulation, as well as the market's own adjustment function – the invisible hand.

Conclusions

The development of China's capital market has been closely supervised and guided by the Chinese government. It has been proven that the government's support and guidance are essential in shaping emerging markets. In China, the governmental intervention into the securities market is made mainly for the purpose of promoting the enterprise reforms and financing state companies. As a result, discrimination between state enterprises and private enterprises has been evident since the very beginning. The governmental control in listing admissions and share issuance has resulted in a high demand in A shares and price distortion on the securities market. The regulatory infrastructure of the securities business and market is still in a process of development and improvement. All of these make China's securities market highly speculative. Speculation has exacerbated irregularities on the market. Breaches by listed companies and market intermediaries have become widespread. Consequently, many Chinese listed companies are inefficient and their

---

73   Before B shares were only for foreigners to subscribe.

74   *See* the Editor, *The Facts in 2.19 B Share Policy Divulgence Incident*, available at <http://stock.163.com/edito/010221/-010221_36369.html>.

75   *See* Li, *supra* note 2, at 195–6.

76   *Ibid*, at 192.

performance is not up to standard. There are also other reasons responsible for the problems, including inefficient listing and delisting rules, increased competition, changes of taxation polices, and poor corporate governance.[77]

China must accelerate its improvements to the securities investment environment in order to ensure a prosperous market in the coming decade. Developing an efficient regulatory framework that works as an independent system is imperative. The government was successful in administrating the securities market at the initial stage. However, with China's capital market growing more mature, overly relying on government intervention has shown increasing ineffectiveness. It is now time for China to make adjustments to its regulatory policies and develop new strategies for regulating its securities market.

---

77   *See* Lu, *supra* note 60.

PART II
Securities Markets
and Corporate Governance

Chapter 4
Capital Market as an External Mechanism of Corporate Governance

As a transitional and emerging economy, the People's Republic of China has merely 20 years of history in the capital market. The Chinese government has been motivated by three major objectives in developing a securities market: (1) encourage securities investments and mitigate the lack of capital resources faced by many Chinese enterprises; (2) maximize employment of idle capital; and (3) establish a modern corporate governance system in listed companies.[1] Unlike some developed countries, China attaches great importance to the monitoring function of the securities market over the management of listed companies.[2] In fact, using the securities market as leverage to speed-up the process of building a modern corporate governance system has been an important reform strategy of the Chinese government.[3] The expectations of the Chinese are based on the two fundamental

---

1   *See* Qingbo Chen, Securities English 161 (Beijing: China Machine Press, 2003). *See* also Daniel M. Anderson, *Taking Stock in China: Company Disclosure and Information in China's Stock Markets*, 88 Georgetown Law Journal (June 2000), at <http://www.findarticles.com/p/articles/mi_qa3805/is_200006/ai_n8889116>.

2   China has a significant number of State-Owned Enterprises (SOEs). Reforming SOEs is the core of China's Economic Reform. The Chinese Authority wishes to improve the corporate governance of SOEs by listing SOEs on the domestic stock exchanges. It is expected that incorporating private interests through listing will provide checks and balance on the management to improve performance. *See* Erika Leung, Lily Liu, Lu Shen, Kevin Taback and Leo Wang, *Financial Reform and Corporate Governance in China*, MIT Sloan School of Management 50th Anniversary Proceedings 11, 14, 15 (Cambridge Massachusetts, June 2002). *See* also Stephen C. Thomas and Chen Ji, *Privatizing China: The Stock Markets and Their Role in Corporate Reform*, 58 China Business Review (1 July 2004) (book review) (2004 WLNR 11626777).

3   I had interesting discussions with the staff members of the China Securities Regulatory Commission and Hong Kong Stock Exchange during conferences in 2001 and 2003. They clarified that by encouraging state-controlled companies to be listed on stock exchanges, the Chinese government hoped that these companies would accelerate the process of modernizing their management and promoting the practice of good corporate governance. They pointed out that these state-controlled companies have state banks to be their financiers and their main purpose of going public was not raising funds from the securities market. *See* Yuwa Wei, *The Role of the China Securities Regulatory Commission in Corporate Law Reforms and Corporate Governance*, Paper Presented at the DEST (CHESI) Melbourne Conference: Corporate Governance in Post WTO China, 11 *passim* (5–6 December 2003).

functions of the securities market: corporate finance and corporate governance.[4] This chapter will examine these two functions in turn.

The first section investigates the role of the securities market in relation to corporate governance. It examines the theoretical aspects of the securities market and its regulations. It also analyzes the important role played by the securities market in the economy, and its value-creating capacity. This section illustrates the rationalities behind the development of the securities market, and then analyzes significance of its supervisory function over the management of listed companies.

The second section reveals the relationship between internal control and external control through a close case study of China. It briefly examines how the Chinese utilize the monitoring functions of the securities market to upgrade their corporate governance systems.

The Market Control Function of the Capital Market

In a highly competitive commercial environment, corporations race for survival. In this race, large corporations have a better chance of surviving.[5] This is because the expansion of business scales can reduce unit costs and increase the total long-run profits.[6] Also, large-scale corporations have the advantage of attracting top managerial talents and skilled workers.[7] Corporations must grow.[8] Consequently, they must expand their business scale and scope to increase their total long-run profits. To facilitate this growth, corporations need funds which energized the development of the Securities Market worldwide.[9]

---

4   *See* Xiao Geng, *China's Securities Market Development: Lessons from Hong Kong and Other Asian Markets* 1, 3 (15 January 2003) available at <www.econ.hku.hk/~xiaogeng/ research/Paper/   Securities%20market%20development%-20in%20China-English.pdf>; *see* also Yuwa Wei, *Seeking a Practicable Chinese Model of Corporate Governance*, 10 Michigan State University-DCL Journal of International Law 393, 426 (2002).

5   *See* Alfred D. Chandler, Jr., Scale and Scope: The Dynamics of Industrial Capitalism 8, 953–6 (Massachusetts: The Belknap Press of Harvard University Press, 1990) (stating that large manufacturing companies enjoyed powerful competitive advantages).

6   *Ibid*, at 953.

7   *See* Edith T. Penrose, The Theory of The Growth of the Firm 95 (1980). *See* also James C. Cooper and Kathleen Madigan, Small isn't Beautiful When Skills are Scarce Business Week: Enterprise Online (2 October 1995), at <http://www.businessweek. net/1995/40/b3444129.htm>.

8   *See* Edith T. Penrose, The Theory of The Growth of the Firm 30 (New York: Oxford University Press, 1959).

9   *See* Colin Mayer, *Stock-markets, Financial Institutions, and Corporate Performance*, in Nicholas Dimsdale and Martha Prevezer (*eds*), Capital Markets and Corporate Governance 179 (Oxford: Clarendon Press, 1994); *see* also Conard, *supra* note,

The securities market is a place where corporations and individuals buy and sell securities. For corporations, issuing securities on a stock exchange is an important means of raising funds.[10] Alternatively, a corporation could also directly borrow funds from financial institutions, or issue shares and debentures to specific investors. Such financial arrangements, however, have limits. For example, bank loans would burden companies with high interest costs. Moreover, it is difficult to find specific investors when the amount of funds needed is extensive. Consequently, raising funds from the general public becomes a crucial means of boosting corporate finance.

The securities market and banks have played important roles at every stage of corporate development, from the early joint stock companies to modern public listing companies, and from early railway, shipping, and mining industries to our modern aviation, space, and information technology industries.[11] In some leading common law systems, the rise of the corporate economy relied a great deal on attracting and utilizing public investments.[12]

The securities market not only enables corporations to raise capital from a wide range of investors, but also acts as a monitoring mechanism over the management of corporations.[13] This is because share prices closely reflect the managerial efficiency of corporations.[14] Specifically, investors are reluctant to invest in a poorly managed company. As a result, the share prices of poorly managed companies are likely to go down, thereby exposing these companies as targets for takeovers. The threat of takeover acts as a deterrent that obliges the board and management to act in the interests of the corporation.[15] In the meantime, the benefits of being listed on a stock exchange provide incentives for corporations to actively improve their

---

at 258, 259; *See* also *ibid*, at 6; *see* also Robert Baxt, Ashley Black and Pamela Hanrahan, Securities and Financial Services Law 268 (Sydney: LexisNexis Butterworths, 2003).

10   *See* James D. Cox, Robert W. Hillman and Donald C. Langevoort, Securities Regulation Cases and Materials 2 (New York: Aspen Law & Business, 2001).

11   *See generally* E. Victor Morgan and W.A. Thomas, The Stock Exchange: Its History and Functions (London: Elek Books Limited, 1969); *See* also Tai Teng, Value Creation and the Growth of Securities Companies 22 (Shanghai: Shanghai University of Finance and Economy, 2003).

12   *See* Morgan and Thomas, *ibid*.

13   *See* Michael C. Jensen and William H. Meckling, *Theory of the Firm: Managerial Behavior, Agency Costs and Ownership Structure*, 3 The Journal of Financial Economics 305, 323 (1976).

14   *See generally ibid.*; R. Ian McEwin, *Law and Economics as an Approach to Corporate Law Research*, 3 Canberra Law Review 40, 41 (1996); William J. Baumol and Alan Blinder, Economics, Principles and Policy 647 (New York: Harcourt Brace College Publishers, 1988).

15   *See* Thomas Lee Hazen, *The Short-Term/Long-Term Dichotomy and Investment Theory: Implications for Securities Market Regulation and for Corporate Law*, 70 North Carolina Law Review 137, 182 (1991).

economic and managerial efficiency to satisfy the listing requirements of stock exchanges.[16]

The securities market is subject to rigorous regulation because of its profit-making function.[17] Over time, the securities market experienced eras of free trade, regulation, and deregulation. Initially, the securities market was basically unregulated, which led to a series of crises and scandals.[18] For instance, the burst of the South Sea Bubble in the early eighteenth century caused the collapse of the entire financial market in the United Kingdom.[19] In the United States, the failure of the securities market added further devastation to the economic depression in the 1930s.[20] Following these failures, rules and regulations were introduced to make the securities market a fair and orderly place for public investments.[21] Now, in a fair and orderly securities market, investors are reasonably informed and the market has the ability to assess the performance of public companies, and supervise their management.[22]

In summary, the securities market has the following functions: (1) it provides a mechanism for companies to sell securities in order to finance corporate expansion; (2) it provides a means for investors to buy and sell their outstanding shares; (3) it establishes share prices that assist in monitoring firms and allocating resources; (4) it encourages risk-taking by spreading risks and rewarding profitable investment; and (5) through corporate control, it allows managerial failure to be corrected through its markets.[23]

---

16   *See* Paul Redmond, Companies and securities law: Commentary and Materials 63 (Sydney: LBC Information Service, 2005); *See also* Baxt, Black and Hanrahan, *supra* note 9.

17   *See* Thomas Lee Hazen, The Law of Securities Regulation 8 (St. Paul, Minnesota: West Group, 1996).

18   *Ibid*, at 6.

19   *See* Lewis Melville, The South Sea Bubble vii (Boston: Small, Maynard & Co, 1921); Peter George Muir Dickson, The Financial Revolution in England (London: Macmillan, 1967).

20   *See* John P. Caskey, The Evolution of the Philadelphia Stock Exchange: 1964–2002 8 (Research Department, the Federal Reserve Bank of Philadelphia, Working Paper No. 03-21, 2003).

21   *See* Louis Loss and Joel Seligman, Fundamentals of Securities Regulation 34, 36 (5th ed. 2004).

22   *See* Arthur R. Pinto, *The United States*, in Arthur R. Pinto and Gustavo Visentini (*eds*) The Legal Basis of Corporate Governance in Publicly Held Corporations: A Comparative Approach 253, 258 (London: Kluwer Law International, 1998); Daniel R. Fischel, *Efficient Capital Market Theory, the Market for Corporate Control, and the Regulation of Cash Tender Offers*, 57 Texas Law Review 1, 9 (1980).

23   *See* Colin Mayer, *Stock-markets, Financial Institutions, and Corporate Performance*, in Nicholas Dimsdale and Martha Prevezer (*eds*), Capital Markets and Corporate Governance 179 (Oxford: Clarendon Press, 1994); Paul Marsh, *Market Assessment of Company Performance*, in Nicholas Dimsdale and Martha Prevezer (*eds*), Capital Markets and Corporate Governance 66–67 (Oxford: Clarendon Press, 1994).

In a well-functioning securities market, companies can raise new funds and investors can buy and sell outstanding securities at a fair price.[24] However, there have always been doubts on the efficiency of the securities market in pricing its securities. Indeed, there has been evidence of mis-pricing.[25] Otherwise, the securities market is efficient.[26] Furthermore, improving financial reporting, disclosure, and quality of investment analysis could improve efficiency.[27] As a result, investors are still confident enough to invest in securities.

A well-functioning securities market also acts as an important mechanism for corporate governance in public companies.[28] It encourages public companies to improve managerial efficiency and correct managerial failures in order to be admitted into a stock exchange and maintain their profiles.[29] This is because companies must comply with the listing rules of the stock exchange.[30] Also, once there, the share price of a company reflects the managerial efficiency of the company.[31] Because of the low share price, a poorly managed company faces the threat of takeover. A takeover inevitably replaces the under-performing management team.[32] Hence, takeovers contribute to the governance process in two ways: (1) the possibility of a takeover encourages management to act in the interests of the shareholders or the corporation as a whole;[33] and (2) most likely, a takeover would seek to remedy the problems caused by an unsuccessful incumbent management by replacing it.[34]

Because of these reasons, takeovers become an effective mechanism for corporate governance.[35] Yet, takeovers themselves merely provide an external mechanism for corporate governance and should be employed only as a last resort. That is they operate after internal governance mechanisms have failed.[36]

---

24   *See* Marsh, *ibid*, at 67.

25   *Ibid*, at 69–70

26   *Ibid.*

27   *Ibid*, at 84–90.

28   *See* Pinto, *supra* note 22, at 258.

29   *See* Clyde E. Rankin III, *United States Corporate Governance: Implications for Foreign Issuers*, in Dennis Campbell and Susan Woodley (*eds*) Trends and Developments in Corporate Governance: The Comparative Law Yearbook of International Business Special Issue 286, 291 (London: Kluwer Law International, 2003).

30   *Ibid*, at 266.

31   *See* Pinto, *supra* note 22, at 258; *See* also Fischel, *supra* note 22, at 1.

32   *See* Fischel, *supra* note 22, at 9.

33   *See* Pauline O'Sullivan, *Governance by Exit: An Analysis of the Market for Corporate Control*, in Kevin Keasey, Steve Thompson and Mike Wright (*eds*), Corporate Governance: Economic and Financial Issues 122, 122–3 (London: Oxford University Press, 1997); *see also* Pinto, *supra* note 22, at 273.

34   O'Sullivan, *ibid*, at 122–3.

35   *Ibid*, at 124; *See* also Yuwa Wei, Comparative Corporate Governance: A Chinese Perspective 47 (London: Kluwer Law International, 2003); Henry G. Manne, *Mergers and Market for Corporate Control*, 71(1) Journal of Political Economy 112–14 (1965).

36   *See* O'Sullivan, *supra* note 33, at 122–3.

On the other hand, many people doubt that takeovers provide a natural remedy to corporate inefficiency.[37] They point out that takeovers do not always push corporations to improve management.[38] They believe that takeovers could encourage corporate managers to focus on short-term performance, since the "pressures from the financial markets often drive them to engage in perverse behaviour that reduces long-term value".[39] Particularly, managers may make business decisions just to frustrate potential takeovers. For example, company managers may try to make themselves indispensable, and therefore, costly to replace.[40] In addition, studies have shown that the shareholders of the bidder company may be worse off after the takeover.[41]

This further suggests that, to enhance the efficiency of the securities market and its control function, it is necessary to introduce regulatory mechanisms over the securities market and securities business. Presently, the regulatory systems in developed countries, particularly the countries of leading economies, are based on longstanding practices, and thus are basically well established.[42]

Currently, the fundamental principle behind the securities market regulations of most jurisdictions is *disclosure*.[43] This principle is based on the economic hypothesis that investors are rational beings. If they possess relevant information, investors could be in a position to make business decisions that are in their best interests. Hence, disclosure of relevant information, relating to specific securities and the issuers, is crucial. According to US Justice Louis Brandeis, disclosure is the most effective cure of the social and industrial diseases, electric light the most efficient police officer.[44] Enhancing their disclosure system requires much effort. This includes improving reporting and auditing regulation and practice and combating fraud, insider trading, and market manipulation.[45]

Fraud directly violates the principle of disclosure.[46] Hence, securities laws universally prohibit fraud.[47] Insider trading upsets the fairness of information disclosure and consequently damages the integrity of the financial market. This is

---

37   *See* Hazen, *supra* note 15, at 182.

38   *Ibid*, at 182–3.

39   *See* Margret M. Blair, Ownership and Control: Rethinking Corporate Governance for the Twenty-First Century 122 (Washington, D.C.: The Brookings Institution, 1995).

40   *See* O'Sullivan, *supra* note 33, at 125.

41   *See also* Hazen, *supra* note 15, at 191.

42   *See* Lin Yie, Securities Law 56–64 (Beijing: People's University Press, 2000).

43   *See* Cox, et al., *supra* note 10, at 8.

44   *See* Louis D. Brandeis, Other People's Money and How the Bankers Use It 92 (New York: A.M. Kelley, 1971).

45   *See* Loss and Seligman, *supra* note 21 at 769; *see also* Hazen, *supra* note 17 at 418.

46   *See* Loss and Seligman, *supra* note 21, at 951–9.

47   *See* Xiaoke Hu, Preliminary Study on the Prohibition System of Securities Fraud 1 (Beijing: Economic Science Press, 2004). The book provides general discussions on antifraud laws and practice of different systems. Also *see generally* John Farrar, Corporate

because market participants should have equal access to the relevant information from the company that issues the securities. Corporate insiders, however, would have access to undisclosed confidential information that affects the value of the company's securities.[48] They could seek to profit from the confidential information by trading their securities based on this information. This creates inequity among securities investors and also injures the company and its shareholders because the insiders profit based upon informational asymmetry.

Market manipulation is a special form of fraud.[49] It is usually an attempt to drive up a stock price on the secondary market by creating demand for the stock through the dissemination of false and misleading information.[50] A number of strategies could be exercised to achieve the purpose of market manipulation, including *pools, churning, runs*, and *short selling*.

Mutual Dependence of Internal and External Corporate Control

Because of the important role played by the securities market in corporate development and corporate governance, it is important to develop sound securities regulations.[51] Some countries have been trying to fully exploit the monitoring function of the securities market in order to improve the governance of their listed companies.[52] China is one of the countries that have employed the supervisory functions of the securities market to assist in corporatizing its state-owned enterprises and establishing an effective governance system in its corporatized enterprises.[53] China has also endeavored to develop a strong legal regime over the

---

Governance: Theories, Principles, and Practice 219–318 (Melbourne: Oxford University Press, 2005).

48   Insider trading in its origin refers to the corporate insider – the director, officer, employee, or associate of the corporation. Now, in same systems, it extends to a tippee – the person who deals in the securities on the basis of information provided to him or her by a corporate insider. *See* Hon. Justice Ipp and W. Weerasooria (*eds*), Butterworths Business and Law Dictionary 264, 265 (NSW: LexisNexis Butterworths, 2002).

49   *See* Cox, et al., *supra* note 10, at 691.

50   *See* Butterworths, *supra* note 48, at 313.

51   "Sound legal rules in company laws and securities regulations are a first step towards effective corporate governance". *See* James D. Wolfensohn, Corporate Governance and the Challenge of Development (President, The World Bank Group, Beijing, 26 May 2002), available at <http://www.worldbank.org.cn/English/Content/-273v6319724.shtml>.

52   *See* Pinto, *supra* note 22, at 269–70; *See* also Alice de Jonge, *Corporate Governance in a Cross-Border Environment: Overseas Listings of Chinese Firms*, in Dennis Campbell and Susan Woodley (*ed.*) Trends and Developments in Corporate Governance: The Comparative Law Yearbook of International Business Special Issue 286, 291 (London: Kluwer Law International, 2003).

53   *Ibid.*

securities market and its activities.[54] In a span of ten years, China has enacted a securities code and a number of regulations.[55]

However, structural defects, along with misconduct and legal violations in the securities business, have undermined this attempt. Two problems persist in the operation of China's securities market. Firstly, China's securities market is extremely volatile. Before July 2001, China's securities market was basically a bull market. From July 2001 to the end of 2005, the market experienced a bear market. In other words, there was more than four years of depression. Between June 2001 and June 2005, the index fell from 2245 points to 998 points.[56] From April 2006, the market began to pick up. Then from the end of 2006, the market became bullish again. However, the market has always been volatile. Within a single trading day, the index could rise more than 100 percent or plunge more than 16 percent.[57] One can acutely sense the degree of volatility of China's capital market when comparing these figures with the record of index fluctuation in a mature market. For instance, the largest single-day increases of the Dow Jones was 4.98 percent, and the largest single-day decreases of the Dow Jones was 7.183 percent.[58]

2007 was an extraordinary year to many Chinese securities investors who witnessed the dazzling flux of the market. The year was called the golden time of China's securities market, in which Chinese investors experienced an unprecedented bull market, with the Shanghai Composite Index moved from 2728.19 points to 5261.56 points and the Shenzhen Composite Index from 6730.12 points to 17700.62 points.[59] However, it was also a year that witnessed the most volatile capital market in the past ten years. The bull market approached China in the beginning of 2007. By the time of Chinese New Year, the Shanghai Composite Index reached a historical high, followed by a dip on 31 January. On 26 February, the market reached another historical high, and then fell specularly on the following day, with the index losing 8.84 percent in a single day.[60] On 14 and 16 March, the market plunged twice. The index fell more than 100 points on 14 March and lost 21.22 points on 16 March.[61] In May the market plunged again

---

54   *Ibid*, at 97.

55   *Ibid*.

56   *See* Baisan Xie, *China Needs not to Go with the Tide on the US Securities Market*, available at <http://cn.biz.yahoo.com/070317/16/l9c6.html>.

57   *See* Dehuan Jin, A Study of Volatility of the Chinese Securities Market and Control 9, 40 (Shanghai: Shanghai University of Finance and Commerce Press, 2003).

58   *Ibid*.

59   *See* the published figures at Xinhua Net, available at <http://news.xinhuanet.com/finance/2008-01/02/content_-7343915.htm>.

60   *See* Xiaobing Wu, Wenjun Liu and Ye Chen, *Who Pulled the Trigger?* available at <http://zhoukan.hexun.com/-Magazine/ShowArticle.aspx?ArticleId=11963>.

61   *See* the Commentator, *The Market on the Two Stock Exchanges Continues to Fall, and the Index Dives More Than 21 Points*, available at <http://finance.people.com.cn/GB/67815/68059/5480901.html>.

and lost more than 300 points. This time, the main cause was the publication of the official news that the stamp duty on securities transactions was increased from 0.1 percent to 0.3 percent.[62] The market was hit heavily again on 11 September. On that day, the Shanghai Composite Index lost 4.5 percent and Shenzhen Composite Index lost 5.3 percent.[63] Fluctuation persisted to the end of the year. On 8 November, influenced by a crash in the US and other Asian capital markets, China's stock market began to tumble. The Shanghai Composite Index fell 271.76 points, representing a loss of 4.85 percent.[64] The prices of some individual shares dropped more than 7 percent.

Since the beginning of 2008, the securities market has become even more volatile. On 21 January, the Shanghai Index opened at 5188.80 points but closed at 4922.80 points, making a loss of 266 points.[65] On the next day, the Index lost another 354 points. The market dipped to its lowest point since 2005.[66] Some began to predict that the bull market was coming to its end.

Why is China's securities market so volatile? Why was there a four-year depression at the beginning of the century? The reasons are many. An important factor responsible for the irregular fluctuation of the capital market is its lack of efficiency. Serious irregularities and breaches exist in China's capital market. It is a common circumstance that listed companies engage in market misconduct including misleading disclosure, insider trading and market manipulation. The breaches are widespread enough to confuse investors. Share prices do not necessarily reflect the economic efficiency or performance of listed companies. Consequently, investors are unable to distinguish between good companies and bad companies. Investment decisions are likely to be made based on distorted information and for speculative purposes. It is true to say that China's securities market is easily manipulated and investors are immature and confused. It is thus not a surprise to see that many Chinese investors often sway between two psychological phenomena: investment mania and panic. The market inevitably goes up and down violently. The inefficient market results in a loss of investment confidence. The four years of depression between 2001 and 2005 could be largely attributed to investors' loss of confidence in the securities market.

---

62   *See* the Editor, *The Mad Cow Panted: Sneak-raid on 30 May*, available at <http://stock.hexun.com/2008-01-06/102652791.html>.

63   *See* Buding New Report, *September 11: The Appears in the A Share Market*, available at <http://www.my1510.cn/-article.php?5c0d885df8520566>.

64   *See* Shaoye Xu, *Farewell 2007: Shanghai and Shenzhen Indices Obtained the Longest Yang Line in China's History*, Shanghai Securities Daily (29 December 2007), available at <http://news.xinhuanet.com/fortune/2007-12/29/content_7333087.htm>.

65   *See* Yan Shen, *Panic Penetrates: Investors Are Confused by the Drastic Fluctuation on the Securities Market*, Shanghai Hot News Online (24 January 2008), available at <http://news.online.sh.cn/news/gb/content/2008-01-24/content_2207433.htm>.

66   *Ibid.*

Another factor that causes irregular fluctuation of China's securities market is the lack of opportunity for market admission. In China's securities market, listing has been subject to strict control. Only a small number of companies is admitted. In the meantime, the public has limited channels of investments. As a result, the demand for shares has always been higher than the supply. It is almost guaranteed that once a company is listed, it will definitely profit from issuance of shares.[67] The high profitability has tempted companies to invest considerable energy in obtaining listing. For achieving this purpose, many of them are willing to engage in illegal conduct including forging accounting records and making misleading disclosure. It follows logically that such companies, once becoming listed, are less interested in improving its corporate governance practice, but are likely to continue to engage in fraudulent conduct. Corporate fraud causes market volatility. Reports show that the market is likely to plunge following the public being informed about an incident of fraud.[68]

It appears that the initial goal of establishing a securities market in order to improve corporate governance in Chinese listed companies is not well achieved. The problems in the corporate governance of Chinese listed companies persist, and eventually have an impact on the securities market. The Chinese experience has proven that a well-functioning securities market and a sound system of corporate governance are mutually dependent: the development of the securities market provides an external monitoring mechanism of corporate governance, and good practice of corporate governance, in turn, ensures the orderly operation of the securities market.[69] An efficient securities market promotes good corporate governance, and good corporate governance enhances the efficiency and transparency of the securities market. The task faced by the Chinese is: how to balance the relationship between the securities market and corporate governance in listed companies.

Improving regulatory framework is an important mechanism of advancing sound corporate governance and curtailing corporate misconduct. However, a good law does not guarantee good practice. China has constantly been learning from other systems, including the US, the UK, Germany and Japan. However, measures effective in some other systems do not necessarily produce desirable results in China. For instance, the Chinese law has institutionalized the two-tiered board system. However, the supervisory boards in Chinese companies have not achieved the monitoring purpose as efficiently as the supervisory boards do in

---

67   *See* Zhijun Li, Government Regulation of the Securities Market 62–3 (Changchun: Jilin People's Press, 2005).

68   *See* Pi Sui, Who is Victimizing China's Stock Market? 12–14 (Beijing: China Economics Press, 2005).

69   *See* Yuwa Wei, *Securities Regulation and Corporate Governance in China*, in Enhancing Corporate Accountability Prospects and Challenges: Conference Proceedings 69 (Corporate Accountability Conference, Monash University, Melbourne, Australia 8–9 February 2006).

German companies. The Chinese then tried to draw inspiration from the concept of independent directors in English-American systems. It is still early to say whether or not it is a good idea to require companies to embrace dual supervisory organs – a supervisory board and independent directors. Hence, developing a legal framework workable in China is another challenge that the Chinese have to face.

Research shows that there is a close relationship between a country's level of capital market development and the quality of its legal system.[70] Therefore, advancing the legal system governing China's securities business must be achieved in conjunction with the promotion of economic efficiency in its financial sectors and enterprises.[71] To build a modern corporate governance system, China needs to make further efforts to rationalize the shareholding structure in its companies. It needs to continue to develop its securities regulation and improve the corporate governance practice in its listed companies.

Conclusions

The capital market has the function of corporate control. The threat of takeover compels managers to act in the interest of shareholders. At least managers and shareholders agree that the share price of their companies must be kept as high as possible.[72] Only when the shares are sold at a high price, is the company relatively safe from takeover by outsiders, and the managers are able to retain control. The result is that corporate managers have to perform relatively efficiently.

The Chinese have placed high hopes on the disciplinary function of the securities market and aspired that the market could substantially improve corporate governance in listed companies. Ironically, the problems of corporate governance in listed companies have persisted and eventually impaired the operation of the stock market. The Chinese experience in the past two decades has shown that establishment of a securities market does not necessarily guarantee good corporate governance in listed companies. China demonstrates that the capital market and

---

70   *See* Frank H. Easterbrook and Daniel R. Fischel, *Mandatory Disclosure and the Protection of Investors*, 70 Virginia Law Review 669–715 (1984); Frank H. Easterbrook and Daniel R. Fischel, The Economic Structure of Corporate Law (Chapter 11: *Mandatory Disclosure*, Massachusetts: Harvard University Press, 1991); Ronald J. Gilson and Reinier H. Kraakman, *The Mechanisms of Market Efficiency*, 70 Virginia Law Review 549–644 (1984); Marcel Kahan, *Securities Laws and the Social Costs of 'Inaccurate' Stock Prices*, 41 Duke Law Journal 977–1044 (1992); Marcel Kahan, *Games, Lies and Securities Laws*, 67 New York University Law Review 750–800 (1992); and Donald C. Langevoort, *Theories, Assumptions, and Securities Regulation: Market Efficiency Revisited*, 140 University of Pennsylvania Law Review 851–920 (1992).

71   *See* Yuwa Wei, *Volatility of Chinese Securities Markets and Corporate Governance*, 29.2 Suffolk Transnational Law Review 215 (2006).

72   *See* Henry Manne, *Our Two Corporation Systems: Law and Economics*, 53 Virginia Law Review 266 (1967).

the efficiency of corporate governance are interactive and interdependent. Whereas a transparent and orderly capital market encourages managerial efficiency, well performed listed companies are crucial to the long-term prosperity of the market.

Chapter 5

Experiences
of Mature Markets

Contemporary discussions on corporate governance generally classify systems of corporate governance into two classical types, "market based" and "bank based", based on ownership structure. While dispersed ownership fosters market-based corporate governance, concentrated ownership nurtures bank-based corporate governance. A bank-based corporate governance is characterized by "controlling blockholders, weak securities markets, high private benefits of control, and low disclosure and market transparency standards, with only a modest role played by the market for corporate control, but with a possibly substitutionary monitoring role played by large banks".[1] A market-based corporate governance system is featured by "strong securities markets, rigorous disclosure standards, and high market transparency, in which the market for corporate control constitutes the ultimate disciplinary mechanism".[2] Practices in different countries are usually pigeonholed according to this dichotomy. For instance, whereas the US and UK models of corporate governance are treated as typical market-based models, the German and Japanese models of corporate governance are generally regarded as bank-based models.

The advantage of the classification above is that it clearly indicates how important the securities market should be in a specific system of corporate governance. This chapter discusses the corporate governance practices in three systems: the US, Japanese and the EU systems. The US and Japanese systems are representatives of the above two general models. The EU is in the dynamic process of creating a unified securities market and a uniform securities regulatory regime. In doing so, this chapter attempts, through exploring the three influential securities markets, to provide a comparative discussion on the securities regulations and practice in these systems. It intends to demonstrate how the securities market is at work in exerting its corporate control function.

---

1 *See* John C. Coffee Jr., *The Rise of Dispersed Ownership: The Role of Law in the Separation of Ownership and Control*, Annual Raben Lecture, Yale Law School, January 2001, available at <http://papers.ssrn.com/-paper.taf?abstractid=254097>.

2 *Ibid.*

Securities Market and Corporate Governance in the US

Traditionally, the US states banned financial institutions from holding significant blocks of shares in industrial firms.[3] This was mainly driven by local-protectionism since no state desired their local firms to be controlled by banks of other states. Large firms had to rely on the capital market for finance.[4] This resulted in dispersed share ownership in large public companies, and stimulated the fast growth of a robust and highly liquid securities market. The enactment of the *Bank Act* of 1933, known as the *Glass-Steagall Act* further restricted banks from engaging in securities business. The *Glass-Steagall Act* banned banks and brokerages from uniting together. In other words, commercial banking must separate from investment banking, and commercial banks were prohibited from underwriting and dealing in securities. The arrangement was based on the concern that there would be conflicts of interest if banks were permitted to engage in comingled investment business. Furthermore, the Great Crash had proven that banks' involvement in the securities business would increase the risk of financial meltdown during economic recession. Although the *Glass-Steagall Act* was superseded by the *Financial Services Modernization Act* of 1999 which eventually knocked down the wall between commercial banking and investment banking by allowing banks to provide mixed services including underwriting securities and insurance brokerage, the long-standing practice of restricting banks from owning controlling share blocks in non-financial companies had effectively shaped dispersed share structure in public companies in the US.

According to Monks and Minnow, a system of market control usually possesses three conditions: (1) a large number of listed companies; (2) a liquid capital market; and (3) a few intercorporate equity holdings.[5] The US meets all these conditions. Research shows that market control in the US has dominated the landscape of corporate governance.

Since the 1930s, the US federal government has extensively exercised its regulatory power to improve corporate governance through market control. Corporate governance has always been a highlight in federal legislation, including the *Securities Act* of 1933 and the *Sarbanes-Oxley Act* of 2002. Promoting sound corporate governance has also been an important task of the SEC. Both the securities legislation and the SEC have the objective of promoting good corporate governance through effectively regulating disclosure, board independence and auditing.

---

3   *See* Yuwa Wei, Comparative Corporate Governance: A Chinese Perspective 135 (London: Kluwer Law International, 2003).

4   *Ibid.*

5   *See* Robert A.G. Monks and Neil Minow, Corporate Governance (Massachusetts: Blackwell Business, 1995).

Disclosure

As discussed elsewhere in this book, disclosure is the cornerstone of the US securities laws. Disclosure is crucial in promoting transparency, accountability and responsibility. A transparent capital market attracts more investments. Companies that disclose timely, accurate, reliable information are able to attract more investors. Furthermore, disclosure places the management of a company under close scrutiny of the stakeholders and public. Hence, disclosure is not only a strategy of enhancing capital market transparency, but also an important mechanism of promoting sound corporate governance.

Section 17 of the *Securities Act* of 1933 forbids a person to make untrue statements in offering and selling securities.[6] However, this section does not catch fraud in purchasing securities. In 1942, the SEC learnt that a company president published untrue pessimistic statements about the company's economic performance and induced existing shareholders to sell the company's shares to himself.[7] To prevent similar fraudulent conduct in the future, the SEC issued Rule 10b-5 under the *Securities Exchange Act* of 1934. Rule 10b-5 stipulates that it is unlawful for any person to engage in fraudulent or deceptive conduct in connection with the purchase or sale of any securities. Since coming into existence, Rule 10b-5 has become one of the most useful rules in the securities law.

In the 1990s, the SEC proposed Regulation Fair Disclosure and received wide support from securities investors. Regulation Fair Disclosure addressed the issue of selective disclosure. Selective disclosure was a practice whereby companies invited a selective audience to explain their most recent performance, namely their quarterly financial results.[8] The selective audience usually comprised securities analysts and institutional shareholders. The SEC believed that selective disclosure bore close resemblance to tipping, and would undermine the integrity of the capital market and result in loss of investors' confidence.[9] In 2000, after inviting comments from a wide range of investors, Regulation Fair Disclosure was finally introduced. Regulation Fair Disclosure requires that when a company makes an intentional disclosure of material non-public information to a person covered

---

6 Section 17 states: "It shall be unlawful for any person in the offer or sale of any securities by the use of any means or instruments of transportation or communication in interstate commerce or by the use of the mails, directly or indirectly – (1) to employ any device, scheme, or artifice to defraud, or (2) to obtain money or property by means of any untrue statement of a material fact or any omission to state a material fact necessary in order to make the statements made, in the light of the circumstances under which they were made, not misleading, or (3) to engage in any transaction, practice, or course of business which operates or would operate as a fraud or deceit upon the purchaser".

7 *See* Larry D. Soderquist, Understanding the Securities Laws 246–7 (Translated by Xuanzhi Ju and Yunhui Zhang, Beijing: Law Press, 2004).

8 *See* Securities and Exchange Commission, *Final Rule: Selective Disclosure and Insider Trading*, available at <http://www.sec.gov/rules/final/33-7881.htm>.

9 *Ibid.*

by the regulation, it must simultaneously disclose the information to the general public.[10]

Disclosure is also used as an important strategy of improving corporate governance in the *Sarbanes-Oxley Act*. The *Sarbanes-Oxley Act* requires that the Chief Executive Officer and Chief Financial Officer must, in relation to the company's every annual and quarterly report, sign certifications regarding the effectiveness of the company's disclosure controls and procedures and internal control over financing reporting, as well as the adequacy and accuracy of disclosure contained in the reports, subject to both civil and criminal penalties.[11] These requirements have led many public companies to create internal "disclosure committees" responsible for considering the materiality of information and evaluating the company's disclosure obligations on a timely basis.

Board Independence

Another regulatory focus has been the enhancement of board independence. A significant amount of reports has identified separation of ownership and control as a primary problem of corporate governance.[12] Preventing corporate controllers from advancing their personal interests at the expense of the shareholders' interests is thus an important task of corporate governance. Based on this argument, it is generally believed that independent directors can reduce abuse of power by management and improve overall corporate governance.[13] The SEC has played a leading role in advocating board independence. In 1978, the NYSE made it a listing requirement that all listed companies of the NYSE should have audit committees

---

10   *Ibid.*

11   *See* section 302, the *Sarbanes-Oxley Act* of 2002.

12   *See* Ronald Coase, *The Nature of the Firm*, in Ronald Coase, The Firm, the Market and the Law 39-41 (Chicago: The University of Chicago Press, 1988). *See* also Henry Manne, *Mergers and Market for Corporate Control*, 71(1) Journal of Political economics 110–20 (1965); Armen A. Alchian and Harold Demsetz, *Production Information Costs and Economic Organization*, 62 American Economic Review 777–95 (1972); Eugene F. Fama and Michael C. Jensen, *Agency Problems and Residual Claims*, 26 Journal of Law and Economics 327–49 (1983); Eugene F. Fama and Michael C. Jensen, *Separation of Ownership and Control*, 24 (2) Journal of Law and Economics 301–25 (1983); Philip L. Cochran and Steven L. Wartick, *Corporate Governance – A Review of the Literature*, in R.I. Tricker (*ed.*), International Corporate Governance, Text, Readings and Cases 9 (New York: Prentice Hall, 1994); and Adolf A. Berle and Gardiner C. Means, The Modern Corporation and Private property (New Jersey: Transaction Publishers, 1991).

13   *See* Eugene F. Fama and Michael C. Jensen, *Separation of Ownership and Control*, 26 Journal of Law and Economics 327–49 (1983). *See* also James A. Brickley and Christopher M. James, *The Takeover Market, Corporate Board Composition, and Ownership Structure: The Case of Banking*, 30 (1) Journal of Law and Economics 161–80 (1987).

comprising independent directors.[14] The National Association of Securities Dealers Automated Quotations (NASDAQ) soon introduced the same requirement.

Following the enactment of the *Sarbanes-Oxley Act*, in August 2002, both the NYSE and the NASDAQ proposed rules elevating their listing standards in relation to board composition and director independence. The NYSE proposed a requirement that a majority of the board of directors of a listed company should be "independent" unless the company was a controlled company, a limited partnership, in bankruptcy proceedings, or was a company listing only preferred or debt securities.[15] Furthermore, companies listed on the NYSE were required to establish audit, nominating (or corporate governance), and compensation committees composed entirely of independent directors. Each of these committees was required to have a formal written charter including minimum content requirements as described in the new NYSE rules.[16] The NYSE recommended that each director should be selected by the nominating (or corporate governance) committee.

The NASDAQ also required that a majority of the board of directors of a listed company must be "independent", unless the company was a controlled company, a management investment company registered under the *Investment Company Act* of 1940, or a limited partnership. In addition, the NASDAQ required listed companies to have audit committees entirely comprising independent directors.

The proposed rules above were approved by the SEC in November 2003. Before long, the SEC published new rules requiring a public company to disclose whether it had a nominating committee or a committee performing similar functions and, if not, a statement of the board of directors justifying why it believed that it was appropriate for the company not to have such a committee, as well as a statement about the identification of each director who participated in the consideration of the director nominating committee.[17]

Auditing

The current regulation on corporate governance in the US has the tendency of imposing increasing responsibilities on boards of directors and chief executive officers in relation to insuring the efficiency of their companies' internal control

---

14   *See* Jonathan Charkham, Keeping Good Company 188 (New York: Oxford University Press, 1995).

15   A controlled company is a company in which more than 50 percent of the voting power is held by an individual, group or another company.

16   A controlled company, a limited partnership, a company that is in bankruptcy proceedings or lists only preferred or debt securities listed are exempt from the requirement of having corporate governance and compensation committees. However, they may be required to have an auditor committee.

17   *See* Securities and Exchange Commission, *Disclosure Regarding Nominating Committee Functions and Communications Between Security Holders and Boards of Directors*, available at <http://www.sec.gov/rules/final/33-8340.htm>.

system. Inevitably, auditors have an increasingly important role to play in corporate governance, since directors and chief executive officers have to rely on the assistance of auditors in discharging their responsibilities.

The internal control of a company refers to the strategies and measures that the company puts in place in order to ensure effective and efficient operations and compliance with laws, regulations and internal policies. Audit is an essential monitoring mechanism assuring effective internal control. There are two types of audit: internal audit and external audit. The traditional responsibilities of internal audit have been evaluating the effectiveness and efficiency of the company's operation, the accuracy of the company's financial reporting, and the compliance with laws by the company.[18] In recent years, increasing importance has been attached to internal audit, and the scope of responsibilities of internal audit has extended to include risk management and entire internal control framework.[19] Due to the concern of conflicts of interest, the law places internal audit under the scrutiny of external audit. The primary concern of external audit is whether the company's financial reports are free from misstatements.[20]

The *Sarbanes-Oxley Act* of 2002 has extensive provisions about increased duties of internal and external auditors and measures of ensuring audit independence. It requires that a public company must, in their annual report, prepare an internal control report stating the responsibility of the management in relation to maintaining adequate internal control and lodging financial reports.[21] The auditor must attest to, and report on, the assessment made by the management in accordance with standards for attestation engagements issued or adopted by the Board.[22] In doing so, the auditor will have to require the management to identify, document and evaluate significant internal controls (the management cannot delegate this function to the auditor). From these requirements, one can see that the US law clearly recognizes the essentiality of audit in warranting accuracy and liability of corporate financial reporting. Only when investors are confident that the information in financial reporting is accurate and reliable, can the prosperity of the securities market be sustainable.

In summary, the US is a market-based economy and has developed a range of strategies of corporate governance through market control. The US government has fully exerted its regulatory influence over corporate governance in public companies through the securities market and regulation.

---

18   *See* Alex Dunlop, Corporate Governance and Control 27–41 (London: Kogan Page, 1998).

19   *See* Institution of Internal Audit, *Definition of Internal Auditing* (Altamonte Springs, 1999). *See* also Paul Coram, Colin Ferguson and Robyn Moroney, *The Value of Internal Audit in Fraud Detection* 5, available at <http://www.afaanz.org/research/AFAANZ%200642.pdf>.

20   *See* Dunlop, *supra* note 18, at 48.

21   *See* sec. 404 of the *Sarbanes-Oxley Act* of 2002.

22   *Ibid.*

Securities Market and Corporate Governance in Japan

The Japanese corporate system is known as a typical banked-based system. Banks and conglomerates have been the two key actors in Japanese corporate life.[23] In its heyday, about 99 percent of Japanese firms existed in a corporate group and mainly relied on banks for finance.[24] The main bank played an essential role in corporate governance.[25] The concentrated share ownership, interlocking shareholding and trading relationship between member companies, and the tradition of life-time employment made takeovers an unpopular practice. Thus, to many, the corporate governance function of the capital market in Japan was negligible.[26]

However, the Japanese securities market is far from being underdeveloped. In fact, the Tokyo Stock Exchange is the second largest stock market in the world.[27] By 31 May 2007, it listed 2,424 domestic companies and 26 foreign companies.[28]

The history of the capital market in Japan can be traced back to 1878. In that year, two stock exchanges were established in Tokyo and Osaka respectively.[29] By 1911 the number of stock exchanges increased to thirteen.[30] National bonds, corporate equities and debentures were traded on the capital market. Transactions of national bonds and corporate equities were firmly supported by Japanese banks through special discounting facilities.[31] Although speculation and abuse were common, the capital market developed and became an important channel for firms to raise funds.

Despite the existence of the arguments that the bank-centered culture of corporate finance was not apparent in pre-war Japan, the mainstream belief has been that the success of the Japanese corporate economy should be attributed to the government's patronage that was eventually delivered in the form of investment by big banks.[32]

---

23 *See* Wei, *supra* note 3, at 149–54.

24 *See* Takeo Hoshi, *The Economic Role of Corporate Grouping and the Main Bank System*, in M. Aoki and R. Dore (*ed.*), The Japanese Firm: The Sources of Competitive Strength 285 (New York: Oxford University Press, 1994).

25 *See* Wei, *supra* note 3, at 151–2.

26 *See* Hideki Kanda, *Trends in Japanese Corporate Governance*, in Klaus J. Hopt (*ed.*), Comparative Corporate Governance, Essays and Materials 190 (Walter de Gruyer, Berlin, 1997).

27 *See* the Editor, *Let's Know about Japanese Stock Market*, available at <http://www.japanese-stockmarket-now.com>.

28 *See* the Editor, *A Brief History of the Japanese Stock Market*, available at <http://thejapanesestockmarket.com>.

29 *See* Norio Tamaki, Japanese Banking: A History 1859–1959 108 (London: Cambridge University Press, 1995).

30 *Ibid.*

31 *Ibid.*

32 *See* relevant discussions in Alexander Gerschenkron, Economic Backwardness in Historical Perspective (Cambridge: Harvard University Press, 1962); William W.

The Japanese securities market was shut down for four years after World War II and reopened in 1949. By the 1950s, five stock exchanges operated in Japan. Today, the Japanese Stock Market is divided into three sections called first section, second section and Mothers. Those listed in the first section are the larger companies; and those in the second section are smaller companies with lower trading volumes. The Mothers section was established in 1999 and includes innovative venture capital companies both in Japan and abroad.[33]

In 1948, Japan introduced the *Securities and Exchange Law* modeled on the *Securities Act* of 1933 (US) and the *Securities Exchange Act* of 1934 (US). The law was amended quite a few times and was renamed as the *Financial Instruments and Exchange Law* in 2007. Generally speaking, the securities market was strictly regulated from the 1950s to the 1970s. Commercial banking and investment banking were separated.[34] Deregulation of the securities market started in the late 1970s. The barrier between different banking sectors were gradually broken down. Financial institutions were allowed to own subsidiaries offering various financial services.[35] In Japan, the 1980s was a decade of investment boom. Bank loans were easier obtained than ever before.[36] Affluent citizens and the strong Japanese yen fueled an investment boom, resulting in a land and securities price bubble.[37] With the burst of the bubble in late 1997, Japan sank into economic recession. To overcome the financial crisis and restore investors' confidence, Japan launched a series of financial reforms.

In 1996, Prime Minister Hashimoto launched the concept of a Big Bang reform of the Japanese financial system, aiming at transforming the Japanese financial market into an international financial market with conditions similar to those in New York and London.[38] Although the program was supposed to be completed by 2001, the reforms are still in progress. More than twenty laws concerning the capital market and corporations were amended to facilitate the reforms. Strategies

---

Lockwood, The Economic Development of Japan: Growth and Structural Change, 1868–1938 (Princeton: Princeton University Press, 1954); Colin Mayer, *New Issues in Corporate Finance*, 32 (5) European Economic Review 1167–1183 (1988); and Masahiko Aoki and Hugh Patrick (*eds*), The Japanese Main Bank System, Its Relevance for Developing and Transforming Economies (New York: Oxford University Press, 1994).

33   *Ibid.*

34   Article 65 of the *Securities and Exchange Act* of 1948 prohibited banks from participating in the domestic securities industry, from holding more than 5 percent of a securities company, and from selling equity or underwriting securities.

35   The *Financial System Reform Act* of 1992 allowed banks to enter underwriting business by setting up securities subsidiaries.

36   *See* Shigeyoshi Miyagawa and Yoji Morita, Lessons from Japan's Prolonged Recession 2 (Working Paper 44, Department of Economics and Accounting, University of Tampere, Finland, 2005).

37   *Ibid.*

38   *See* Ernest T. Patrikis, Japan's Big Bang Financial Reforms (1998), available at <http://www.newyorkfed.org/-newsevents/speeches/1998/ep980427.html>.

seeking to revitalize the capital market have been introduced. Firstly, measures have been put in place to encourage citizens and corporations to invest in securities.[39] An important approach was to increase stockbrokers' sales channels and make it easier for investors to invest in securities. Secondly, trials of securitizing bad loans are underway and banks are expected to make prudent loans in the future. Hopefully, this will lead to more market oriented investments.[40] Thirdly, more market mechanisms have been introduced to allow the capital market, particularly the secondary market to function efficiently according to market rules; and finally, securities regulations have been improved to confine irregularities on the securities market.[41]

All this indicates that the Japanese government is determined to move from the bank-centered financial system into a market-centered system. How successful the transformation will be is anybody's guess. Theoretically speaking, a market-centered financial system requires a few preconditions. The most important precondition is the existence of dispersed investors in companies. Only when ownership is dispersed, a liquid market is likely to exist and market control becomes necessary and effective. However, currently, Japanese stock exchanges are affected by cross shareholdings and by stagnant individual stock ownership.[42]

Another important precondition of having a dynamic market-based financial system is the existence of a workable legal framework in favor of takeovers. The disciplinary function of the capital market lies much in the threat of takeover. If takeovers are unduly restricted, the effectiveness of market control will be compromised. However, takeovers have never been a popular practice in Japan.

In addition, to promote a market-based financial system, a strictly enforced regulatory regime governing disclosure has to be established. Disclosure is an essential element ensuring the efficiency of market control. Disclosure must be timely and accurate. Before the new rules of disclosure were introduced by the *Financial Instruments and Exchange Law* in 2007, either requirement was met by Japanese laws. Firstly, the Japanese law required companies to disclose twice a year. A three month lag was allowed.[43] Secondly, companies were under no obligation to update information in the disclosure documents.[44] The *Financial Instruments and Exchange Law* has imposed a quarterly report obligation on companies. The law has also introduced rules concerning managerial assessment of internal controls,

---

39   *See* Sadakazu Osaki, *Reforming Japan's Capital Markets*, 1(1) Public Policy Review 7 (2005).

40   *Ibid*, at 10.

41   *Ibid*, at 12–13.

42   *See* the Editor, *Let's Know about Japanese Stock Market*, available at <http://www.japanese-stockmarket-now.com>.

43   *See* Hideki Kanda, Disclosure and Corporate Governance: A Japanese Perspective (Paper at A Conference on Corporate Governance in Asia: A Comparative Perspective, Seoul, 3–5 March 1999) 7.

44   *Ibid*.

equivalent to the requirements in the US *Sarbanes-Oxley Act*. It is interesting to see how the rules will be implemented and enforced in the coming years.

The road to a market-based corporate finance system was not smooth. Despite the determination and efforts of the Japanese government, the performance of the Japanese securities market in the past ten years was not entirely satisfactory. One problem was that the prices in the stock market have been extremely volatile.[45] Volatility itself both reflected the instability of, and posed a challenge to investors' confidence in the capital market. The volatility of securities prices inevitably has had and will continue to have an impact on the overall economic development of Japan.

Securities Market and Corporate Governance in the EU

An exploration of the integration of EU securities markets is always a good starting point when evaluating the regulation and practice concerning the capital markets in the current EU. This section will begin with a brief review of the development of economic integration in the EU, and then discuss the programmatic document guiding the current practice of corporate governance in the EU – the Modernizing Company Law and Enhancing Corporate Governance in the European Union – A Plan to Move Forward in 2003 (the Plan).

The pace of economic integration in the EU has accelerated since the 1980s. In 1985, the EU tabled the White Papers on Completion of the Internal Market. In 1987, the commission submitted to the European Council and the European Parliament its Second Report on Implementing the Commission's White Paper on Completion of the Internal Market. The *Single European Act* (SEA) was also introduced in 1987. This Act aimed at tearing down the barrier against establishing an internal market in which persons, goods, services and capital could move freely among member states. The SEA has been an important step towards an integrated market. It introduced four important changes in the Community's strategy for advancing the integration process. Firstly, it made harmonization of national laws more achievable by simplifying the requirements of harmonization. Member states were required to meet certain essential standards of harmonization and adopt those mutually recognized national norms and regulations.[46] Secondly, it introduced a voting system favorable to promotion of harmonization by extending the scope of qualified majority voting. This allowed the main decisions required for a single market to be decided faster and more efficiently.[47] Thirdly, it gave the European Parliament a greater role in the legislative process.[48] Finally, it clarified

---

45   *Ibid.*

46   *See* the Committee for the Study of Economic and Monetary Union, section 3 of the *Report on economic and monetary union in the European Community* (1989).

47   *Ibid.*

48   *Ibid.*

that its major objectives included enhancing economic and social cohesion, strengthening the European Monetary System, implementing a European research and technology policy, harmonizing working conditions with respect to health and safety standards, encouraging the dialogue between management and labor, and initiating action to protect the environment.[49]

In 1989, the European Council summit accepted the *Report on economic and monetary union in the European Community* submitted by the Committee for the Study of Economic and Monetary Union.[50] The report proposed that the economic and monetary union might be achieved in three steps over a ten-year period.[51] In the following few years the Treaty of Maastricht on the European Union (1992) and the Investment Services Directive (1995) were promulgated. The official launch of the Euro as the single currency in the Eurozone in 1999 has brought the EU into a new era of economic integration.

The economic integration requires the assistance of an integrated securities market. This is because the main task of economic integration is to allocate resources according to comparative advantages of member states in order to achieve economics of scope, reduce costs and obtain competitive advantages.[52] In this process, merger and acquisition play an imperative part. Acquisition requires a liquid capital market. A liquid capital market is characterized by active trading, well informed investors and an adequate number of listed companies.[53] Furthermore, an efficient corporate governance system is a major building block in boosting sustainable public confidence in the capital markets. A sound corporate governance system is thus essential to the single market program.

In an effort to promote good corporate governance, the EU introduced the Modernizing Company Law and Enhancing Corporate Governance in the European Union – A Plan to Move Forward in 2003 (the Plan). The Plan put forward the following initiatives: firstly, listed companies should be required to disclose key elements of their corporate governance structures and practices in disclosure documents. Secondly, practicable measures of advancing shareholder activism should be designed and introduced. Thirdly, directors' remuneration needed to be subject to stricter shareholders' scrutiny. Finally, a European Corporate Governance Forum should be established to promote coordination and convergence of national corporate governance codes and practices.[54]

---

49 *Ibid.*

50 It is also known as the Delors Report after the name of the president of the Commission of the European Communities, Jacques Delors.

51 *See* the Committee for the Study of Economic and Monetary Union, *supra* note 46.

52 *See* Shaozhou Qi, The Integration of EU Securities Market 5 (Wuhan: Wuhan University Press, 2002).

53 *Ibid.*

54 *See* Part 3 of the Modernizing Company Law and Enhancing Corporate Governance in the European Union – A Plan to Move Forward (2003).

The current approach of corporate governance in the EU is a mix of regulatory intervention and self-regulation. The regulatory traditions relating to corporate governance in the EU are divided. While the UK, Holland, Ireland, Finland and Sweden are basically self-regulatory regimes, countries such as France and Italy adopt a centralized regulatory approach. Countries like Germany and Belgium have adopted a compromise approach by treating self-regulation and binding regulation as mechanisms of equal importance.[55] Within the EU, the issue of whether or not those bank-based economies should be encouraged to embrace the market-based financial system, and *vice versa*, is not on the agenda. Rather, the diverse traditions and preferences have decided that the regulation of corporate governance in the EU has to be a compromise. This is typically demonstrated by the recommendation in the Plan that companies can make a choice between the one-tier and two-tier board structures. Another example is that the Plan does not require the audit committee to be consisted exclusively of independent directors.[56]

Nevertheless, the capital markets and regulation in the EU are moving towards the direction of free market prevalence. More regulatory changes facilitating takeovers are expected to be made. In fact, there has been an increase in the number of takeover cases since the new millennium.[57] It is clear that the capital market will have to shoulder considerable tasks in the course of developing a single market in the EU. Consequently, the corporate control function of the capital market has been attracting increasing attention.

Conclusions

The Asian financial turmoil directly led a super economic power (Japan) to overhaul its practice of corporate governance. The market based corporate governance system re-gained its superiority over the bank-based system. However, in recent years, market control has failed spectacularly. A number of high profile scandals including the Enron case has revealed serious defects in corporate governance in the market-based system. In the post-Enron era, the general trend has been the increase of regulatory intervention. The US initiatives of enhancing regulation over the capital market have mostly been embraced by Japan. The Japanese are eager to adopt the US style of practice and regulation in developing its securities market. The outcomes of the Japanese efforts will remain to be seen over the coming years.

In the EU, the development of the capital market in member countries is uneven. The UK has established a highly liquid capital market, whereas Germany has been the model of a bank-based economy. Though the capital markets are comparatively

---

55   *See* Qi, *supra* note 52, at 191–5.

56   *See* Chapter 3 of the Modernizing Company Law and Enhancing Corporate Governance in the European Union – A Plan to Move Forward (2003).

57   *See* Qi, *supra* note 52.

less active in most member countries, increased attention has been given to the role of market control. Due to the essential role of the capital market in promoting a single market, the EU has strived to develop and harmonize the rules governing corporate governance and financial markets. Importance has been attached to the areas of disclosure, board and audit independence, and shareholders' participation. These regulatory focuses are concordant with those of the US regulation.

Chapter 6

Experiences of Some
Transitional Economies

This chapter examines corporate governance in two transitional economies: Russia and Czechoslovakia. Transition here refers to transformation from a planned economy to a market economy. In a market economy, the market acts as the adjustment between demand and supply through pricing and capital flow mechanisms.[1] It possesses at least the following conditions: (1) decentralized decision-making in economic units; (2) division of social labor; and (3) free competition.[2] These conditions do not exist in a planned economy. In a planned economy, the decision-making powers are concentrated in the hands of the government and the state claims ownership of most enterprises. Economic units merely implement plans and free competition basically does not exist. Economic transition usually starts from privatizing state ownership and introducing market mechanisms.

Russia and Czechoslovakia, like China, adopted the planned economy before the 1950s and launched economic reforms after the 1970s with enormous energy and determination. The difference of their experiences lies in their social and political costs of carrying out the reforms. An analysis of Russian and Czechoslovakian experiences will lead to an interesting comparison with the case of China. This is helpful in understanding the Chinese system.

Securities Market and Corporate Governance in Russia

Development of the Capital Market

Russia built the largest communist empire and a leading planned economy between the 1920s and the beginning of 1990s. The modern Russian market economy started its economic reforms in the 1990s. Privatization was believed to be the essential step of transition from a planned economy to a market economy.[3] It followed the

---

1 *See* Yoshiaki Nishimura, *Economic Policy for Transition to Market Economy: Overview* 2 (2001), available at <http://www.esri.go.jp/en/tie/russia/russia1-e.pdf>.

2 *Ibid.*

3 *See* the World Bank, *Transition, The First Ten Years: Analysis and Lessons for Eastern Europe and the Former Soviet Union* 70 (Washington D.C.: 2002), available at <http://siteresources.worldbank.org/ECAEXT/Resources/-complete.pdf>.

theory that privately owned firms produced better economic performance, and in a huge country with a weak central government and uncooperative enterprise managers, only rapid and mass privatization could guarantee the success of such a massive economic transition.[4] Based on this belief, the Russian government opted for mass privatization instead of traditional privatization. A voucher scheme was adopted as the major mechanism of implementing the mass privatization, and Russia began its "sale of the century". It was hoped that privatization would revive the stagnant economy through introducing profit incentives.[5] In this course, a model of interaction between enterprises and investors, and between owners and managers would be introduced into the Russian environment.[6]

Regrettably, because supportive institutions and a compatible regulatory framework for securing fair and transparent transition were not established, the privatization was tainted with insider dealing, corruption and organized crime.[7] Worst of all, corrupt officials and company insiders then formed a joint force resisting future reforms.[8] All of this caused the development of the securities market and corporate governance in Russia to be a complicated, rough, even traumatic process, disparate from the one that many Russian people initially expected.

The first Russian stock exchange was established in 1991. At that time, the legal framework was incomplete and the securities market was somewhat chaotic.[9] The trading activity was low because there were few private companies that existed to offer shares. The trading volume grew significantly due to the rapid privatization program in the following years. A secondary market also emerged for citizens to transfer vouchers. Forming a regulatory regime for ensuring the orderly operation of the securities market was on the reform agenda.[10] The year 1994 saw a dramatic increase in trading activities, due to massive issues of securities by privatized enterprises stimulating active transactions on the capital market. Nonetheless, the unprecedented supply merely matched the demand for securities, due to increased bank investments and foreign funds flowing into the Russian capital market in 1994.[11]

---

4   *See* Bernard Black and Reinier Kraakman, Russian Privatization and Corporate Governance: What Went Wrong? 8 (Stanford Law School John M Olin Program in Law and Economics Working Paper No. 178, 1999), available at <http://papers.ssrn.com/paper. taf?abstract_id=181348>.

5   *Ibid*, at 1.

6   *See* Andrei Yakovlev, *Evolution of Corporate Governance in Russia: Government Policy Vs. Real Incentives of Economic Agents*, 16(4) Post-Communist Economies 1 (2004).

7   *See* Black and Kraakman, *supra* note 2, at 4.

8   *Ibid*.

9   *See* Fulin Shang (*ed.*), Securities Market Regulatory Regimes: A Comparative Study 485–6 (Beijing: China Finance Press, 2006).

10   *See* D. Vasiliev, *Capital Market Development in Russia* 4, available at <http://siteresources.worldbank.org/-ECAEXT/Resources/VassilievPaper.pdf>.

11   *Ibid*.

In 1993, the Russian president's Order No. 163-rp "On Commission for Securities and Exchanges under the Russian President" endorsed the establishment of the Federal Commission for the Securities Market of Russia (FCSM).[12] It was renamed as the Russian Federal Securities Commission in 1996. The year 1996 also saw the promulgation of the first Russian securities law, the 1996 *Federal Securities Law* (FSL).[13] In the meantime, the *Law on Joint Stock Companies* was enacted. With further amendments made to the existing laws and introductions of the 1998 *Bankruptcy Law*, the 1999 *Law on Protection of Investors' Rights*, the 2001 *Investment Funds Law*, and 2003 *Law on Mortgage Securities*, a comprehensive legal framework was built up. The legislation endorsed a regulatory structure resembling the US practice.[14]

In practice, the Russian capital market experienced the most disordered and turbulent period between 1991 and 1996. Frauds frequently attacked the market. The MMM event was one of the most notorious fraudulent cases that severely upset the Russian capital market. Founded in 1989, MMM was involved in a few businesses with limited success. The year 1993 was the turning point for the company, when it decided to attract public investment on the securities market by offering high dividend returns. The promise was a sham and MMM declared bankruptcy in 1996. The company was later found guilty of tax invasion and misleading and deceiving investors.[15] MMM was not alone. Similar companies including Tibet, Chara, Khoper-Invest, Selenga, Telemarket, and Germes dominated the capital market at that time.[16] The chaotic securities market gravely shook Russia's economy. Yet, this was not the end of the story. The financial market crash in 1998 brought Russia further to the brink of economic crisis.

The Russian financial crisis of 1998 was caused by a number of connected factors. Firstly, the decline of the crude oil price sharply reduced the government's revenue income and weakened the government's financial capacity of handling economic crises. Secondly, the newly privatized enterprises were plagued by asset stripping problems resulting in low economic efficiency of Russian industries. Thirdly, the inefficient capital market provided a hotbed for imprudent speculative conduct, which posed high risks of triggering further crises. Finally, the announcement made by the Russian Federation and the Central Bank of Russia on 17 August 1998 regarding the devaluation of the ruble further anguished the financial market. The value of the ruble rapidly declined, which led to a collapse in the value of equity stocks in Russian companies and the virtual cessation of the offerings of international fixed income securities by both the Russian government

---

12   *See* the Editor, *History/Competence*, available at <http://www.fcsm.ru/catalog. asp?ob_no=1438>.

13   *See* Shang, *supra* note 9, at 486.

14   *Ibid*, at 487.

15   *See* the Editor, *MMM (pyramid)*, Wikipedia, available at <http://en.wikipedia.org/ wiki/MMM_(pyramid)>.

16   *Ibid*.

and corporations.[17] All these factors had an impact on the Russian economy and eventually brought Russia into an economic breakdown.

The privatization was completed through a non-transparent process and created an insider market.[18] Russia's economy collapsed in August 1998, the ruble lost 75 percent of its value and the main index of the Russian stock market lost 93 percent of its value in half a year.[19] Hence, Russia's experience in its first decade of economic reforms was not a happy one.

The mainstream literature has attributed the market failure in Russia to a lack of regulatory infrastructure and legal enforcement in its economic reforms. For instance, the World Bank stated:

> [I]f countries choose methods of rapid privatization that lead to diffuse or insider ownership, strengthening and enforcing the regulatory and supervisory framework are crucial to enhance the accountability of corporate boards and managers, to protect the rights of minority shareholders, to promote disclosure, and to ensure that secondary trading is conducted at fair and transparent prices.[20]

In the 1990s, institutional and legislative infrastructure in Russia was described as extremely feeble. The areas of commercial and corporate law were not governed by the rule of law in general.[21]

The disastrous aftermath of the financial market crash caused the Russian government to realize the importance of regulatory intervention. Since 1998, legislative efforts have been enhanced. The regulatory organization, the FCSM, was given extensive powers in penalizing market misconduct and breaches. The FCSM subsequently released a series of policies aimed at maintaining stability and sustainable development of the market.[22]

In 2004, the Federal Financial Markets Service (FFMS) was established in accordance with President Vladimir Putin's Decree No. 314 "On the System and Structure of Federal Executive Branch Agencies". The FFMS took over the functions of controlling and supervising the financial market formerly performed by the FCSM and Ministry of Labor and Social Development. It also inherited the

---

17   *See* Wayne P.J. McArdle, *Russian Financial Crisis*, available at <http://library. findlaw.com/1998/Sep/1/-128169.html>.

18   *See* Alexander Koliandre, *A Decade of Economic Reform*, BBC News (24 December 2001), available at <http://news.bbc.co.uk/1/hi/business/1727305.stm>.

19   *Ibid.*

20   *See* the World Bank, Transition – The First Ten Years: Analysis and Lessons for Eastern Europe 73 (Washington D.C.: The World Bank Publications, 2002).

21   *See* the secretariats of the United Nations Conference on Trade and Development and the United Nations Economic Commission for Europe, *The Russian Crisis of 1998* (Geneva, October 1998), available at <http://www.twnside.org.sg/title/1998-cr.htm>.

22   *See* Shang, *supra* note 9, at 487.

responsibility to control the activity of stock exchanges from the former Ministry of Antitrust Policy, and the responsibility to control and supervise pension reforms from the Ministry of Finance.[23] The FFMS has the power to issue relevant regulations. The FFMS's key objectives are to maintain stability in the financial markets, make the markets more efficient and attractive to investors, increase market transparency, and reduce investment risks.[24]

The defects in corporate governance have been regarded as another cause for the capital market failure in Russia. Good corporate governance facilitates corporate access to capital markets and thus helps the development of capital markets and stimulates economic growth.[25] In Russia, mass privatization has resulted in massive insider self-dealing. The insiders have opted for stripping the assets of the privatized enterprises, instead of improving their economic and managerial efficiency.[26] The insider controlled firms in a weakly controlled capital market are prone to making questionable profits. This has been evidenced by cases like MMM. Hence, improving corporate governance has been a high priority of the Russian government in the post crisis era.

Corporate Governance

The principle features of the corporate governance structure in Russia are basically decided by the Russian model of privatization. The privatization has resulted in insider control and dispersed ownership.[27] Insider control has resulted in economic inefficiency. Dispersed ownership requires a liquid capital market and compatible regulatory infrastructure. The mainstream theory suggests that dispersed ownership is the essential condition for developing a market-based corporate governance system. However, it is too early to say that Russia has developed a market-centered corporate governance system. Russia's capital market does not act as an effective monitoring mechanism over listed companies either. Currently, the Russian capital market is far from liquidity and the influence of institutional investors is limited. It is important for the country to develop effective internal and external corporate governance mechanisms in order to improve performance of its firms and the efficiency of its capital market.

---

23   *See* the Editor, *About Us* (the Federal Financial Market Service website), available at <http://www.fcsm.ru/eng/>.

24   *Ibid.*

25   *See* the International Finance Corporation and US Department of Commerce, *The Importance of Good Corporate Governance for Russia*, The Russia Corporate Governance Manual v (2004), available at <http://trade.gov/-goodgovernance/adobe/CGMEnPart_1/p1_importance_of.pdf>.

26   *See* Black and Kraakman, *supra* note 2, at 4.

27   *See* D.V. Vasilyev, *Corporate Governance in Russia: Is There Any Chance of Improvement?* 2–3, available at <http://www.imf.org/external/pubs/ft/seminar/2000/invest/pdf/vasil2.pdf>.

Soon after the initial stage of privatization, the control in Russian firms became more and more concentrated in the hands of managers and a few corporate groups, the so called oligarchs. The fact suggested that the effort of creating dispersed ownership in public companies had been frustrated.[28] Since vouchers were allowed to be traded on the secondary market immediately after their issuance, company managers and some intermediaries were able to acquire shares from employees and citizens by paying cash, and thus become controlling owners of the companies in the initial stage of privatization.[29] This resulted in the culture of insider control in Russian firms. Soon the Russian government joined in the game of sale for cash. It auctioned off its shares in the most profitable and promising firms mainly in the sectors of energy, telecommunications and metallurgy for bank loans. As a result, a small group of selected banks grasped control of these enterprises. This group of oligarchs was reported as being responsible for the later opaque dealings in Russia's capital market and corporate breaches.

From 1991 to 1995, very few regulatory efforts were made to scrutinize the corporate governance practice and the securities market. The legislative basis for the development of the securities market was basically absent.[30] Since 1995, there was a joint effort of the President, the government and the federal parliament to establish a regulatory regime for corporate and securities activities. The most remarkable achievement was the promulgation of the 1995 *Law on Joint Stock Companies* and the FSL. The FCSM has been active in promoting regulations controlling all aspects of market functioning.[31] In 2002, Russia introduced its first Corporate Governance Code (the Code). The Code was an important step of boosting good corporate governance. It embodied international standards of corporate governance. For instance, the Code required companies to have independent directors and committees, and provided guidelines for transparent operation.

It appears that monitoring mechanisms have gradually been introduced. However, the effectiveness of these mechanisms remains uncertain due to weak enforcement. Currently, the legal system is subject to abuses in many ways. Corruption has severely undermined the Russian judicial system. For instance, it is not uncommon for legal enforcement agencies to be unlawfully engaged in corporate conflicts.[32] As a result, investors have less confidence in the Russian judicial system. It is reported that only 20 percent of the investors who had

---

28   *See* Bruno Dallago, *Corporate Governance in Transformation Economies*, in Bruno Dallago and Ichiro Iwasaki (*eds*), Corporate Restructuring and Governance in Transition Economies 29 (New York: Palgrave Macmillan, 2007).

29   *Ibid.*

30   *See* Vasilyev, *supra* note 27, at 15.

31   *Ibid.*

32   *See* Julia Kochetygova and Oleg Shvyrkov, *Corporate Governance Practices in Russia and the Implementation of the Corporate Governance Code* 75, available at <http://www.ebrd.com/pubs/legal/lit061j.pdf>.

encountered problems sought judicial relief, and only very few of them managed to win.[33]

The imperfect legal framework and weak enforcement have negative effects on the practice of corporate governance. The area most impacted has been ownership disclosure. Russian companies are not required to disclose indirect shareholdings. Although listed companies are required to disclose their ownership in their quarterly reports to the regulatory authority, the disclosure is limited to immediate shareholders.[34] Furthermore, due to the absence of many corporate governance institutions, the implementation of the laws and the Code may only result in superficial changes.[35]

To summarize, although progress has been made, Russia has a long way to go to fundamentally improve the corporate governance practice in its enterprises.

Securities Market and Corporate Governance in the Czech Republic and the Slovak Republic

The Czech Republic and Slovakia split from Czechoslovakia, which existed as a socialist country since 1948, and launched their transitional reforms in 1993. The reformers firmly believed that the first necessary step of bringing market mechanisms into the economy was to privatize state-owned enterprises. In fact, privatization started even before the dissolution of Czechoslovakia. Since 1989, the Czechoslovakian government initiated privatization through three programs: restitution, small-scale privatization, and large-scale privatization.[36]

Restitution allowed the former owners to reclaim their ownership over assets and properties nationalized by the communist government since 1948. Small-scale privatization referred to selling out small businesses through public auctions. Large-scale privatization was a program, in which medium and large sized state-owned enterprises were transferred into private hands. To achieve the goal of rapidly privatizing large enterprises, investment vouchers were introduced as the effective method of mass privatization. Large state-owned enterprises were transformed into joint stock companies. Czechoslovakian citizens were given the opportunity to purchase vouchers for a nominal fee and they could bid for shares of the joint stock companies. Investment Privatization Funds (IPFs) were created to facilitate

---

33   *Ibid*, at 76.

34   *Ibid*.

35   *Ibid*, at 78.

36   *See* Ladislav Venys, *The Political Economy of Privatization in Czechoslovakia* 2–5 (Carnegie Council/DRT International Privatization Project, 1991), available at <http://www. cceia.org/resources/publications/-privatization_project/0002.html/_res/id=sa_File1/2_ Ladislav_Venys.pdf >. *See* also Barbara Blaszczyk, Iraj Hoshi and Richard Woodward, Secondary Privatisation in Transition Economies: The Evolution of Enterprise Ownership in the Czech Republic, Poland and Slovenia 172 (New York: Palgrave Macmillan, 2003).

the voucher privatization. Citizens who did not want to bid for shares themselves could assign their voucher points to an IPF for a share in it.[37] According to the law authorizing the mass privatization, large firms were to be privatized in two waves. The first wave of privatization was completed by the end of 1992. Shares in 988 firms were available for bidding.[38] When Czechoslovakia split up into the Czech Republic and Slovakia in January 1993, enterprises subject to the second wave of voucher privatization were divided between the two new states. As a result the second wave of privatization was delayed about six months and was completed in the beginning of 1994.

Upon independence, both the Czech Republic and Slovakia inherited an economy that had experienced two years of intensive economic reforms. A large number of citizens in each country were ready to trade the shares acquired in the first wave of voucher privatization during the Czechoslovakian regime. Consequently, securities markets were established in both countries. In the Czech Republic, the Prague Stock Exchange started to trade in April 1993. The stock exchange offered two trading systems: the SPAD for big and medium investors, and the trading modules auction and continual for small investors.[39] By 1997, the Czech Republic had over 2,100 listed joint stock companies, with a market capitalization of around 30 percent of GDP.[40] Nowadays, the Prague Stock Exchange has become the second largest stock exchange in Central and Eastern-Europe. Since 2004, the SEC has officially recognized the stock exchange as a "designated offshore securities market" and included it in the list of offshore exchanges reliable for investors.

Important laws regulating the Czech securities market include the *Bonds Act* (1990); the *Commercial Code* (1991); the *Securities Act* (1992); the *Stock Exchange Act* (1992); the *Investment Fund Code* (1992); and the *Securities Commission Act* (1998).[41] In 1998, the Securities Commission was established to supervise the securities market, particularly in the areas of securities issuance and trading.

Since 1993, three official securities markets have existed in the Slovak Republic. They are Bratislava Stock Exchange, Bratislava Options Exchange, and the RM-System (the electronic exchange market).[42] In addition, there is an

---

37   *See* Jan Hanousek and Randall K. Filer, *Lange and Hayke Revisited: Lessons from Czech Voucher Privatization*, 21(3) Cato Journal 493 (2002).

38   *Ibid.*

39   The SPAD is the Czech acronym for System Supporting the Market for Shares and Bonds. *See* the Editor, SPAD (the Prague Stock Exchange website), available at <http://www.pse.cz/Obchodovani/SPAD>.

40   *See* the *International Monetary Fund, Report on The Observance of Standards and Codes (ROSC): Czech Republic* (2000), available at <http://www.imf.org/external/np/rosc/cze/securit.htm>.

41   The *Commercial Code* and the *Securities Act* were amended in 1996.

42   *See* Mikael Olsson, *Corporate Governance in Economies of Transition – The Case of the Slovak Republic* 1 (Uppsala Papers in Financial History, Report No. 5, Department of Economic History, 1995), available at <http://www.diva-portal.org/diva/getDocument?urn_nbn_se_uu_diva-2357-1__fulltext.pdf>.

unofficial securities market – the "off market" trading or the "street market". The regulatory authority of the Slovak capital market has been the Ministry of Finance. The securities business and the stock market are mainly regulated by *Law No. 600/1992 Coll. On Securities*, *Law No. 191/1950 on Bills of Exchange and Cheques*, *Law No. 385/1999 Coll. on Bonds*, *Law on Collective Investments*, *Law No 330/2000 on the Stock Exchange*, and *Law No. 600/2000 on Securities*.[43]

Nearly two decades have passed since the privatization movements in the Czech Republic and Slovakia. Looking back the development of the securities markets in the Czech Republic and Slovakia, one can conclude that the capital markets in both countries are still volatile, non-transparent, and lacking liquidity.[44] It is therefore unsurprising that the capital markets have a limited part to play in relation to encouraging good corporate governance in the listed companies of both countries. In fact, both the Czech Republic and Slovakia have a problem with the absence of external corporate governance. Originally, it was expected that voucher privatization would result in dispersed ownership in large corporations, and the control power in these companies would be concentrated in the hands of management. In such a circumstance, it would be very necessary to fully exert the monitoring functions of the securities market. However, in reality, the securities markets in the Czech Republic and Slovakia are inefficient and have become an arena of tunneling, looting and corruption.[45]

Although privatization resulted in scattered shareholding in large firms, many shareholders are merely passive owners.[46] This largely attributed to a lack of shareholder activist culture and a lack of legal protection for investors. The legal framework regulating the capital market and corporate conduct in the two countries is lax and has lagged behind the practice. Both the legislative system and judicial institutions are ill prepared to effectively constrain market defectiveness and corporate misconduct.[47] As a result, investors' interests are not adequately protected, and expropriation of small shareholders' wealth is rampant.

---

43 These laws were amended on certain occasions in *See* Sovak Investment and Trade Development Agency (SARIO) and Johanthan Beuvid, *Capital Markets*, in Jonathan Beuvid (*ed.*), Doing Business with Slovakia 106–9 (London: Kogan Page and Contributors, 2004).

44 *See* Olsson, *supra* note 38, at 46. *See* also Edward Glaese, Simon Johnson and Andrei Shleifer, *Coase Versus the Coasians*, 116(3) The Quarterly Journal of Economics 882 (2001).

45 *See* Robert Cull, Jana Matesova and Mary Shirley, *Ownership and the Temptation to Loot: Evidence from Privatized Firms in the Czech Republic*, 30(1) Journal of Comparative Economics 1–24 (2002). *See* also Simon Johnson, Rafael La Porta, Florencio Lopez-de-Silanes and Andrei Shleifer, *Tunneling*, 90 American Economic Review 22–7 (2000).

46 *See* Martin Myant, Transforming Socialist Economies 134 (Aldershot: Edward Elgar Publishing Limited, 1993).

47 *See* Cheryl Gray, In Search of Owners: Lessons of Experience with Privatization and Corporate Governance in Transition Economies 59 and 109 (World Bank Policy Research Working Paper No. 1595, 1996).

Due to the limited monitoring function of the securities market, it is recommended that the Czech Republic and Slovakia may adopt a concentrated ownership structure in order to mitigate the malfunctioning of the external governance mechanisms.[48] This is because internal governance mechanisms can compensate for weak market supervision and improve corporate efficiency through enhancing internal supervision over the management.[49] Large shareholders are able to influence the structure of the board through their voting powers so as to ensure the independence of the board. An independent and efficient board is essential to hold the management accountable.

In the beginning, the governments of the Czech Republic and Slovakia intended to prevent large blocks of shareholdings for the purpose of minimizing the influence of the former insiders in the planned economy. As a result, ownership in newly privatized companies was dispersed. On the other hand, the governments only made modest efforts to regulate securities transactions and improve the liquidity and efficiency of the capital markets. The defused ownership in combination with underdeveloped capital markets and weak regulation led to poor performance of their public companies.[50]

In recent years, the ownership in Czech and Slovak companies has tended to become more concentrated in the hands of investment funds. To an extent, this has been achieved through methods that are unlawful in some other countries, including two-tier tender offers, auctioning of on-tendered shares at below-market prices, and transfers of company assets to offshore accounts owned by large shareholders.[51] There have been reports that the increasingly concentrated ownership in Czech and Slovak companies has led to improved corporate governance.[52] This strongly

---

48   *See* Tomas Jandik and Graig G. Rennie, The Evolution of Corporate Governance and Firm Performance in Emerging Markets: The Case of Sellier and Bellot 9 (European Corporate Governance Institute Finance Working Paper No. 59/2004, 2005), available at <http://www.fma.org/Chicago/Papers/jandik_rennie_fmae05.pdf>.

49   *See* Andrei Shleifer and Robert W. Vishny, *A Survey of Corporate Governance*, 52 The Journal of Finance 737–83 (1997). *See* also Julian Franks and Colin Mayer, *Ownership and Control of German Corporations*, 14(4) Review of Financial Studies 934–77 (2001). *See* also Alexander Dyck and Luigi Zingales, *Private Benefits of Control: An International Comparison*, 59 The Journal of Finance 537–99 (2004).

50   *See* Jandik and Rennie, *supra* note 47, at 10.

51   *See* John C. Coffee Jr., *Inventing a Corporate Monitor in Transitional Economies: The Uncertain Lessons from the Czech and Polish Experience*, in Klaus Hopt et al (*eds*), Comparative Corporate Governance: The State of Emerging Research 96–9 (Oxford: Clarendon Press, 1998).

52   *See* Stijn Claessens, Simeon Djankov and Gerhard Pohl, Ownership and Corporate Governance: Evidence from the Czech Republic 1, 8–15 (The World Bank, Policy Research Working Paper Series, No. 1737, 1997), available at <http://www.worldbank.org/html/dec/Publications/Workpapers/WPS1700series/wps1737/-wps1737.pdf>. *See generally* Jandik and Rennie, *supra* note 47.

supports the argument that concentrated ownership improves corporate governance in a system of legal, market and accounting inefficiency.

It is noteworthy that in the Czech and Slovak Republics, banks have a positive influence on corporate governance.[53] This is because banks are significant shareholders in companies, particularly in investment funds. Like the German arrangements, commercial banks in the Czech and Slovak Republics not only hold large blocks of shareholdings in other companies, but also are allowed to act as other shareholders' proxy. As a matter of fact, investment funds sponsored by banks are usually institutional shareholders holding controlling blocks of shares in newly privatized companies. Consequently, the banks have no choice but to assume the monitoring functions of a main bank.[54] Research has found that firms with concentrated share blocks in the hands of investment funds sponsored by a bank deliver better economic performance.[55]

Conclusions

Different transitional economies have adopted different reform strategies. Russia relied on a voucher scheme and a "loans for shares" scheme to complete mass privatization. The initial purpose was to create dispersed ownership. However, control in privatized firms soon became concentrated in the hands of managers and a few financial institutions. Whereas the voucher scheme resulted in insiders obtaining control in privatized firms, the "loans for shares" scheme saw ownership concentration in the hands of a few banks or of some oligarchs controlling these banks. Since the 1998 financial crisis, new significant owners in Russian firms have emerged. They are termed as external shareholders who acquired shares either inside or outside the capital market.[56] It is hoped that the newly emerged external investors will be helpful in advancing good corporate governance.

The Czech Republic and Slovakia present another interesting case of economic restructure. Their reform process was an experiment in transplanting a market economy of a specific model based on mainstream economic theories. Their economic transition is, therefore, labeled as a case of textbook reform. Again, the effects of privatization in the Czech Republic and Slovakia were less than satisfactory. Their privatization represents a case of technological success with undesired consequences.[57] The fundamental problem is that there has been absence of a basic legal and institutional framework accommodating the transition. As a result, fraud, theft and market misconduct have undermined the reform efforts and

---

53   *Ibid*, at 1.
54   *Ibid*, at 14.
55   *Ibid*, at 12–15.
56   *See* Dallago, *supra* note 28.
57   *Ibid*, at 30.

deprived the Czech Republic and Slovakia of the benefits of the economic reform considerably.

The development of the securities markets in the Czech Republic and Slovakia is closely linked to the mass voucher privatization program, which was the focus of the governments' economic reform efforts from the late 1980s to mid-1990s. The two countries have all opted for voucher privatization as a strategy of introducing dispersed ownership in their public companies in order to create a competitive market economy. However, the dispersed ownership did not last long. Nor did it lead to improved practice of corporate governance. Since dispersed ownership did not lead to improvement of corporate performance in the current economic and legal environments, concentration is welcomed and regarded as a legitimate solution to the corporate governance problems. Furthermore, investment funds and banks are expected to play an active part in promoting corporate efficiency.

The experiences of Russia, the Czech Republic and Slovakia demonstrate that regulatory and institutional support is an essential element in relation to ensuring successful economic transformation.

PART III
Securities Markets and Corporate Governance in China

Chapter 7
A Historical Review of the Development of China's Capital Market

This chapter traces the tortuous path of the development of the securities market in China. In doing so, it demonstrates that the development of the securities market and regulation is shaped by the particular social, political, and economic circumstances of a particular country. It also reviews the development of securities companies and investment funds in China to offer readers a full picture of China's securities market.

The Development of China's Securities Market before 1949

The earliest securities dealings in China took place in the 1860s. The first securities market was established in Shanghai in 1903. It subsequently evolved into the largest capital market in Asia.[1] However, strictly speaking, the Shanghai Stock Exchange was not an officially recognized Chinese stock exchange, since it was a company registered in Hong Kong with foreign stock brokers as the majority members.[2] In the meantime, some Chinese scholars and entrepreneurs advocated creation of Chinese stock exchanges. However, the Qing government ignored such calls.

Like all capital markets in their early stage of development, China's capital market was not closely monitored or regulated. Fraudulent conduct within the market was rampant. The most notorious abuse events included the Rubber Booms. The impact of these events on the Chinese society was similar to those of the South Sea Bubble event in the London Stock Exchange or the Railway Boom and Land Boom in the US securities market.

Rubber booms plagued China twice, the first in the 1910s and the second in the 1930s. The first rubber boom started from the beginning of the twentieth century and ended in July 1910. In the early 1900s, rubber manufacturing was a prosperous industry. Rubber products were highly demanded in China. Consequently the shares of the companies manufacturing rubber products became popular on the

---

1 *See* Jiangyu Wang, *China's Securities Experiment: The Challenge of Globalization*, available at <http://www.eastlaw.net/research/securities/securities-no1.htm>.

2 The stock exchange had 100 members. Among them 87 were foreign members. *See* Zhong Chen, Wind and Cloud on The Securities Market in China 6–7 (Shanghai: Shanghai Transportation University Press, 2000).

securities market. This was deemed as an exploitable opportunity in the eyes of market raiders. They registered phony rubber companies. Meanwhile, they manipulated the market by creating false transactions of the shares of these phony companies and by releasing misleading information. The sky rocketing prices of rubber shares soon induced a rubber mania in the city of Shanghai. The holders of rubber shares even extended to include rickshaw wheelers and maidservants, not to mention banks, companies and those well off.

Foreign banks and business people were the main force driving this rubber boom. When the majority of speculators fled abroad with mighty profits, the bubble eventually burst. The aftermath was disastrous. More than a dozen local banks became insolvent, resulting in thousands of bank depositors falling into bankruptcy. It was a painful memory in the minds of millions of Chinese of that generation.

Nevertheless, the securities business steadily developed and laws regulating the stock market gradually came into effect. When the Republic regime replaced the Qing Dynasty, the Chinese government began to pay more attention to the development of the financial market. In 1914, the first Chinese law regulating securities markets, the 1914 *Stock Exchange Law*, was promulgated. According to the *Stock Exchange Law*, a Chinese stock exchange was a company limited by shares, carrying on the business with the approval of the Agriculture and Trading Ministry. Only Chinese citizens could become brokers and staff of the stock exchange.[3] In the following year, the Chinese government published the 1915 *Detailed Regulations for Implementation of the Stock Exchange Law*. After the enactment of the laws, stock exchanges were established in major Chinese cities including Beijing, Shanghai and Tianjing. The introduction of the financial market provided a channel for the large amount of idle money concentrated in major Chinese cities. Soon, the number of stock exchanges mushroomed. Shanghai was a city that attracted most securities businesses. By 1921, about 136 stock exchanges were established in Shanghai.[4] More than half of them mainly dealt with government bonds.

When Mr Sun Zhongsan, the founding father of the Guomindang Party and the Republic of China, fought for building a new China, he tried to raise funds for funding the revolution through issuing bonds in China, Japan and the US. These bonds were called "revolution bonds" and they stated that upon the success of the revolution, the holders would be entitled to an amount of repayment equaling to ten times the subscribed amount. Since the amount raised was far less than that needed, Mr Sun decided to establish a stock exchange in Shanghai. His application was finally approved by the Agriculture and Trading Ministry. Consequently, the

---

3   *See* Zhong Chen, Wind and Cloud on The Securities Markets in China 16 (Shanghai: Shanghai Transportation University Press, 2000).

4   *See* Zhiying Liu, *A Review of Chinese Stock Exchanges in Old China*, 15 Modern Bankers (2006), available at <http://www.modernbankers.com/modernbankers/jrws/20060 9/20060926153010.shtml>.

Shanghai Securities and Commodity Stock Exchange came into existence in July 1920.[5] The stock exchange dealt with securities and futures. About seven types of goods were traded on the futures market. The Shanghai Securities and Commodity Stock Exchange was the first stock exchange fully comprised of Chinese members. In the early years, its business was successful and the prices of the shares of the Stock Exchange increased by almost 500 percent.[6]

The success of the Shanghai Securities and Commodity Stock Exchange inspired many to seek the same achievement. Within a few months, more than 100 stock exchanges were opened. In the meantime, a number of trust companies were registered.[7] However, most of them were closed down before the end of 1921 due to a lack of business. In the end only two trust companies and six stock exchanges survived. This was the so called "trust and stock exchange boom".[8] In the aftermath of the trust and exchange boom, numerous firms became bankrupt and many investors committed suicide. The business of the Shanghai Securities and Commodity Stock Exchange declined substantially after the boom and was eventually closed down ten years later.

The trust and stock exchange boom resulted in investors losing confidence in stock investments. Subsequently, government bonds became popular securities. Before the Guomindang government came into power, China was experiencing a period of civil war among war lords. Although the Northern War Lords controlled the central government, the political environment was unstable. Some speculators affiliated with government officials had opportunities of manipulating the capital market by releasing military or politically sensitive information. By July 1924, the prices of government bonds reached a historical high. Soon, the bond market plunged due to the spread of the rumor that a war between Xiangsu and Zhejiang local forces was likely to break out. The crash of the bond market resulted in the Beijing Stock Exchange being closed for four months and the Huashang Stock Exchange (Shanghai) stopping trading twice within ten days.[9] This event was termed as "government bond boom" in the present Chinese financial history.

The situation did not improve substantially during the Guomindang regime. Since 1928, Japan started military penetration in Northern China, which eventually developed into military invasion in 1931. China approached the brink of political and economical crisis. The government issued a large amount of government bonds.

---

5   *See* Chunting Zhang, *A Brief History of China's Securities Market: The Republican Period (1)*, The Forum of China's Economic History, available at <http://www.zlunwen.com/financial/stock/4079.htm>.

6   *See* Chen, *supra* note 3 at 21.

7   *See* Liu, *supra* note 4.

8   *See* Chunting Zhang, *A Brief History of China's Securities Market: the Late Qing Period*, The Forum of China's Economic History, available at <http://economy.guoxue.com/article.php/71>.

9   *See* the Editor, *The History of Stock Exchange and Trust Companies in Old China*, China Net of Finance and Securities, available at <http://www.zj365.cn/zj4.htm>.

For strengthening the public's faith in the investments, all bonds were guaranteed by the government's revenue income. In order to obtain the banks' support, the government sold the bonds to those acting as the underwriters at a price much lower than the face value. The government hoped that in doing so, it could reduce military expenditure and expand the government's financial resources.[10]

However, the object was never achieved due to rampant corruption in the government and flagrant fraud upon the capital market. The capital market was controlled by gangsters, mafia and, worst of all, corrupt officials. It is interesting to note that the three well-known master manipulators of the market constituted the Head of the Monetary Department of the central government, the Deputy of the Central Bank, and the General Manager of China Constructive Bank. The big brother was the Minister of Finance.[11] A typical practice of market manipulation was for these important officials to divulge the information that the government was going to replace the old bonds with a new type of bond and in the meantime would change the tax rate in order to maintain the order of the market. Before long, the information was leaked to the market that the government planned to stop paying interest to the holders of the previously issued bonds. Bondholders rushed into underselling their bonds to avoid the worst. These manipulators took the opportunity to purchase the bonds at the bottom price. After that, they bid up the price of the bonds. Through such games they made many bankrupt within a few days.

Between 1937 and 1945, Shanghai was occupied by Japanese invaders. Stock exchanges were forbidden from trading not only government bonds, but also foreign securities, gold, silver, foreign currency, cotton, and gauze. Investment capital could only flow to stocks of Chinese companies.[12] However, the capital market under the control of the corrupt puppet government was impossible to revive. At that time, the most powerful speculators in the Shanghai securities market were the wives of the three top figures in the puppet government including the President. They appeared to have enormous resources for speculation since they could utilize the reserve money of the puppet government under their husbands' management. It was a time of outrageous speculation and swindle.

After the Japanese occupation ended, all stock exchanges approved by the puppet government were forced into liquidation. In April 1946, the Chinese government decided to re-establish a stock exchange. Following some preparation, the Shanghai Stock Exchange was formally opened. Unfortunately, the government was in a hurry to make the stock exchange a ready source of money. The Ministry of Finance and the Ministry of Economy required the brokers of the stock exchange

---

10   *See* Chunting Zhang, *A Brief History of China's Securities Market: The Republican Period (2)*, The Forum of China's Economic History, available at <http://www.zlunwen. com/financial/stock/4079_1.htm>.

11   They were Xu Kan, Chen Xing and Song Ziliang. The Minister of Finance was Kong Xiangxi. *See* Chen, *supra* note 6, at 40–41.

12   *See* Zhang, *supra* note 10.

to pay an amount up to 5 billion yuan of bond and 40 percent of it must be in the form of gold.[13] The total amount of bond submitted by the 230 qualified brokers reached 46 billion yuan, which was ten times the government investments in the capital market.[14] This bond went directly to the treasury.

It was not a surprise that the business of the securities market never thrived after the recovery. The securities market continued to be a place where interested groups imposed all types of scams on ordinary investors. The worst market manipulators were again government officials. From 1946 to 1948, rumors about changing exchange rates, increase of gold, and current price reforms caused wild volatility on the securities market. The most notorious event was the direct involvement of the army. Since the end of February 1947, the capital market went up. Although it was against the wish of some important figures, the market continued to rise. In the beginning of March, the soldiers of the Shanghai Garrison Headquarters suddenly rushed into the Shanghai Stock Exchange and the price of the stock exchange eventually went down. In the end, even brokers were victimized. The government issued public bonds in May 1947 and stipulated that new bonds must be purchased in US dollars. Because investors were not interested in the new bonds, brokers were required to purchase a certain amount of the bonds.[15] It was clear that the government resorted to killing the goose that lays the golden eggs. This resulted in a brokers' strike. In August 1948, the Shanghai Stock Exchange stopped business and finally closed down by the end of that year.[16]

China's Securities Market between 1949 and 1986

In 1949, the Communist Party took over the government and the People's Republic of China came into existence. The new government was facing an economy that was close to collapse. The financial market was extremely chaotic. Industry was under stress and inflation was serious. To recover the order of the market, the new government introduced a number of policies aimed at recovering the economy. One of them was reorganizing the capital market in order to eliminate black markets and restrict speculation.

In June 1949, with the support of the government, the Tianjin Stock Exchange was reopened. The stock exchange successfully absorbed substantial idle money. In the following year, the Beijing Stock Exchange was established. The operation of these stock exchanges was helpful in stabilizing currency, utilizing idle funds, and controlling inflation.

With the establishment of the planned economy, the significance of the capital market gradually faded. In the beginning of 1952, the stock exchanges in Tianjin

---

13   *See* Chen, *supra* note 3, at 65.

14   *Ibid.*

15   *Ibid.*

16   *See* Zhang, *supra* note 10.

and Beijing were closed down. In the meantime, with the progress of the socialist enterprise reform, most existing companies were transformed into state-owned and collectively-owned enterprises. The rest became joint state-private enterprises. Since 1956, according to the provisions in the 1956 *Provisional Regulations for Fixed Interest in Joint State-Private Enterprises*, the private shareholders in joint state-private enterprises would receive fixed dividends quarterly for a certain period of time before fully transferring their shares to the state.[17] In the following 23 years, the government became the only fund provider for enterprises and fully controlled production activities. Companies and the securities market disappeared from China's economic life. In 1978, China was preparing for the reforms of transforming the planned economy into a market economy. The investment structure underwent changes. Before the reforms, it was the central government allocating funds to enterprises. After 1978, banks became the main investors, assisted by local governments. This was described as a transition "from government allocation to bank loans". Since 1978, Chinese citizens' living standard improved significantly and the amount of public savings increased substantially. From 1978 to 1990, the amount of public saving in China increased from 210.6 billion yuan to 7034.2 billion yuan.[18] The annual rate of increase was 33.96 percent. In 1978, the percentages of public saving, enterprise saving and government saving were 11.8 percent, 14.9 percent and 73.3 percent respectively.[19] In 1990, these percentages became 40.1 percent, 38.9 percent and 21 percent.[20] This demonstrated that public saving gradually became an important source of industrial finance. This provided an important foundation for future financial changes.

In January 1981, the State Council of China promulgated the *Regulations of the People's Republic of China on Government Bonds*. From 1981, the government would issue government bonds. The *Regulations* provided methods for subscribing for bonds. Considering the public's reluctance in relation to investing in bonds, in the beginning, government bonds were only allocated to state-owned enterprises, collectively-owned enterprises, government departments, local governments, armies, and rich communes.[21] After 1988, the government introduced market mechanisms by establishing the bond market in some cities, allowing transfer of bonds on the market. The issuance of government bonds effectively directed the idle funds to the most needed sectors.

With the deepening of economic reforms, some enterprises began to seek new channels of fund raising. In 1984, due to the emergence of over-investment and

---

17   *See* the State Council, the 1956 *Provisional Regulations for Fix Interest in Joint State-Private Enterprises.*

18   *See* Qingquan Ma, The History of Securities Business in China 8 (Beijing: OITIC Publishing House, 2003).

19   *Ibid.*

20   *Ibid.*

21   *See* the State Council, the 1981 *Regulations of the People's Republic of China on Government Bonds.*

inflation, the government decided to reduce financial investments. Under such a circumstance, some enterprises attempted to seek other channels of funds. In November 1984, Shanghai Feile Acoustics Company decided to issue shares to the public.[22] It consequently became the first share company in the history of the People's Republic of China. Since then, many share companies came into existence. However, there was confusion about the concept of shares. Strictly speaking, the shares issued at that time were not shares in a true sense. For example, Shanghai Feile Acoustics Company provided that the holders of its shares were entitled to a fixed amount of annual interest and the interest should be paid in cash. In addition, the company was obliged to return the principal to the shareholders.[23] Some companies even promised "three types of return", i.e. return of principal, interest and bonus. Some enterprises even distributed shares to their employees as a means of welfare. On some occasions, the value of the shares did not represent the value of the enterprises' assets. Furthermore, in some companies the same shares did not carry the same rights.[24]

It was necessary for the government to provide policy guidance and legislative regulation in order to eliminate the confusion in bond and share issuances and transactions. In 1987, the State Council enacted the *Provisional Regulations for Managing Enterprise Bonds*. In 1990, the People's Bank of China published the *Measures of Regulating Securities Companies*, the *Provisional Methods of Regulating Securities Trading across Administrative Areas*, and the *Circular on Strictly Restricting Share Issuance and Transfer*. The laws and regulations at this stage were scatted and there was not a uniform regulatory authority nationwide.

In 1984, the first over-the-counter securities market in China since the economic reforms came into existence. It was the Jinjan Branch of the Shanghai Trust Company. In 1986, John Phelan, the Chairman of the Board of the New York Stock Exchange (NYSE) visited China. He was received by the president of China, Deng Xiaoping.[25] Mr Phelan sent an emblem of the NYSE as a gift to Mr Deng. Mr Deng in return sent him a green card. This green card was the first stock certificate in the history of the People's Republic of China. It was issued in 1984 by Shanghai Feile Acoustics Company.[26] Mr Phelan was excited to know that China had established its first over-the-counter securities market and requested to visit it.[27] The host did not think the stock exchange would be impressive to Mr Phelan since it was located in an eleven square meter room and had merely one

---

22   *See* Carl E. Walter and Fraser J.T. Howie, Privatizing China, The Stock Markets and their Role in Corporate Reform xxii (Singapore: John Wiley & Sons (Asia) Pty. Ltd., 2003).

23   *See* Unknown Grass, *A Hundred Years' History of China's Capital Market*, East Blog, <http://blog2.eastmoney-.com/wswzfy123,528407.html>.

24   *Ibid.*

25   *See* Chen, *supra* note 3, at 92.

26   *Ibid.*

27   *Ibid.*

staff member.[28] Nevertheless the host organized the trip and Mr Phelan visited the Jinjan Branch of Shanghai Trust Company in Nanjing Xilu Road, Shanghai.[29] Mr Phelan met the manager of the Jinjan Branch, Mr Guixian Huang. The meeting was described as the meeting of the chairs of the largest stock exchange and the smallest stock exchange.[30] Mr. Phelan commented that the Jinjan Branch, in its nascency, was superior to the NYSE due to the fact that the initial transactions of the NYSE were completed under a buttonwood tree.[31]

It is important to note that unlike some transitional economies such as Russia and Czechoslovakia, in China, market mechanisms were not introduced as part of the package of massive privatization. In the beginning of the economic reforms, privatization was intensively debated. The idea of privatizing state-owned enterprises was not favored by the majority of the Chinese people. Many believed that public ownership was superior to private ownership, in the sense of upholding social justice and maintaining social stability in the course of economic reforms.[32] To most of the Chinese, economic reforms were means but not ends. The principal goal of China's economic reforms was to develop the economy and improve people's living standards. In other words, the goal was to realize a common enrichment in China. For this purpose, there was a need to uphold social justice. As public ownership was the economic foundation of social justice, it was necessary to maintain the dominance of public ownership in China. If the dominance of public ownership was eroded by the economic reforms, polarization would be inevitable.[33] This would exacerbate all conflicts, including those between different areas, different levels of governments, and different ethnic groups, and bring about a disastrous outcome.[34]

Nevertheless, the Chinese policy-makers understood that corporatization and gradual privatization of some industrial sectors were necessary steps in the course of the enterprise reforms. Moreover, there was the need to direct idle funds, particularly public savings, to the most efficient economic sectors. The introduction of the capital market was perceived inevitable. The initial political and economic conditions determined that the development of China's capital market would have to follow the path of building up a bond market first and then gradually establishing a stock market.

---

28   *Ibid.*

29   *Ibid.*

30   *Ibid.*

31   *Ibid.*

32   *See* Shangqing Sun, *The Dominance of Public Ownership is the Foundation of Fairness*, Economic Reference (Jing Ji Can Kao Bao, 24 September 1994). *See also* Mingwu Chen's remarks in Wenmin Zhang et al. (*eds*), The Great Economic Debate in China 69–70 (Publishing House of Economic Management: Beijing, 1997).

33   *See* Yuwa Wei, Comparative Corporate Governance: A Chinese Perspective 30 (London: Kluwer Law International, 2003).

34   *Ibid.*

China's Securities Market after 1986

China has made impressive progress in the development of its financial markets and securities business since the 1980s. Within a few years after Mr Phelan's first visit, China established two national stock exchanges – the Shanghai Stock Exchange and the Shenzhen Stock Exchange.[35]

At the very beginning of China's enterprise reforms, the Shanghai City Council had the plan of establishing a stock exchange in Shanghai. On 2 February 1989, the Shanghai City Council instructed the Shanghai Branch of the People's Bank of China to propose the blue print for the establishment of a stock exchange. On 27 February 1987, the Shanghai Branch of the People's Bank of China organized a study group for the purpose. Based on the detailed proposal drafted by the study group, the Shanghai Branch of the People's Bank of China submitted a report on preparing for establishing the Shanghai stock exchange.

In the meantime, with the support of the State Council and the People's Bank of China, the Stock Exchange Executive Council (SEEC) was established.[36] The SEEC was an institution sponsored by nine state-owned companies including SINOCHEM Corporation, China Foreign Economy and Trade Trust Investment Co. Ltd (FOTIC) and the China Economic Development Trust Investment Company. The object of the SEEC was to provide project research, consultation, training and information exchange services to participants of the securities market for the purpose of increasing market efficiency.[37]

Originally, the organizers and sponsors of the SEEC had a view of launching a stock exchange in Beijing. However, after making investigations in China's major cities, the SEEC believed that Shanghai was in a better position for founding a stock exchange. This conclusion further boosted the confidence of the Shanghai government. At the end of 1989, the Mayor of Shanghai invited two members of the SEEC to participate in the preparations for launching the Shanghai Stock Exchange.[38] A preparation committee was formed.

After research into the practices of some mature markets, the preparation committee of the Shanghai Stock Exchange finalized the following principles guiding the operation of the upcoming stock exchange: (1) the Shanghai Stock Exchange should be a non-profit entity. Its functions included: providing facilities for securities trading, making the listing rules of the stock exchange, examining and approving listing applications, monitoring members and listed companies and supervising securities transactions, and publishing market information; (2) the Shanghai Stock Exchange should be a mutual organization, owned by its

---

35   *See* Yuwa Wei, *The Development of the Securities Market and Regulation in China*, 27.3 Loyola of Los Angeles International and Comparative Law Review 480 (2005).

36   *See* the Editor, *The History*, at the SEEC homepage, available at <http://www.cei. gov.cn/doc/lhcjjg/seec/-doc01.htm>.

37   *Ibid.*

38   *See* Ma, *supra* note 18, at 132.

members. A member should be a securities company with the status of a legal person. An individual did not qualify for membership; (3) the stock exchange would mainly facilitate the trading of government bonds in the initial stage and gradually become a market accommodating both stocks and bonds; (4) for promoting healthy investment activities, the stock exchange would encourage spot transactions and prohibit fictitious transactions; and (5) the stock exchange would focus on securities activities in Shanghai, with a view to becoming a nationwide stock exchange.[39]

The preparation committee also drafted the Shanghai Stock Exchange Constitution, the Shanghai Stock Exchange Business Rules, and the Administrative Rules of the Members of the Shanghai Stock Exchange.[40] The formation of these rules was essentially based on the fundamental principles of justice, fairness and revelation.[41]

The last task of the preparation committee was deciding the initial members of the stock exchange and organizing its physical location. It was finally confirmed that about 16 securities companies were qualified as the initial members of the Stock Exchange. On 26 November, the People's Bank of China declared that the first stock exchange since the economic reforms, the Shanghai Stock Exchange, formally came into existence. On 19 December 1990, the Shanghai Stock Exchange started to operate. The stock exchange was located at Pujiang Hotel and equipped with a first class facility. The shares of eight listed companies were traded. In the first trading week, the share prices increased at a rate of 5 percent per day.[42]

Whilst the Shanghai government worked hard to found the Shanghai Stock Exchange, Shenzhen, the earliest special economic zone, was making the same efforts. As a special economic zone, Shenzhen was in an advantageous position to develop a securities market. Firstly, Shenzhen possessed foreign investment banks at a very early stage of the economic reforms. Secondly, a number of financial institutions emerged in Shenzhen. By 1988, there were 15 financial institutions including banks, trust companies and credit cooperatives in Shenzhen.[43] Thirdly, it was convenient for Shenzhen to learn from Hong Kong's successful experience in building stock exchanges, due to its geographical proximity to Hong Kong. By the mid-1990s, the plan of creating a stock exchange was on the agenda of the Shenzhen government. When the Shenzhen government heard the news that the authority had endorsed the establishment of the Shanghai Stock Exchange, it decided to open its local stock exchange without official approval. On 1 December

---

39   *Ibid*, at 133.

40   *See* the Editor, *Notice to Members*, The Shanghai Stock Exchange website, available at <http://www.sse.com.cn/-sseportal/en_us/ps/member/nm.shtml>.

41   *See* Ma, *supra* note 18, at 137.

42   *See* Yong Zhang, *Shanghai Stock Exchange 1990*, Economic Observation Daily (5 August 2007), available at <http://www.p5w.net/stock/news/zonghe/200708/t1131816.htm>.

43   *See* Ma, *supra* note 18, at 137.

1990, the Shenzhen government declared that the Shenzhen Stock Exchange had started to operate. Because of a lack of official endorsement, the operation of the stock exchange was defined as a trial.[44] Unlike the Shanghai Stock Exchange, the business of the Shenzhen Stock Exchange in the beginning was quite sluggish. A few months later, the operation of the stock exchange gradually became orderly. Upon the approval of the State Council, the Shenzhen Stock Exchange officially opened on 3 July 1991.[45]

With the establishment of the two national stock exchanges, securities business in China developed rapidly. Encouraged by the success of A shares, China introduced B shares and H shares in 1993. A shares are shares issued by companies listed on the Shanghai and Shenzhen Stock Exchanges, and quoted and traded in Renminbi.[46] Originally only Chinese citizens were allowed to trade A shares. Since 2002, international investors are also able to trade A shares under the laws regulating Qualified Foreign Institutional Investors (QFIIs).[47] B shares are shares issued by Chinese companies listed on the Shanghai and Shenzhen Stock Exchanges, quoted in US dollars (in the Shanghai Stock Exchange) and HK dollars (in the Shenzhen Stock Exchange).[48] Both Chinese investors and foreign investors are able to trade B shares in the prescribed currencies. H shares refer to shares issued by Chinese companies qualified for listing on the Hong Kong Stock Exchange. Such shares are traded in Hong Kong dollars. They are not available to Chinese citizens.[49] Since 1994, qualified Chinese companies are allowed to issue N shares. N shares are shares issued by companies incorporated in China and listed on the New York Stock Exchange. They are quoted and traded in US dollars.[50]

The two stock exchanges also introduced their indices. Since 15 July 1991, the Shanghai stock Exchange compiled and published the Shanghai Stock Exchange Composite Index, Shanghai Stock Exchange A Share Index, Shanghai Stock Exchange B Share Index, Shanghai Stock Exchange Industrial Index, Shanghai Stock Exchange Commercial Index, Shanghai Stock Exchange Real Estate Index, Shanghai Stock Exchange Utilities Index, Shanghai Stock Exchange

---

44   *Ibid.*

45   *See* Su Chen, Special Research on Securities Law 31 (Beijing: Tertiary Education Press, 2006).

46   *See* the Editor, *Share Glossary*, available at <http://www.denguang.com/html/98/6098-9048.html>.

47   *See* China Securities Regulatory Committee, the People's Bank of China and State Administration of Foreign Currency, article 18 of the 2006 *Measures of Administrating Investments in Chinese Securities by Qualified Foreign Institutional Investors. See* also China Securities Regulatory Committee and the People's Bank of China, article 18 of the 2002 *Provision Measures of Administrating Investments in Chinese Securities by Qualified Foreign Institutional Investors.*

48   *See* the Editor, *supra* note 46.

49   *Ibid.*

50   *See* the Editor, *The Forum of Electricity and Gas*, Electricity and Gas Net, available at <http://bbs.chinaaba.com/-archiver/showtopic-6591.aspx>.

Conglomerates Index, Shanghai Stock Exchange Fund Index, Shanghai Stock Exchange Government Bond Index, Shanghai Stock Exchange Corporate Bond Index, Shanghai Stock Exchange 180 Index, Shanghai Stock Exchange 50 Index, Shanghai Stock Exchange Dividend Index, Shanghai Stock Exchange New Composite Index, Shanghai Stock Exchange 180 Financial Index, and Shanghai Stock Exchange Governance Index.[51] These indices can be categorized into four types of indices: constituent indices, composition indices, sector indices and other indices. They have provided indicators for measuring the performance of China's securities market including equity, fund and bond markets. The core index is the Shanghai Stock Exchange 180 Index.[52] The Shenzhen Stock Exchange has introduced the Shenzhen Stock Exchange Composite Index, Shenzhen Stock Exchange Agriculture Index, Shenzhen Stock Exchange A Share Index, Shenzhen Stock Exchange B Share Index, Shenzhen Stock Exchange Component Index, Shenzhen Stock Exchange Component A, Shenzhen Stock Exchange Component B, Shenzhen Stock Exchange 100 Index, and Shenzhen Stock Exchange New Index.[53]

By the end of 1996, the number of listed companies in the two national stock exchanges reached 530 (Shanghai had 293 and Shenzhen had 237). The trading value amounted to 9,842 billion Reminbi yuan. There were 94 securities companies and 224 trust investment companies. Their branches reached 2,419.[54] In 2006, the number of listed companies increased to 1,359.[55] In the beginning of the 2000s, the trading value of the two national stock exchanges accounted for 50 percent of China's GDP.[56]

Coming into the 2000s, share reforms have been on the agenda of the Chinese government. The main objects of the share reform are improving the efficiency of the securities market and effectively protecting public investors through easing the lack of liquidity caused by share split. Share split refers to the situation where share structure of Chinese listed companies is such that shares are divided into state shares, legal person shares and public shares. State shares and legal person shares are not freely transferable. Only public shares are tradable on the market. Before the share reform, large volumes of non-tradable shares existed in Chinese listed companies. By the end of 2004, of 7,149 billion listed shares, 4,543 billion

---

51   *See* the Editor, *SSE Index*, the Shanghai Stock Exchange website, available at <http://www.sse.com.cn/sseportal/-en_us/ps/sczn/zstx_home.shtml> and <http://www.sse.com.cn/sseportal/en_us/ps/sczn/zstx.jsp>.

52   *Ibid.*

53   *See* the Editor, *Indices List*, the Shenzhen Stock Exchange website, available at <http://www.szse.cn/main/-en/marketdata/Indiceslist/>.

54   *See* Ma, *supra* note 18, at 251.

55   *See* Jinqing Zhu, Securities Law 53 (Beijing: Beijing University Press, 2007).

56   By September 2001, trading value of the stock exchanges accounted for 51.26 percent of China's GDP. *See* Dehuan Jin, A Study of Volatility of the Chinese Securities Market and Control 4 (Shanghai: Shanghai University of Finance and Commerce Press, 2003).

shares were non-tradable shares, accounting for 63.55 percent.[57] More than 74 percent of non-tradable shares were state shares.[58]

Share split resulted in vulnerability of small public shareholders and caused distortion of share prices. It was also responsible for inefficient corporate governance practice in some listed companies. The Chinese government has been seeking device on solving the problem. Reducing non tradable shares, particularly state shareholdings, in listed companies has been regarded as a way out. The four-year recession on the securities market from 2001 to 2005 further reinforced the Chinese government's determination to carry out the share reform. In 2001, the State Council enacted the *Provisional Methods of Administering Reduction of State Shares and Financing of Social Welfare Funds*, which encouraged selling state shares at market prices. Only 16 listed companies participated in the trial. However, due to the lack of support mechanisms, the reform was not satisfactory and the State Council soon circulated an announcement to stop the share reform.[59] In 2004, the State Council put the share reform on the agenda again. With the publication of the *Opinions about Successfully Completing the Pilot Projects to Undertake the Share Reform* and the *Administrative Measures on the Share Reform in Listed Companies* in 2005, the share reform was formally launched. Currently, the share reform pilot projects are in process. The effect remains to be seen. It is expected that the share reform will improve the corporate governance of listed companies and capital liquidity in the long run. After the share reform, the conflict of interests between majority shareholders and minority shareholders should be mitigated, and the cost of decision-making will be reduced. This will lead to the improvement of the quality of listed companies and the confidence of the shareholders in the companies' shares. Fast growing companies will be able to engage in mergers and acquisition through the capital market. In the meantime, it is important for China to continue to perfect the laws regulating listed companies and introducing mechanisms to hold company controllers and managers accountable. Only so, the supervisory strength can be enhanced and an orderly securities market may be maintained.[60]

In summary, China has made impressive progress in developing its capital market. However, the development of China's securities market has never been smooth. In fact, China's securities market has been plagued by irregularities and bubbles since the very beginning. Chapter 8 and Chapter 9 will give a detailed

---

57   *See* Zhengrong Chen, *What is Share Split?* Daily Economy News, available at <http://finance.sina.com.cn/-stock/t/20050531/02561638152.shtml>.

58   *Ibid*.

59   *See* the Editor, *Share Slip: Capital Looks at Valuable Opportunities*, Zhongying Investment website, available at <http://www.zysg.net/Article_1735.aspx>.

60   *See* Xudong Zhang, *How to Evaluate the Effect of the Share Reform?* Xinhua News Net (15 May 2005), available at <http://news.xinhuanet.com/stock/2005-05/15/content_2961394.htm>.

review on the problems existing in China's capital market and the measures implemented and proposed for tackling these problems.

The Development of Securities Companies

Generally speaking, securities companies refer to financial intermediaries including brokerage firms, securities dealers and traders, investment banks, and advisory firms. In China, securities companies are non-bank financial intermediaries. The business scope of securities companies includes underwriting bonds and shares, trading securities on behalf of customers, and speculating securities for profits.[61] The functions of securities companies in China are close to those of investment banks in some developed countries.

In China, many financial institutions engage in the securities business. The Chinese classify these securities institutions into two types. The first type refers to those specialized in securities dealings. They are securities companies approved by the People's Bank of China. The second type is those dealing in both securities businesses and other financial businesses. They are usually branches of banks and trust investment companies.

A Historical Review of the Development of Securities Companies in China

Between 1981 and 1987, the institutions dealing with the business of securities brokerage and trading were mainly trust investment companies and special branches of banks. In 1985, the first securities company specializing in securities business, the Securities Company of Shenzhen Special Economic Zone, was established. Since then, the number of securities companies increased significantly. By 1990, 44 securities companies emerged.[62] In the meantime, the People's Bank of China enacted the *Provisional Measures for Administrating Securities Companies*.

Because of substantial profits associated with the securities business, banks, trust companies, financial departments of governments and other financial institutions competed to set up and invest in securities companies. For instance, the People's Bank of China held shareholdings in more than 40 securities companies.[63] Some even made investments when they were short of funds and technology. This increased the operational risks of these institutions. Since 1990, the government embarked on separating the securities business from the banking business. The People's Bank of China circulated the *Official Letter of the People's Bank of China regarding Forbidding Banks from Directly Engaging in Securities*

---

61   *See* Chen, *supra* note 44, at 182.

62   *See* Kemin Zhu, Theoretical Analysis on Share Structure in China's Securities Companies 106 (Shanghai: Shanghai University of Finance and Economy Press, 2006).

63   *See* Gong Chen, Shengye Zhou and Xiaoqiu Wu, Securities Issuance and Transaction 179 (Beijing: the People's University of China, 1996).

Business (11 August 1990). The Letter stated that from this day, banks should not directly deal in the securities business. Banks were prohibited from setting up securities transaction counters. Nevertheless, those securities transaction counters previously set up by banks could continue to carry on their business. Hence, the Letter only restricted banks from further engaging in mixed businesses, but did not finally eliminate the phenomenon of dealings in securities by banks. Moreover, trust investment companies were not restricted from setting up branches dealing in securities.[64]

From 1991 to 1995, with the establishment of the two national stock exchanges, the number of securities companies and other institutions carrying on securities business increased dramatically. However, because the securities market was in its early stage of development and the scope of securities business was relatively small, many of these securities companies and institutions engaged in property speculation or directly invested in industry. The government was called to introduce measures for regulating the financial sector. In 1996, the People's Bank of China issued the *Notice of Separation of Banks from Their Branches Handling Securities Business*. Commercial banks, insurance companies, credit cooperatives and other financial institutions were required to either terminate or assign their branches carrying on securities businesses.[65] At the same time, the People's Bank of China brought in methods of disciplining securities companies. Securities companies were required to improve their internal governance and were forbidden from using their customers' insurance funds. Since November 1997, the China Securities Regulatory Commission replaced the People's Bank of China and began to exercise administrative powers over securities companies.[66]

The enactment of the 1998 *Securities Law of the People's Republic of China* further clarified the legal status of different types of securities institutions. Apart from commercial banks and insurance companies, the *Securities Law* also prohibited trust development companies from dealing in the securities business.[67] In other words, securities companies became the only financial institutions qualified to engage in the securities business. The State Council subsequently decreed that trust development companies could carry on securities business in only three ways: (1) setting up a subsidiary company; (2) jointly setting up a securities company; and (3) assigning the business to an outside third party.[68] At the same time, the central government required relevant ministries to relinquish the profit-making entities owned by them.

---

64   *Ibid.*
65   *See* Zhu, *supra* note 62, at 110–11.
66   *Ibid*, at 111.
67   *See* the People's Congress, the 1998 Securities Law of the People's Republic of China, sec. 7.
68   *See* Zhu, *supra* note 62, at 112.

The 1998 *Securities Law* divided securities companies into two categories – comprehensive securities companies and brokerage securities companies.[69] Their business permits should be issued by China Securities Regulatory Commission. A comprehensive securities company must meet the following conditions: (1) to have a minimum registered capital of 500 million yuan; (2) to have chief administrators and business persons who are qualified to engage in securities business; (3) to have a fixed place of business and up-to-standard trading facilities; and (4) to have a sound management system and a standardized system for the separate administration of business on its own account and brokerage business.[70] A brokerage securities company has to satisfy the following requirements: (1) to have a minimum registered capital of 50 million yuan; (2) to have chief administrators and business persons who were qualified to engage in the securities business; (3) to have a fixed place of business and up-to-standard trading facilities; (4) to have a sound management system.[71] The existing securities companies were required to adjust their organizational and financial structures within a certain period in order to qualify as either a comprehensive securities company or a brokerage securities company. By 2004, China had 129 securities companies and among them, 97 qualified as comprehensive securities companies.[72]

Since the enactment of the 1998 *Securities Law*, securities companies have come into an era of orderly development. A number of efficient and large-scale securities companies have emerged. They have attracted high quality management staff and professional experts, and introduced advanced technical and managerial mechanisms. Through strengthening self-regulation, building up market reputation and introducing risk prevention strategies, they have attained an advantageous position in the market. Generally speaking, Chinese securities companies have the following characteristics:

Firstly, significant blocks of shareholdings in Chinese securities companies are owned by the state. This is the result of implementing a planned economy prior to the economic reforms. In China, some large securities companies are joint stock companies invested in by the state-owned commercial banks, insurance companies and other financial institutions. Some securities companies are wholly owned subsidiaries of the above institutions. Some other securities companies are either invested in by financial institutions owned by local governments, or by trust development companies owned by the state or local governments.[73]

Secondly, unlike the ownership structure in those investment banks in the US and the UK, the share structure in Chinese securities companies is concentrated. Large shareholders in Chinese securities companies normally hold about 50 percent of the shares in their companies. Large blocks of shares are usually state

69   *See* the People's Congress, *supra* note 67, sec. 119.
70   *Ibid*, sec. 121.
71   *Ibid*, sec. 122.
72   *See* Zhu, *supra* note 62, at 112.
73   *Ibid*, at 114.

shares and legal person shares, which are non-tradable shares. Consequently, most securities companies are unlisted companies.[74]

Thirdly, the gearing of Chinese securities companies is very low.[75] Due to a lack of channels available for raising loan capital, Chinese securities companies mainly obtain their operational capital through raising equity. However, the ability of China's securities companies to raise sufficient equity capital is limited by the size of the capital market and the investment environment. As a result, most Chinese securities companies are under capitalized. For instance, amongst securities companies, Haitong Securities Company is reported to have the highest registered capital. However, its registered capital only reached RMB 87 billion yuan in 2004. Under capitalization inevitably affects the business scopes of Chinese securities companies.[76] In practice, some securities companies attempt to raise funds through dubious channels. This has increased the business risks of these institutions.[77]

With China's entry into the WTO, securities services businesses in China are open to international competitors. An important task faced by Chinese securities companies is to utilize fund-raising channels in order to enhance their competitive strength. Possible strategies have been discussed and debated. Some suggest creating dispersed ownership structures in China's securities companies by increasing private shareholdings or by allowing securities companies to take the form of partnerships.[78] Some recommend that extensive commercial bank loans should be more accessible to securities companies.[79] Another strategy is to allow securities companies to issue large amounts of debentures.

Universal Banking versus Separate Fragmented Banking

Financial institutions are important participants in the securities markets. Significant securities investors and dealers are usually banks or other financial institutions. In different jurisdictions, the practices of financial institutions in relation to investing and dealing with securities are divided into two situations: universal banking and separate fragmented banking. Universal banking refers to the situation where banks not only provide saving and loan services, but also engage in investment services.[80] Universal banking is more common in European countries. For example, German commercial banks accept deposits, make loans,

---

74 *Ibid*, at 115–16.

75 *Ibid*, at 117.

76 *Ibid*.

77 *See* Shunyan Zheng, *The Legal Analysis of Fund Raising by China's Securities Company*, in Zhipan Wu and Jianjun Bai (*eds*), Law and Practice of Securities Transaction 191 (Beijing: China University of Political Science and Law, 2000).

78 *See* Zhu, *supra* note 54, at 150–66.

79 *See* Zheng, *supra* note 69, at 201–2.

80 *See* Ning Zhang, Study of Allfinanz Model 37 (Beijing: China Social Science Press, 2006).

underwrite corporate stocks, and provide investment consultation to corporations. Universal banking usually results in concentration of corporate shareholdings in the hands of large banks.

Separate fragmented banking is a different banking model characterized by division of commercial and investment banking. Commercial banking mainly deals with banking activities including accepting deposits, making loans, and other fee-based services.[81] Investment banking concerns capital markets activities such as underwriting, issuing and distributing stocks, bonds, and other securities.[82] The US has the tradition of implementing separate fragmented banking. This tradition came after the Great Depression. Before the Great Depression, US Commercial banks heavily invested in the securities market. During the Stock Market Crash, more than 10,000 banks failed and resulted in losses of millions of depositors.[83] Investigation concluded that banks' imprudent investments in speculative business had exposed depositors to huge financial risks.[84] In 1933, The US Congress passed the *Banking Act* of 1933, also known as the *Glass-Steagall Act*, imposing a separation between commercial banks and investment banks.[85] US banks had to choose to become either a commercial bank or an investment bank. The effect of the *Glass-Steagal Act* went beyond the US border and has influenced the banking structures of many other countries. For instance, Japan adopted the same practice in 1948.[86] Furthermore, in 1956, Congress passed the *Bank Holding Company Act* to restrict financial services conglomerates' powers of dealing with insurance business. Banks were not allowed to underwrite insurance any more.

In the 20 years following the enactment of the *Glass-Steagall Act*, the business of commercial companies was more profitable than that of investment banks. Since the 1960s, the business of investment companies began to flourish. This resulted in constantly lobbying by interested groups for repealing or introducing exceptions to the requirement of separating commercial banking from investment banking in the *Glass-Steagall Act*.[87] In the meantime, the US investment banks also wished to expand into commercial banking in order to increase their operational capital and enhance their competitive strength in the international market. As a result, in 1984, the US amended the law and commercial banks were allowed to provide services

---

81 *See* Pan Pan, *Legal Restrictions on the Right of Commercial Banks in Making Securities Investments*, in Zhipan Wu and Jianjun Bai (*eds*), Law and Practice of Securities Transaction 44 (Beijing: China University of Political Science and Law, 2000).

82 *See* general Robert Lawrence Kuhn, Investment Banking: The Art and Science of High Stakes Dealmaking (London: Longman, 1990).

83 *See* the Editor, Stock Market Crash, available at <http://www.stock-market-crash. net/1929.htm>.

84 *See* Reem Heakal, What Was The Glass-Steagall Act?, available at <http://www. investopedia.com/articles/-03/071603.asp>.

85 *See* sec. 20 of the *Glass-Steagal Act*.

86 *See* Tai Teng, Value Creation and the Growth of Securities Companies 106 (Shanghai: Shanghai University of Finance and Economy, 2003).

87 *Ibid*, at 107.

in bonds and mortgage ensured debentures.[88] In 1987, bank holding companies were permitted to deal in stocks and bonds.[89] Eventually, in November 1999, the US Congress repealed the *Glass-Steagal Act* with the enactment of the *Financial Modernization Act* (also known as the *Gramm-Leach-Bliley Act*), which eliminated the *Glass-Steagal Act* restrictions against affiliations between commercial and investment banks by allowing commercial and investment banks to consolidate. Today, the separation between commercial and investment banking in the US is no longer mandatory. Japan soon followed suit.

When China's capital market was in its initial stage of development, securities institutions engaged in both commercial and investment banking. In fact, most securities institutions were invested or wholly owned by banks. Whether or not banking should separate from the securities business or *vice versa* was a topic intensively debated in China. Those in favor of separation believed that non-separation would substantially increase financial risks.[90] Those opposed to the practice believed that the risk caused by non-separation was limited because Chinese banks were state-owned and thus had sufficient capital reserves to resist financial risks.[91] Considering that China's securities market was in its early stage of development and the regulatory infrastructure was not perfect, Chinese policy-makers elected separate fragmented banking in order to reduce financial risks. This was finalized in the 1998 *Securities Law*. Section 6 of the 1998 *Securities Law* stated that commercial banking, securities investments and insurance must be separate.

Moreover, the 1998 *Securities Law* further fragmented investment banking by classifying securities companies into comprehensive securities companies and brokerage securities companies. A brokerage securities company was only permitted to engage in securities brokerage business. A comprehensive securities company, apart from brokerage business, was also permitted to engage in the securities business on its own account, securities underwriting business; and other businesses verified by the securities regulatory authority under the State Council.[92] The *Securities Law* implied a connection between the reliability and the registered capital of a company. Because comprehensive securities companies are required to subscribe a considerably higher amount of registered capital, they were hence permitted to engage in various securities dealings. However, research suggested that the credibility and the registered capital of a company were not necessarily connected.

The implementation of separation between commercial banking and investment banking resulted in some negative feedback. In addition, universal banking gained

---

88   *Ibid.*

89   *Ibid.*

90   *See* Chen, *supra* note 44, at 180.

91   *See* Zhihua Yang, A Study of Securities Regulatory System 157 (Beijing: China University of Political Science and Law, 1995).

92   *See* the People's Congress, *supra* note 67, sec. 130.

momentum worldwide since the 1980s. Calls to abolish the separation between commercial banking and investment banking began to increase. In 2005, the People's Congress made extensive amendments to the 1998 *Securities Law*. The amended *Securities Law* upheld the principle of separating commercial banking from investment banking on the one hand, and introduced exceptional rules on the other. Section 6 of the amended *Securities Law* stated that the securities companies and the business organs of banks, trust and insurance shall be established separately, "unless otherwise provided for by the state". This, in fact, has made universal banking possible. In the same year, the People's Bank of China, the China Bank Regulatory Commission, and the China Securities Regulatory Commission jointly published the *Administrative Measures on Pilot Projects of Establishing Fund Management Companies by Commercial Banks*, which loosened the control on commercial banks in relation to their investment in the securities business. Since then, it has been expected that universal banking would become a trend in China in the coming years.[93]

The amended *Securities Law* has also annulled the division between comprehensive securities companies and brokerage securities companies. Instead, it classifies securities businesses into seven categories: securities brokerage; Securities Investment consultation; financial advising relating to activities of securities trading or securities investment; underwriting and recommendation of securities; self-operation of securities; securities asset management; and any other business operation concerning securities. A securities company may apply for permission to carry on one or more of these businesses. The securities regulatory authority will then examine and approve the application based on the conditions and business records of the securities company. Upon approval by the securities regulatory authority, a securities company may undertake some or all of those securities businesses.[94] The new classification is beneficial to securities companies in relation to expanding their businesses in accordance with their conditions.

The Development of Securities Investment Funds in China

A securities investment fund is a form of collective investment, which absorbs funds from the public and invests them in stocks, bonds and other types of securities.[95] Securities investment funds may take the form of a trust, a corporation or a contractual arrangement. The US counterparts of securities investment funds

---

93   *See* Linying Shen, *The Great Acceleration of the Banking Reform in 2005: From Separation Fragmented Banking to Universal Banking*, Securities Daily, (21 December 2005), available at <http://news.xinhuanet.com/fortune/2005-12/31/content_3991701. htm>.

94   *See* the People's Congress, *supra* note 67, sec. 125.

95   *See* Di Zhao, *What Are Securities Investments Funds*, available at <http://book.jrj. com.cn/book/TextBookDetail/-12467.htm>.

are mutual funds. According to the 2003 *Law of Securities Investment Funds of the People's Republic of China*, a securities investment fund is managed by a manager and is under the administration of a trustee.[96] In China, there are two types of investment funds: close-ended funds and open-ended funds. A close-ended fund has a fixed number of shares or units and the investors of such a fund can not withdraw their shares/units of investment.[97] Its shares are listed and traded on a stock exchange. An open-ended fund does not have a fixed amount of shares/units and the investors are able to purchase and redeem shares/units within the agreed time stipulated in their investment contracts.[98] The shares/units of open-ended funds are unlisted and can not be traded on the securities market.

Chinese investment funds can also be divided into old investment funds and new investment funds. Old investment funds refer to those established before the promulgation of the 1997 *Provisional Administrative Measures on Securities Investment Funds*. New investment funds are those established thereafter.

The advantage of investing in securities investment funds is that these funds are managed by professional managers. Therefore, investment risks are reduced and small investors are better protected under such an investment scheme.[99] Furthermore, since securities investment funds are generally looking for long-term or medium-term investment returns, they have the function of restraining speculative investments and reducing bubbles on the capital market.[100] The development of Chinese securities investment funds, therefore, concerns the long-term stability and prosperity of China's securities market.

The Development of Securities Investment Funds

The first old securities investment fund came into existence in October 1991. It was Zhuxin Commodity Trust Number 1, which was soon renamed as Zhugxin Fund. The second securities investment fund, Nanshan Fund, was established in Shenzhen a few days later. In 1991 and 1992, the People's Bank of China and the State Council all decreed that the establishment of investment funds was subject to the approval of the Central Bank of the People's Bank of China.[101] Because the requirement was not strictly complied with, in 1993, the People's Bank of China demanded its branches in provinces to immediately stop any contradictory

---

96   *See* the People's Congress, the 2003 Law of Securities Investment Funds of the People's Republic of China, sec.2.

97   *Ibid*, sec. 5.

98   *Ibid*.

99   *See* Shiping Li, Case Studies of Essential Issues Concerning the Securities Law 246 (Beijing: China Economics Press, 2001).

100   *Ibid*.

101   *See* the People's Bank of China, the 1991 *Announcement about Strengthening the Administration over the Examination and Approval of Securities Investment Funds in China*. *See* also the State Council,

activities in approving securities investment funds.[102] Since then, the pace of establishing securities investment funds slowed down. The People's Bank of China and its local branches focused on standardizing the operation of the existing securities investment funds.

By the end of 1994, the number of investment funds reached 75. Four of them were approved by the central bank of the People's Bank of China, 68 by its branches, and three by local governments. All the securities investment funds were close-ended. Among them, 73 funds were contractual arrangements, and three took the form of corporations.[103] The terms of the contractual securities investment funds varied from two years to 20 years.[104] The promoters of old securities investment funds were usually investment banks, securities companies, trust companies and large manufacturing enterprises. The managers of these funds were commonly trust investment companies, securities companies and administrative companies of investment funds.

At this stage, many Chinese including some promoters and managers of these old securities investment funds did not fully understand the functions and significance of a securities investment fund. Some local governments treated a securities investment fund as a welfare instrument. Some managers were not aware of the risks associated with securities investments and heavily invested their funds in securities of high risk and low liquidity. Investors were unable to distinguish between the shares/units of a securities investment fund and stocks or bonds. Some mistakenly believed that they would be entitled to both interest and principal, as a bondholder would be.[105]

During this period, the management of these old securities investment funds was far from standardized. Many securities investment funds were not independently managed, instead, they were run by branches of some financial institutions. It was believed that they would benefit from relying on these financial institutions in relation to obtaining funds and developing a commercial reputation. On some occasions, the managers and the trustees were affiliated. Such practices increased the risk of fraud on investors. Furthermore, due to the absence of effective regulation, most securities investment funds failed to disclose their performance properly. This further harmed investors' interest.

Most of the shares/units of the old securities investment funds were traded local stock exchanges or the two national stock exchanges. Since 1993, some Sino-foreign securities investment funds emerged. Sino-foreign securities investment funds include those jointly invested by both Chinese and foreign promoters and

---

102   *See* the People's Bank of China, the 1993 *Emergency Announcement about Prohibiting the Activities of Irregularly Issuing Shares of Investment Funds and Trust Units.*

103   *See* Ma, *supra note* 18, at 215.

104   *Ibid.*

105   *Ibid*, at 217.

those invested by foreign investors.[106] The first Sino-foreign securities investment fund was registered in Shanghai, China.

Generally speaking, old securities investment funds had the following features: Firstly, most of them were small in capital scale. The largest securities investment funds had an amount of capital of 5.8 billion yuan. The amount of capital of an average-sized securities investment fund was around 300 million yuan. The lack of capital limited the ability of these securities investment funds to resist risk and stabilize the capital market.

Secondly, most securities investment funds did not have investment focuses. They invested in each type of securities including government bonds, other bonds, corporate shares, futures, and real estate. This increased the level of management difficulty. At a stage where proficient managers of securities investment funds were hard to find, this practice posed further challenges to the management in these institutions.

Thirdly, although the law required the establishment of securities investment funds to be approved by the central bank of the People's Bank of China, most old securities investment funds were, in fact, approved and administered by local governments or branches of the People's Bank of China. This resulted in multi-levels of administration and caused confusion.

In November 1997, the State Council enacted the first law regulating securities investment funds, the *Provisional Administrative Measures on Securities Investment Funds*. In December of the same year, China's Securities Regulatory Commission introduced the *Detailed Regulations on Implementing the Provisional Administrative Measures on Securities Investment Funds* and some other complementary regulations. According to the 1997 *Provisional Administrative Measures on Securities Investment Funds* and relevant regulations, the establishment of a securities investment fund was to be approved by China's Securities Regulatory Commission. The promoter(s) could either apply for establishing a close-ended or an open-ended securities investment fund.[107] A promoter must meet the following requirements: (1) must be a securities company, trust investment company or fund management company; (2) in the case where the promoters were not fund administration companies, each promoter should have pooled an amount of capital no less than three billion yuan, and the main promoters should have at least three years' experience in securities business and have a record of consecutive profitability; (3) the promoters, managers and trustees should have complete organizational and administrative structures, sound financial conditions, and standard business conduct; and (4) managers and trustees should

---

106 *See* Xinying Yang et al, *The Report on Performance Evaluation of Sino-Foreign Securities Investment Funds*, in China Securities Association, The Research on Innovative Topics concerning the Development of China's Securities Market 236 (Beijing: China Press of Finance and Economy, 2005).

107 *See* the Securities Commission of the State Council, the 1997 *Provisional Administrative Measures on Securities Investment Funds*, sec. 6.

have business addresses and other infrastructure necessary for the operation of their businesses.[108]

The 1997 *Provisional Administrative Measures on Securities Investment Funds* also stipulated that the term of a close-ended securities investment fund should not be less than five years and the capital pooled should not be less than two billion yuan. Once established, a close-ended securities investment fund might submit an application for being listed on a Chinese stock exchange.

After 1997, a number of new securities investment funds were formed. By June 2007, the number of securities investment funds increased to 330, with about 20,000 fund investors.[109] Since 2001, China began to promote open-ended securities investment funds. The first open-ended securities investment fund, Huaan Innovation, come into existence in 2001.[110] It was an immediate success, and about 50 billion yuan worth of its shares was purchased within a single day. By 2005, the number of open-ended securities investment funds increased from three to 114.[111]

In 2003, China enacted the Law of Securities Investment Funds of the People's Republic of China. With the enactment of the Law of Securities Investment Funds, the 1997 Provisional Administrative Measures on Securities Investment Funds lost its significance, since many of its provisions were contradicted in the Law of Securities Investment Funds. The new law provided that the manager of a securities investment fund must be a fund management company.[112] A fund management should satisfy the following conditions: (1) having the articles of association which are in conformity with the present law and the Company Law of the People's Republic of China; (2) having a registered capital of no less than 100 million yuan and all of the capital being paid in monetary capital; (3) principal shareholders having good business performance and public reputation in the securities business, securities investment consultation, trust assets management or other financial assets management, having no record of violation of the law within the last three years, and having a registered capital of no less than 300 million yuan; (4) the number of persons having fund practice qualification reaching the statutory requirements; (5) having business sites, securities facilities and other facilities relating to the fund management business that comply with the requirements; (6)

---

108   *Ibid*, sec. 7.

109   *See* Shuming Du, The Development of Securities Investment Funds: A Great Leap in Ten Years' Time, Yinhe Securities, (9 September 2007), available at <http://www.p5w.net/stock/lzft/jjyj/200709/t1229655.htm>.

110   *See* Baoli Jia, *Looking Back the Past Ten Years*, Shanghai Securities Newspaper (10 September 2007), available at <http://www.p5w.net/fund/fxpl/200709/t1204772.htm>.

111   *See* Bin Yan and Xia Wang, *The Study of the Fee Rate of Open-ended Securities Investment Funds in China*, in China Securities Association, The Research on Innovative Topics concerning the Development of China's Securities Market 345 (Beijing: China Press of Finance and Economy, 2005).

112   *See* the People's Congress, *supra* note 67, sec. 12.

having sound internal auditing, monitoring and risk control systems; and (7) other conditions provided for by laws and administrative regulations and those provided for by the securities regulatory department under the State Council and approved by the State Council.[113] By June 2007, there were 58 fund management companies in China.[114]

In recent years, the business of securities investment funds has developed rapidly. From 2003 to 2006, the capital scale of securities investment funds increased 65 percent annually, which doubled the annual increase rate of insurance business.[115] Consequently, securities investment funds have become the largest investors in China's securities market. In 2006, securities investment funds held more than 19 percent of the total tradable shares in the securities market.[116] This figure increased to 24.12 percent in 2007.[117] The rapid progress of securities investment funds is largely a result of the bullish securities market since 2006. In the first half of 2007, securities investment funds in China made a net profit of 3640.67 billion yuan, which is equal to the total sum of the net profits in the past nine years.[118]

The Current Situation of Securities Investment Funds in China

An important development of Chinese securities investment funds is that the number of individual investors has constantly increased. In 2004, individual investors accounted for 59 percent of the total fund investors.[119] In 2007, this percentage increased to 86 percent.[120] This indicates the increasing popularity of securities investment funds as a new channel of investment.

Various types of securities investment funds have been developed. There are not only open-ended and close-ended funds, but also equity funds, bond funds, money market funds, active management funds, and index funds. New types of funds such as exchange-traded funds and listed open-ended funds have been constantly introduced to China's capital market. Investors are able to choose a wide range of investment choices.

Today, open-ended securities investment funds have become the main investing force in the capital market. In June 2006, the total number of securities investment funds was 266. Among them, 212 were open-ended funds and only 54 were close-ended funds. The net asset value of closed-end funds amounted to 119.615 billion yuan, accounting for 23.39 percent of the total net asset value; and the share scale

---

113   *Ibid*, sec. 13.
114   *See* Du, *supra* note 109.
115   *Ibid.*
116   *Ibid.*
117   *See* Jia, *supra* note 110.
118   *Ibid.*
119   *Ibid.*
120   *Ibid.*

reached 81.7 billion units, accounting for 19.14 percent of the total. The net asset value of 212 open-end funds reached 391.8 billion yuan, accounting for 76.61 percent of the total and the share scale reached 345.209 billion units, accounting for 80.86 percent of the total.[121]

The fast development of securities investment funds requires a compatible legal framework. Unfortunately, the law regulating the funds industry has lagged behind the practice. There are calls for the update of the 2003 *Law of Securities Investment Funds*. It is expected that the amended law will further loosen some restrictions encumbering the healthy development of the funds industry.[122]

It is anticipated that in ten years time, China's funds industry will reach a scale of 70,000 to 90,000 billion yuan, and the number of investors will increase to 1.5 billion.[123] This prediction is based on the forecast of the development of China's economy, since the future development of securities investment funds rely on the steady growth of China's economy and the profitability of Chinese enterprises. Low interest rates and low inflation are also crucial to the prosperity of securities investment funds.

Conclusions

Since the economic reforms, China's capital market has made remarkable progress. The trading value of the capital has increased constantly and substantially. The quality of services provided by securities intermediaries and specialized personnel has improved dramatically. Nevertheless, as an emerging market with less than 20 years of history, China is facing many difficulties on the way to success. It has made and will continue to make efforts to tackle the problems associated with securities issuance, listing requirements, corporate governance, intermediaries, accounting standards, and accommodation of modern technologies in securities transactions.

Since China's entry into the WTO, its securities market has opened further to foreign investors. China's securities market has attracted worldwide attention. The admission of QFIIs into China's securities market indicates that China has accelerated the pace of internationalization.

Today, the economic reforms in China have come into a crucial stage. More and more Chinese enterprises need the support of a healthy and efficient securities market for sustainable development. The healthy growth of the capital market will relieve the burden of state banks and improve China's financial structure.

---

121   *See* the Editor, *China Fund Industry Report 2006–2007*, available at <http://www.okokok.com.cn/Abroad/-Class126/Class106/200701/115045.html>.

122   *See* Yuling Wang, *Wang Lianzhou: the Amendments to Securities Investment Fund Law*, Xinhua News Net (10 January 2008), available at <http://news.xinhuanet.com/newscenter/2008-01/10/content_7400682.htm>.

123   *Ibid.*

Although China's capital market is very volatile and appears to overprice securities, the general opinion about the future trend of the market is optimistic. Some have estimated that in the coming two to three years, China's capital market should continue to prosper.[124] The environment for securities investments in China requires further improvement. The quality of securities services also needs to be further enhanced. Unless these tasks are completed, the long-term prosperity of the securities market may not be achieved.

Currently, China's economic performance is sound. The Chinese government has formulated strategic plans for the development of China's capital market in the coming ten years. It is predicted that China's economy will continue to grow steadfastly. This will require large amounts of capital investment. On the other hand, the income of Chinese citizens will continue to increase and the social welfare system will further develop. The capital market will consequently attract more investments. These will provide the necessary environment for building an efficient, transparent, integrated and sustainable capital market.[125]

---

124   *See* the Editor, *Experts Forecast China's Capital Market: The Economy Needs a Stable Securities Market* (Liaowang News Weekly, 16 April 2007), available at <http:// news.xinhuanet.com/fortune/2007-04/16/content_5982891.htm>.

125   *See* Daojong Zhou, *The Securities Market is Facing Good Opportunities* (Securities Daily, 19 November 2007), available at <http://stock.jrj.com.cn/news/2007-11-19/000002940708.html>.

Chapter 8
Securities Regulation in China

This chapter examines the regulatory framework of China's securities market. It gives an overview of the regulatory infrastructure of China's securities market and business, and then gives detailed discussions on the laws and regulations governing stock exchanges, securities intermediaries and securities issuance. It analyzes the characteristics and identifies the problems of securities laws and practices in China. In doing so, a comparison is drawn between the practice in China and the practices in some mature markets. After identifying the distinct characteristics of China's securities market and regulation, it suggests that it is necessary for China to further promote the role of banks in corporate finance.

In conclusion, it is pointed out that China's securities market has come into a crucial stage of development. Designing a securities regime in China is an uphill task. China must reduce governmental intervention in order to allow the market to operate under market rules. Additionally, China should develop a securities regime that combines the strengths of both the market-based and bank-based approaches.

A Historical Review

Like many other legal systems, China's securities market experienced a progression from non-regulation to regulation. Since the economic reforms, securities regulation has progressed steadfastly. This indicates that a competent regulation regime is the foundation of an efficient securities market. It is then necessary to first review the development of securities regulation in China.

The Regulatory Framework at the Initial Stage of Development

Although having a long history of utilizing partnership, traditional China had never developed a business vehicle akin to a modern company.[1] Consequently, there was not a market for company stocks. The history of using financial instruments, including notes, drafts and pawn tickets, in China is very long and can be traced to around two thousand years ago. However, this did not lead to the creation of a securities market.

As introduced in Chapter 7, modern incorporation and securities business in China started after the Opium War. The first modern stock exchange was initiated by

---

1 *See* Sujian Huang, Companies 71 (Beijing: People's University Publishing House, 1989).

foreign merchants during the 1860s. The corporate activities of foreign companies and merchants inspired the modernization movement in China. Some officials in the Qing government suggested China had to learn modernization experiences from some industrialized countries. The Qing government subsequently funded some Chinese companies and sought public investment for financing these enterprises.[2] The central purpose of this initiative was to vitalize China's industry, particularly the military industry. This initiative together with the subsequent implementation activities were later described as the "modernization movement".

Since the Qing government was unable to sufficiently finance the emerging industry, the organizers of the new enterprises decided to utilize non-governmental resources for fundraising. In 1872, with the support of the government, the Shanghai Merchant Invested Shipping Company was established. The company was partly financed by some merchants in return for a certain number of shares. The company was the first Chinese joint stock company.[3] Since then, a number of Chinese joint stock companies were set up. Securities transactions subsequently emerged.[4]

At that time, the transactions involving Chinese companies' shares were commonly completed in private. Such transactions were not subject to any regulatory rules. The parties of the transactions might set up the share prices with reference to that of foreign companies. With the creation of more and more Chinese enterprises and establishment of privately-owned banks, a securities market gradually came into existence. In addition, the Qing government began to issue bonds for easing its financial difficulties.[5] This further boosted securities trading.

In response to the securities trading, stock exchanges began to emerge. The first stock exchange initiated by foreign merchants in 1903 in Shanghai was created, where securities of foreign founded companies were traded. Later, Chinese stock exchanges were established, and the securities business developed significantly.

It was interesting to note that at that time laws regulating the establishment and operation of companies and securities transactions did not exist. Ordinarily, a company was created by undergoing the following steps: (1) entering into international agreements or contracts; (2) applying for government approval of the operational rules; and (3) granting the approval. The contract clauses and operational rules in the application would then become binding rules governing the company's future activities. These governing rules differed on a case by case basis.

---

2   *See* Chi-kong Lai, *The Qing State and Merchant Enterprise: The China Merchants' Company 1872–1902*, in R. Ampalavanar Brown (*ed.*), Chinese Business Enterprise, Volume 6 100 (London: Routledge, 1999).

3   *See* Chunting Zhang, *A Brief History of China's Securities Market: the Late Qing Period*, The Forum of China's Economic History, available at <http://economy.guoxue.com/article.php/71>.

4   *Ibid.*

5   *See* Yi Xu, The History of Debts Borrowing by the Qing Government 672 (Beijing: China Press of Finance and Economy, 1996).

Due to the lack of uniform rules regulating incorporation activities, business people and reformers began to call for a legal framework supporting the fledgling modern industry. In 1904, the Qing government enacted the first Chinese *Company Law*. The law had 11 divisions and 131 articles, and was based on the 1855 *Companies Act* (UK), the 1862 *Companies Act* (UK), and the 1899 *Commercial Code* (Japan). It was therefore a hybrid of common law and civil law.[6] The 1904 *Company Law* contained fundamental principles of corporate practice. It had provisions about corporate registration procedure, shareholders' rights and meetings, directors' duties and board meetings, amendment of constitutions, accounts, dissolution, and penalties. The law provided for four types of company, *hezi gongsi* (partnership), *hezi youxian gongsi* (limited partnership), *gufen gongsi* (joint stock company with limited and unlimited shareholders), *gufen youxian gongsi* (company limited by shares). The main contribution of the law was the introduction of the last type of company, *gufen youxian gongsi*, which was truly a modern company. Companies were required to have at least two or seven members with no top ceiling. Separate personality was recognized for the first time. All companies had to be registered with the Ministry of Commerce in Beijing.[7]

The enactment of the law further encouraged industrial activities. Up until the end of the Qing dynasty in 1911, there were 615 factories.[8] Among them, 521 factories were set up by Chinese entrepreneurs.[9] In 1908, the Qing Government decided to amend the *Company Law* with a view to improve some ambiguous provisions in the law. The fact that the law was "badly translated from two other nations' experience" had engendered mistrust.[10] The amendment work began in 1908. A revised version of the *Company Law* was finalized but never enacted, as the Qing government collapsed and China became a republic in 1911.[11]

The early republican government maintained the 1904 *Company Law* until 1914. In 1914, the government enacted the *Company Regulations*. The new law was based on the unpublished revision of the 1904 *Company Law*. The 1914 *Company Regulations* adopted the German model of corporate legislation, and it was a clearer corporate code compared to the 1904 *Company Law*. The new code provided for four types of company including *wuxian gongsi* (unlimited company), *lianghe gongsi* (joint company), *gufen lianghe gongsi* (joint share company),

---

6   *See* Yuwa Wei, Comparative Corporate Governance: A Chinese Perspective 86 (London: Kluwer Law International, 2003).

7   *See* Jiansheng Xu, *Commercial Laws and Enterprise Development in the Republican China*, China History Education Net, available at <http://hist.cersp.com/kczy/sxdt/200705/6394_2.html>.

8   *See* Yipeng Liu, Guilong Zhang and Chi Meng (*eds*), Complete Works on the Company Law of the People's Republic of China for Practice 15 (Harbin: Harbin Publishing House, 1994).

9   *Ibid.*

10   *See* William C. Kirby, *China Unincorporated: Company Law and Business Enterprise in Twentieth-Century China*, 54 The Journal of Asian Studies 48 (1995).

11   *See* Wei, *supra* note 6.

and *gufen youxian gongsi* (company limited by shares).[12] It provided that banks should be companies limited by shares (*gufen youxian gongsi*). The new law had a considerable effect on the promotion of corporate activities. The period from 1914 to 1927 was a time during which commercial activities developed rapidly in China. In 1920, the number of factories reached 1759.[13] From 1911 to 1920 there were 807 registered companies.[14]

In the meantime, the first securities law, the 1914 *Securities Exchange Law* in China's history came into effect. The *Securities Exchange Law* contained 35 provisions. It provided the fundamental principles and rules for securities transactions. A stock exchange was defined as a market established for accommodating transactions involving government bonds, shares, debentures, and other securities and for measuring and standardizing the prices of those securities.[15] The law clarified that a stock exchange should take the form of a joint stock company. In 1915, the *Detailed Regulations for Implementation of the Stock Exchange Law* and other related regulations were enacted. A few years later, the republican government enacted the 1921 *Commodity Exchanges Regulation*. The 1914 *Securities Exchange Law* and the 1921 *Commodity Exchange Regulation* were replaced by a single code – the 1927 *Exchange Law* that combined and amended the two laws. The 1927 *Exchange Law* abolished the provisions prohibiting women from becoming brokers and clarified that incorporated bodies were allowed to engage in brokerage businesses. The 1927 *Exchange Law* was amended once in 1935. The company legislation also made impressive progress. A new *Company Law* based on the 1914 company code was also introduced in 1929.

Apart from the legislative efforts, a supervisory system was also gradually built up. In 1926, the government began to appoint supervisory officers responsible for monitoring activities on stock exchanges.[16] In 1927, the government terminated the practice of appointing supervisory officers, and established the Supervisory Bureau of Finance as the regulatory authority of stock exchanges.[17] The practice of appointing supervisory officers was re-introduced in 1931.

Despite the above regulatory efforts, China's capital market was extremely disorderly. Breaches by listed companies were common. It appeared that the laws were not effectively enforced and complied with. There were a number of reasons

---

12   A joint company had at least one limited liability shareholder and one unlimited liability shareholder. The later would manage the company, whereas the former only provided capital. The difference of a joint share company from a joint company was that a joint share company issued shares to the general public.

13   *See* Liu, Zhang and Meng, *supra* note 8, at 17.

14   *See* Zhengao Chen, The Historical Materials of Present Chinese Industries, Volume 4, 55–6 (Beijing: Living, Reading and New Acknowledge Three Joint Publishing House, 1961).

15   *See* Zhiying Liu. *A Review of Chinese Stock Exchanges in Old China*, 15 Modern Bankers (2006), available at <http://www.modernbankers.com/modernbankers/jrws/20060 9/20060926153010.shtml>.

16   *Ibid.*

17   *Ibid.*

responsible for this. At the economic aspect, the establishment of the securities market was not a result of economic development, but the pressure of foreign powers and the need to raise funds either for the government-sponsored military enterprises which facilitated the government's civil war and world war efforts, or for the government's expenditure. A genuinely supportive economic environment did not exist. The national industry was too fragile to support a prosperous securities market. The banking sector was not designed to facilitate the securities business. The number of institutional investors was negligible. Many investors were ignorant of the full economic consequences associated with investing in securities. As a result, the securities market operated in a chaotic environment and was subject to excessive speculation.

Furthermore, the political environment in which China's securities market operated was hostile. During this period, China experienced its most corrupt and commercially ineffectual governments in its present history. The late Qing Dynasty was a weak feudal regime that was even reluctant to recognize commerce as a respectable trade. It finally accepted the idea of incorporation and securities trading because it was compelled to do so by industrial powers and desperately needed to develop industries and obtain necessary funds in order to resist the military and economic invasion of some imperial powers. During the early republican period, the government was controlled by several warlords in succession. The warlord governments were more concerned themselves with expanding their territories and enhancing their military strength. They were rarely interested in matters involving the national economy and the people's livelihood. In their eyes, the securities market was no more than a place of extracting money. The government officials responsible for supervising and managing the securities market in the republican governments treated the securities market as an arena to seek their personal financial benefits and abused their powers by relentlessly exploiting the securities market. Their conduct severely damaged the stability of the securities market. In the meantime, China's securities market was a target of foreign speculative money. Foreign speculators saw the Chinese securities market as a paradise of speculation and orchestrated turmoil on the market.

During the period when the Guomindang Party was in power, China experienced Japanese invasion and a civil war between the Guomindang force and the communist army. For funding military expenditure, the Guomindang government issued large amounts of government bonds. Between 1927 and 1936, the government issued 26 billion yuan's worth of bonds, four times as much as the total amount of the bonds issued by previous warlords' governments.[18] During the Japanese invasion, the securities business was interrupted and the securities market rapidly declined.

---

18   *See* Chunting Zhang, *A Brief History of China's Securities Market: The Republican Period (2)*, the Forum of China's Economic History, available at <http://economy.guoxue.com/article.php/71>.

In Japanese occupied areas, both the Japanese and the puppet governments tried to manipulate the securities market to fund their needs.[19]

In addition, the legal system was not well equipped to accommodate the development of the securities market. While the legal infrastructure needed further improvement, most laws, particularly the early legislation, were directly transplanted and thus did not integrate effectively into China's practice and increased the difficulty of enforcement. Judicial corruption further undermined the implementation of the laws. Many people in the securities regulatory authority and related government departments involved themselves in activities resulting in conflicts of interest. This caused not only laxity in supervision over the stock exchanges, but also widespread confusion and frustration.

The Securities Regulation Before 1978

The People's Republic of China ("the PRC") was founded in 1949. The new government faced a country where the economy was feeble, industries were ravaged, speculation was rampant, and inflation was serious. The urgent task was to recover the economy. The new government was determined to build a socialist economic system. This would be a centrally planned economy where economic activities would follow administrative plans of the state rather than market demand and the price system. In the agricultural sector, the strategy was to establish people's communes and introduce state ownership over rural land. In the industrial sector, the reform comprised two steps. The first step taken by the government was for the state to confiscate bureaucratic enterprises (the enterprises owned by the previous government). The next step was to transform private enterprises into joint state-private enterprises and then convert them into state-owned or collectively-owned enterprises. The state-owned enterprises would then play the dominant role in the nation's economy.[20]

This economic policy of completing the reform tasks in the first step was formed according to Mao's thoughts on a new democratic economy.[21] The essence of the policy was to eliminate bureaucratic capitalism in China by confiscating the enterprises owned by the previous government. The private sector was allowed to continue to operate and was not subject to confiscation. The government believed that the private sector could contribute to the country's economy, and could be reformed in a less drastic fashion. Hence, the government's principal policy of

---

19   *Ibid.*

20   *See* Wei, *supra* note 6, at 91.

21   *See* Zedong Mao, *The Chinese Revolution and the Chinese Communist Party* (1939), *New Democratic Economy* (1940), *The Coalition Government* (1945), and *The Current Situation and Our Duties* (1947), in Zedong Mao, Selected Works of Mao Zedong (Beijing: Foreign Languages Press, 1965).

enterprise development at the time was to confiscate bureaucratic enterprises and protect private enterprises.[22]

Within the new democratic economy, economic structure was divided into different components according to ownership. Thus there was a state economy, a semi-state economy, a mixed economy, a capitalist economy, an individual economy, and a state capitalist economy. These economic components co-existed during the economic recovery period. Accordingly, enterprises were classified as state-owned enterprises, collective enterprises, private enterprises, individual enterprises and mixed enterprises. The traditional categories of enterprises including companies, partnerships and sole traders were largely ignored. The new enterprise categories gave clearer indication of which enterprises were subject to ongoing socialist reform.[23]

In order to regulate private enterprises, which were still large in number, the government enacted the 1950 Interim Regulations Concerning Private Enterprises and the 1951 Implementing Methods of the Interim Regulations Concerning Private Enterprises. In accordance with the legislation, private enterprises were divided into sole traders, partnerships and companies. An important characteristic of the 1950 legislation was that it introduced a provision that enabled the state to incorporate productive activities of private enterprises into its economic plan.

In the beginning of the economic recovery period, stock exchanges were closed down. However, speculation of commodities in black markets was rampant.[24] To revive the economy, the government decided to recover the securities market and utilize available idle money present in society. Consequently, the Tianjin Stock Exchange was re-opened in June 1949. Shares of more than ten companies were listed on the Tianjin Stock Exchange. In 1950, the Beijing Stock Exchange was re-opened for the same reasons.[25] Shares of six companies including Qixin Cement, Kailuan Mining, Jiannan Cement, Dongya Enterprise, Renli and Yuehua were traded on the Beijing Stock Exchange.

The trading activities were quite active in the beginning. Later, the market became volatile due to excessive speculation. The government introduced reform mechanisms and increased regulation over the stock exchange and stock brokers. With the recovery of the economy and restoration of financial orders, more and more idle funds were attracted to other areas of investment. In addition, an increasing number of private enterprises were transformed into joint state-private enterprises. As a result, the securities business became sluggish. Many brokers ceased doing business. On the other hand, with the progress of the socialist reform,

---

22   *Ibid.*

23   *See* Jianmin Dou, Research on the History of Corporate Ideology in China 84 (Shanghai: Publishing House of Shanghai University of Finance and Economics, 1999).

24   *See* Chunting Zhang, *A Brief History of China's Securities Market: Before the Economic Reforms*, the Forum of China's Economic History, available at < http://economy. guoxue.com/article.php/73>.

25   *Ibid.*

144   *Securities Markets and Corporate Governance*

the 1950 *Interim Regulations for Private Enterprises* had a decreasing number of entities to regulate. The types of companies defined in the legislation gradually became extinct, except for the limited company, which was still used by joint state-private enterprises. Consequently, the government closed down the Tianjin and Beijing stock exchanges in July and October 1952 respectively.[26]

During this period, the government relied considerably on the bond market for balancing its income and expenditure. In December 1949, the government published the *Decision of Issuing People's Victory Convertible into Goods Bonds*. The bonds were called "convertible into goods bonds" because their prices were calculated according to the value of certain goods. The bonds were distributed twice in 1950.[27] The receivers were mainly rich citizens, business people and retired government officers in previous governments.

Since 1953, China came into an era of rapid economic development. The socialist reform went further. The government launched its first five-year economic plan in 1953, and the process of reforming private enterprises accelerated. The government introduced new methods of reforming private enterprises, which included ordering goods, unified purchase and sale by the state, and restructuring private enterprises into joint state-private enterprises.

In 1954, the country enacted the *Interim Regulations for Joint State-Private Enterprises*. The *Regulations* provided guidance for the organization of joint state-private enterprises. It was provided that joint state-private enterprises were invested by both the state and private investors, and it should take the form of limited companies. All shareholders had limited liability to the value of their shares.[28] The state would appoint representatives to participate in management. If a joint state-private enterprise was large in both size and shareholders, it needed to have a board of directors to discuss and decide business affairs. There were no general meetings in joint state-private enterprises. Private shareholders would hold private shareholders' meetings to decide matters concerning the relationship between private shareholders.[29] Consequently, the board of directors in such a company became the only authority exercising control over the company affairs. This organizational arrangement enabled the state to enhance its control over large joint state-private enterprises since the state could easily achieve control or domination over the boards. To further enhance this control, the 1954 *Interim Regulations for Joint State-Private Enterprises* stipulated that "joint state-private enterprises are subject to the leadership of the state, and are jointly managed by state representatives and private agents".[30]

---

26 *Ibid.*
27 *Ibid.*
28 *See* the State Council, the 1950 *Interim Regulations for Joint State-Private Enterprises*, art. 8.
29 *Ibid*, art. 22.
30 *Ibid*, art. 20.

Before the enactment of the 1954 *Interim Regulations for Joint State-Private Enterprises*, the state and the private shareholders of a joint state-private company appointed directors respectively. The number of directors was distributed to each side according to their share proportions. The 1954 regulations discarded this practice by providing that the number of directors to be appointed by each side should be decided through negotiation. In addition, the law stipulated that the issues should be submitted to the authoritative department for resolution if shareholders could not reach agreement on important matters. The 1954 regulations thus made the operation of joint state-private enterprises further depart from traditional corporate practice and brought their activities closer to those of state-owned enterprises.[31]

In the meantime, the government continued to utilize the bond market to assist the socialist reform and economic development. In the beginning of the first five-year plan, the government needed to invest large amounts of funds in large economic projects and therefore decided to raise part of the funds by issuing government bonds. In 1953, the government enacted the 1953 *Regulations on the National Construction Bonds*. Between 1954 and 1958, more than 35 billion yuan worth of bonds were issued.[32] This time, citizens purchased the bonds based on their free will.

In 1956, the State Council enacted new rules that fixed the dividends of private shareholdings in joint state-private enterprises at five percent per year.[33] The rules also required dividends to be paid for a period of either seven years or ten years regardless of whether the enterprise made profits or not.[34] The new rules, in fact, converted private shareholders into creditors. As a result, the majority of joint state-private enterprises (the only remaining limited companies) were converted into state-owned enterprises, and the remainder were transformed into collectively-owned enterprises.

In a state-owned enterprise, the state claimed absolute ownership as well as managerial powers. In a collective enterprise usually a local government had ownership and managerial rights. China adopted a method of "uniform ownership, but hierarchical control" to manage state-owned enterprises. Thus, there existed state-owned enterprises that were owned by the central government but controlled by local governments.[35] By the end of 1956, all private enterprises were converted

31 *See* Wei, *supra* note 6, at 94.

32 *See* Zhang, *supra* note 23.

33 The two piece of legislation were: the *Provisions regarding the Promotion of Fixed Dividends in Joint State-Private Enterprises* and the *Instructions on Some Questions about Reforming Private Industrial and Commercial Sector, Private Handicraft Sector, and Private Transportation Sector*.

34 *See* Baoshu Wang and Qinzhi Cui, The Theory of the Chinese Company Law 15 (Beijing: Social Science Literature Publishing House, 1998).

35 *See* Peizhong Gan, The Law of Enterprises and Companies 102 and 152 (Beijing: Beijing University Publishing House, 1998). *See also* Xiaohong Chen, *Chinese and Japanese Enterprise System: Some Descriptions and Analyses*, in Liming Li (*ed.*), The

into joint state-private enterprises. Stock exchanges and securities markets, together with all types of private ownership, lost their significance and disappeared from China's economic life.[36] A centrally planned economy dominated China for the following twenty years.

The laws governing enterprises and the securities market during this period had the following characteristics: firstly, this period did not produce any comprehensive code regulating the capital market and enterprises. The laws and regulations promulgated were mostly special laws. Secondly, these laws aimed at assisting the social project of establishing a planned economy in China. Some had the goal of raising necessary funds for the economic projects in the economic plans, while others provided guidance for reforming existing companies into state-owned or collectively-owned enterprises. Thirdly, although the laws supplied rules for regulating the securities market and companies, they served the fundamental purpose of diminishing and eventually eliminating the role of the securities market and the private sector in the economy. For instance, the laws regulating enterprises went through utilizing, limiting and removing private ownership in reforming enterprises. The laws regulating the securities market clearly demonstrated the fact that the government only intended the securities market to exist during the period in which the government had no other financial resources to rely upon.

The Securities Regulation After 1978

Since the end of the 1970s, China initiated the market economic reforms. The primary goal of the reforms was to reform the planned economic into a market economy. The essence of the economic reforms was to reform China's enterprise system. It was about introducing market mechanisms into China's enterprises. The Chinese were aware of the fact that reforming a planned economy into a market economy was an unprecedented social project and there was no existing model for them to follow. The guiding policy for the reforms was the old Chinese saying "crossing the river by feeling stones under feet and stepping on the stones".

Under the planned economy, enterprises were basically factories. They didn't own assets or make profits. They produced whatever the state instructed them to produce.[37] There were no incentives for innovation and technological upgrade. The essence of the enterprise reforms was to introduce competition, modern technology and modern management skills into the enterprise system in order to improve the economic performance of the state-owned enterprises. At first, the government

---

Comparison of Chinese and Japanese Enterprise Systems 122–57 (Beijing: Law Publishing House, 1998).

36   *Ibid*; *See also* Zhong Chen, Wind and Cloud on the Securities Market in China 91 (Shanghai: Shanghai Transportation University Press, 2000).

37   *See* Shenshi, Mei, Research on the Structure of Modern Corporate Organs' Power: A Legal Analysis of Corporate Governance 3 (Beijing: Publishing House of China University of Political Science and Law, 1996).

tried to reform the enterprise without changing the state ownership.[38] Some market mechanisms including contracting out were introduced. However, strategies of this kind had proven to be ineffective. In the last resort, the Chinese government turned to corporatization. By the 1980s, the government was determined to reform the enterprise system by corporatization and privatization.[39] Gradually, state-owned enterprises were transformed into corporations, and securities activities revived.

Nearly 30 years later, in 1981, the PRC revived its securities activities.[40] By then, the PRC had already given up the idea of a planned economy and initiated economic reforms aimed at establishing a market economy throughout China.[41] First, the State Council issued national treasure bonds in 1981.[42] Then in 1983, a Shenzhen company issued shares for the first time in the PRC's history.[43] In 1984, Shanghai Feile Acoustics made the first public share offering. In 1986, Shenyang opened the first over-the-counter market,[44] which was authorized by the People's Bank of China.[45] Additionally, in December 1990, the People's Bank of China authorized the establishment of two national stock exchanges: the Shanghai Stock Exchange and the Shenzhen Stock Exchange.[46] The two stock exchanges were defined as non-profit legal entities.[47] From the late 1980s to the early 1990s, a number of local stock exchanges in conjunction with the two national stock exchanges (Shanghai and Shenzhen) started operating in China.[48]

With the development of corporate activities, China endeavoured to establish an efficient regulatory framework to govern its corporations and securities markets. In 1993, the first company code of the People's Republic of China – the *Company Law*, was introduced and took effect in 1994. The 1993 *Company Law* incorporated many principles and practices of both Anglo-American systems and civil law systems. It was influenced by the laws and practices in leading corporate economies including Germany, Japan, the UK and the US. For instance, the law

---

38   *Ibid.*
39   *See* Wei, *supra* note 6, at 98–9.
40   *See* Sanzhu Zhu, Securities Regulation in China 5 (New York: Brill, 2001).
41   *Ibid*, at 4–5.
42   *See* Changjiang Li, The History and Development of China's Securities Markets 61 (Beijing: China Wuzi Publishing House, 1998); *See also* I.A. Tokley and Tina Ravn, Company and Securities Law in China 62 (Hong Kong: Sweet & Maxwell Asia, 1998).
43   *Ibid*, at 61.
44   *Ibid*, at 61.
45   *See* Zhu, *supra* note 41, at 10 and 29.
46   *Ibid*, at 67.
47   *See* Carl E. Walter and Fraser J.T. Howie, Privatizing China: The Stock Markets and Their Role in Corporate Reform 31 (Singapore: John Wiley & Sons (Asia) Pty Ltd, 2003). *See* also China Securities Regulatory Commission, *China's Securities and Futures Markets* (April 2004), available at <http://www.csrc.gov.cn/cms/-uploadFiles/introduction2004edition.1087888443500.doc>.
48   *See* Zhu, *supra* note 40, at 7.

adopted a two-tier board system on the one hand,[49] and required listed companies to have independent directors/executive directors on the other.[50]

Chinese scholars and practitioners were dissatisfied with the 1993 *Company Law*. They believed that the law required substantial improvement. For example, the *Company Code* did not clarify whether derivative and class actions were available; it did not clarify if directors had fiduciary duties; it did not even provide a statutory quorum for a shareholder meeting. Some practices introduced by the *Company Law* were also problematic. For instance, in a Chinese company, the board of directors had the power to make business decisions. However, the board did not make those decisions on a day-to-day basis. The power of day-to-day management was given to the general manager of the company. This meant that the board could potentially become a mere figurehead of the company.[51] Furthermore, although the supervisory board had the function of monitoring the board of directors, it did not have any input in the election of directors. This reduced the supervisory strength of the supervisory board. In addition, the *Company Code* stipulated that the chairperson of the board of directors was the legal representative of the company. Without that person's signature, a legal document did not bind the company. This could have created inconvenience in practice. The *Company Code* was amended in 2005. The amended *Company Code* had improved regulatory mechanisms over corporations including enhancing the monitoring power of the supervisory board. However, the amended *Company Code* did not eliminate all the problems of its predecessor.

While improving its corporate law, China has also been enhancing another force to regulate corporate activities and promote good corporate governance. This new force is the China Securities Regulatory Commission (CSRC). Since its establishment in the 1990s, the CSRC has been very active in producing regulations and rules relating to the issue and trade of securities and the operation of stock exchanges. For example, the CSRC has endeavored to fill the gaps of the *Company Code* and *Securities Law* by producing detailed provisions on corporate governance including the *Guidelines for Introducing Independent Directors to the Board of Directors of Listed Companies* (2001) and the *Code of Corporate Governance for Listed Companies* (2002). The CSRC also stipulates detailed requirements for shareholders' general meetings in listed companies. It requires a listed company to lodge a report with the stock exchange to explain the reasons of not holding the annual general meeting on time, and authorizes stock exchanges to delist a company that fails to hold the annual general meeting on time without

---

49   *See* the People's Congress, the 1993 Company Law of the People's Republic of China, secs 52, 71 and 118.

50   *Ibid*, sec. 123.

51   *See* Yuwa Wei, *Volatility of China's Securities Market and Corporate Governance*, 29.2 Suffolk Transnational Law Review 117 (2006).

reasonable excuses.[52] It suggests that the board of directors should invite lawyers specialized in securities to attend general meetings, and provide and publish their opinions on matters involving the validity of the procedure of the meetings and the qualification of the attendees.[53] It further suggests that the board may also invite public notaries to attend the meetings.[54]

Apart from enacting detailed regulations on corporate governance and general meetings, the CSRC has vigorously promoted greater disclosure by listed companies. Listed companies are required to prepare half yearly reports and annual reports. In addition to periodic reporting, listed companies are also required to make continuous disclosure.

Regulatory framework of securities industry   In China, the legal framework of the securities industry has developed in its own special social and historical environment.[55] In other words, the evolution of securities regulation in China has followed a unique path.[56] In the beginning, a number of piecemeal legal and administrative documents regulated stock exchanges.[57] People hoped that the enactment of the *Securities Law* would supersede most, if not all, of the piecemeal regulatory documents.[58] The 1998 *Securities Law*, however, did not live up to expectations. The fact was that the *Securities Law* mainly regulated the issuing and trading of shares, corporate bonds, and other such securities lawfully recognized by the State Council.[59] The provisions of the 1993 *Company Law* and other laws and administrative regulations covered those areas outside the reach of the securities law.[60] It seemed that the operation of some earlier laws and legal documents should continue to apply.[61] Nevertheless, the 1993 *Company Law* and the 1998 *Securities Law* substantially improved the earlier piecemeal situation by establishing a unified regulatory framework over China's securities industry.[62] Both the 1993 *Company Law* and the 1998 *Securities Law* were amended extensively in 2005.

Today, the sources of securities regulation include the following:

- The 1993 *Company Law* (revised in 2005) provides provisions governing the establishment and operation of stock companies; it also sets provisions

---

52   *See* China Securities Regulatory Commission, the 2000 *Suggestions on Regulating the General Meetings of Listed Companies*, art. 3.
53   *Ibid*, art. 7.
54   *Ibid*.
55   *See* Zhu, *supra* note 40, at 8.
56   *Ibid*.
57   *See* Tokley and Ravn, *supra* note 42, at 66; *See* also Zhu, *supra* note 40, at 207.
58   *See* Zhu, *supra* note 40, at 13.
59   *See* the People's Congress, 1998 Securities Law of the People's Republic of China, sec. 2.
60   *Ibid*.
61   Zhu, *supra* note 40, at 79–80.
62   *Ibid*, at 103.

over the conduct of companies operating on securities markets. For example, it forbids the conduct of short-swing trading and the conflicts of interest of company directors.[63]

• The 1998 *Securities Law* (revised in 2005) regulates the establishment and operation of stock exchanges and brokering firms; issuing and trading of securities; and securities registration and clearing institutions.[64] The 1979 Criminal Code deals with corporate and securities market offences.[65]

• Special Regulations of the State Council; it is noteworthy that the *Securities Law* only applies to the issuing and trading of shares, bonds, and other securities recognized by the State Council within China. It applies neither to shares listed abroad, nor to shares of Chinese companies reserved for foreign investment.[66] Neither does the *Securities Law* apply to government bonds. The State Council regulates the above exempt securities.

• The 1997 *Methods of Administrating Securities Investment Funds* are other relevant State Council regulations.

• Ministry Rules. They are relevant administrative rules and regulations over the securities industry; they were enacted on behalf of some ministries and commissions, including the CSRC, directly under control of the State Council.

• Finally, self-regulation, including rules of self-regulation made through the Articles of Association of China Securities Association, business rules of the Shanghai and Shenzhen stock exchanges, represents the final set of relevant regulations.[67]

By taking a close look at these regulations, one can see that the *Securities Law* and the *Company Law* primarily regulate the issuance of securities. These two laws also regulate shares and stock companies. Furthermore, insider trading, market manipulation, and disclosure are largely regulated by the *Securities Law*.

It is interesting to note that a large part of the Chinese *Securities Law* focuses on the establishment and operation of stock exchanges, stock brokering companies, and market intermediaries.[68] Because of this, Chinese *Securities Law* transgresses

---

63   Such regulations are mainly contained in Company Law Of The People's Republic Of China, chs 4 and 5 (1994), available at <http://www.cclaw.net/download/companylaw.asp>.

64   *See* the People's Congress, *supra* note 59, arts 5–7.

65   Such provisions are mainly contained in 1979 Criminal Code Of The People's Republic Of China, chs 3, 4.

66   These refer to B shares, H shares, L shares and N shares. B, H, N, L shares are RMB denominated shares, but should be purchased by foreign or domestic investors by using foreign currency.

67   *See* Xianyi Zeng, Securities Law 26–8 (Beijing: the Publishing House of the People's University, 2000).

68   *See* the People's congress, *supra* note 59, arts 5 and 6.

the territory of company law.[69] Such an overlap seldom occurs in the securities laws of western countries.[70]

The enactment of the *Company Law* in 1993 was a milestone in China's enterprise reform.[71] Notably, the *Company Law* affirmed the policy of developing a market economy.[72] Since the implementation of the law, China has experienced an unprecedented wave of corporatization and privatization.

However, ongoing corporate practice revealed some aspects of inefficiency in the *Company Law*, even from the very beginning of its enactment.[73] Since the enactment of the *Company Law* in 1994, scholars and practitioners wanted to amend the *Company Law*.[74] This was because the *Company Law* left many gaps or loopholes to be filled.[75] Many issues were not clearly addressed by the *Company Law*, such as directors' fiduciary duties, classification of shares, shareholders' derivative actions, and class actions.[76] Nevertheless, the 1993 *Company Law* has stood for ten years without any significant amendments.[77] During this decade, China increased the role of the CSRC and reinforced securities legislation.[78] Consequently, the CSRC has become very active in effectively regulating listed companies to improve corporate governance.

The 1993 *Company Law* was eventually overhauled in 2005. The amended *Company Law* introduced fundamental changes in five core areas. Firstly, the threshold of registered capital was reduced significantly. The current minimum registered capital of a limited liability company is RMB 30,000 yuan, 94 percent to 70 percent less than the required amount in the early versions of the *Company*

---

69   *See* Jiangyu Wang, *China's Securities Experiment: the Challenge of the Globalization*, Chapter I, available at <http://www.eastlaw.net/research/securities/securities-intro.htm>.

70   *Ibid.*

71   *See* Anna M. Han, *China's Company Law: Practicing Capitalism in a Transitional Economy*, 5 Pacific Rim Law and Policy Journal 457, 459 (1996).

72   *See* Zhu, *supra* note 40, at 88–9.

73   *See* Han, *supra* note 71, at 460.

74   *See* Xiqing Gao, *Some Regulatory Issues of the PRC Securities Market*, in China 2000: Emerging Investment, Funding and Advisory Opportunities for a New China, OnlineBooks, available at <http://www.asialaw.com/-bookstore/china2000/chapter01.htm>; *see also* Walter Hutchens, *PRC Amends Company Law and Securities Law*, Walter Hutchens.com, available at <http://rhsmith.umd.edu/faculty/whutchens>.

75   *See* Sonja Opper, et al., The Power Structure in China's Listed Companies: The Company Law and its Enforcement 26 (H.K. Institute of Economics and Business, Strategy Working Paper No. 1039, 2002).

76   *See* Gao, *supra* note 74.

77   *See* Walter Hutchens, *Major Revision to PRC Company Law Moving Forward*, Walter Hutchens' Blog (25 February 2005), available at <http://www.rhsmith.umd.edu/faculty/whutchens/2005/02/major-revision-to-prc-company-law.html>.

78   *See generally* Han, *supra* note 71, at 457.

Law.[79] The minimum registered capital of a joint stock limited company is currently RMB 5 million yuan, reduced 50 percent compared with the mandatory amount before the law was amended.[80] The amended company law also gives legal recognition to a single person company. These changes were made for the purpose of encouraging investment, creating more business opportunities, and promoting economic development.

Secondly, the revised company law introduced the notion of lifting the corporate veil. This allows courts to hold controlling shareholders and directors liable in the case of abusing the corporate personality. The law states that the People's Supreme Court is responsible for supplying the guidance for implementing the principle of lifting the corporate veil.

Thirdly, the new version of the company law has increased protection for minority shareholders. It has new provisions stipulating that shareholders are entitled to inspect the accounting books of the company, and have a right to require the company to buy back their shares in the case where the company does not distribute dividends for a long time.[81] The revised company law formally recognizes the shareholders' derivative action.[82] Furthermore, the current law provides for detailed statements on directors and managers' duties of loyalty, care and diligence.[83]

Fourthly, the amended company law has improved the rules of corporate governance. The role of the supervisory board has been enhanced. Nowadays, having independent directors in listed companies is a mandatory requirement.[84] This is an important change, since it guarantees board independence and combats the insider control problem.

Finally, the amended law has added provisions to protect employees' lawful rights and interests, including that companies should purchase social insurance for employees, enhance labor protection and workplace safety, improve employees' life quality through reinforcing vocational education and in-service training.[85] The law goes further and states that employees are encouraged to organize unions, and companies should provide necessary conditions for their labor unions to carry out union activities. The law provides that the labor union has the power to, on behalf of employees, negotiate and conclude a collective contract with the company

---

79   *See* the People's Congress, the 1994 Company Law of the People's Republic of China (Revised in 2005), sec. 26. Before the 2005 amendment, the minimum register capital of a limited liability company was RMB 500,000, 300,000, or 100,000 yuan, depending on the trade of the company. The minimum register capital of a joint stock limited company was RMB 10 million yuan.

80   *Ibid*, sec. 81.

81   *See* the People's Congress, *supra* note 79, secs 34 and 75.

82   *Ibid*, sec. 152.

83   *Ibid*, sec. 148.

84   *Ibid*, sec. 123.

85   *Ibid*, sec. 17.

with respect to remuneration, working hours, welfare, insurance, work safety and sanitation, and other matters.[86] Companies are required to implement the requirements of democratic management in relevant laws and their constitutions including assuring the labor representatives at meetings, soliciting the opinions and proposals of the employees through the meeting of the representatives of the employees and other ways when making a decision that concerns important issues.[87] Importantly, the revised company law expressly stipulates that a company should provide necessary conditions for the activities of the organization of the Chinese Communist Party established by the employees of the company.[88] These provisions illustrate the intention and determination of the Chinese law makers to uphold social justice and welfare through introducing legal rules reflecting socialist value and Chinese characteristics.

In 1998, the Standing Committee of the People's Congress passed the *Securities Law of the People's Republic of China*. With the enactment of the 1998 *Securities Law*, China, for the first time since 1949, possessed a comprehensive code regulating the securities business and securities market. Due to the limitation of practice, the 1998 *Securities Law* did not give sufficient attention to many details and therefore left gaps. For instance, it failed to provide adequate remedies to investors. Furthermore, the law did not introduce effective strategies to control market misconduct including insider trading and other types of market manipulation.

Significant amendments were made to the 1998 *Securities Law* in 2005. The amended *Securities Law* made improvements to the rules governing disclosure, securities issuance, investor protection, stock exchanges, and securities intermediaries. The amended law introduced new mechanisms relating to public offering, disclosure in applications for an initial public offer, establishment of a securities investor protection fund, recommended requirements for public issuance of securities, and the responsibility of directors and senior managers relating to information disclosure in the listed company's prospectus and financial reports.[89] Changes were made to enable transactions of new species of securities including futures, and to allow securities companies to provide securities financing services through securities transactions for their clients.[90] Generally speaking, the revised *Securities Law* has made the following important improvements to the regulation of securities:

Firstly, the law has set up new requirements for issuers to meet in order to control the quality of listed companies and securities, and prevent unlawful issuance of securities. The revised law introduces a recommendation system to improve

---

86   *Ibid*, sec. 18.

87   *Ibid*.

88   *Ibid*, sec. 19.

89   *See* the People's Congress, the 1998 Securities Law of the People's Republic of China (revised in 2005), secs 10, 11, 21, 68, 134, and 188.

90   *Ibid*, secs 42 and 142.

administration over securities issuance and to ensure standard operation of listed companies. The law states that any issuer filing an application for public issuance of stocks or convertible corporate bonds by means of underwriting according to law, or for public issuance of any other securities should employ an institution with the qualification of making recommendations as its recommendation party. A recommendation party should, based on the principles of honesty, creditworthiness, diligence and accountability, carry out a prudent examination of the application documents and disclosure materials from the issuers for the purpose of supervising and urging the issuer to operate in a standard manner.[91] To prevent frauds in the course of an initial public offering, the law stipulates that an issuer submitting an application for an initial public offer of stocks must disclose the relevant application documents in advance.[92] The law also adds new restrictions on advertising, public inducement or public issuance in any disguised form in cases where securities are not issued in a public manner.[93] Furthermore, the current *Securities Law* introduces the concept of issuance failure. Section 35 states that a public offer of stocks through sale by proxy will be deemed a failure, if the quantity of stocks fails to reach 70 percent of the planned quantity when the term of sale by proxy expires. The relevant issuer must return the issuing price plus interest calculated at the current bank deposit rate to the subscribers of stocks.

Secondly, the revised law increases the protection of investors. It stipulates that the state must establish the "securities investor protection fund". The capital of the fund is contributed by securities companies or raised in other lawful manners.[94] The fund will be managed according to the instructions and guidance provided by the State Council. A securities company is required to withdraw a "trading risk reserve" from its annual after-tax profits to cover any losses from securities transactions. The specific proportion for that withdrawal should be prescribed by the securities regulatory authority.[95] The current law also has provisions forbidding investment consulting institutions and practitioners in the trade of securities services from committing frauds on their clients or exploiting their clients by engaging in activities such as entering into an agreement with a client to share the gains of securities investment or to bear the loss of securities investment, purchasing or selling any stock of a listed company, for which the consulting institution provides services, or providing or disseminating any false or misleading information to investors through media or by any other means.

Thirdly, the amended law has enhanced supervision and regulation over listed companies and securities transactions. It extends the scope of directors and managers' responsibilities in ensuring the accuracy of companies' reports and other disclosure documents by stating that directors and senior managers of a listed

91 *Ibid*, sec. 11.
92 *Ibid*, sec. 21.
93 *Ibid*, sec. 10.
94 *Ibid*, sec. 134.
95 *Ibid*, sec. 135.

company must give their opinions for recognition in the written periodic reports of their company. The supervisory board of a listed company must examine the company's periodic reports formulated by the board of directors and produce their opinions in writing.[96] Moreover, the directors, supervisors and senior managers of a listed company have to guarantee the authenticity, accuracy and integrity of the information disclosed by the company.[97] The law goes further to require listed companies to disclose information concerning important events or matters that affect the trading price of the company's shares and are unknown to the public.[98] The disclosure can be made by immediate submission of a temporary report outlining the relevant major event to the securities regulatory authority and the stock exchange, as well as making an announcement to the general public. In particular, the amended *Securities Law* prescribes the situations amounting to "important events", which include the case where a company or any director, supervisor or senior manager is involved in any crime or under criminal investigation.[99] This is because criminal investigation or a crime is an event likely to affect the stock price of the company.

Fourthly, the amended law has enhanced the strength of the securities regulatory authority. It gives the authority, in the course of performing its duties and functions, the power to inspect and photocopy securities trading records, transfer registration records, financial statements and other relevant documents or materials of any entity or individual relating to a case under investigation. The regulatory authority can also seal any document or material that may be transferred, concealed or damaged. It may consult the capital account, security account or bank account of any relevant party, entity or individual concerned in a case under investigation.[100] Where evidence suggests that certain property may be in illegal proceeds, or securities have been or may be transferred or concealed, any important evidence has been or may be concealed, forged or damaged, the regulatory authority is able to freeze or seal-up the property, securities or evidence.[101] When investigating into any major securities irregularity such as manipulation of the securities market or insider trading, the securities regulatory authority may restrict the securities transactions.[102] On the other hand, to prevent abuses of power by the securities regulatory authority, the current *Securities Law* contains provisions stating that staff of the securities regulatory authority, in the course of performing their duties, should be dutiful and impartial, should handle matters according to law, and

---

96   *Ibid*, sec. 68.
97   *Ibid.*
98   *Ibid*, sec. 67.
99   *Ibid.*
100 *Ibid*, sec. 180.
101 *Ibid.*
102 *Ibid.*

must not take advantage of their post to seek any unjust interests or divulge any commercial secret of a relevant entity or individual.[103]

Finally, the revised *Securities Law* leaves more room for further financial reforms. Although the law upholds the principle that the securities business, banking, trust and insurance should operate separately, it goes further and states that this does not include the case where the state has different provisions.[104] This leaves open the possible practice of universal banking in the future. Furthermore, the revised *Securities Law* repeals the provisions prohibiting banks to speculate in the stock market by stating that "the channel for capital to enter into the stock market should be broadened".[105] Nevertheless, it still forbids unqualified capital to flow into the stock market. It appears that the law intends to leave the matter to be clarified by banking legislation. The new law has also removed the provisions prohibiting transactions of securities of state-owned enterprises and state-dominated enterprises, and thus eliminates the legal hurdle for share reforms.[106] Furthermore, the law no longer restricts securities companies from engaging in securities transactions that are financed by funds or securities obtained from their clients.[107] This change allows Chinese securities companies to adopt the current mainstream practice in the world, increase the efficiency of capital utilization in securities companies, as well as improve the liquidity of the capital market. The law goes further to clarify that such practice must be subject to close supervision by the relevant laws and supervisory authorities.[108]

The legislative efforts in the areas of corporate law and securities law in recent years suggest that China has endeavored to improve the corporate governance practice of Chinese listed companies, as well as enhance the regulatory strength over the securities market. With the progress in the financial reforms and regulatory improvement, China's securities issuance and trading system has continued to develop, and the conduct of its listed companies and the practice of the securities business have become more standardized. Today, the most challenging task faced by Chinese people is law enforcement.

The regulatory activities of the China Securities Regulatory Commission over corporate governance   In the beginning, the stock exchanges were regulated by different organizations, including the People's Bank of China, the State Council,

---

103   *Ibid*, sec. 182.
104   *Ibid*, sec. 6.
105   *Ibid*, sec. 81.
106   *Ibid*, sec. 83.
107   Section 142 of the revised 1998 *Securities Law* states that a securities company engaging in securities transactions that are financed by funds or securities obtained from their clients must do so in accordance with the requirements of the State Council and should be subject to the approval of the securities regulatory authority.
108   *Ibid*.

the Ministry of Finance, and local governments.[109] This practice caused regulatory inefficiency and corruption. A number of incidents on the securities market illustrated this, of which the 8.10 Incident was a typical example. The incident happened on 10 August 1992 (It was thus named 8.10). On that day, some 700,000 would-be investors of a new issue rushed into Shenzen to subscribe to the new issue. The prescribed five million subscription forms were used up within four hours, left many empty handed. It was clear that the officials of the People's Bank of China corrupted the process of handling the subscription forms. This resulted in violent protest which led to riots. The government restored order by distributing an additional five million forms the next day.[110] It was apparent from this incident that too many organizations claiming authority over the operation of securities market and securities activities was likely to cause confusion and corruption. Incidents relating to the operation of the stock exchanges, particularly the 8.10 Incident on the Shenzhen Stock Exchange in 1992, alerted the State Council to ambiguity in securities regulation and administration.

The State Council soon clarified the regulatory authority over the securities market by establishing a specialized body to be the sole regulator of the securities market.[111] Consequently, by the end of that year, the State Council established the China Securities Regulatory Commission.[112] The State Council intended to create a single market regulatory body. The influence, interests, and focus of this regulatory body depended on the future development of the securities market.[113] But, there was strong resistance from all the other existing regulators.[114] The People's Bank, the local governments, and even the stock exchanges did not want the CSRC to be their sole regulator.[115] As a result, for four years, the CSRC struggled to consolidate its authority, before eventually obtaining full control over the stock exchanges and the securities industry.[116]

The first important step made by the CSRC was to retain staff and gradually strengthen its influence over the securities markets.[117] During 1992 to 1993, the CSRC gained extended power of investigation and enforcement.[118] The next step, during 1996, was to assume full control over the two national stock exchanges.[119] Since 1997, with the exclusion of the People's Bank of China and local governments' participation in the securities industry, the CSRC has

---

109   *See* Zhu, *supra* note 40, at 8–10.
110   *See* Walter and Howie, *supra* note 47, at 30.
111   *See* Tokley and Ravn, *supra* note 42, at 64.
112   *Ibid.*
113   *See* Walter and Howie, *supra* note 47, at 9.
114   *See* Zhu, *supra* note 40, at 188–9.
115   *Ibid.*
116   *Ibid*, at 192.
117   *See* Walter and Howie, *supra* note 47, at 54–60.
118   *Ibid*, at 9.
119   *Ibid*, at 9–10.

secured and retained its status as the single regulatory power of the securities market and the securities industry in China.[120] The 1998 *Securities Law* further clarified and affirmed the status and powers of the CSRC as the sole regulatory authority of the securities industry in China. The State Council directly oversees the CSRC.[121]

Since its establishment, the CSRC has been given an increasingly active role in regulating the issuance and trade of securities and the operation of stock exchanges.[122] For example, the CSRC enacted the *Announcement of Prohibition of Market Manipulation* and the *Provisional Rules of Prohibition of Entry into the Securities Market*.[123] In October 2003, the CSRC enacted five more legal documents, including:

- The Disclosure Standard of Securities Companies Issuing Shares to Particular Investors;[124]
- The Standard of Reports on Assessing the Credibility and Ranks of Securities Companies;[125]
- The Standard of Application Form for Issuance of Securities by Securities Companies; and[126]
- The Standard of Prospectus of Securities Companies, and the Standard of Announcement of Being Listed.[127]

Additionally, just one month before, on 29 August 2003, the CSRC promulgated the *Provisional Methods of Administrating the Securities of Securities Companies*.[128]

---

120   *Ibid*, at 10.

121   *See* the People's Congress, *supra* note 59, arts 7 and 166.

122   *See* Gao, *supra* note 74.

123   The Announcement of Prohibition of Market Manipulation was promulgated in 1996, and the Provisional Rules of Prohibition of Entry into the Securities Market was promoted in 1997.

124   *See* Qiaoning Li, *The Regulatory Framework of Issue of Securities Has Been Build Following the Publication of Five Supplementary Documents*, Securities Times (2 September 2003), available at <http://www.china.com.cn/-chinese/2003/Sep/396047.htm>.

125   *Ibid*.

126   *Ibid*.

127   *Ibid*. The regulations (Chinese version) can be found at the following websites: <http://www.sol.net.cn/law/-law_show.asp?ArticleID=15832>;   <http:// www.sol.net.cn/law/law_show.asp?ArticleID=16026>;   <http://www.ccn86.com/news/ policy/20050226/9952.html>;   <http://sol.net.cn/law/law_show.asp?ArticleID=15365>; <http://www.sol.net.cn/law/law_show.asp?ArticleID=15367>.

128   *See* China Securities Regulatory Commission, the *Provisional Methods of Administrating the Securities of Securities Companies*, available at <http://www.jincao. com/fa/law09.50.htm>.

The regulatory power of the CSRC trespassed into the traditional territories of both the *Company Law* and *Securities Law*.[129] This was particularly true in the area of corporate governance.[130] For instance, because the Company Law did not provide detailed provisions on corporate governance, the CSRC endeavored to fill this gap. In 2001, the CSRC produced the *Guidelines for Introducing Independent Directors to the Board of Directors of Listed Companies* and the *Code of Corporate Governance for Listed Companies*.[131] Since July 2003, the CSRC further required that at least one third of the members of the board of directors be independent directors.[132] At the same time, the CSRC took steps to organize training classes for independent directors.[133]

Furthermore, the CSRC stipulated detailed requirements for shareholders' general meetings in listed companies.[134] According to the *Suggestions on Regulating the General Meetings of Listed Companies 2000*, listed companies should lodge a report with the stock exchanges to explain their reasons for not holding an annual general meeting within the prescribed timeframe.[135] This was important as stock exchanges might delist a company that failed to hold an annual general meeting on time without a reasonable excuse.[136] Thus, the CSRC further suggested that the board of directors might invite securities lawyers to attend the general meetings and publish their expert opinions on the validity of the procedures of the meetings, and the qualifications of the attendees and shareholders who called the meeting.[137] It was further suggested that the board might also invite public notaries to attend the meetings.[138]

Apart from independent directors and the detailed requirements on general meetings, the CSRC has vigorously promoted greater disclosure by listed companies. Listed companies are required to publish half yearly reports[139] and annual reports.[140] In addition to these periodic reports, listed companies must also

---

129   *See* Tong Lu, *Corporate Governance in China* 8 (China Center for Corporate Governance), available at <http://www.iwep.org.cn/cccg/pdf/Corporate%20Governance%20in%20China%20%20Prof.pdf>.

130   *Ibid*, at 8–9.

131   *See* Wei, *supra* note 6, at 120. China Securities Regulatory Commission and State Economic and Trade Commission, *Code of Corporate Governance for Listed Companies in China* (7 January 2001) available at <http://www.csrc.gov.cn/en/jsp/detail.jsp?infoid=1061968722100&type=CMS.STD>.

132   *See* Walter and Howie, *supra* note 47, at 66.

133   *See* Lu, *supra* note 129 at 7.

134   *Ibid*, at 4.

135   *See* Li, *supra* note 96.

136   *See* China Securities regulatory commission, *Suggestions on Regulating the General Meetings of Listed Companies*, art. 3 (2000).

137   *Ibid*, art. 3, 122.

138   *Ibid*, art. 7, 122.

139   *See* the People's Congress, *supra* note 89, secs 65 and 66.

140   *Ibid*, art. 61.

make continuous disclosure.[141] Whenever a major issue arises, a listed company must announce it publicly.[142] The method of disclosure required is to publish information or documents in specified newspapers, periodicals and gazettes. In addition, information should be made available for public inquiry at the company and the stock exchange.[143] Recently, the CSRC has published a set of five documents relating to disclosure.[144] These documents provide detailed requirements on the preparation of a prospectus and expert report, and the standard of disclosure.[145]

Before 2005, the CSRC had the power to delist non-profitable or poorly performing companies.[146] The CSRC might give the companies an opportunity to improve their performance before delisting them.[147] In the meantime, the CSRC would give warnings to potential investors in those companies. In China, poorly performing or non-profitable companies were formally labeled as either "PT Companies" or "ST Companies".[148] PT stood for Particular Transfer, which indicated that the company had made losses in the past three consecutive years.[149] ST meant Special Treatment, which indicated that the companies had made losses in the past two consecutive years.[150] Since 2001, delisting has been subject to stricter rules. Stock exchanges are able to delist the securities of a company that has operated at a loss for the latest three consecutive years and fails to gain profits in the year thereafter, or fails to meet other requirements in relevant laws.[151]

In 2001, the CSRC and the State Economic and Trade Commission jointly initiated a program inspecting the establishment and development of a model corporate governance system in listed companies.[152] The aims of the inspection scheme were to gain a clear understanding of the current situation of listed companies in developing their modern corporate mechanisms, to identify

---

141   *Ibid*, art. 62.

142   *Ibid*.

143   *Ibid*, art. 64.

144   *See* Li, *supra* note 96. *See* China Securities Regulatory Commission, *Implementing Procedure on Listing Suspension and Termination of Listed Companies Operating at Loss*, available at <http://www.csrc.gov.cn/en/-jsp/detail.jsp?infoid=1061948161100&type=CM S.STD>.

145   *Ibid*.

146   *See* Walter and Howie, *supra* note 47, at 66, 67.

147   *Ibid*, at 67.

148   *Ibid*.

149   *Ibid*. Since 2001 the term "PT" was repealed with the enactment of the *Revised Measures Concerning Suspension and Termination the Listing of the Shares of Lose Making Listed Companies* (the CSRC, 2001).

150   *Ibid*.

151   *See* the CSRC, the 2001 *Revised Measures Concerning Suspension and Termination the Listing of The Shares of Lose Making Listed Companies*. *See* also the People's Congress, *supra* note 89, sec. 56.

152   *See* China Securities Regulatory Commission, *Code of Corporate Governance*, available at <http://www.csrc.gov.cn/en>.

problems, and to propose effective solutions.[153] The Chinese authorities expected that the program would further promote the establishment of a modern corporate system in listed companies, protect the rights of investors, and advance the healthy development of the securities market.[154] The matters to be inspected included:

- whether controlling shareholders influenced staff, or financial arrangements;
- the appropriation of funds of listed companies by controlling shareholders;
- whether controlling shareholders interfered in the decision-making processes relating to the appointments of directors, supervisors, managers, and other senior officers, and the business affairs of the listed companies;
- matters relevant to enterprise reforms;
- operation of the general meeting, the board of directors and the supervisory board;
- the use of funds raised on the securities market; and
- statements in periodic and interim reports.[155]

The inspection took six months and was carried out in three phases. The first phase was the *Self-Inspection Phase* which lasted about two months. The second phase was the *Emphasis Inspection Phase*. In this phase, the branches of the CSRC and the Commission of Economy and Trade randomly selected some listed companies as targets of inspection. And finally, the CSRC and the Commission of Economy and Trade analyzed the outcomes of the inspection and drew conclusions based on the analyzes.[156]

The Chinese *Company Law* and *Securities Law* did not provide securities investors with sufficient remedies. For instance, it did not provide for a right to commence class actions.[157] In 2002, the People's Supreme Court of China ruled that investors could sue the company or the directors of the company, if an investigation of the CSRC revealed fraudulent activities.[158] Since then, officials

---

153 *Ibid.*

154 *See* China Securities Regulatory Commission, *Announcement of Carrying out the Inspection of the Development of Modern Corporate System in Listed Companies* 2002, available at <http://www.csrc.gov.cn/en>.

155 *Ibid.*

156 *See* China Securities Regulatory Commission and China Economy and Trade Commission, *Announcement of Carrying Out Inspection on the Governance of Listed Companies* (13 May 2002). *See* also Laura M. Cha, *Speech at Video and Telephone Conference on Inspection on the Governance of Listed Companies*, available at <http://www.cnstock.com/shzqb/shiwuban/200205130056.htm>.

157 *See* Wenhai Cai, *Private Securities Litigation in China: Of Prominence and Problems*, 13 Columbia Journal of Asian Law 135, 143–8 (1999).

158 *See* Susan V. Lawrence, *Ally of the People*, Far East Economic Review 26 (9 May 2002).

of the CSRC began calling for the introduction of Class Actions.[159] In 2005, the People's Supreme Court of China ruled that courts might accept securities investors' class actions where those investors sought remedies for misleading statements.[160] This new ruling indicates a great step forward towards formally recognizing class actions. Unfortunately, both the current *Company Law* and *Securities Law* remain silent on the topic.

It can be seen, therefore, that the CSRC has been playing an increasingly active role in promoting the practice of sound corporate governance. Its important role in China's corporate and securities systems will be further examined.

A closer view of the China Securities Regulatory Commission (CSRC)   The wording in the *Securities Law* implies that a securities regulatory authority should not be a public institution, but only a body or a commission under direct control of the State Council.[161] Interestingly, the CSRC only has the status of a ministry in China.[162] At present, it does not quite fit the description of a securities regulatory authority under securities law. In reality, the CSRC is clearly a public institution.

Generally speaking, there are basically three types of securities regulatory practice. The first type is the Australian model discussed above. The second is the US style, with a centralized regulatory authority (the SEC) with extensive power of administration and regulation over securities activities and operation of stock exchanges.[163] The final type is that of Germany. China presents a different type of securities regulatory practice from those three classical types.

The CSRC is different from the Australian Securities and Investments Commission (ASIC) and the Securities and Exchange Commission (SEC) in the United States. In Australia, the ASIC is a government body and administers Australian corporations law.[164] Under the supervision of the ASIC, the Australian Stock Exchange produces its own listing and business rules.[165] If there is a breach,

---

159   *See* Bei Hu, *China Urged to Adopt Class Action Suits,* South China Morning Post (21 November 2002), at 1.

160   *See* Zhiwu Chen, *Class Action Is an Effective Means of Protecting Securities Investors,* New Fortune (11 April 2005), available at <http://www.p5w.net/scoop/xcfwz/200504/t307823.htm>.

161   *See* the People's Congress, *supra* note 89, secs 178–86.

162   *See* China Securities Regulatory Commission, *About Us,* available at <http://www.csrc.gov.cn/en/homepage/-about_en.jsp>.

163   *See* Paul Redmond, Companies and Securities Law: Commentary and Materials 58 and 59 (Sydney: LBC Information Service, 2005).

164   *See* Australian Securities and Investment Commission (ASIC) *ASIC at a Glance,* available at <http://www.asc.gov.au>; The ASIC, *The Laws ASIC Administers,* available at <http://www.asc.gov.au>.

165   *See* Alan Shaw and Paul von Nessen, *The Legal Role of the Australian Securities Commission and the Australian Stock Exchange,* in Gordon Walker (*ed.*), Securities Regulation in Australia and New Zealand 163–85 (Sydney: LBC, 1998).

the stock exchange itself decides whether to delist a company.[166] In the United States, the SEC administers the stock exchanges, has authority to administer and supervise securities activities in that country, and is given extended power of investigation.[167] Under the administration and supervision of the SEC, stock exchanges, clearing houses and the National Association of Securities Dealers also make their own rules of self-regulation.[168]

In China, however, the CSRC deals with the market more directly.[169] For instance, for a long period, the CSRC retained the power of delisting poorly performing companies and promulgated detailed requirements on general meetings and disclosure.[170] In a sense, its regulatory power eroded some traditional territory of the *Company Code* and *Securities Code*, as well as some territory of self-regulation of the stock exchanges. This practice ceased at the beginning of 2006, as a result of revision made to the 1998 *Securities Law* in 2005.

In Germany, banks play an important role in regulating securities activities.[171] Banks are members of stock exchanges, essentially monopolizing the stock broking business[172] and underwrite most securities issued by companies.[173] Consequently, Germany has comparatively relaxed rules of disclosure.[174] As sophisticated investors, banks have the means and skills to obtain necessary commercial information.[175]

In the past decade, China persistently strengthened the power of the CSRC.[176] Based on this, it seems that the country is going in the direction of the US practice by building a strong securities-regulatory regime. China's situation, however, is not exactly the same as that of the United States. Historically, the reason for a strengthened securities regime in the United States is that the states pre-empted the regulatory power over corporations.[177] Building a robust securities legal regime is an effective strategy of federal control over US corporate and securities systems.[178]

---

166 *Ibid*, at 188.

167 *See* U.S. Securities and Exchange Commission (SEC), *The Investor's Advocate: How the SEC Protects Investors and Maintains Market Integrity*, available at <http://www. sec.gov/about/whatwedo.shtml>.

168 *Ibid*.

169 *See* Zhu, *supra* note 40, at 51.

170 *Ibid*, at 51–2 and 192.

171 *See* Wei, *supra* note 6, at 142.

172 *See* Brian R. Cheffins, *Mergers and Corporate Ownership Structure: The United States and Germany at the Turn of the 20th Century*, 51 American Journal of Comparative Law 473, 498 (2003).

173 *Ibid*.

174 *See* Anupama J. Naidu, *Was Its Bite Worse Than Its Bark? The Costs Sarbanes-Oxley Imposes on German Issuers May Translate into Costs to the United States*, 18 Emory International Law Review 271, 282 (2004).

175 *Ibid*, at 282 and 75.

176 *See* Zhu, *supra* note 40, at 8–9.

177 *See* Wei, *supra* note 6, at 134–5.

178 *Ibid*, at 135.

China, on the other hand, is motivated by some contrasting factors regarding promotion of the securities market and securities regulation.

The introduction of modern corporate mechanisms into the Chinese enterprise system is the essential component of the economic reform package. As mentioned above, since 1996, the pace of corporatization in China has accelerated dramatically. An important objective of the Chinese authority is to encourage companies to be listed on the securities market, thus placing these companies under the supervision of the market.[179] It is expected that disciplinary function of the capital market will aid more rapid establishment of a modern corporate governance system in listed enterprises.[180]

The CSRC has aggressively promoted sound corporate governance that assists Chinese companies to withstand scrutiny.[181] In this way, the CSRC acts as a separate leverage for accelerating enterprise reform in China. Hence, China's unique social and economic environment has tightly linked the development of the CSRC to China's enterprise reform.[182] The CSRC plays an extremely important and special role in China's enterprise reform. It is expected to continue to vigorously bring changes and improvement to China's corporate and securities systems. The CSRC Vice Chairperson, Laura Cha, pronounced: "For our part, the CSRC is committed to be a pro-active regulator in fostering corporate governance, in enforcing our rules, in safeguarding the integrity of our markets, and in championing the rights of our investors."[183]

The current development of the securities legal regime and the securities' regulatory authority in China suggests that the status of the CSRC as the centralized and powerful regulatory and administrative authority over the securities market is firmly established. How far it will go in that direction remains to be seen. The activities pursued by the CSRC have yielded and will continue to yield significant influence on the law and practice of corporations and securities in China.

---

179   *See general* Lu, *supra* note 129.

180   *See* Laura M. Cha, *The Future of China's Capital Markets and the Role of Corporate Governance*, Luncheon Speech at China Business Summit (18 April 2001), available at <http://www.csrc.gov.cn/en/jsp/detail.jsp?-infoid=1061948105100&type=CM S.STD>. *See generally* also Zhipan Wu and Jianjun Bai (*eds*), Law and Practice of Securities Transaction I-VIII (Beijing: China University of Political Science and Law Press, 2000).

181   *See* Daochi Tong, *Securities Market Reform in China: Advancing Corporate Governance*, at Asia Perspective Seminar: Advancing Corporate Governance Reform in Asia 12–14 (28 February . 2002). *See* also Daochi Tong, *Building Up a Clean Corporate Culture in an Era of Economic Growth and Development: The Role of Corporate Governance*, China Securities Regulatory Commission Luncheon Speech at 2005 Leadership Forum: Successes Through Ethical Governance.

182   *See* Walter and Howie, *supra* note 47, at 47.

183   *See* Laura M Cha, The Future of China's Capital Markets and the Role of Corporate Governance, Luncheon Speech at China Business Summit (18 April 2001), at <http://www.csrc.gov.cn/en/jsp/detail.jsp?-infoid=1061948105100&type=CMS.STD>.

Regulation of Listed Companies

The important regulations disciplining listed companies in the early stage of the financial market reforms mainly included: (1) the *Methods of Initiating the Pilot Projects of Establishing Stock Companies* (1992, jointly promulgated by the State Commission for Restructuring the Economy, the State Commission of Economic Planning, the Ministry of Finance, the People's Bank of China, and the State Council); (2) the *Provisional Regulation Administering Share Issuance and Trade* (1993, the State Council); (3) the *Announcement of Suspending Acquiring Enterprises Abroad and Enhancing Administering Overseas Investment* (1993, the State Council); (4) the *Announcement of Further Enhancing the Administration of Foreign Investment* (1993, the State Council); (5) the *Company Law* (1993, the People's Congress); (6) the *Instructive Opinions about Shareholders' Meetings* (1995, the CSRC); (7) the *Announcement of Standardizing Shareholders' Meetings in Listed Companies* (1995, the CSRC) and; (8) the *Announcement of Enhancing the Administration of the Shares Held by the Company's Directors, Supervisors and Managers* (1996, the CSRC). These rules provided timely directions for listed companies in relation to organizing their international affairs, preparing for issuance of stocks, and complying with standard finance and accounting rules. They supplied effective principles and mechanisms for tackling the problems which arose in enterprise reforms and capital market development during that period. Among them, the 1994 *Company Law* was the first comprehensive code that supplied the fundamental principles and detailed rules regulating corporate conduct in compliance with international standard and practice.

Further attempts to more strictly regulate the conduct of listed companies have been made since the late 1990s. The State Council and other legislative bodies enacted a series of laws and regulations by the end of the 1990s. In 1997, the State Council, the People's Bank of China, and the Committee of Economy and Trade jointly promulgated the *Provisions about Strictly Prohibiting State-Owned Enterprises and Listed Companies from Speculating Shares*. The law prevented listed companies from using bank loans and share capital to speculate stocks, as well as lending such funds to securities companies or other institutions for the purpose of speculation. In the same year, the CSRC also published the *Guidelines for Listed Companies* (Guidelines). The *Guidelines* gave detailed guidance on construction of the internal rules of listed companies. They contained 12 chapters including general provisions, objects, shareholders meetings, the board of directors, the supervisory board, finance, accounting and auditing, acquisition, dissolution, liquidation, alteration to the constitution, and supplementary provisions.[184] The CSRC required listed companies to amend their constitutions in compliance with the principles in the *Guidelines* at their first shareholder meeting of the year.

In 1998, the CSRC published further two binding documents calculated to standardize the procedure of shareholders' meetings and regulate listed companies

---

184   *See* the CSRC, the *Guidelines for Listed Companies* (1998).

regarding verification of their businesses and disposal of their assets. The *Opinions about Standardizing Shareholders' Meetings* stipulated that listed company should hold shareholders meetings at least once a year. The shareholders were to be given 30 days' notice of the meeting. Matters subject to the examination and approval of the CSRC had to be decided by specific resolutions. Where a shareholder had an interest in a related transaction, the shareholder was not permitted to vote on the resolution when the matter was decided.[185] The *Announcement of Alteration of Main Businesses and Disposal of Assets in Listed Companies* stated that listed companies must re-submit issuance applications in the event of a change of business and disposal of important assets.

Apart from the above regulatory steps, the CSRC paid considerable attention to issues essential to share issuance and disclosure with a view to ensuring orderly operation of the securities market. Between 1997 and 1998, the CSRC issued and amended a number of regulations providing guidance for share issuance and disclosure in company reports and other documents. Of those regulations, the *Contents and Format of the Prosperous* (Rule No. 1, 1997), the *Contents and Format of the Annual Report* (Rule No. 2, 1997), the *Contents and Format of the Half Year Report* (Rule No. 3, 1997), and the *Contents and Format of the Book Listing Notice* (Rule No. 7, 1997) were of most importance.

The above rules and regulations had great historical significance in the development of China's securities market. They filled the regulatory vacuum present before the introduction of the comprehensive securities code in 1998. This contributed significantly to the dynamic operation of China's securities market. The enactment of the 1998 *Securities Law* brought regulation over listed companies into a new era, with disciplining listed companies as the focus of securities regulations.[186] In the 1990s, breaches by listed companies had become a serious problem. Listed companies would commonly release misleading information. The conflict of interest between the controlling shareholder and other investors was acute. This severely damaged the apparent fairness of the securities market and unsettled investors' confidence. In order to control the problem, the 1998 *Securities Law* attached great importance to regulating the conduct of listed companies.[187] For further implementing the principles in the *Securities Law*, the CSRC published a number of more detailed rules in the following years, namely including the *Opinions about Standardizing the Shareholders' Meetings in Listed Companies* (2000), the *Measures of Inspecting Listed Companies* (2001), the *Instructive Opinions on Establishing the System of Independent Directors* (2001), and *Some Provisions concerning Enhancing the Protection of the Interests of Public Shareholders* (2004), etc.

---

185   *See* the CSRC, the *Opinions about Standardizing Shareholders' Meetings* (1998).

186   *See* Su Chen, Special Research on Securities Law 36 (Beijing: Tertiary Education Press, 2006).

187   *Ibid.*

However, the problem of misconduct by listed companies persisted. It was believed necessary to raise the degree of penalties for corporate breaches and increase protection for investors. This was achieved through revision to the *Securities Law* in 2005. The revised *Securities Law* broadened the civil remedy regime and clarified principles of imputation. In relation to misleading disclosure, parties were liable either on a no-fault liability, fault liability, or presumption of fault basis. The particular ground was determined according to their role in the breach. Persons guilty of insider trading, market manipulation and fraud on clients were not only subject to criminal penalties, but also liable to render civil remedies.[188]

Although, technically, the securities regulation has been improved substantially, the regulatory development and the pace of the reforms in China's corporate system and financial sector are not completely harmonized.[189] Currently, the enterprise and financial reforms are still in the process of development. Share reforms have only recently been initiated. Some reports point out that the capital market is hindered by split of shares in listed companies. As long as shares in listed companies are divided into tradable and non-tradable, or state shares, legal person shares and public shares, the problems of abuse of power by large shareholders and share price distortion will continue to exist. Many believe that it is time for China to finally eradicate the negative effect of share split in its listed companies. However, it has to be borne in mind that retaining an appropriate proportion of state-owned companies or state ownership is necessary in terms of maintaining the stability and sustainability of the nation's economy at the level of macro-economy, particularly at the current stage of economic development. How to maintain the balance in an era of reform and development is a challenge still faced by the Chinese today.

Regulation of Stock Exchanges

A stock exchange is generally accepted as an organization of self-governance, and adopts one of two forms – a member-owned mutual organization (a membership organization) or a public company.[190] Traditionally, stock exchanges took the form of a mutual or a membership organization. They were, in fact, companies limited by guarantee. Since the 1990s, demutualization has become more prevalent, with many stock exchanges were transformed into for-profit, shareholder-owned public companies.[191] These demutualized stock exchanges would list and trade their own shares. The most influential stock exchanges such as those in New York, London, Tokyo, Hong Kong, and Australia have all undertaken demutualization. Stock

---

188 *See*, the People's Congress, *supra* note 89, secs 73–82.

189 *See* Chen, *supra* note 186, at 38.

190 This is true even in the countries of regulatory tradition such as the US. *See* Chapter 19 of the US *Securities Exchange Act* of 1934.

191 *See* Chen, *supra* note 186, at 167.

exchanges in some emerging markets including Hungry, Singapore and Malaysia have similarly adopted the form of a public company.[192]

However, a stock exchange is different from an ordinary for-profit public company. It has the function of a public body, and also has the responsibility of a supervisor. A non-mutual stock exchange is therefore a public institution on the one hand, and a for-profit organization on the other. Inevitably, non-mutual stock exchanges frequently encounter conflict between their commercial gains and public interests.[193] This has resulted in increased regulatory intervention aiming at curbing such conflicts. Nevertheless, it is generally accepted that stock exchanges operate far better if they are substantially governed by their own rules. This approach has been adopted by many jurisdictions such as the UK.

Prior to 2005, although the securities laws in China did not expressly define the nature of a stock exchange, relevant provisions indicated that a Chinese stock exchange was intended to be a member-owned/mutual organization. For instance, the 1998 *Securities Law* stated a stock exchange was a non-profit legal person that provided a place for the centralized trading of securities at competing prices.[194] It further provided that gains accumulated by a stock exchange belonged to its members, and its rights and interests should be shared by the members. However, the accumulated gains were not to be distributed to the members while the stock exchange was in existence.[195] The 2001 *Measures of Administering Stock Exchanges* contained provisions expressing the members' meeting to be the highest authority of the stock exchange.[196] Through reading them conjunctively, one could be certain that stock exchanges established in compliance with these laws possessed the characteristics of a mutual. As a result, it was widely accepted that stock exchanges in China took the form of a mutual. However, upon closer examination, it was evident that a Chinese stock exchange did not possess all the characteristics of a mutual. The reasons were as follows: firstly, a Chinese stock exchange was not promoted by members themselves but by the government; secondly, it was not fully owned and controlled by its members, but rather an institution pertaining to the government and under the government's control; and thirdly, to a certain extent, it was financially supported by the government.

Many Chinese commentators took the view that there was no need for China to reject the prevailing contemporary trend by requiring stock exchanges to adopt the traditional organizational structure – a member-owned mutual.[197] This view was accepted by the legislature and manifested in a statement contained in the revised

---

192   *Ibid.*

193   *See generally* Zengyi Xie, Conflicts of Interest in Demutualized Stock Exchanges (Beijing: Social Sciences Academic Press, 2007).

194   *See* the People's Congress, *supra* note 59, sec. 95.

195   *Ibid*, sec. 98.

196   *See* the State Council, the 2001 *Measures of Administering Stock Exchanges*, sec. 17.

197   *See* Chen, *supra* note 186, at 172.

Securities Law (2005): "The gains accumulated by a stock exchange that adopts a membership system shall belong to its members". This statement, in a sense, recognizes the possibility of establishing a stock exchange that elects to adopt a business structure that is not a mutual in nature.[198]

The current *Securities Law* confirms that stock exchanges may make their own listing rules, trading rules, regulations administering members and other rules in accordance with laws and relevant administrative regulations.[199] This has provided the basis for shaping a regime of self-regulation in stock exchanges. However, the developmental path of China's securities market has decided that the stock exchanges in China are unable to possess absolute independence. The CSRC maintains control over Chinese stock exchanges in all important respects. Firstly, the CSRC has control over the arrangement of important personnel in stock exchanges. The non-member directors, the general manager and the vice general manager of a stock exchange are appointed and dismissed by the CSRC. The appointment and dismissal of the chief financial officer and the head of the human resources department are subject to the approval of the CSRC. The appointment and dismissal of other senior and middle level managerial officers must be reported to the CSRC.[200]

Secondly, the making of and alteration to the listing rules and the articles of association of a stock exchange must be approved by the CSRC.[201] Furthermore, the CSRC can order the stock exchange to amend its listing rules and articles of association.[202]

Thirdly, the CSRC has the right to examine and approve the businesses of the stock exchange. For instance, the stock exchange needs to obtain the approval of the CSRC for listing new species of securities and for providing services to securities listed on other stock exchanges.[203] In addition, the CSRC supervises the daily business of the stock exchange, and has the power to monitor and investigate its business, finance and other matters. Stock exchanges must, upon the demand of the CSRC, lodge market information, business documents and other data and materials to the CSRC.[204]

The above discussions highlight that in China, the regulatory authority's intervention into the administration of stock exchanges is extensive, when compared with the dominate practice throughout the world. For instance, although it is accepted in many jurisdictions that some members of a stock exchange may be appointed by the regulatory authority, it is highly uncommon that a chief manager or a deputy chief manager of a stock exchange would be subject to such

---

198   *Ibid.*
199   *See* the People's Congress, *supra* note 89, sec. 118.
200   *See* the State Council, *supra* note 195, secs 24 and 25.
201   *See* the People's Congress, *supra* note 89, sec. 103 and 118.
202   *See* the State Council, *supra* note 195, sec. 89.
203   *Ibid*, secs 13, 14 and 87.
204   *Ibid*, secs 87 and 90.

an appointment. In mature markets, matters such as conditions of being listed and types of securities to be listed are usually decided by stock exchanges themselves, instead of regulatory authorities.

It is necessary for China to fully implement the self-regulatory function of stock exchanges. This can only be achieved by bringing the regulatory practice of Chinese stock exchanges to the wider international standard. It would be beneficial to bring Chinese exercise closer to the mainstream practice. For example, the current rules authorize the CSRC to appoint the general manager and vice general manager of a stock exchange on the one hand, and allow them to be assessed and monitored by the board of directors of the stock exchange on the other. This arrangement does not permit the stock exchange to effectively exercise its power to monitor the general manager and vice general manager. Some suggest returning the power of appointing the general manager and vice general manager to the stock exchange.[205] It is expected that senior officers will be more efficiently supervised and assessed if they are appointed by the stock exchange rather than the CSRC.

Regulation of Securities Companies

The earliest laws regulating securities companies were local laws made after the mid-1980s, such as the 1988 *Guidelines of Securities Companies in Beijing*. The first uniform laws regulating securities companies were the 1990 *Provisional Measures of Administering Securities Companies* and the 1991 *Measures of Administering Branches of Securities Companies*. However, these laws only provided general guidance for creation and registration of securities companies. Pursuant to the laws, creation of a securities company had to be approved by the People's Bank of China. A financial institution with capital of more than RMB 10,000,000 yuan could apply for establishing a securities company.[206] The total value of securities in the account of a securities company should not exceed 80 percent of the amount of the company's total capital.[207] A securities company's shareholdings in a company should not exceed 5 percent of the total shares in that company.[208] Moreover, the value of shares purchased by the securities company from another company must be less than 10 percent of the securities company's total capital. A securities company was required to submit an amount of money that accounted for 3 percent of its profits to the People's Bank of China for the purpose of covering possible trading losses.[209]

See Chen, *supra* note 186, at 176.
    206   *See* the People's Bank of China, the 1990 *Provisional Measures of Administering Securities Companies*, sec. 6.
    207   *Ibid*, sec. 15.
    208   *Ibid*.
    209   *Ibid*, sec. 16.

Due to the fact that securities companies were directly regulated by the People's Bank of China and were usually promoted by banks, the securities and banking businesses were not clearly separated during the mid-1980s and the early 1990s. As a result, during this period, securities companies did not exclusively deal with the securities business, and trust companies and commercial banks were also able to carry on the business. However, the government always preferred separating the banking business from the securities business. Thus, in 1995, the People's Bank of China and the Ministry of Finance jointly issued the *Announcement of Inspecting Securities Institutions in the Financial System*, and decided to check up each securities institution in the financial system and allow those qualified to carry on the securities business to sever relations with the financial authorities.[210]

At the same time, the People's Congress passed the *Commercial Banking Law* which clarified that the banking, insurance and securities businesses should be carried out separately and should be subject to the administration of different authorities.[211] It was clarified that the direct administering authority of securities companies was the People's Bank of China. In the meantime, securities companies were subject to the supervision of the CSRC in the course of operation. In 1996, the People's Bank of China published the *Announcement of Requiring the Branches of the People's Bank of China to Cut the Ties with Their Invested Securities Companies* and ordered all securities companies to terminate any form of affiliation with their patronage banks before the end of 1996. Since then, the principle of separating banking from the securities business has been firmly entrenched.

Since entering the 2000s, the competition of securities business has intensified. In 2001 alone, a large number of securities companies went into liquidation.[212] This brought substantial losses to both the state and public investors. The government engineered a rescue strategy by enhancing regulation over securities companies. When the *Securities Law* was amended in 2005, a great deal of attention was paid to improving the rules concerning administration of securities companies.

The current *Securities Law* has improved the rules governing securities companies' registered capital, in order to ensure the capital adequacy of a securities company. The amount of registered capital of a securities company is higher than that of an ordinary company. The required amounts of registered capital in securities companies differ depending on the scope of their businesses. The amount of registered capital of a securities company should be at least RMB 50 million yuan, where its business is limited to securities brokerage, securities investment consulting and financial advising relating to activities of securities trading or securities investment.[213] The sum of registered capital increases to

---

210   *See* the 1995 *Announcement of Inspecting Securities Institutions in the Financial System*, arts 2, 3, 4, and 5.

211   *See* the People's Congress, the 1995 Commercial Banking Law of the People's Republic of China, secs 43 and 74.

212   *See* Chen, *supra* note 186, at 196.

213   *See* the People's Congress, *supra* note 89, secs 125 and 127.

RMB 100 million yuan or more, if a securities company engages in any of the following businesses: (1) underwriting and recommendation of securities; (2) self-operation of securities; (3) securities asset management; and (4) any other business operation concerning securities.[214] In addition, the law stipulates that the CSRC has the power to increase the minimum amount of registered capital of securities companies in light of risk rating in relation to business operations. The *Securities Law* particularly emphasizes that the registered capital of a securities company must be the paid-in capital. This is in contrast to the system of paying in installments contained in the *Company Law*, which applies to other types of companies.[215]

Furthermore, a limit of indebtedness has been imposed on securities companies to boost their capacity of risk resistance. The *Securities Law* authorizes the CSRC to formulate the risk control indicators of a securities company. Important indicators include the ratio between net capital and liabilities, the ratio between net capital and net assets, and the ratio between current assets and current liabilities.[216] Before the amendment to the *Securities Law* in 2005, the CSRC also introduced rules to control the ratio between capital and liability in a securities company. For instance, the 1999 *Some Opinions about Further Strengthening the Administration over Securities Companies* stipulated that the total amount of debt of a comprehensive securities company should not exceed eight times its net assets.

The current *Securities Law* prescribes additional measures to reinforce securities companies' risk resistance capacity by requiring them to set up a trading risk reserve fund. A securities company is required to withdraw a certain amount of trading risk reserve from its annual after-tax profits to cover any loss from securities transactions.[217] The specific proportion for withdrawal is prescribed by the CSRC. For further strengthening the requirement in the *Securities Law*, the CSRC obliges securities companies to withdraw at least 10 percent trading risk reserve from their after-tax profits.[218]

In order to prevent securities companies from shifting their trading risk to investors, the *Securities Law* promotes the establishment of an investor protection fund. Unlike the trading risk reserve fund, the investor protection fund is created and managed by the state. Securities companies remain, however, obliged to make financial contribution to the investor protection fund.[219]

Today, securities companies are under much greater obligations to make timely continuous disclosure. A securities company must, in compliance with the relevant provisions in law, report the information and materials regarding its operation and

---

214   *Ibid.*

215   *Ibid.*

216   *Ibid*, sec. 130.

217   *Ibid.*

218   *See* the CSRC, the 1999 *Some Opinions about Further Strengthening the Administration over Securities Companies*, sec. 3.

219   *See* the People's Congress, *supra* note 89, sec. 134.

management to the CSRC. The information and materials reported or provided by a securities company must be authentic, accurate and complete. A securities company must report to the CSRC within three business days and provide reasons, if its net assets fall below the amount provided in relevant law, or the ratio between current assets and current liabilities does not meet the requirement in the *Securities Law*.[220]

The law also imposes further requirements in respect of appointing directors and managers aiming at lifting the quality of management in securities companies. The directors, supervisors and senior managers of a securities company must have honesty and integrity, have sound moral standards, be familiar with the laws and administrative regulations on securities, possess the ability of operation and management as required by the performance of their functions and duties, and should have obtained the post-holding qualification as verified by the securities regulatory authority under the State Council before assuming their posts.[221] Furthermore, the directors and managers take much more draconian liabilities for breaches. The CSRC is given additional powers to penalize securities companies and their controllers for fraud and other misconduct.[222]

In summary, Chinese securities companies are operating in a progressively more competitive environment. Facing fierce competition, a securities company in a disadvantageous situation is likely to adopt unlawful business strategies, such as misappropriation of clients' funds in desperation. When securities companies engage in such misconduct, investors, the community, even the country's financial safety are severely jeopardized. It is therefore very necessary to strengthen regulation over securities companies in contemporary China.

The Future

Markets Have to be Regulated by Market Rules

China's securities practice emerged from the economic reforms of the late 1970s.[223] By 2000, the Shanghai Stock Exchange was one of the best performing markets in the world.[224] In general, the Chinese capital market operated reasonably well before the collapse in July 2001.[225] The market continued to decline in the following four years. The government's plans of raising social securities funds remained under threat, and many private companies were adversely affected.[226]

---

220   *See* the CSRC, *supra* note 218.
221   *See* the People's Congress, *supra* note 89, sec. 131.
222   *Ibid*, sec. 150.
223   *See* Chen, *supra* note 36, at 148.
224   *Ibid*.
225   *Ibid*.
226   *Ibid*.

By September 2001, the trading value of the Shanghai and Shenzhen stock exchanges accounted for 51.26 percent of GDP.[227] Unlike the developed markets, however, the Chinese capital market fluctuates irregularly, and the volatility of the market follows a drastic pattern. From 1990 to mid-2001, the Chinese securities market soared to an historic high, though suffered several periods as a flat market along the way.[228] Since mid-2001, the market could be classified as a bear market.[229]

In the past, the Chinese government produced a number of interventional strategies to control the flux on the securities market and to prevent crises that could devastate the market as a whole. When the market soared to an unprecedented high, the government suspended the issuance and trade of new shares to prevent the formation of an investment bubble.[230] Adjusting financial policies was another way of intervening in the securities market.[231] For example, in 1996, the government cut the interest rate twice and the market reacted positively.[232] It was estimated that around RMB 500 million yuan flowed into the securities market after the first interest cut.[233]

The government also tried to use the media to cool down an overheated market. This was successful in some cases, but not always. For instance, in 1994, the market in Shanghai skyrocketed.[234] The government sensed the danger of a market crash and released a large quantity of news warning investors.[235] Investors, however, did not hear the warning and share prices continued to soar.[236] Eventually, the market crashed spectacularly, dropping 70 percent from its peak.[237] Such a sharp fall had rarely been seen in the modern world.[238] In contrast to the experience in the Shanghai Stock Exchange, the Chinese government successfully intervened into the feverish speculation in shares of Shenzhen Development Bank (SDB) through the media in 1996.[239]

---

227   *See* Dehuan Jin, A Study of Volatility of the Chinese Securities Market and Control 4 (Shanghai: Shanghai University of Finance and Commerce Press, 2003).

228   *See* Walter and Howie, *supra* note 47, at 207.

229   *See* Xinhua News Agency, *Chinese Stock Market Witnesses Unexpected Bear Period,* available at <http://english.people.com.cn/200406/16/eng20040616_146483. html>.

230   *See* Chen, *supra* note 36, at 118.

231   *See* Jin, *supra* note 228, at 39 and 63.

232   *Ibid*, at 154.

233   *Ibid.*

234   *Ibid*, at 138.

235   *Ibid.*

236   *Ibid.*

237   *Ibid.*

238   *Ibid*, at 139.

239   *See* Walter and Howie, *supra* note 47, at 211, 212.

Since mid-1996, the robust trading of shares in SDB catalyzed a bull market in both the Shanghai and Shenzhen stock exchanges.[240] Concerned about the ultimate outcome, the government intervened and issued a warning through a "special correspondent" in a *People's Daily* editorial on 16 December.[241] Due to the political status of the *People's Daily* and the historically significant role played by that editorial in China's political and economic life, not many investors could allow themselves to ignore the message conveyed in the editorial.[242] Within three weeks, the Shenzhen market was down 30 percent.[243]

Generally speaking, government intervention was an effective means of control over the volatility of China's securities market in the 1990s. It seems, however, that government intervention is less likely to achieve the goal of control in China today. Since the bear market started in 2001, Chinese authorities sought to control the fall in the market.[244] but intervention had proven to have little effect.[245] For example, one strategy adopted was to limit the size of new offerings.[246] A listing application would not be approved if the company sought to sell shares at a price of more than 20 times its earnings.[247] The strategy proved to be unsuccessful. Reports found that many well-performing companies decided not to issue new shares and a significant number of promising private companies moved to Hong Kong, as its market looked more attractive.[248]

This suggests that it is time for the Chinese to address the problems in the securities market and discern solutions to improve market performance. At present, the main problems in the securities business include undue government intervention, lack of regulatory leverage, and poor corporate governance.[249] Excessive government interference is a proven problem that burdens the securities business in China.[250] Theoretically, China's system of control over the securities market and its transactions has become a combination of governmental supervision and self-regulation. In practice, governmental supervision is the

---

240   *Ibid.*

241   *Ibid.*

242   *Ibid*, at 212.

243   *Ibid*, at 212; *see also* Chen, *supra* note 36, at 161–3.

244   *See* Xinhua News Agency, China Selects Firms for Experiments to Tackle Major Problem Facing Sluggish, available at <http://english.people.com.cn/200505/10/eng20050510_184242.html>. *See* also Chen, *supra* note 36, at 148.

245   *See* Chen, *supra* note 36, at 148.

246   *Ibid.*

247   *Ibid. See* also Jin, *supra* note 227, at 4.

248   *See* Chen, *supra* note 36, at 149.

249   *See* Stephen Green, *Something Old, Something New*, 18 China Review (2001), available at <http://www.cmagic.co.uk/home-fp01/g/b/www.gbcc.org.uk/crcon.htm>. *See* also Baisan Xie, Xuelai Dai and Lan Xu, *A Comparative Study of Chinese and US Securities Markets*, in Baisan Xie (*ed.*), International Comparison of Securities Market 3 (Volume 1, Beijing: Qinghua University Press, 2003).

250   *See* Jin *supra* note 227, at 201.

paramount influence.[251] Consequently, the self-regulatory function of the stock exchanges remains marginal.[252] For example, currently, the authority to investigate misconduct of listed companies is given to the government body, the CSRC, not the stock exchanges.[253] As a result, the stock exchanges are unable to swiftly impose liability on companies that have issued misstatements.[254]

Furthermore, the supervisory functions of the CSRC and the stock exchanges are not clearly divided. The CSRC, in practice, has considerable power to intervene in the securities market and its transactions.[255] Moreover, to be eligible to be listed on a stock exchange, a company must obtain approval from the CSRC.[256] In other words, a stock exchange cannot finally determine whether a company should be granted admission. Nevertheless, the stock exchanges provide listing requirements, and companies have to meet these requirements to qualify to trade on these stock exchanges.

The stock exchanges are closer to the securities market than any government body could be, and are better placed to receive market information. Hence, it is desirable to fully implement a self-regulatory capacity within China's stock exchanges. Furthermore, the self-regulation approach is more acceptable and business friendly to listed companies. Put simply, China needs to determine how to enhance the self-regulatory function of its stock exchanges, or suffer continued inefficiency.

The lack of efficient regulation over the securities market and business represents another serious problem that is hindering the healthy development of the securities market.[257] China does not have detailed legislation regulating securities transactions, protecting investors and supervising securities services. The current *Securities Law* provides general principles relating to securities markets and transactions, but it leaves many issues to be remedied. These loopholes allow undesirable dealings on the market and increase difficulties in enforcing the *Securities Law* and other regulations. For example, the *Securities Law* does not provide civil remedies that could be made available to victims of insider trading.[258] It only provides that the insider may receive a fine of a specific amount.[259] Regarding disclosure, the law states that a company has the duty to make complete and actual

---

251   *Ibid.*

252   *Ibid.*

253   *Ibid. See* also Securities Law, *supra* note 82, art. 167. "The securities regulatory authority under the State Council shall perform the following functions in regulating the securities market: …(7) according to law, to investigate and deal with violations of laws and administrative regulations concerning the regulation of the securities market."

254   *See* Jin *supra* note 227, at 201.

255   *Ibid*, at 201–2.

256   *See* the People's Congress, *supra* note 89, sec. 10.

257   *See* Chen, *supra* note 36, at 138, 199.

258   *See* Lu, *supra* note 129, at 2.

259   *See* the People's Congress, *supra* note 89, sec. 202.

disclosure.[260] It seems, however, that the law neglects to require companies to make timely disclosure – disclosure within a prescribed time.[261] Because of such gaps in the legislation, market misconduct is not dealt with efficiently.[262] Efforts need to be made to further complete the securities legislation.

It is noteworthy that in China, many incidents of market misconduct are connected to poor corporate governance. The volatility of the securities market is frequently associated with corporate governance problems.[263] This distinguishes the Chinese securities market from more mature markets. Many listed Chinese companies still experience insider control problems.[264] In China, insider control problems usually result from the shareholding structure in its state-controlled listed companies.[265] Most listed companies are corporatized, state-owned, or controlled enterprises with the state being the dominant shareholder.[266] Minority shareholders in those companies do not have the power to change the management nor the boards.[267] The state, as the dominant shareholder, has to rely on its agents to exercise its shareholders' rights.[268] The directors of these companies are appointed by the relevant authorities or state agents. There are opportunities for directors to entrench themselves in their positions and make themselves *de facto* owners of the companies.[269] As insiders, once they seize control of the company, they may pursue private goals other than maximizing shareholders' interests. For example, insiders may excessively increase their remuneration and other private benefits without fear of intervention from other shareholders. Moreover, members of the supervisory board in such companies may also be insiders.[270] Such a supervisory board cannot efficiently exercise supervision over its management. In many cases, poor corporate governance leads to misconduct on the securities market, and *insider trading* has become the typical example.[271] Insiders deal with the securities of their own companies based on undisclosed, price sensitive information, or supply the information to other parties.

---

260   "The documents for the issuing and listing of shares or corporate bonds announced by companies shall be truthful, accurate and complete; they may not contain any falsehoods, misleading statements or major omissions." *See* People's Congress, *supra* note 89, sec. 59.

261   *See* Li Shiping, Case Studies of Essential Issues Concerning the Securities Law 47–8 (Beijing: China Economics Press, 2001).

262   *See* Baisan Xie and Meiting Lu, *The Pricing Approaches of IPO in Some other Countries and the Arduous Reforms of Issuance of New Shares in China*, Xie, *supra* note 249, at 175.

263   *See* Jin, *supra* note 227, at 217.

264   *See* Wei, *supra* note 6, at 120.

265   *Ibid.*

266   *Ibid.*

267   *Ibid.*

268   *Ibid.*

269   *Ibid*, at 117.

270   *Ibid*, at 120–21.

271   *See* Jin, *supra* note 227, at 217.

Recent years have seen the emergence of a few privately owned and listed companies in China.[272] Such companies are usually in the hands of a single individual or family. In such a company, the dominant shareholder may obtain excessive personal profit by exploiting minority shareholders.[273] It appears that both state-controlled companies and individual or family-controlled companies have troubles in adhering to the ethical practice of corporate governance.[274] Improving corporate governance of listed companies has become the Chinese government's most imperative task in business.

China has much to do to improve its securities practice and regulation. Thus, its securities system is still in the process of development. How China will shape its securities regime is an issue stimulating much interest.

Different jurisdictions have different styles of securities regulation. The divergence of securities regulation and practices illustrates the fact that different social, political, economic, and historical environments foster different systems of securities regulation and practice, suitable to the specific circumstances. In some cases, differences merely lie in technical divergences. Experiences in different systems provide valuable resources for the Chinese to use for reference in order to find their own path of developing an efficient fund-raising mechanism for their newly corporatized state-owned enterprises and their fledgling private enterprises. At the moment, some people conjecture that China is following suit with the United States, while others predict that the German-Japanese bank-based model will finally be accepted by the Chinese.

Will China Follow the US Path?

Current US regulation of the securities market can be traced to ancient England.[275] However, the UK securities market is no longer the largest.[276] The privilege of maintaining the largest securities market and the most influential securities regulatory regime is claimed by the United States.[277]

---

272   "[About] 20% of the 1259 companies are private firms, without the State being the controlling shareholder." *See* Zhiwu Chen, *Capital Market and Legal Development: the China Case*, 11 (2003), available at <http://icf.som.yale.edu/research/china/files/Cap ital%20Markets%20and%20Legal%20Development.pdf>. *See* also Dr. John D. Sullivan, *Corporate Governance and the Market System*, available at <http://www.cipe.org/china/-keynotes.htm>.

273   *See* Wenkui Zhang, *The Role of China's Securities Market in SOE Reform and Private Sector Development*, 6–7, available at <http://www.tcf.or.jp/data/20020307-08_ Wengkui_Zhang.pdf>.

274   *See* Wei, *supra* note 6, at 198–200.

275   *See* Louis Loss and Joel Seligman, Fundamentals of Securities Regulation 1 (New York: Aspen Publishers, 2004).

276   *See* Amir Licht, *David's Dilemma: A Case Study of Securities Regulation in a Small Open Market*, 2 Theoretical Inquiries Law 673 and 684 (2001).

277   *Ibid.*

Current securities regulation in the United States is the result of long-term development and oftentimes painful experience.[278] In the beginning, the US securities market was not adequately regulated.[279] After World War I, vast sums of money were being invested into the securities market.[280] Consequently, share prices were pushed to an historical high and created a "bubble" in securities investment.[281] The bubble burst, numerous corporations collapsed, and the whole country slipped into economic depression.[282] The *Securities Act* of 1933 and the *Securities Exchange Act* of 1934 were enacted primarily to bring activities on the securities market under close control.[283]

The *Securities Act* of 1933 focused markedly on public distribution of securities.[284] It required companies to disclose necessary information when issuing securities to the public.[285] The *Securities Exchange Act* of 1934 gave the SEC power to regulate all aspects of the securities industry, as well as to investigate and punish illegal dealings.[286] It regulated insiders' transactions in securities, proxy solicitations, and tender offers; provided anti-fraud provisions, and prohibited manipulation in securities dealings.[287]

One of the most distinctive features of US securities regulation is the development of rigorous securities laws and rules.[288] The securities market and its transactions are under close regulatory surveillance[289] and a strong legal regime, separate from the Corporations Code, exists over securities.[290] Historically, the power of making corporations law has been entrenched in state jurisdictions due to constitutional implications.[291] In efforts to attract more corporations to their own

---

278   *See generally* Joel Seligman, The Transformation of Wall Street: A History of the Securities and Exchange Commission and Modern Corporate Finance (New York: Aspen, 2003).

279   *Ibid*, at 349.

280   *Ibid*, at 1–2.

281   *Ibid*, at 2–3.

282   *See* John P. Caskey, The Revolution of the Philadelphia Stock Exchange: 1964–2002 8 (Research Department Federal Reserve Bank of Philadelphia, Working Paper No. 03-21, 2003).

283   *See* the SEC, *The Laws that Govern the Securities Industry*, available at <http://www.sec.gov/about/laws.shtml>.

284   *See* David L. Ratner and Thomas Lee Hazen, Securities Regulation in A Nutshell 34 (St. Paul, Minnesota: West Group, 2002).

285   Securities Act of 1933, 15 U.S.C. §§ 77a–8lll (2004); *See* also the SEC, *supra* note 283.

286   Securities Exchange Act of 1934, 15 U.S.C. §§ 78a–8mm (2004).

287   *Ibid*.

288   *See* Alfred F. Conard, Corporations in Perspective 39 (New York: The Foundation Press 1976).

289   *Ibid*, at 42.

290   *Ibid*, at 46.

291   *Ibid*, at 22, 41–2.

states, the states initially raced to produce relaxed rules for corporate operation in their jurisdictions.[292] The federal attempt at securities regulation followed.[293] The question facing the states was whether they were willing to impose stringent securities regulation on corporations in their jurisdiction at the risk of driving corporations to incorporate elsewhere.[294] For regulating securities effectively, it was necessary to establish a strong securities regulatory regime at the federal level.[295] Accordingly, the *Securities Act* of 1933 and the *Securities Exchange Act* of 1934 became federal law.

The spirit of US securities laws is disclosure.[296] The *Securities Act* of 1933 requires the issuer of securities to file timely a registration statement with the SEC before issuing new securities.[297] Disclosure is made by including relevant statements in the prospectus and registering those statements with the SEC.[298] The *Securities Exchange Act* of 1934 requires periodic reports from the issuers,[299] as well as requiring the issuing companies to file a statement disclosing their shareholdings.[300]

Another distinctive aspect of US securities regulation is that it established an efficient, hierarchical system of regulatory bodies.[301] At the apex of the regulatory system is the SEC, the administrator of the *Securities Act* of 1933, the *Securities Exchange Act* of 1934, and five other securities statutes.[302] The SEC is an administrative agent of the US government and has legislative, executive, and judicial functions.[303] It has the power to enact rules and regulations for implementing the securities laws, including the *Securities Act* of 1933 and the *Securities Exchange Act* of 1934.[304] It enforces securities laws and regulations, investigates violation of the laws and regulations, and pursues legal actions against violators.[305] Beneath the SEC are the self-regulation bodies including stock

---

292   *See* Liggett Co. v. Lee, 288 U.S. 517, 558–9 (1933) (Brandeis, J., dissenting) (noting that "[c]ompanies were early formed to provide charters for corporations in states where the cost was lowest and the laws least restrictive. The states joined in advertising their wares. The race was one not of diligence but of laxity").

293   *See* Conard, *supra* note 288, at 22.

294   *Ibid*, at 42.

295   *Ibid*.

296   *See* Marc I. Steinberg, Understanding Securities Law 1 (USA: Lexis Nexis Matthew Bender, 1996).

297   *Securities Act* of 1933, 15 U.S.C. § 77e (2004).

298   *Ibid*.

299   *Securities Exchange Act* of 1934, 15 U.S.C. § 78m (2004).

300   *Securities Exchange Act* of 1934, 15 U.S.C. § 78p (2004).

301   *See* Lin Yie, Securities Law 56–7 (Beijing: People's University Press, 2000).

302   *See* Steinberg, *supra* note 296, at 2.

303   *See* the SEC, *supra* note 150.

304   *Ibid*.

305   *Ibid*.

exchanges and the National Association of Securities Dealers, Inc.[306] The base of the regulatory hierarchy comprises the supervisory bodies of listed companies.[307] Hence, the United States has adopted a regulatory system of central administration based on the self-regulation groundwork.

The US influence is evident throughout China's securities system and legislation. China has established a US-style regulatory regime over its securities system.[308] Like the United States, the Chinese securities regulations are provided in a separate code. The code itself models the US securities law in many aspects.[309] For instance, it emphasizes transparency and prevention of market manipulation and forbids the involvement of commercial banks in securities investments.[310] China has also established a concentrated regulatory and administrative system over securities markets and business, which resembles the US regulatory system. The CSRC's functions are similar to those of the SEC.[311] In addition, the Chinese are calling for further importation of the US principles and constraints in areas of disclosure, investor protection, and regulating securities companies.[312]

Nevertheless, it is too early to say that a US-style securities system will take root in China. Significant differences exist in the corporate systems of the two countries. In China, the most important and well-performing companies remain wholly owned by the state, and their shares cannot be traded on the stock

---

306   *Ibid.*

307   *See* Maureen O'Hara, *Searching for a New Centre: US Securities Markets in Transition*, Q4 the Federal Reserve Bank of Atlanta Economic Review 47 (2004).

308   *See* Daniel M. Anderson, *Taking stock in China: Company disclosure and information in China's stock markets*, Geo. L.J., (June 2000), available at <http://www.findarticles.com/p/articles/mi_qa3805/is_200006/ai_n8889116>.

309   When drafting the Securities Law, China's legislators closely studied US, Japanese, and Taiwanese legislation, and drew inspiration from their experiences. Japanese and Taiwanese securities laws are all substantially influenced by US legislation. *See generally* Zhipan Wu, *Seeing the Designation of the Administrative System of Securities Business Through the Definition of Securities,* in Wu and Bai, *supra* note 180, at 4; *see also* Bing Peng, *The US Experience in Regulating Conflicts of Interests of Stock Brokers*, in Wu and Bai, *supra* note 180, at 119.

310   Since 1995, the United States has relaxed the rules that forbid banks' involvement in securities investments. Japan has followed suit.

311   *See* Chao Wang, *Redesigning China's Regulatory System over Securities Business in Law*, in Wu and Bai, *supra* note 180, at 35.

312   *See* relevant discussions in Zhenzhong Huang, Civil Litigation and Remedies in US Securities legislation (Beijing: Law Press, 2003); Xuejun Sheng, Research on Disclosure System in Securities Business (Beijing: Law Press, 2004); *see also* Liang Yang, *A Comparison of the Regulatory Systems of the Capital Adequacy of Securities Companies*, in Wu and Bai, *supra* note 180, at 143–64.

exchanges.[313] These companies rely substantially on state banks for finance.[314] Conversely, the largest US companies are all listed public companies. Large Chinese companies usually have the state as the dominant shareholder, while large US companies have dispersed shareholdings. Furthermore, in China, not all shares are freely transferable.[315] State shares and legal person shares are only allowed to be transferred among state-owned companies or legal persons.[316] They are not tradable on the securities market.[317] As a result, only 34.13 percent of the total issued shares are freely tradable on the securities market.[318]

China's current situation of corporate development and its policy of keeping important trades and companies under state control suggest that the country's aspiration to develop a US-style securities market is constricted by its social, political, and economic systems. It may, therefore, be more desirable for China to promote the role of its banks in corporate finance at the present stage, and to gradually carry out the transition from a bank-based system to a US-style market-based system.[319]

Can any Inspiration be Drawn from the German Experience?

In Germany, it is not a popular practice for companies to raise funds by issuing securities on the securities market.[320] Historically, German banks have been the main source of corporate finance in the country.[321] Banks charge a low interest rate on bank loans[322] and usually underwrite the shares of companies.[323] Consequently,

---

313 *See* Wei, *supra* note 6, at 197. *See also* Erika Leung, Lily Liu, Lu Shen, Kevin Taback and Leo Wang, *Financial Reform and Corporate Governance in China*, MIT Sloan School of Management 50th Anniversary Proceedings 11, 14, 15 (Cambridge Massachusetts, June 2002). *See also* Stephen C. Thomas and Ji Chen, *Privatizing China: The Stock Markets and Their Role in Corporate Reform*, 58 China Business Review (1 July 2004) (book review) (2004 WLNR 11626777).

314 *See* Wei, *supra* note 6, at 202.

315 *See* Xinhua News Agency, Poor Governance Blamed for Securities Market, at http://english.people.com.cn/-200504/03/eng20050403_179230.html. *See* also Chengxi Yao, Stock Market and Futures Market in the People's Republic of China 18 (1998).

316 *Ibid.*

317 *Ibid.*

318 *See* Zhiguo Han, *The Mechanisms of Development and Innovation of China's Corporate Economy*, 1 Securities Law Review 320 (2001).

319 *See* David Eu, *Financial Reforms and Corporate Governance in China*, 34 Columbia Journal of Transnational Law 472 (1996).

320 *See* Robert Edesess, *The End of Innocence: An Actual Knowledge Threshold for Intermediaries Holding Fiduciaries/Clients' Assets*, 2 DePaul Business and Commercial Law Journal 377, 418 and 19 (2004).

321 *See* Wei, *supra* note 6, at 142.

322 *See* Economist Intelligence Unit, Country Commerce Germany § 9.1 (2004), available at 2004 WLNR 13986210.

323 *See* Cheffins, *supra* note 172, at 498.

Germany has a less active securities market and fewer listed companies than both the United States and the United Kingdom.[324]

Historically, debentures were subject to double taxation. Shareholders had to pay tax on the dividends they received, after the companies had been taxed on the profits out of which the dividends had been paid.[325] Loan interest, however, was not taxed in this fashion.[326] As a result, many investors chose to deposit their money in a bank, rather than invest in securities. This was also an important factor which negatively affected the vitality of the securities market in Germany.[327] The German experience is in contrast with other major modern economic regimes such as the United States and the United Kingdom, but shares some common characteristics with the Japanese financial system.[328]

At a time when nations are fiercely competing for capital investment, Germany has gradually shown interest in the idea of enhancing the function of the securities market in corporate development.[329] Since the 1970s, Germany reduced the tax rate on dividends[330] and took important steps to establish US-style regulation of the securities market.[331]

In China, some scholars are contemplating the benefits of promoting a banks-based financial system or a hybrid system that combines the strengths of banks and markets.[332] Presently, Chinese banks are generally prohibited from engaging in speculative activities.[333] The core reasons behind the policy mainly include:

---

324   *See* Edward S. Adams, *Corporate Governance After Enron and Global Crossing: Comparative Lessons for Cross-National Improvement*, 78 Indiana Law Review 723, 761 (2003).

325   *See* Sigurt Vitols, *The Transition from Banks to Markets in the German and Japanese Financial Systems* 10 (Working Group on Insts., States, and Mkts., Discussion Paper No. P 02-901, 2002).

326   *See* Yie, *supra* note 301, at 62–4.

327   *See* Caroline Fohlin, *Regulation, Taxation, and the Development of the German Universal Banking System*, 6 European Review of Economic History 221, 252 (2002).

328   Both German and Japanese financial systems are bank-based. In that sense, the two systems have certain common characteristics. *See generally* Sigurt Vitols, *The Origins of Bank-Based and Market-Based Financial Systems: Germany, Japan and the United States* (Discussion Paper FS 101–302). *See generally* Vitols, *supra* note 325.

329   *See* Vitols, *supra* note 325, at 18.

330   *See* Francene M. Augustyn, *A Primer for Incorporating Under the Income Tax Laws of France, Germany, or the United Kingdom*, 7 Northwestern Journal of International Law and Business 267, 281 (1985).

331   *See* Vitols, *supra* note 325, at 12.

332   *See*, for example, Amy Wu, *PRC's Commercial Banking System: Is Universal Banking a Better Model?* 37 Columbia Journal of Transnational Law 623, 633 (1999).

333   *See* the People's Congress, the 1995 Commercial Banking Law of the People's Republic of China, sec. 43, *reprinted in* Asia Law and Practice, Commercial Banking Law in the PRC: Establishing a Foreign Commercial Banking Operation in China 68 (1995).

- First, to protect the customers of banks.[334] If banks were allowed to participate in stock market activities, they would be likely to invest in high risk and high return businesses. With funds locked in such investments, banks might be unable to perform their primary function of repaying principal and interest on time. In addition, when the companies in which the banks hold shares or other securities experience difficulties, the depositors would be likely to withdraw their money from the banks, in the fear that the banks could be adversely affected. This would, in turn, trigger a series of crises. In order to protect the depositors of banks, it is necessary to separate banks from the securities market;
- Second, to avoid amplification of risks.[335] Banks are likely to rescue poorly performing companies in which they themselves hold securities by continuing to purchase the securities of these companies, in order to avoid losses. Or the banks may want to help out the companies by making loans to them. Such decisions would not be made in the best interests of the depositors. Furthermore, such actions of the banks would increase the risk to investments; and
- Third, to avoid the banks' conflicts of interests.[336] When banks perceive difficulty of assisting the companies by taking further securities, they may encourage their customers to purchase securities of the companies in which the banks themselves hold securities. Such behavior could shatter public confidence in banks.

On the other hand, many in China see the benefits of banks' involvement in the securities business and in corporate finance generally. It has been pointed out that the advantages of including banks in the securities business definitely outweigh the disadvantages.[337] Forbidding banks to participate in securities activities is a very expensive method of avoiding the risks that banks' participation could bring to securities business.[338] An absolute restriction of banks' involvement in securities business would bring economic inefficiency.[339] Cheaper methods should be used to avoid or mitigate such risks. Bank participation in securities activities can reduce costs of services and encourage competition. When banks strategically invest their money in different trades and companies, their ability to withstand risks is actually strengthened.[340] Most importantly, bank participation in the securities business

---

334   *See* Pan Pan, *Legal Restrictions on the Right of Commercial Banks in Making Securities Investments, in* Wu and Bai, *supra* note 180, at 50.

335   *Ibid,* at 50–51.

336   *Ibid,* at 50.

337   *Ibid,* at 72.

338   *See,* for example, Wu, *supra* note 332, at 630.

339   *See* Pan Pan, *supra* note 334, at 72.

340   *See* Art Alcausin Hall, *International Banking Regulation into the 21st Century: Flirting with Revolution,* 21 New York Law School Journal of International and Comparative Law 41, 74 (2001).

would enhance the competitive capacity of China's enterprises in the international market.

Since China's entry into the WTO, Chinese enterprises and financial institutions have been further exposed to international competition.[341] Chinese banks should play a more strategic role in supporting national enterprises and protecting national industries. In the meantime, Chinese banks face challenges from foreign banks.[342] Further restricting Chinese banks' business activities could do them more harm than good. Therefore, the German experience of establishing a bank-based financial system and gradually introducing market factors does seem a useful reference for the Chinese.

Conclusions

The development of the securities market since 1978 in China has been driven by two primary purposes: first, to utilize domestic savings to facilitate social funds and private companies; and second, to establish a modern corporate governance system in the listed companies.

Significant achievement has been made. Within ten years, China established two national stock exchanges, enacted the *Securities Law* and a number of relevant regulations, and founded the administrative body, the CSRC. By 2000, about 1,211 Chinese companies were listed on domestic and international stock exchanges.[343] The total amount of capital traded on the two national exchanges accounted for 50 percent of China's GDP.[344]

Despite these achievements, the development of the Chinese securities business has also unearthed some serious regulatory and practical problems, inherent in the securities business in China. The accumulation of those problems has markedly contributed to the current stock market slump. It is time for the Chinese to think purposefully and plan the future development of the securities market carefully. First of all, China must address the question: should China follow the US model by developing a sophisticated securities market as the main resource of corporate finance? It seems that Chinese securities law and practice have been substantially influenced by US laws and practice. Yet, in the process of building a modern corporate system and a financial system, China has faced different social, political, and economic challenges and has followed its own path of development. China's particular social, political, and economic situations suggest that China may not wholeheartedly embrace a US style of corporate financial system and securities

---

341   *See China's Resource Bid*, Editorial, The Globe and Mail (22 October 2004) at A18.

342   *See* Brian Kelleher, *Foreign Banks Target China*, Australian Banking and Finance (17 November 2004), at 2.

343   *See* Jin, *supra* note 227, at 217.

344   *Ibid*, at 11.

regulatory regime. At the current stage of development, it may be more desirable that China develop a financial system that combines the strengths of the market-based approach and the bank-based approach.

To ensure that the securities market becomes a fair and reasonable trading place for investors, the Chinese government does need to reduce direct governmental intervention to allow the market to operate under market rules. Efforts should also be made to improve the current securities law and corporate governance of listed companies. It is interesting to note that China expected its securities market to promote sound practice of corporate governance in listed companies, to help it speed up the establishment of a modern corporate governance system. It appears that this does not necessarily follow in such a unilateral way. In fact, the development of the securities market and the progress in corporate governance are interactive. The bad practice of corporate governance in listed companies will, sooner or later, have an impact on the efficiency of the securities market. To build a modern corporate governance system, however, China needs to make further efforts to rationalize the shareholding structure in its companies. It needs to curtail inside control and improve its securities regulation.

Chapter 9
Volatility of China's Securities Markets and Corporate Governance

Too many anomalies exist in China's capital market. For example, shares in China's capital market are divided into A shares and B shares. A shares are traded in Reminbi, and B shares in foreign currencies. The price of a company's A shares is always much higher than the price of the same company's B shares. Furthermore, the share prices in the secondary market are unreasonably higher than that in the primary market. In addition, China's capital market is extremely volatile, accompanied by frequent irregularities and widespread breaches of securities regulations. Many are puzzled by these anomalies, and by the fact that despite these anomalies, China's capital market has developed rapidly in the past two decades and investors have enjoyed a relatively high investment return.[1] This chapter aims to explain the causes of the puzzles and proposes solutions by investigating the special social and economic environment in which China's capital market has developed. It analyzes the interaction between corporate governance and market volatility, as well as assessing the impact of corporate governance on the volatility of China's securities market, and examines whether China can accelerate the modernization of governance practice through the securities market. Based on the analyses and finding, it deliberates on controlling the volatility of China's capital market.

The analyses and arguments proceed in four parts. The first part studies the development of China's securities market in the context of its economic reforms, and identifies the factors that have contributed to the irregular fluctuation of the securities market. The second investigates China's capital market regulatory framework. It analyzes how corporate governance interacts with the volatility of the securities market and examines the impact of poor corporate governance on China's securities market. It acknowledges the significance and necessity of governmental regulation, and the perils of excessive governmental intervention. The third looks closely at mechanisms for controlling market volatility in China by investigating past efforts and considering its current options. The final part concludes the discussions of this chapter.

---

1   *See* John Fernald and John H. Rogers, *Puzzles in the Chinese Stock Market*, 84(3) The Review of Economics and Statistics 416–32 (2002).

The Securities Regulation and Corporate Governance in China

The Chinese securities market developed in tandem with its economic and enterprise reforms. In the late 1970s, China initiated economic reforms aimed at restructuring its planned economy into a market economy. The central goal of the economic reforms was to replace the state-owned enterprise system with a modern, corporate system. In 1980, Liaoning Fushun No. 1 Brick Factory issued the first stock shares in post-1949 China.[2] Four years later, Shanghai Feile Acoustics made the first initial public offering.[3] In 1986, the first securities exchange opened and by 1993 the Chinese legislature officially endorsed China's massive corporatization by passing the 1993 *Company Law*. The enactment of the *Company Law* coincided with the establishment of the two national stock exchanges, Shanghai and Shenzhen. China's securities market has performed impressively in the 20 years since its inception, particularly before the July 2001 plunge. The trading value of the two national stock exchanges accounted for 53.79 percent of China's gross domestic product (GDP) in 2000.[4]

Having emerged from the economic reforms of the late 1970s, the Chinese securities market is barely 20 years old. Unlike the developed markets, however, the Chinese capital market fluctuates irregularly, and market volatility follows an erratic pattern.[5] From July 2001 to the end of 2005, China's securities market experienced a serious downturn, nearly freezing the country's equity markets and attracting considerable attention.[6] There have been a significant number of discussions focusing on the crisis and its causes, with commentators identifying and examining many problems in securities regulation and practice.

Many factors contribute to the fluctuation of a securities market: international competition, financial policies and laws, administrative governance, and corporate governance of the listed companies all influence the movements of the securities market. Reports on China's securities market indicate that many incidents of Chinese market misconduct correlate to poor corporate governance.[7] Problems with corporate governance also contribute to the volatility of the securities market. This distinguishes the Chinese securities market from other mature markets

---

2 *See* Carl E. Walter and Fraser J.T. Howie, Privatizing China, The Stock Markets and their Role in Corporate Reform xxii (Singapore: John Wiley & Sons (Asia) Pty. Ltd., 2003).

3 *Ibid*, at xxiii.

4 *See* Meilun Shi, Vice-Chairperson, China Securities Regulatory Commission, Speech at the Conference on Supervising Investment Funds (28 November 2001), available at <http://www.csrc.org.cn/en/jsp/detail.jsp?infoid=-1059880761100&type=CMS.STD>.

5 *See* Dehuan Jin, A Study of Volatility of the Chinese Securities Market and Control 12 (Publishing House of Shanghai University of Finance and Economy, 2003).

6 *See* Qingbo Chen, Securities English 148 (Beijing: China Machine Press, 2003).

7 *See* Zhong Chen, Wind and Cloud on the Securities Market in China 197 (Publishing House of Shanghai University of Transportation, 2000); *see* also Xuejun Sheng, Research on Disclosure System in Securities Business 236 (Law Press, 2004).

where volatility is less extreme and rarely triggered solely by flaws in corporate governance.[8]

There were historical causes for the irregular fluctuation on China's securities market. Initially, China decided to establish the securities market for achieving two primary purposes: (1) to utilize domestic savings to facilitate social funds and private companies; and (2) to discipline the listed companies and accelerate the pace of building a modern corporate governance system.[9] In other words, the Chinese government expected the securities market to play two roles:

First, the Chinese securities market would channel domestic savings to facilitate corporatization. By the 1980s, Chinese domestic savings represented an enormous capital resource, constituting 40 percent of China's GDP.[10] Traditionally, domestic savings could only be deposited at state banks that channeled the money into state-owned enterprises as loans. This method was the least efficient use of the money, because a substantial number of the loans were bad. By channeling them to the securities market instead, the government hoped that domestic savings could be allocated more efficiently.[11] It was expected that allowing and encouraging citizens to invest in securities would increase the likelihood that the money would go to the best performing or most efficient enterprises. These enterprises would, in turn, further advance their economic efficiency.

Second, the securities market would discipline and monitor the newly incorporated state-owned companies. The key task for the Chinese government in establishing a modern enterprise system was introducing modern management mechanisms into China's state-owned enterprises. After experiencing a series of strategies, corporatization represented the only effective method of modernizing China's enterprise system.

New problems did emerge, however, during corporatization and privatization. Although state-owned enterprises were subject to corporatization early on, state ownership in important industries and trades was not challenged. Consequently, the government converted many important state-owned enterprises into wholly state-owned companies, with the state as the sole shareholder, or state-controlled companies, with the state as the dominant shareholder.[12] Following the conversion, insider control became a persistent disease in these newly corporatized companies. The boards of directors and the supervisory boards were all controlled by insiders. This insider control had eroded the supervisory strength over the management in

---

8   *See* Jin, *supra* note 5, at 9 and 216.

9   *See* Chen, *supra* note 6, at 161.

10   *Ibid.*

11   Before, the savings were mainly deposited in state banks and were lent to state-owned enterprises. Many of these state-owned enterprises were loss-making enterprises. The banks' loans were not used in an efficient way.

12   *See* Yuwa Wei, Comparative Corporate Governance: A Chinese Perspective 117 (Kluwer Law International, 2003).

such companies.[13] As a result, the government's plan to systemically introduce sound corporate governance practices into Chinese companies was slow. To minimize insider control problems and promote the establishment of a modern corporate governance system, the Chinese government encouraged state-owned companies to be listed on stock exchanges, primarily to ensure the involvement of minority shareholders in these companies and promote improved governance, transparency and competitiveness.[14]

The situation in privately-owned or privately-controlled companies was no better. Impropriety at shareholder meetings and abuse of power by directors and supervisory boards were frequently reported.[15] The absence of a clear statutory framework, in the form of laws, regulations, and rules for corporate behavior caused these problems. Furthermore, given corporate development's short history in China, corporate participants might not properly understand their roles, rights, and duties.[16]

Despite the government's high expectation of developing an efficient capital market, the securities business in China was by no means prosperous before 1990. Since June 1990, however, citizens in Shanghai, Shenzhen, and other business centers began to show great enthusiasm for share investments. In the early 1990s the market displayed spectacular fluctuations. Record highs were followed by sharp declines. In early 1996 a bull market emerged and the market remained stable for nearly two years. This was followed by another record high which lasted until 2001, when the market once again tumbled and a bearish market surfaced. This bear market lasted about four years until the end of 2005. Since 2006, the market has become bullish again.

Tracing back 20 years' history of the securities market in China, one can see that the securities market frequently experienced volatile fluctuations. When the market fell, the stock exchange index tumbled by up to 79.2 percent, and when the market rose, the stock exchange index increased by more than 138 percent within three days.[17] In a single trading day, the index could rise more than 100 percent or plunge more than 16 percent.[18] Compared with mature markets such as the New York Stock Exchange and the Hong Kong Stock exchange, the Chinese securities market appeared to fluctuate more often and more severely. From 1991 to 2000, the largest single-day increases of the Dow Jones and Hengsheng indexes were 4.98 percent and 18.82 percent respectively, and their largest single-day decreases were 7.183 percent and 13.70 percent respectively.[19]

---

13   *See* the World Bank, China's Management of Enterprise Assets: The State as Shareholder 49 (Report No. 16265-CHA, June 5, 1997).

14   *See* Chen, *supra* note 6, at 161.

15   *See* Wei, *supra* note 12, at 200.

16   *Ibid.*

17   *See* Jin, *supra* note 5, at 9.

18   *Ibid.*

19   *Ibid.*

The uncertainty in securities investments eventually took its toll. China's securities market was fragile between mid-2001 and the end of 2005. China's sluggish stock market during this period posed a huge problem because the Chinese government desperately needed to tap the potential in equity market funding. Bolstering the securities market thus became crucial. Since 2006, although the securities business has become flourishing, the capricious movements of the capital market and widespread breaches have shown the signs of instability and vulnerability. China's economic reforms have entered into a new phase in which setting up social-security funds, on which a modern corporate system is premised, has become the central task. The flourish of social investment funds rely greatly on a prosperous securities market. It is thus crucial to find solutions of controlling irregularities in the capital market in order to maintain investors' confidence. In seeking solutions, it is necessary to examine the causes of irregular volatility in the Chinese securities market.

It is important to note that the volatility of China's securities market has followed an irregular pattern. This irregularity lies in its frequency, range and timing of volatility. Compared with some well-developed markets, the Chinese securities market fluctuates more frequently and sometimes in an illogical fashion. Empirical studies focusing on China's volatile securities market suggest that a lack of regulatory control, changes in financial policies, and poor corporate governance have been the primary cause of the volatility.[20]

In the initial stage of development of the securities market, from 1990 to 1994, speculative conduct and government policies primarily drove market fluctuations. During this period, the number of listed companies with transferable securities available to the public was small. The supply of issued shares fell short of demand. In addition, most Chinese investors were inexperienced and motivated by speculative desire. Consequently, the market fluctuated drastically, characterized by rocketing gains and drastic losses.[21]

Since 1994, market volatility has resulted from a range of complex and interrelated elements, including excessive administrative intervention, the defective legal framework and the remnants of a planned economy that cannot accommodate a securities market.[22] Furthermore, China has also accelerated its financial reforms. The volatility of the securities market has also been influenced by changes in the laws and in financial policies. It is noteworthy that much of the irregular movement in the Chinese securities market is caused by poor corporate governance. Poor corporate governance such as fraudulent disclosure, market manipulation and insider trading leads to increased market volatility.[23] Notorious

---

20 *See* Baisan Xie, Xuelai Dai and Lan Xu, A *Comparative Study of Chinese and US Securities Markets*, in Baisan Xie (*ed.*), International Comparison of Securities Markets 1, 3–4 (Volume 1, Beijing: Qinghua University Press, 2003).

21 *Ibid.*

22 *Ibid*, at 4.

23 *See* Jin, *supra* note 5, at 217.

cases involving false statements, misleading disclosure, insider trading, and market manipulation, such as the Qiong Min Yuan case, the Chengdu Hongguang case, and the Zheng Bai Wen case, have devastated many investors and shaken public confidence in China's domestic market.

The Chinese experience demonstrates the existence of an interactive relationship between corporate governance and securities markets. As part of its efforts to fix the corporate governance problems, China has relied on the monitoring function of the securities market over the management of listed companies. The Chinese government has resolved to use the securities market as leverage to expedite building a modern corporate governance system within its enterprise system.[24] It is believed that the securities market enables corporations to raise capital from a wide range of investors, and to act as a monitoring mechanism over corporate management.

The monitoring function relies on the fact that share prices closely reflect corporate managerial efficiency.[25] Poorly managed companies face the threat of takeover, and the actual occurrence of takeover inevitably replaces the under-performing management team. The takeover threat deters improper behavior and forces the board and management to act in the interests of the corporation.[26] A listed corporation's benefits provide incentives for companies to actively improve their economic and managerial efficiency, if only to satisfy listing requirements and rules under which the exchanges operate.[27] Good corporate governance, in turn, promotes fairness and transparency in the securities business and enables the securities market to function properly.[28]

On the other hand, even though admission to a stock exchange acts as an incentive for sound corporate governance, and the threat of delisting and takeover restrains companies from irresponsible conduct, poor corporate governance practice could hinder the efficient operation of the securities market. The impact of poor corporate governance on the securities market mainly derives from the fact that poorly governed companies are likely to engage in market misconduct. Market misconduct, in turn, may cause confusion and volatility on the securities market. The securities market, as an external corporate governance mechanism, must work in collaboration with

---

24   *See generally* Yuwa Wei, *The Development of the Securities Market and Regulation in China*, 27 (3) Loyola of Los Angeles International and Comparative Law Review (2005).

25   *See* Frank H. Easterbrook and Daniel R. Fischel, The Economic Structure of Corporate Law 18 (Massachusetts: Harvard University Press, 1991). *See generally* also Michael C. Jensen and William H. Meckling, *The Theory of the Firm: Managerial Behavior, Agency Costs and Ownership Structure*, 3 Journal of Financial Economics 305–60 (1976).

26   *See* John C. Coffee Jr., *Regulating the Market for Corporate Control: A Critical Assessment of the Tender Offer's Role in Corporate Governance*, 84 Columbia Law Review 1145–8 (1984).

27   *See* Wei, *supra* note 24, at 483.

28   *See* Pauline O'Sullivan, *Governance by Exit: An Analysis of the Market for Corporate Control*, in Kevin Keasey et al. (*eds*), Corporate Governance: Economic and Financial Issues 122–3 (London: Oxford University Press, 1997).

internal corporate governance mechanisms. For instance, takeovers merely provide an external mechanism for corporate governance and should be employed only as a "last resort", and only after internal mechanisms have failed.[29]

In China, the development of a securities market has helped encourage and promote sound corporate governance practices. Securities regulation and practice play a significant role in China's enterprise reforms. The efforts to monitor the Chinese securities market have been weak, however, because transferable shares account for only a small percentage of issued shares. In the meantime, due to structural defects, regulatory inefficiency and other reasons, many listed companies fail to adhere to good practice of governance practice. Their weaknesses in corporate governance result in rampant misconduct and legal violations in the securities business. This has undermined attempts to reform the Chinese financial sector and enterprise system. Whereas the inefficient capital market has jeopardized China's efforts to promote sound corporate governance in its listed state-owned enterprises, the poor corporate governance of the listed companies has imposed negative impact on the securities market. Promotion of good corporate governance is, therefore, essential, not only to the improvement of China's corporate system, but also to the efficient operation of its securities market.

Volatility of the Securities Market and Corporate Governance

In China, corporate governance has affected the fluctuations of the securities market. Irresponsible corporate conduct on the securities market, stemming from flawed corporate governance practices, has had a great impact on market performance and investor confidence. The volatility of the securities market is frequently associated with problems of corporate governance such as nondisclosure, misleading disclosure, insider trading, and market manipulation. For example, the market may become volatile *before* the publication of price sensitive information but remarkably stays calm *after* the disclosure.[30] In this case, information has been leaked before the official disclosure. Reports suggest that insider control has been a main cause of these corporate governance problems in listed companies.[31]

Information Disclosure

In 1993, the Hainan Minyuan Company was listed on the Shenzhen Stock Exchange. On the first trading day, its share price increased 16 points, from RMB 3.25 yuan to RMB 27.25 yuan.[32] Since then, the performance of the share

---

29   *Ibid.*
30   *See* Jin, *supra* note 6, at 192.
31   *See* Wei, *supra* note 12, at 129.
32   *See* Qilin Fu, Well-Known Cases relating to China's Securities Market in the Past Ten Years 70 (Beijing: Publishing House of China University of Political Science and Law, 2002).

was ordinary. By 1996 the price fell to RMB 2.08 yuan.[33] In January 1997, the company's 1996 annual report was published in the *Securities Times*.[34] The report falsely declared the company made an annual profit of more than RMB 570 million yuan in 1996, and the accumulation funds of the company had increased by RMB 657,330,000 yuan.[35] With the publication of this information, the company's share price increased to RMB 26.18 yuan.[36] In conjunction with the false and materially misleading disclosure, the company had manipulated the market by borrowing from Shenzhen Bank to purchase its own shares at increasing prices. In the meantime, the company and its affiliate, Shenzhen Nonferrous, acquired more than 10 percent of the issued shares. This further boosted the company's capacity to affect the market. In March 1997, the China Securities Regulatory Commission (CSRC) investigated Hainan Minyuan's published claims. The CSRC found that the company had made profits of only RMB 30 million yuan, and that the RMB 657,330,000 yuan increase in accumulation funds was entirely fabricated.[37]

Consequently, the directors and accountant of the Hainan Minyuan Company were found civilly and criminally liable, and the company was subjected to delisting. However, the CSRC eventually decided to suspend the company from trading and restructure it. They worried that a complete delisting would cause a depression of investor confidence or some other crisis for the securities market. Instead of delisting, a new company, Beijing Zhongguancun Technology Development Limited Company, was established. The shareholders of Hanan Minyuan sold their shares in return for an equal number of shares in Beijing Zhongguancun Technology Development.[38]

In the following years, more cases involving nondisclosure and misleading statements were reported, and it appeared that such cases pervaded China's securities market.[39] These cases unveil serious problems in China's securities and corporations regulatory regime and in its corporate-governance system. The disclosure provisions in China's securities laws and regulations are close to those of mature markets such as the United States. Chinese listed companies are required to lodge their annual reports, half-year reports, and quarterly reports with the securities regulatory authority.[40] The law also differentiates between initial

33   *Ibid.*
34   *Ibid.*
35   *Ibid.*
36   *Ibid.*
37   *Ibid*, at 70–71.
38   *Ibid*, at 72.
39   *See* Li Qiang and Liang Han, Cases and Important Issues of Securities Law 12 (Beijing: China Economy Press, 2001).
40   *See* the People's Congress, the 1998 Securities Law of the People's Republic of China (revised in 2005), secs 65 and 66; the People's Congress, the 1994 Company Law of the People's Republic of China (revised in 2005), sec. 146; the CSRC, the 1993 *Detailed Regulations concerning Information Disclosure*, arts 4, 15 and 16; the CSRC, *Standard Contents and Forms of Information Disclosure* (No. 2, 2001); the CSRC, *Standard Contents*

disclosure and continuing disclosure. Matters subject to continuing disclosure include: (1) a major change in the business or business scope of the company; (2) a decision of the company on any major investment or major asset purchase; (3) an important contract concluded by the company, which may have an important effect on the assets, liabilities, rights, interests or business achievements of the company; (4) any incurrence of a major debt in the company or default on an overdue major debt; (5) any incurrence of a major deficit or a major loss in the company; (6) a major change in the external conditions for the business operation of the company; (7) a change concerning the directors, or no less than one-third of the supervisors or managers of the company; (8) a considerable change in the holdings of shareholders or actual controllers who each hold or control no less than 5 percent of the company's shares; (9) a decision of the company on capital decrease, merger, division, dissolution, or application for bankruptcy; (10) Any major litigation involving the company, or where the resolution of the general assembly of shareholders or the board of directors has been cancelled or announced invalid; (11) where the company is involved in any crime, which has been filed as a case as well as investigated into by the judicial organ or where any director, supervisor or senior manager of the company is subject to compulsory measures as rendered by the judicial organ; and (12) any other matter as prescribed by the CSRC.[41] Chinese law forbids false statements, misleading statements, and omissions of important information. The law provides consequences for breaches of these rules. Nevertheless, compared with some mature markets, the Chinese laws regulating information disclosure need further improvement. For instance, the 1998 *Securities Law* (revised in 2005) fails to clarify the rules for disclosure of information concerning related parties and competition.[42] Moreover, serious problems exist in law enforcement, resulting in widespread breaches of the disclosure requirements.

Currently, about 250 laws, regulations, standards, and decrees regulate securities.[43] The 1998 *Securities Law* and 1994 *Company Law* are the primary laws governing securities, stock markets and listed companies. These two laws provide rules yet lack detailed operational provisions. As a result, the CSRC, the Supreme Court, and other authorities have enacted supplementary regulations and provisional rules to deal with practical issues not addressed by these laws. Loopholes in the laws, and the lack of coordination between different laws and regulations increase the difficulty of implementing rules and procedures relating to information disclosure and supervision of China's securities activities.

---

and Forms of Information Disclosure (No. 3, 2002); and Reporting Regulations (No 13, 2002).

41   *See* the People's Congress, the 1998 Securities Law of the People's Republic of China (revised in 2005), sec. 67.

42   *See* Fu, *supra* note 32, at 153.

43   *See* Qiang and Han, *supra* note 39, at 135.

Cases involving false statements reveal defects in the corporate governance of listed Chinese companies. The companies involved in these cases repeatedly made false and misleading statements to the public and the regulatory authority without being questioned by a company supervisory organ. Their shareholders' meetings, supervisory boards, independent directors and internal auditors were totally illusory. Several reasons exist for the malfunctions at the shareholder meetings. Insider control is one primary cause. The shareholding structure of China's state-controlled listed companies offers a typical example. The state is the dominant shareholder in most listed companies. Small or minority shareholders in those companies do not have the power to change management or corporate boards. The state, as the dominant shareholder, has to rely on its agents to exercise its shareholder rights. The relevant authorities or agents of the state appoint the directors. The directors work as representatives of the state's agents and are likely to remain loyal to the department that appointed them. Furthermore, directors may have the opportunity to entrench themselves as *de facto* owners of their companies.[44] Insiders in control of the company can pursue private goals without regard to shareholders' interests. For example, the insiders may excessively increase their compensation and other private benefits without fear of intervention from other shareholders. Moreover, members of the supervisory board (appointed by the same government authorities or agents) are also insiders and, therefore, do not efficiently supervise the directors.

A few privately owned listed companies in China have emerged in recent years. A single individual or family usually controls or owns these companies. Majority shareholders in such companies can exploit minority shareholders to obtain excessive personal profits. Hence, both state-controlled and individual- or family-controlled companies have trouble adhering to ethical corporate-governance practices. Today, one of the most important tasks for the Chinese government is to improve corporate governance in listed companies by eliminating insider control that allows for deceptive conduct on the securities market.

Shareholders' lack of participation in company affairs also encourages insider control problems. Shareholders, and particularly individual shareholders, in most Chinese companies are passive investors. Shareholder participation, therefore, must be addressed.

Compared with the two-tier board practice in Germany, the supervisory board in China has less ability to monitor management. Unlike Germany, where shareholders meet to elect a supervisory board that then elects directors, in China, company shareholders elect both the supervisory and management board members.[45] In China, the supervisory board may lose considerable power because it does not

---

44   The situation is described as "agents use agents". *See* Wei, *supra* note 12, at 117.

45   *See* Yuwa Wei, *The Historical Development of the Corporation and Corporate Law in China*, 14 Australian Journal of Corporate Law 258.

elect the management board. Insider control further weakens the supervisory board in a state-controlled Chinese company.[46]

The board of directors in a Chinese company makes only business decisions and is not responsible for day-to-day operations.[47] The company's general manager has the power to direct day-to-day operations. In many listed companies, the same person takes both the post of board chairperson and the position of general manager. This practice considerably compromises the board of directors' ability to supervise day-to-day management. Moreover, the law does not clarify the status of internal auditors. Total subjection to a general manager's will substantially weaken an auditor's monitoring power.

Current Chinese corporate and securities law does not provide a set of practicable, comprehensive rules for internal corporate governance. In many cases, the organs of corporate governance do not function effectively. This has, to a certain extent, encouraged misconduct on the securities market.

Some other Chinese social, historical and cultural elements do not accommodate the concept and practice of rational information disclosure. For instance, the traditional Chinese code of conduct conflicts with the norms of modern disclosure. Disclosure is based on the impersonal relationships in a modern, commercialized society. In traditional China, however, transactions were based on personal relationships, and trading rules varied according to the parties' relationship.[48] Disclosure also departs from the concept of "face saving", which retains deep roots in Chinese society.[49]

Insider Trading and Other Market Manipulative Activities

Insider trading occurs when personnel, basing their decisions on undisclosed and price-sensitive information, deal with the securities of their own companies for personal gain, or supply undisclosed information to other parties. Chinese law forbids insider trading. The *Shares Regulations*, *Antifraud Regulations* and the *Securities Law* all stipulate that a person with knowledge of inside information on securities trading or a person who has illegally obtained such inside information must not purchase, sell, or divulge such information, or counsel another person to purchase or sell such securities.[50] A breach may incur pecuniary and administrative

---

46   A state-controlled company is a company in which the state is the dominant shareholder. *See* Wei, *supra* note 12, at 199.

47   *See* the People's Congress, the 1994 Company Law of the People's Rerpublic of China (revised in 2005), secs 47 and 50.

48   *See* Sheng, *supra* note 7, at 262–3.

49   *See* Sheng, *supra* note 7, at 262–3.

50   *See* the State Council, the 1993 *Shares Regulations*, art. 72; the State Council, the 1993 *Antifraud Regulations*, arts 3, 5 and 6; and sec. 202 of the 1998 Securities Law (revised in 2005).

penalties.[51] Illegal income is subject to disgorgement, and a fine up to five times the illegal income may be imposed on the insider.[52] In the case where the wrongdoer is an entity, the person-in-charge of the entity and any other person directly responsible may be given a warning and imposed a fine up to 300,000 yuan.[53]

According to Chinese law, insiders are persons who possess or have illegally obtained knowledge of inside information on securities trading. Persons subject to insider-trading law include: (1) directors, supervisors, managers, deputy managers, and other senior management personnel in a company that issues shares or bonds; (2) shareholders who hold at least 5 percent of the shares in the company; (3) the holding company, as well as the directors, supervisors and senior management of the holding company of the issuer; (4) persons with access to securities-trading information by virtue of their positions in the company; (5) staff members of the securities regulatory authority, and other persons who administer securities issuance and transaction pursuant to their statutory duties; (6) the relevant personnel of recommendation institutions, securities companies engaging in underwriting, stock exchanges, securities registration and clearing institutions and securities trading service organizations; and (7) other persons specified by the securities regulatory authority under the State Council.[54] Persons illegally obtaining inside information include those who obtain it by defrauding, monitoring, bugging, and stealing, through private dealings, extortion, or other methods.[55] The law does not, however, address whether insider-trading provisions apply when a person is no longer an insider at the time of trading. In addition, the law does not prohibit a tippee from trading securities.[56]

The deterrent effect of China's law forbidding insider trading is limited. Insider trading and other market-manipulating activities are reported to be widespread.[57] However, due to the lack of practicability of the early laws in handling insider trading, the covert nature of insider trading activities, and the difficulty of proof, only a limited number of cases was investigated and dealt with accordingly by the regulatory authorities in the past fifteen years. These cases include the Huayang company and Longgang company case, the Xiangfan Agricultural Bank Case, the Zhangjiajie Tourist company case, the Southern Securities company versus the

---

51   *See* the People's Congress, *supra* note 41, sec. 202.

52   *Ibid.*

53   *Ibid.*

54   *See* the People's Congress, *supra* note 41, sec. 74.

55   *See* the State Council, the 1993 *Provisional Methods of Prohibiting Securities Fraudulence*, art. 4.

56   *See* Legal Dictionary (defining tippee as person who receives tip), available at <http://www.answers.com/library/Legal %20Dictionary;jsessionid=315obodddmmog-cid-447479963-sbid-lc01a>.

57   Nearly every share has a speculator or has some element of insider trading associated with it. *See* Xiaoke Hu, Preliminary Study on the Prohibition System of Securities Fraud 250 (Beijing: Economy and Technology Press, 2004).

Beida Motor corporate group case, the Wang Chuan case, the Dai Lihui case,[58] the Yu Meng Wen case,[59] and the Gao Fa Shan case. These cases commonly involved dealing with securities based on inside information by dominant shareholders, senior managerial personnel including directors, chairpersons, and general managers in listed companies.

The Huayang company and Longgang company case happened in 1993. It was not only the first case involving insider trading, but also the earliest case concerning hostile takeover. Huayang and Longgang were two subsidiaries of the Bao-an Shanghai company. The three companies repeatedly aqcuired the shares of the Yanzhong company. By 29 September 1993, the three companies had acquired 10.65 percent of the total shares in Yanzhong, greatly exceeding the allowed percentage stipulated in the law.[60] While none of the three companies made necessary disclosure, on 30 September, Bao-an Shanghai purchased an additional 1,147,700 shares from a related party, bringing the total shareholdings of the Bao-an corporate group to 17.07 percent. At the same time, the related party sold 246,000 shares to the public. By then, the Bao-an corporate group, for the first time, disclosed the information about their shareholdings in Yanzhong by publishing an announcement. Soon, the Bao-an corporate group acquired another 2.73 percent of Yanzhong's shares, and became a significant shareholder holding 19.80 percent of the total shares in Yanzhong.[61] Bao-an Shanghai subsequently exercised its large shareholder's rights to inspect the books of Yanzhong and to call a shareholder meeting to change the company's business plan and the composition of the board. Yanzhong reacted strongly once being aware of the fact and claimed that the Bao-an group had acquired a majority of its shares through illegal methods and thus refused to accommodate requests of Bao-an Shanghai.[62]

The CSRC investigated the case and ruled that Bao-an Shanghai breached the law in the course of acquiring Yanzhong's shares. Bao-an Shanghai was fined RMB 1 million yuan.[63] In this case, the Bao-an corporate group engaged in nearly every prohibited securities activity including non-disclosure, insider trading, and illegal acquisition.

---

58   In 1997, the Sichuan Changzheng Company and the Sichuan Tuopu Technology Development Company planned to restructure the main business of Sichuan Changzheng. Dai Lihui was the executive director of Sichuan Tuopu Technology Development at that time. He took advantage of the inside information and purchased 572,600 shares of Sichuan Changzheng, earning considerable profits. *See* Fu, *supra* note 32, at 211.

59   Yu Meng Wen was an officer of the Pan Zhi Hua Iron and Steel Company. He utilized the inside information that Pan Zhi Hua was going to issue new A shares following a restructure scheme and gained RMB 80,000 yuan in illegal profits. *See* Fu, *supra* note 32, at 222.

60   *See* the Editor, *The Legal Framework of the Credibility of Listed Companies*, available at <http://www.xingzhi.org/law/civillaw/6538_3.html>.

61   *Ibid.*

62   *Ibid.*

63   *See* Fu, *supra* note 32, at 383.

The Wang Chuan case was a typical example of senior managerial personnel dealing with securities based on inside information. Wang Chuan was the Vice Chairperson of the board of Beijing Beida Fangzhen corporate group. In February 1998, the corporate group lodged an application with the CSRC for equity participation in Shanghai Yanzhong group. Based on this inside information, Wang Chuan purchased 68,000 shares of Yanzhong in February and made RMB 610,000 yuan by selling the shares on the market two months later. He was fined RMB 100,000 yuan and his illegal profits were confiscated.[64]

The case of the Southern Securities company versus the Beida Motor corporate group involved a company and a senior officer trading the securities of another company based on insider information. Mr Xiong Shuangwen was the Vice Chairperson of the Southern Securities company. In October 1996, he visited Beida Motor and spoke with the Chairperson, Vice Chairperson and the general manager of the company. The officers then gave him information about Beida Motor's business operation. They told Xiong Shuangwen that each share of Beida Motor would make RMB 0.60 yuan profits and the company planned to issue a significant amount of new shares soon. The parties agreed that Southern Securities would act as the main consignee of the shares of Beida Motor. Southern Securities and Xiong Shuangwen then borrowed large sums of money to speculate Beida Motor's shares. By January 1997, Southern Securities and Xiong Shuangwen controlled 15.62 percent of transferable shares in Beida Motor. The price of Beida Motor then doubled. In the end, Southern Securities earned RMB 74,558,900 yuan net profits and Beida Motor earned RMB 850,000 yuan net profits. The CSRC found that both companies had breached the *Anti-Fraud* and *Shares Regulations*.[65]

Chinese law also forbids market manipulation activities. The 1998 *Securities Law* prohibits such activities as wash sales, match orders, manipulation by actual purchases, pool operation, corners, and false rumors.[66] Market manipulation on several occasions caused irregular volatility on China's securities market, exemplified by the Su San Shan case. In that case, Mr Dingxing Li negotiated a loan with a company, using the money to purchase Su San Shan shares listed on Shenzhen Stock Exchange at prices of RMB 9.60 yuan and RMB 9.85 yuan. The share price fell. To recover his loss, Li forged a company seal and disseminated documents from the non-existing company to several journals and newspapers to publish information that the company held more than 5 percent of Su San Shan.[67]

---

64   *Ibid*, at 205.

65   *See* Fu, *supra* note 32, at 226–9.

66   *See* the People's Congress, *supra* note 41, secs 77, 78 and 79; the State Council, *supra* note 55, arts 7 and 8; and the State Council, the *Shares Regulations*, art. 74.

67   *See* the People's Congress, the 1998 Securities Law of the People's Republic of China, sec. 79. The law required an investor who had more than 5 percent of the shares in a company to disclose the information.

On the first trading day following the publications, the Su San Shan share price increased from RMB 8.30 yuan to RMB 11.50 yuan.[68]

Another notorious case of manipulation involved misconduct by four companies all holding Yian Technology shares: Guangdong Xinsheng, Zhongbai, Baiyuan, and Jinyi. These companies collaborated on trading Yian Technology shares. By trading amongst themselves, between 1999 and 2001, they created the false trading impression in Yian Technology shares, cornered the market, drove up the price of the shares, and earned a legal profit of RMB 449 million yuan.[69]

The widespread breach of the law prohibiting insider trading and market manipulation again reveals the lack of deterrence in China's securities legal and supervisory regimes. It also reveals corporate governance system deficiencies in Chinese listed companies. In many cases, independent directors and supervisory boards turned a blind eye to insider trading and market manipulative activities by executive directors and officers, or negligently failed to notice the irregularities inside their companies.

When Yian Technology shares rocketed from RMB 26 yuan to RMB 126 yuan within 70 trading days, a reasonable person could sense price manipulation. This did not, however, alarm any securities supervisory or regulatory authority, suggesting lax securities law enforcement. This observation is particularly true when considering remedial aspects relating to securities market misconduct. Commentators point out that in many cases the misconduct of listed companies and responsible individuals has been punished lightly.[70] Moreover, before 2002, there was not a single case where a securities investor victim of market misconduct received a remedy. During this time, China's courts made several unusual legal judgments relating to remedies. In 1999, for example, the Chengdu Gongguan company was found liable for making false statements and engaging in deceptive conduct, and the responsible directors and officers were sentenced and fined. The court, however, rejected an investor's claim for damages on the ground that the court lacked jurisdiction over such cases.[71] Even more unusual, in September 2001, the Supreme Court of China decreed *Some Rules about Hearing False Statements on the Securities Market*, which stated that because of legislative ambiguity and a lack of limited enforcement resources, the court would not hear civil cases relating to insider trading, false or misleading statements, or market manipulation. The Supreme Court first advised that the problems in such cases were usually caused by some factors relevant to economic reforms and organizational restructure, and thus had to be solved through a number of different mechanisms and strategies.

Furthermore, the statute has not provided adequate guidance for investors' civil compensation. Most 1998 *Securities Law* provisions (revised in 2005) stipulating

---

68   *See* Qiang and Han, *supra* note 39, at 234–6.

69   *Ibid*, at 254–6.

70   *See* Hu, *supra* note 57, at 242–3.

71   *See* Zhenzhong Huang, Civil Liability and Civil Litigation in US Securities Law 7 (Beijing: Law Press, 2003).

liability for breach of the law concern administrative sanctions and criminal penalties. The law seldom mentions civil liability for breach.[72] The Supreme Court's decree deciding not to handle civil cases concerning misleading disclosure, insider trading and market manipulation caused an outcry among investors. In 2002, the Supreme Court eventually issued the *Announcement about Hearing Civil Cases Relating to False Statements on the Securities Market*, clarifying that victims in false statement cases could receive civil remedies. Although this provision is a step forward in compensating investors, it does not satisfactorily mitigate securities law defects. In China, law enforcement poses an even more serious problem relating to preventing securities misconduct. The *Announcement* came into effect on 1 February 2003. After the enactment of the *Announcement*, the courts heard a considerable amount of cases involving claims for compensation due to securities breaches. The cases of far-reaching effect included the Daqing Lianyi case, the Lantian case, the Kelong case, the Ying Guang Xia case, and the Dongfang Electron case.

The Daqing Lianyi case was the first case concerning a claim for civil remedies due to securities frauds.[73] In January 2002, Harbin Intermediate People's Court accepted and heard 250 lawsuits against the Daqing Lianyi Petrochemistry company which committed frauds and misleading disclosure in share issuance and transactions.[74] The cases involved 788 shareholders of the company.[75] The claimed amount of the compensation was over RMB 17 million yuan.[76] In the end, 106 cases were settled out of court.[77] The court heard the remaining cases and upheld most of the shareholders' claims. The Daqing Lianyi Petrochemistry company subsequently made 98 appeals to the Higher People's Court of Heilongjiang Province. Nearly all the appeals were dismissed.

The Lantian Case was the first case where an accounting firm was held being jointly and severally liable for disclosing misleading information in a company's prospectus.[78] About 83 Shareholders of the Lantian company brought some lawsuits against the company and the related parties including Hualun Accounting firm for misleading disclosure.[79] In July 2006, Wuhan Intermediate People's Court

---

72 *See generally* the Supreme Court, *Some Rules about Hearing False Statements on the Securities Market* (2003).

73 *See* Jiuguang Zhao, *Important Cases concerning Civil Remedy Claims for Fraudulent Disclosure*, 2 Securities Lawsuits (6 November 2007), available at <http://www.sipf.com.cn/bin/FrontPage?m=s&channelFlag=-CASES&articleId=24352010877F1 1DCA010EECFECFC9828>.

74 *Ibid.*

75 *Ibid.*

76 *Ibid.*

77 *Ibid.*

78 *See* the Editor, *the First Case in Which An Accounting Firm Takes Joint and Severable Liability for Securities Frauds*, Shenyang Daily (3 August 2006), available at <http://news.pinsou.com/news/-2006/8/3/2006831103582203.htm>.

79 *Ibid.*

delivered its decision and held that Hualun Accounting Firm should take joint and several liability for the amount of compensation owed to the plaintiffs.[80]

The Kelong Case was a case in which the parties employed an unprecedented large number of lawyers. The Kelong Electric Appliance company was sued in Guangzhou Intermediate People's Court for misleading disclosure in securities transactions. The number of plaintiffs reached 1,000, and the claimed compensation amount was proximately RMB 100,000 yuan per person.[81] By July 2006, 59 lawyers across 45 law firms in 18 provinces were hired, creating a record of the scale of legal service in a single case in the legal history of the People's Republic of China.[82]

The Ying Guang Xia Case was the first case where share reform strategies were bound with the discharge of a company's civil liability arising from securities lawsuits. In 2004, 103 lawsuits were brought against the Ying Guang Xia company for misleading disclosure in Yinchuan Intermediate People's Court. Before most of the trials started, the company released its share reform plan which proposed to increase the shareholdings of its shareholders. The plan stated that after the share restructure, the non-transferable shareholders would repay the company's debts arising from the lawsuits between the company and its minority shareholders.[83] The plan was approved in March 2006. Since April 2006, some shareholders involved in the lawsuits accepted the court initiated mediation and entered into reconciliation agreements with the company.

The Dongfang Electron Case registered a new record in regard to the number of plaintiffs and the claimed compensation amount. The Dongfang Electron company was sued for disclosing misleading information in its financial reports. Between February 2003 and the end of 2005, 2,716 actions were brought to Qingdao Intermediate People's Court by 6,989 shareholders.[84] The company sought to settle most of the disputes through its share reform plan. In August 2006, the share reform plan was passed by the general meeting.[85] Negotiations and mediations started thereafter.

---

80   *See* Zhao, *supra* note 73.

81   *See* the Editor, *The Lawyers Have Reached the Common Understanding and Kelong and Deqing Are Facing Claims over A Billion Yuan*, Dongfang Morning Paper (24 July 2006), available at <http://www.sonhoo.com/-info/html/2006-7-24/833730.htm>.

82   *Ibid.*

83   *See* the Editor, *Some Shareholders Accepted Compensation after Reconciliation*, East Money (31 March 2006), available at <http://news2.eastmoney.com/060331,386856. html>. *See* also Jiang Yu and Zhun Fu, *The Full Story of Ying Guang Xia's Binding its Share Reforms with Civil Liabilities*, Xinlang Finance (14 December 2007), available at <http:// finance.sina.com.cn/stock/t/20071214/11484292875.shtml>.

84   *See* Hai Du, *The Court Has Resumed the Trial of the Dongfang Electron Case*, Economic Guidance (1 December 2006), available at <http://jjdb.dzwww.com/ xinwen/200612/t20061201_1897981.htm>.

85   *Ibid.*

Overall, China's securities market is still in a development stage. Unlike investors in mature markets Chinese investors are in a vulnerable state. The reputation of China's securities market and its listed companies has been severely tarnished by the rampages of fraudulent and misleading conduct. Such conduct has seriously damaged Chinese investors' confidence in the securities market. A long time may pass before the market can win back the investors' confidence. Public confidence in securities investments depends on a securities system with a combined force of fairness, justice and effectiveness.[86] To build such a securities market system in China, the Chinese government and relevant authorities must strive to improve the legal regime regulating securities business, the corporate governance system, and other monitoring mechanisms.

Control of Market Volatility

Between July 2001 and December 2005, the securities market in China experienced a serious downturn. The country's equity markets were nearly frozen.[87] Government plans to raise Social Securities Funds were under threat, and many private companies were adversely affected. Since February 2003, the market was more or less stagnant.

Chinese authorities sought to control the falling market, but their intervention had little effect. For example, Chinese authorities adopted a strategy limiting the size and price of new offerings. A listing application would not be approved if the company sought to raise more than 20 times its earnings.[88] This strategy was impractical because the earnings-related cap was insignificant for companies in

---

86   *See* Hu, *supra* note 57, at 83.

87   *See* China Securities Regulatory Commission, Report on the Development of China's Securities Industry 358 (Beijing: China Finance and Economy Press, 2004).

88   *See* Baisan Xie, *Huge Deficits of Shen Kang Jia Reveal the Serious Problem in the Company's Share Issue*, in Baisan Xie (*ed.*), International Comparison of Securities Markets 180–81 (Volume 1, Qinghua University Press, 2003). Before 1999, new shares were issued at fixed prices. Between 1999 and 2001, China adopted the book-building method in deciding the share prices for initial public offerings. The price of an initial public offering was not fixed at a particular price, but had a price range. The final share price was decided at a point within the range according to market demand. Although the benefit of the book-building method is widely perceived and increasing numbers of developed economies have adopted the method, China's practice proved that this method did not suit the situation of China's securities market. Since November 2001, China has imposed a limit on the price flexibility range. A share price is limited to 20 times earnings. Some argued that the adoption of the book-building method was caused partly by the depression of China's securities market.

fast-growing sectors.[89] Facing an arid market, a significant number of promising private companies moved to Hong Kong's more fertile market.[90]

Nevertheless, the continuing growth of China's economy provided a favorable external environment for China's capital market to eventually break away from the recession. With a number of strategies including reducing interest rates and the share reform were brought into effect, China's securities market began to pick up since 2006, and finally embraced an unprecedented bull market in 2007. However, the market has been extremely volatile, and there are not enough signs suggesting that the problems that have plagued China's securities market and listed companies for so long have been effectively tackled or controlled.

Issues concerning China's securities market have attracted considerable attention. Numerous discussions have focused on the market crisis and its causes. Some commentators have suggested that the shareholding structure of Chinese listing companies has contributed to the irregular fluctuation in China's securities market. Under Chinese law, state-owned shares, legal-person shares, and even employee shares are classified as non-tradable shares. As a result the majority of shares in Chinese listed companies are non-transferable and illiquid. Usually, only one-third of the shares can be traded freely on the securities market.[91] The scarcity of transferable shares distorts share prices. The share prices of Chinese companies on the domestic securities market are many times higher than their prices on overseas securities markets.[92] The large profits gained by issuance of new shares on China's securities market, in conjunction with the trend of insider control in Chinese listed companies, have tempted some listed companies to engage in misleading and deceptive conduct on the securities market.

The Chinese government has attempted to enhance shareholders' supervision over listed companies by introducing a dispersed ownership structure. This strategy has gradually reduced the proportion of state shareholdings in some listed companies. However, the "trimming down" of state ownership in these listed companies has caused a rapid increase in the appropriation of state assets by management.[93] Management Buy Out (MBO) effectively has reduced state ownership in listed companies. In practice, however, MBOs have exacerbated appropriation of state assets in listed companies. Appropriation of state assets in listed companies usually occurs in tandem with other instances of fraudulent conduct related to accounting practices, financial reports, prospectuses, and other

---

89   *See* Chen, *supra* note 6, at 149.

90   *Ibid.*

91   *See* Xie, *supra* note 88, at 170.

92   Some Chinese companies are allowed to issue shares on both domestic securities markets and overseas securities markets.

93   *See* Yiwen Deng, Cross Swords: Great Debate on State Ownership Reforms 156 (Beijing: Ocean Press, 2005).

misconduct on the securities market.[94] With the introduction of the share reform, it is expected that the problems of split of shares in listed company and the division of the capital may be eased to a certain degree. It is of interest to see how far the share reform will go.

Furthermore, research indicates that a dispersed ownership structure may itself be inefficient in curbing abuses of power by management. In other emerging markets such as Russia and the Czech Republic, efforts to improve corporate efficiency by creating a dispersed ownership structure in newly corporatized state enterprises have failed considerably.[95] Although corporatized companies in these countries enjoy a great degree of privatization, serious insider control problems emerge when a small number of shareholders gradually seize ownership and control. Corporate scandals have also severely eroded investors' confidence in these companies. Ironically, some studies note that privatized firms with concentrated ownership outperform companies with dispersed ownership.[96] Some commentators conclude that concentrated ownership helps improve the profitability and efficiency of these companies.[97]

Further studies show that a system providing insufficient legal protection to minority shareholders is unable to weather market crises. Investors believe that managers and controlling shareholders appropriate more shares when a company experiences a setback, thereby reducing investment returns.[98] The tendency of these investors to sell shares quickly during economic downturns exacerbates a precarious situation, and can trigger capital market crises such as the Asian financial crises of the late 1990s.[99]

Company misconduct and deficient corporate governance are interrelated. Improved corporate governance is essential to limiting the irresponsible company

---

94   *See* Wenying Shen, *MBO in the U.S. and European Countries and Trouble Caused by the Practice of MBO in China*, in Baisan Xie (*ed.*), International Comparison of Securities Markets ,Volume 1, 249 (,Beijing: Qinghua University Press, 2003).

95   *See* Bernard Black, Reinier Kraakman and Anna Tarassova, Russian Privatization and Corporate Governance: What Went Wrong? (Stanford Law School, Working Paper No. 178, 2000).

96   *See* Stijn Claessens, Simeon Djankov and Gerhard Pohl, Ownership and Corporate Governance: Evidence From the Czech Republic (World Bank, Policy Research Working Paper Series, No. 1737, 1997), available at <http://www.worldbank.org/html/dec/ Publications/Workpapers/WPS1700series/wps1737/wps1737.pdf>.

97   *See generally* Roman Frydman, Marek Hessel and Andrej Rapaczynski, Why Ownership Matters? Politicization and Entrepreneurship in the Restructuring of the Enterprises in Central Europe (C.V. Starr Center, Working Paper No. 98-14, April 1998). *See* also Juliet D'Souza and William Megginson, *The Financial and Operating Performance of Privatized Firms During the 1990s*, 54 Journal of Finance 1397 (1999).

98   *See generally* Simon Johnson, Peter Boone, Alasdair Breach and Eric Friedman, Corporate governance in the Asian Financial Crisis (Rutgers University Department of Economics, Working Paper No. 279, 1999).

99   *Ibid.*

conduct and ensuring the successful operation of the securities market, and vice versa. To control the volatility of the Chinese securities market, China must improve its legal and regulatory framework and develop a sound corporate governance system for listed companies. While such an effort is truly a comprehensive project, this endeavor may generate revolutionary reforms positively affecting the social, cultural, economic, and legal climate in China.

Enhancing Legal Regulation of Securities Dealings and the Securities Market

Theoretically, China's system of control over the securities market and its transactions has combined legal regulation, governmental supervision, and self-regulation. In practice, governmental intervention played the primary influence. China's government continues to closely monitor the securities business and intervenes more frequently and to a greater degree than governments in most other markets.[100] Consequently, the self-regulatory function of the stock exchanges remains marginal.

In any jurisdiction, the rules governing the securities market are a combination of public laws and regulations, by-laws of private industry organizations, industry custom, and private agreements.[101] For example, the United States is a jurisdiction that has developed a comprehensive securities regulation regime, while the United Kingdom enthusiastically promotes self-regulation. An issue for the Chinese to consider is whether or not the US system of regulation is a desirable model. Evidence shows that the Chinese have attempted to transplant elements of US law and regulatory practice into its system. For example, China is following the US lead in establishing a strong regulatory securities regime. The CSRC, a government body, currently has the authority to investigate alleged misconduct by listed companies rather than the stock exchanges. Consequently, the stock exchanges are unable to impose liability on companies that issue misstatements. In the early developmental stages of the market in the 1990s, the Chinese Government exercised effective administrative control over the securities market.[102] Comparable administrative control by the government seems less likely today, however, in light of calls for improving securities regulation, enhancing the ability of stock exchanges to self-regulate and curtailing excessive government interference in the securities business.[103]

---

100   *See generally* Katharina Pistor and Chenggang Xu, Governing Stock Markets in Transition Economies Lessons from China 25–6 (Center for Law and Economics Studies, Columbia Law School, Working Paper No. 262, 2004).

101   *See generally* Edmund W. Kitch, Regulation of the Securities Market (University of Virginia Law School, Working Paper No. 5660, 1999).

102   *See* Pistor and Xu, *supra* note 100, at 15–26.

103   *See* Feng Guo, *A Research on the Establishment of Good Faith Principle in Chinese Securities Market*, 2 Securities Law Review 1 (2002).

Significant gaps currently exist in Chinese securities law, for instance, the law currently forbids future contract transactions. Existing laws fail to provide sufficient remedies to compensate defrauded securities investors, and establish only limited regulatory oversight of securities companies and intermediaries. In addition, Chinese law does not provide adequate mechanisms for constraining misconduct such as nondisclosure, misleading disclosure, insider trading, and market manipulation.

Chinese authorities have introduced piecemeal legislation to address these deficiencies. As a result, Chinese securities markets are regulated by an uncoordinated jigsaw puzzle of more than two hundred laws, regulations, and Supreme Court decrees. This proliferation of legislation has not, however, sufficiently filled the gaps, with new laws creating confusion and additional problems. In his research on emerging markets, Jack Coffee has found that the refinement of securities law is essential to the healthy development of a securities market. Coffee highlights the Czech experience as a paradigmatic market failure caused by inefficient regulation.[104] The Chinese have recognized the importance of reforming existing securities law in order to establish an efficient regulatory framework.[105] Owing to the fact that many critics were calling for a general review of the *Company Law* and the *Securities Law*, the People's Congress made substantial amendments to both the company code and securities code in 2005. Though some regulatory deficiencies are addressed in the revised laws, the law requires further improvement. Some reformers are now advocating enhanced civil remedies and the introduction of class action lawsuits to protect minority shareholders' interests.[106] Some suggest imposing fiduciary duties on company directors and filling gaps in the law.[107] Others call for increased self-regulation. Regardless of the reform mechanism chosen, investors' confidence will be boosted only when they believe that the market is organized to protect them.[108]

Although Chinese adoption of foreign legal concepts may not require exceptional efforts, enforcement of the law poses a serious challenge for the Chinese Government. As mentioned earlier in this section, China has been transplanting US securities legislation. However, significant differences exist in the management and control structures of companies in the two countries. In China, the most important and successful companies remain wholly owned by

---

104　*See generally* John C. Coffee Jr., Privatization and Corporate Governance: The Lesson from Securities Market Failure 18–21 (Columbia Law School Center for Law and Economics Studies, Working Paper No. 158, 1999), available at <http://papers.ssvn.com/paper.taf?abstract_id=190568>.

105　*See* Huang, *supra* note 71, at 7.

106　*See* Hu, *supra* note 57, at 255.

107　*Ibid.*

108　*See generally* Adam C. Pritchard, Self-Regulation and Securities Markets 33 (John M. Olin Center for Law and Economics, Working Paper No. 03-004, 2003), available at <http://www.law.umich.edu/centerand-programs/olin/papers.htm>.

the state, and their shares are not tradable on the stock exchanges. Conversely, the largest US companies are listed public companies. China's current policy of retaining state control will undermine aspirations to develop a US-style securities market and legal framework. Even if China adopted securities laws resembling the US legislation, the laws may not function effectively in such a different environment. Coffee emphasizes that substantive differences in corporate law have significantly less impact on the market than differences in enforcement practice.[109] Successful enforcement depends more upon the strength of the incentives to assert legal remedies than upon the availability of those remedies.[110] Advances in the legal and regulatory structure governing the Chinese securities market must be complemented by the promotion of efficiency in China's financial sector and important enterprises.

Improving Corporate Governance

In many cases, poor corporate governance leads to misconduct on the securities market.[111] In China, insider control usually causes market misconduct. To curtail the insider control problem, mechanisms should be introduced to enhance shareholders' supervisory power and to ensure the efficacy and independence of the supervisory board and independent directors.

The government has sold state shares to reduce its ownership in state-dominated companies. When management strips the assets of state-owned enterprises, however, this process is eroded. Some Chinese economists are calling upon the state to suspend its program of divestiture in listed companies.[112] Although the Chinese government has not presently endorsed reform of its divestiture program, it has become more cautious in moving forward. Debating state ownership reform raises the issue of whether China should draw more inspiration from the administrative intervention economic model practiced in France, instead of transplanting the US free market model or the German/Japanese collective consent economic model.[113] In France, state ownership accounts for a significant portion of its economy. Some economists indicate that it may be more feasible for China to mirror the French system because China's economic basis is more closely related to that of France and Italy.

Many listed companies in China are state-controlled or state-dominant companies in which the state is the dominant shareholder. In such companies, the members of the supervisory board are typically insiders. Where members of supervisory boards and management boards are all insiders, the dedication to supervisory duties is substantially compromised.[114]

---

109   *See* Coffee, *supra* note 104, at 1.
110   *See* Coffee, *supra* note 104, at 1.
111   *See* Jin, *supra* note 5, at 217.
112   *See* Deng, *supra* note 93, at 49–51.
113   *See* Deng, *supra* note 93, at 51.
114   *See* Wei, *supra* note 12, at 121.

Conflicts of interest are expected to be addressed in future company law reforms.[115] The Chinese government needs to develop effective strategies to improve the oversight of supervisory boards in listed companies. Under the current approach, the government attempts to mitigate this ineffectiveness by introducing independent directors.[116] This practice has been codified in relevant legal documents promulgated by the CSRC since 2001 and in the amended Company Law in 2005. In practice, however, independent directors in most listed companies are ineffective because they are used as mere figureheads by their companies and because many do not understand their roles within the company or their legal duties.

In Yian Technology, the chairperson of the board and four significant institutional shareholders aggressively manipulated the company's stock price. The independent directors did not exercise any supervision or intervention to curb the manipulation and subsequently pecuniary penalties were imposed on the independent directors individually. One of the independent directors, a 71-year-old retired university professor, protested that he accepted the role because the company promised him that the position would be honorary, that he would not be expected to participate in the business of the company, and that he would not receive any compensation.[117] The professor believed that by taking the position he could contribute to protecting the minority shareholders in the company. His appointment, moreover, was approved by the CSRC and he considered it a great honor.[118] He accepted the appointment only when the above preconditions were satisfied. Forcing the professor to pay RMB 10,000 yuan was a personal tragedy and a great injustice because he received absolutely no compensation from the company.

The case illustrates that mere transplantation or introduction of modern corporate governance mechanisms does not predict success in China. The operation of a modern corporate system needs a supportive economic environment. Supporting reforms in relevant areas, including financial sector reforms, pricing system reforms, labor policy reforms, and legal reforms are required.[119]

---

115   *See* Zhunhai Liu, *The Important Issues Relating to Corporate Law Reforms*, in Liming Wang (*ed.*), Forum of Civil and Commercial Laws 32, 42 and 46 (Volume 3, Beijing: People's Court Press, 2004).

116   *See* Code of Corporate Governance for Listed Companies in China, art. 49 (promulgated by China Sec. Regulatory Commission and State Economic and Trade Commission, 7 January 2001), available at <http://www.csrc.gov/-cn/en/jsp/index_en.jsp?path=ROOT>EN>laws %20and %20regulations>. *See generally* Guidelines for Introducing Independent Directors to the Board of Directors of Listed Companies (promulgated by China Securities Regulatory Commssion, 16 August 2001), available at <http://www.csrc.gov.cn/en/jsp/detail.jsp?infoid=106194786400+type-cms.std>.

117   *See* Shiling Ma and Zhongfu Yao, *The Case of Lu Jiahao (Former Independent Director of Zheng Bai Wen) Versus the CSRC Will Be Heard Next Thursday*, in Baisan Xie (*ed.*), International Comparison of Securities Markets 497–8 (Volume 2, Beijing: Qinghua University Press, 2003).

118   *Ibid.*

119   *See* Wei, *supra* note 12, at 187–91.

Other Elements

China's financial sector retains many of the features that caused financial crises throughout Asian countries in the 1990's although the country was only moderately affected because of protective financial policies that insulated its financial sector and securities market from external influence.[120] China's entry into the WTO has accelerated the process of integrating China's financial sector and securities market into the world economy. Globalization of financial services and the capital market, however, could be a double-edged sword. Chinese banks are facing fierce competition from international financial institutions, and China's capital market is becoming an arena where international investors are racing to exploit new opportunities. China's financial sector and listed companies will encounter unprecedented challenges in the course of survival and expansion. Chinese policy-makers and corporate elites must determine how to use WTO accession as a vehicle to accelerate the reforms of China's financial sector as well as the modernization of its capital market and corporate governance system. The goal is to enhance the competitive strength of China's financial sector and national industries while also attracting a large influx of international capital.[121]

Problems associated with regulating China's securities business and instilling corporate governance in listed companies reflects systematic defects in China's securities market. State-owned and state-controlled companies rely extensively on external funds but pay insufficient attention to internal accumulation of wealth. This reliance stems from protective and preferential considerations given to state-owned and state-controlled companies upon admission to the securities market and on approval of new share issuance.[122]

Before 1999, securities issuance in China was subject to a strict quota and examination and approval system, which reflected the influence of planned economy.[123] Between 1999 and 2006, companies proposing to issue securities on a stock exchange must meet all the requirements in the Securities Law and file an application with the CSRC. The CSRC opposed and/or ratified applications according to the law. Through the approval and ratification process, preference was usually given to state-controlled companies.[124] The revised Securities Law has further improved the issuance practice by bringing in the recommendation

---

120   *See generally* William H. Overholt, *The Lessons of the Asian and Latin American Financial Crises for Chinese Bond Markets* (2004), available at <http://www.rand.org/pubs/occassional_papers/2005/RAND_OP117.pdf>.

121   *See* Buyun Li and Ping Jiang, WTO and China's Legal Development 16 (Beijing: China Fanzhen Press, 2001).

122   *See* Ting Chen, *The Institutional Defects in China's Securities Market*, in Baisan Xie (*ed.*), International Comparison of Securities Markets 647 (Volume 2, Beijing: Qinghua University Press, 2003).

123   *See* Qiang and Han, *supra* note 39, at 7.

124   *See* Chen, *supra* note 122, at 647.

system. The revised *Securities Law* states that a securities issuer employs an institution with the qualification of recommendation as its recommendation party. The recommendation party will be based on the principles of being honesty, creditworthy, diligent and accountable, carry out a prudent examination of application documents and information disclosure materials of its issuers, as well as supervise and urge its issuers to operate in a regulative manner.[125] It is expected that the recommendation practice will be helpful in ensuring the quality of listed companies and enhance the credibility of securities issuers.

However, nothing can stop state-dominated companies from continuing to enjoy priority in listing. Today, state-controlled companies can not only raise handsome amounts of capital on the securities market, but also request government subsidies and reduced interest for state bank debts when recording a loss. This safety net encourages state-controlled companies to raise increasing external funds. According to a World Bank investigation, Chinese state-controlled companies are keen on spending rather than asset accumulation.[126] These companies tend to distribute a significant amount of profit in the form of bonuses.

Monopolistic practices within the Chinese securities market also stifle sufficient competition. Consequently, many listed companies are unsuccessful companies and are poor candidates for long-term investment.[127] Most investors purchasing shares of these companies are largely motivated by speculation, further adding instability to the securities market.

The third defect is that the Chinese securities market does not provide diversified services. There is no futures market, and the types of tradable securities are extremely limited. As a result, investors have limited opportunity to diversify in order to reduce or avoid investment risks.[128] The risk of investing in China's securities markets is disproportionately high, which has encumbered the development of investment funds in the country.

The involvement of investment funds, including mutual funds, pension funds, and social-securities funds, can efficiently reduce irregular volatility on the securities market. The development of investment funds, however, depends on an efficient and transparent securities market. Financial products traded on Chinese securities markets are limited. Many types of bonds, shares, derivatives, and interests are not available on China's securities market. Chinese investment funds do not have a range of investment choices and, thus, lack the means to limit investment risks. Furthermore, Chinese listed companies devote most of their effort to raising funds from the securities market, but thereafter ignore their financial performance. They lack the capacity or willingness to reward investors by distribution of dividends. As a result, they are hardly regarded as the destination of long-term investments. In such circumstances, Chinese investment funds can only

---

125   *See* the People's Congress, *supra* note 41, sec. 11.
126   *See* Chen, *supra* note 122, at 647.
127   *Ibid*, at 654.
128   *See* Xie, Dai and Xu, *supra* note 20, at 13.

expect to profit from the securities market through speculation, rather than through long-term stock appreciation. The current climate in China's securities market is less than favorable to the development of investment funds. The interdependent relationship between the growth of investment funds and the performance of the securities market highlights the need to develop and maintain a healthy securities market. Failure to do so could delay the final success of the enterprise and financial sector reforms.

Facing unprecedented difficulty in the development of an efficient securities market, commentators question if it is worthwhile investing enormous energy in China's developing securities market or if alternative instruments should be utilized. Many writers argue that banks could replace the role of the securities market in fundraising and improving corporate governance.[129] This argument is evidenced by the performance of bank-based financial systems in Germany and Japan. Chinese banks were prohibited from engaging in speculative activities for a long time. There were debates on the benefit of promoting a bank-based financial system or a hybrid system that combines the strengths of banks and markets.[130] Some Chinese writers noted that China's entrance into the WTO had exposed Chinese enterprises and financial institutions to international competition. Under such circumstances, the banks' role in supporting national enterprises and protecting national industries was even more important.[131] With the provisions prohibiting banks from speculating securities being repealed in 2006, the barrier against banks' participation in the securities business has been removed. It is of interest to see how Chinese banking laws will define the business scope of banks in dealing with securities in the future. Increasing bank involvement in corporate finance is an alternate way to restrain irregularities in the securities market. China may look to fully exploiting the potential of its banks, while developing its securities market. A high degree of bank involvement, however, could increase instability in the financial sector and eventually trigger financial disaster and social turmoil, because of the high risk associated with China's securities market.[132]

China will have to make critical decisions in shaping its capital market over the next three to four years. The role of banks in corporate finance must be clarified. The listing of the best state-owned companies should be carefully considered. The

---

129   *See generally* Michael Jacobs, Short-Term America: The Causes and Cures of Our Business Myopia (Boston: Harvard Business School Press, 1991). *See generally* Michael Porter, Capital Choices: Changing the Way America Invests in Industry (Washington D.C.: Council on Competitiveness and Harvard Business School, 1992).

130   *See* Pan Pan, *Legal Restrictions on the Right of Commercial Banks in Making Securities Investments*, in Zhipan Wu and Jianjun Bai (*eds*), Law and Practice of Securities Transaction 115–16 (Beijing: China University of Political Science and Law, 2000).

131   *Ibid.*

132   *See* Xing Hang and Hunran Pan, *A Comparative Analysis of the Efficiency of US, Japanese and German Securities Markets and What Inspiration China Can Get From It*, in Baisan Xie (*ed.*), International Comparison of Securities Markets 147–8 (Volume 1, Beijing: Qinghua University Press, 2003).

regulatory framework must be improved. More practicable strategies of advancing corporate governance must be introduced and implemented.

Efficient control of irregular volatility on its securities market is unrealistic if China does not substantially improve its financial and corporate environments, and introduce adequate risk-transfer and risk-avoidance mechanisms into the securities business.

Some Recommendations

It is predictable that the Chinese will continue to improve their corporate governance and securities regulation through drawing insights from US experiences and in a manner closely mirroring the US regulatory philosophy and strategies. This is evidenced by the current trend of corporate and securities law making in China and by the fact that China has heavily relied on the US model in shaping the country's corporate and securities regulation. The Chinese attach increasing importance to disclosure requirements in developing their securities regulation. Attention has also been paid to foster dispersed ownership and minority shareholders protection. All these demonstrate the US effect on the theory and practice of securities regulation in China. However, such an approach may not serve China's practice productively. Even in the US, there are voices arguing that the US model of corporate governance is the wrong approach for developing countries. Troy Paredes believes that developing countries should focus on developing mandatory corporate law, instead of imitating the US regulatory strategies. This is because the US corporate governance system relies much on institutions that developing countries do not have, such as proxy advisers, the press and the SEC's mandatory disclosure rules, other supervisory bodies. Hence, only strong legal rules can provide necessary protection for shareholders in developing countries.[133]

Furthermore, some strategies heavily relied on by the US in exercising corporate control, such as establishing a powerful disclosure regime and creating dispersed ownership in corporations, may not bring dramatic improvement to the corporate governance in Chinese companies. The assumption that more information is better than less has been dominant philosophy of US securities regulation. However, with the growth in the number of cases of corporate fraud in recent decades, the magical power of disclosure is subject to increasing doubt. Troy Paredes argues that disclosure does not necessary eliminate informational asymmetries existing between companies and investors, and thus promote capital market integrity and efficiency. On the contrary, undue disclosure may be counterproductive and may not help investors to make informed decisions. In contrast to the famous statement

---

133   *See* Troy Paredes, *The Importance of Corporate Law: Some Thoughts on Developing Equity Markets in Developing Economies*, Speech at the Symposium on Judicial Independence and Legal Infrastructure at the University of the Pacific, McGeorge School of Law (October 2005).

"sunlight is said to the best of disinfectants", Troy Paredes points out "sunlight can also be blinding".[134] He believes that in today's US, "investors, analysts and other securities market participants are subject to information overload", and the "model of mandatory disclosure that says more is better than less is incomplete and may be counterproductive".[135] He thinks that the mandatory disclosure system may need to be scaled back. Samuel DiPiazza suggests making improvements to the disclosure system in order to maintain public confidence and building public trust in the US corporate system. He proposes a three-tier framework for corporate disclosure, which is able to better identify and communicate the information indicating a company's ability to enhance shareholders' value.[136] He emphasizes the importance of investors having confidence or trust in the information disclosed.[137] Investors are motivated to carefully analyze information and make responsible decisions only when they know that their decisions are based on information prepared and disclosed in a transparent and accountable manner.[138]

In addition, the disclosure regulation needs to take investors' biases into consideration. The US disclosure regime is based on the assumption that investors and other participants are perfectly rational. However, investors and other participants are not perfectly rational. Rather, they are plagued by behavioral biases. The current disclosure regulation in the US and elsewhere does not give adequate attention to investor biases. Taking investor cognitive biases into account, one has to acknowledge that information disclosure needs to be adequate but not excessive or undue, since people tend to adopt simplifying decision strategies that require less cognitive efforts when they are overloaded by information.[139]

At present, an important task faced by Chinese policy-makers is to innovatively combine the US regulatory experience with China's practice in order to maximize the function of the capital market as an instrument of external corporate control. In the meantime of transplanting the US securities regulation, the Chinese need to carry out thorough investigation into the rationalities and feasibility of promoting these regulatory philosophy and rules in China. It is also necessary for the Chinese to carefully work out the strategies for implementing these rules. Any regulatory regime is developed against particular social, economic, political and historical backgrounds, and is thus jurisdiction specific. What works for the US, may not work for China. For instance, the evolution of a strong securities regulatory system in the US is a response to dispersed ownership. However, the shareholdings in

---

134 *See* Troy Paredes, *Blinded by the Lights: Information Overload and Its Consequences for Securities Regulation*, 81 Washington University Law Quarterly 419 (2003).

135 *Ibid.*

136 For details *see* Samuel A. DiPiazza and Robert G. Eccles, Building Public Trust: The Future of Corporate Reporting 9–32 (New York: John Wiley and Sons, 2002).

137 *Ibid*, at 9.

138 *Ibid.*

139 *See* Paredes, *supra* note 134, at 419.

Chinese public companies are comparatively concentrated. This is a significant factor that China needs to take into account when designing its securities regulatory system for the purpose of utilizing the external governance function of the securities market. It is commendable that China may take steps to develop a corporate governance approach that gives equivalent emphasis on both internal and external governance mechanisms. While developing a transparent, efficient securities market, efforts have to be made to effectively exploit the supervisory functions of majority shareholders, including the state asset management company, banks and other institutional shareholders.

Furthermore, when developing its securities regulatory proposals, China should fully take the advantage of a latecomer to the market economy. China does not need to go through some trials and errors that the US has gone through. For example, China may focus on proposing a securities disclosure framework that acknowledges investor cognitive biases and promotes effective use of information disclosed. Such a system gives adequate attention to not only the matters and items to be disclosed, but also the way by which the information would be processed by the users.

The next imperative mission for the Chinese is to ensure the enforcement of securities laws and regulations. The past experience of regulating the capital market in China suggests that many regulatory efforts have tumbled in the process of enforcement. The main problems existing in the regulatory enforcement process are: (1) there is a lack of centralized and uniform enforcement power to carry out investigation and punishment relating to securities fraud and market misconduct; and (2) there is a lack of centralized inspection system to supervise the enforcement process. To enhance the regulatory enforcement system, China needs to endeavor to complete the following tasks: (1) optimizing the law enforcement resources; (2) enhancing the law enforcement forces; (3) conducting centralized and uniform investigation; and (4) setting up a centralized inspection system that can enhance quick response capability and overall operational function.

Conclusions

The above discussions and analyses have revealed the relationship between corporate governance and market volatility in China, and the extent that poor corporate governance has caused market malfunction and has lowered investor confidence.

After opening its doors to investment from the rest of the world in the late 1970s, China itself has become a rising corporate economy. During the 1980s, the country accelerated economic reforms leading to greater corporate investment and privatization. After disappearing for a few decades, securities transactions and stock exchanges revived in China during the late 1980s and the early 1990s.

Since the establishment of the first stock exchange in 1990, in Shanghai, the Chinese securities market has experienced intermittent volatility with periods of growth, decline, and stagnation.[140] By 2000, the Shanghai Stock Exchange became one of the best performing stock markets in the world and fared reasonably well before the plunge of July 2001.[141] By September 2001, the trading value of the Shanghai and Shenzhen stock exchanges accounted for 51.26 percent of GDP.[142] By July 2001, however, the market plummeted. At present, the market is still extremely volatile. An unstable financial market may trigger industrial recession and lead to economic depression. The Asian financial crises at the end of the last century should serve as a lesson to China. Currently, the economic and financial reforms in China have reached another crucial moment. The flux in China's securities market has heightened the tensions among interested groups pursuing economic, financial, and enterprise reforms.

Generally, the main factors affecting fluctuations in China's securities market include trading and stock exchange policies, information disclosure, laws and regulations, disciplinary supervision and internal market elements. The internal elements refer to misleading information, manipulative activities and machination of the market. These factors are closely associated with governance problems existing in China's corporate system.

The Chinese government developed a number of interventionist strategies to control volatility in the securities market and avoid financial crises that could devastate the market as a whole. This intervention was initially helpful to aid development of the nascent market. The evolution of an inefficient legal framework and excessive administrative regulation, however, reveal the negative aspects of such a policy.

In the process of reforming its enterprises into modern corporations and establishing a modern securities market, China has impressed the world through its dazzling practice of piecing all possible mechanisms together. This reform is a process of transplantation and innovation. The Chinese experience of developing a modern capital market presents an excellent social laboratory in which the diversified theories and practices of corporate finance and capital markets interact. The reform provides an excellent case study for assessing the interrelationship between poor corporate governance and the volatility of the securities market.

International capital flows, including securities investment, are 60 times greater than trade flows.[143] The speculative nature and volatility of securities markets

---

140   From 1990, to the beginning of 1993, the Chinese market was largely a "bull" market. Then, the market fell from February 1993 to July 1994 (approximately one and a half years). After that, the market remained flat from July 1994 to February 1996. From February 1996 to May 1997, the market rose. The market remained flat again until 1999. From May 1999, the securities market rose and kept soaring until July 2001. This was followed by four years' recession. Since 2006, the capital market has recovered.

141   *See* Chen, *supra* note 6, at 148.

142   *See* Jin, *supra* note 5, at 4.

143   *See* Peter Sutherland, Chairman, Goldman Sachs International and Chairman, Overseas Development Council, *The 1998 Per Jacobsson Lecture: Managing the*

affects national and global economies and also the lives of most individuals. China's fast economic and industrial growth has irrevocably altered international trade, investment, and production patterns at the global and regional levels as the country becomes a market of immense proportion and potential.[144] Many economies are positioning themselves for the next stages of China's growth.[145]

After China joined the World Trade Organization, its domestic securities market became increasingly important as a channel for attracting international investments. Today, foreign investors purchase shares in companies of which the state also owns shares, and foreign investors can obtain control over Chinese companies. Although currently subject to administrative approval schemes, analysts forecast the removal of these barriers to foreign investors' securities investments and takeovers.[146] International investors also participate in speculative and takeover activities through joint ventures or wholly foreign-owned Chinese enterprises. The development and volatility of China's securities market are therefore a focus of worldwide interest.

International Economy in an Age of Globalisation (21 October 1998), available at <www. imf.org/external/am/1998/perj.htm>; *see also* Department of Foreign Affairs and Trade (Australia), Asia's Financial Market: Capitalizing on Reform 15 (1999), available at <www. dfat.gov.au/eaau>.

144   *See* Department of Foreign Affairs and Trade (Australia), Australia – China Free Trade Agreement Joint Feasibility Study 5 (2003), available at <www.dfat.gov.au/geo/china/fta>.

145   *Ibid.*

146   *See* Peihua He and Minzhang Wu, *Issues Concerning Takeovers by Foreign Investors and Citizenship Treatment After China's Entrance Into the WTO*, in Ping Jiang and Zhenshan Yang (*eds*), Civil and Commercial Law Review 472–3 (Beijing: China Fangzheng Press, 2004).

PART IV
China's Capital Market in an Era of Globalization

Chapter 10
Economic Globalization

The term "globalization" generally refers to the increasing integration and interdependence of the human societies across the globe.[1] Globalization has many dimensions including social, economic, cultural, political, technological and ecological dimensions. In economics, globalization essentially means the economic interpenetration of nations.[2]

Economic globalization is basically measured by capital flows, cross border trades, labor movement, and the spread of knowledge and technology.[3] The current economic globalization has been campaigned and guided by powerful transnationals and international organizations including the World Trade Organization (WTO), the International Monetary Fund (IMF), the International Bank for Reconstruction and Development (IBRD or the World Bank), the World Economic Forum (WEF), and the Organization for Economic Cooperation and Development (OECD) towards a free market direction marked by the greatest privatization and corporatization.[4]

Globalization is a new term but not a new thing. In history, significant economic integration took place in a few periods, including the rise of the Mongol empire, the establishment of the Silk Road, and the expansion of the Portuguese and Spanish Empires.[5] During the nineteenth century, globalization took the form of colonization. These earlier forms of globalization were backed by military force and stained by unfair trade treaties, exploitation and slavery. In the first half of the twentieth century, globalization was interrupted by the two world wars. With the end of World War II, the world came into a period of "cold war". In the Cold War, the world economies were generally divided into two camps: the plan economies and the market economies. The focus of the plan economy was to enhance a nation's capacity of import replacement

---

1   *See* Global Policy Forum, *Defining Globalization*, available at <http://www.globalpolicy.org/globaliz/-define/index.htm>.

2   *See* Robert Heilbroner and Lester Thurow, Economics Explained 195 (New York: Touchstone, 1998).

3   *See generally* Joseph E. Stiglitz, Globalization and Its Discontent (New York: Norton, 2002).

4   *See* Brian Barrett-Lennard, Anti-Globalisation 11 (Mornington: Beach Box Books, 2001).

5   *See* Greg Buckman, Globalisation: Tame It or Scrap It? Mapping the Alternatives of the Anti-globalization Movement (NY: St Martin's Press, 2004) 6–7. *See* also Wikipedia, available at <http://en.wikipedia.org/wiki/Globalization>.

in order to achieve self-sufficiency.[6] Socialist countries uniformly adopted the system of plan economy. While socialism took the reins in a significant number of countries including most East European countries and many Asian countries, the idea of globalization was hardly feasible. However, the technologies developed during this era provided important means for closer contact between nations in the coming reform era. On the other hand, closer economic ties were built between the countries adopting the market economy. The barrier to globalization was, therefore, the ideological differences. Consequently, at that time, some avoided using the term "globalization" to describe economic interdependence between nations, and preferred the terms of "harmonization" and "regionalization".

With the end of the Cold War, the pace of globalization dramatically accelerated.[7] The rapid development in transportation and communication technologies has closed geographical gaps. This enables powerful multinationals and transnationals to shape their global business strategies and expand their markets worldwide. These super corporations enter into countries to expand their businesses. They are international entities, but usually direct their allegiance to a specific country.[8] Consequently, the world economy is heavily influenced by a few central cities where multinationals and transnationals establish headquarters and strategize their business decisions.[9] In this process, state sovereignty and government authorities are eroded. The WTO and other international organizations of pro-globalization have been advocating a free trade system in which an independent country's power in trade regulation and currency and tariff control are considerably compromised. International organizations such as the WTO and the IMF have also gained increasing power to monitor national trade policies, to handle trade disputes between member states, and to impose economic sanctions on independent states. Countries, particularly those of transitional economies, are facing unprecedented challenges.

Anti-globalization Movements

Who are the winners of globalization? Who are the losers? Globalization is hailed by many politicians, academics and journalists, and they assert that globalization leads to economic growth and eventually benefits all.[10] Some

---

6   *See* Peter Brain, Beyond Meltdown: The Global Battle for Sustained Growth 84 (Melbourne: Scribe Publications, 1999).

7   *See generally* Joseph E. Stiglitz, The Roaring Nineties, Why We're Paying the Price for the Greediest Decade in History (London: Penguin Books, 2003).

8   *See* Simona Yiannaki, *Redefining Approaches of Globalization for Today's Corporate and State Governance* 2, available at <http:papers.ssrn.com/so13/papers.cfm?abstract_id=980961>.

9   *See* Stiglitz, *supra* note 3.

10   *See* Global Policy Forum, *supra* note 1. *See* Joseph E. Stiglitz, *Social Justice and Global Trade*, 169 (2) Far Eastern Economic Review 18 (2006).

have claimed that globalization is inevitable.[11] However, increasing evidence suggests that developing countries and the poor are worse off in this new round of globalization.[12] Developing countries are forced to eliminate trade barriers and open their markets to developed countries, whereas the developed countries retain their trade barriers.[13] Furthermore, developing countries are instructed to remove regulations designed to stabilize volatile international money.[14] Consequently, developing countries not only lose out in economic competition, but also are vulnerable to the inflow and outflow of foreign hot money aiming at speculating in their financial and property markets.[15] This asymmetrical globalization agenda has greatly contributed to the crises in developing economies, and has been creating instability worldwide.[16]

Millions of workers in both developed and developing countries are left worse off. Workers in developing countries work long hours for a wage as low as 0.25 dollar (US) per hour.[17] Meanwhile, the labor markets of many developed countries are subject to increasing flexibility associated with weakened worker protection and diminished welfare and safety investment.[18] In the 1990s, the number of people living in poverty worldwide increased by 100 million.[19]

The current economic globalization practice has a devastating impact on the fragile world environment. Factors including global warming caused by the use of fossil fuels, the damage to the ozone layer resulting from use of chlorofluorocarbons, and loss of rainforest caused by over logging have led to the worst environmental deterioration of the past few decades.

Moreover, the free trade and investment promoted by the globalization engines such as the IMF and the WTO have generated today's "casino economy". That is hot money chasing short-term profits. In this process, huge amounts of capital are transferred from one market to another to take advantages of a rise in interest rates or to speculate on stock markets.[20] The inflow of enormous amounts of speculative money can destabilize a country's currency, and may

---

11   For instance, in 1998, British Prime Minister Tony Blair said 'globalization is irreversible and irresistible'.

12   *Ibid. See* also Joseph E. Stiglitz, *Globalization and Growth in Emerging Markets and the New Economy*, 25 Journal of Policy Modeling 505–6 (2003). *See* also Stiglitz, *supra* note 3, at 6.

13   *Ibid. See* also Stiglitz, *supra* note 3, at 6–10.

14   *Ibid*, at 10.

15   *Ibid*.

16   *Ibid*, at 6.

17   *See* Kevin Watkins et al., Rigged Rules and Double Standards: Trade, Globalisation and the Fight Against Poverty 91 (Washington D.C.: Oxfam International, 2002).

18   *See* Joseph E. Stiglitz and Thea Lee et al., *Taming Global Capitalism Anew*, The Nation (17 April 2006), available at <http://www.thenation.com/doc/2006417/forum>.

19   *Ibid*, 5.

20   *See* Buckman, *supra* note 5, at 28–9.

even destabilize its economy when such money is pulled out from the country.[21] It has been pointed out that international speculation was an important factor that triggered the "Asian Meltdown" in 1997.[22]

The winners of the current globalization are a few developed countries and big transnational corporations supported by these developed countries. At present, transnational corporations are operating in a more liberal trade environment than previously experienced. Worldwide deregulation allows transnationals to enter into and withdraw from a market more easily than occurred before. Diminution of subsidies to local industries gives transnationals the advantage in trade competition. In addition, transnational corporations are able to dominate a market through a monopoly of technology and intellectual property. For instance, the WTO allows private companies to patent plants, genetic materials and public property in another country. The WTO is an advocate of allowing a private company the right to take a country to court.[23] Consequently, the world has begun to observe illogical and strange occurrences. For instance, some US companies have already patented things concerning other people's livelihood including the Mexican Yellow Enola Bean and Basmati rice; a European company has patented a process of extracting medical substances from the Indian Neem tree, which was known to and practiced by Indian farmers for centuries; and South Korea has patented the Chinese Dragon Boat Festival, a traditional Chinese festival commemorating an ancient Chinese poet, Qu Yan (340–278BC).[24]

During the nineteenth century, the golden age of capitalism, the benefits of industrialization did not follow the wave of globalization and go beyond the few industrialized countries. In fact, the majority of the world population actually became the victims of industrialization.[25] People now see a similar picture in the current globalization development. In this second golden age of globalization, only a few elite developed countries and transnational corporations are enjoying the enormous profits. To many ordinary people, globalization appears to merely bring unsecured employment conditions, reduced freedom, and increased environmental crises. Some economists and academics have sensed the danger of the current trend of globalization and called for "reversing" globalization,

---

21   *Ibid*, at 32.

22   *See* Stiglitz, *supra* note 3, at 99–100.

23   The Multilateral Agreement on Investment (MAI) allowed a transnational corporation investor to take a country to court. *See* Barrett-Lennard, *supra* note 4, at 73. The Uruguay Round of international trade negotiations produced the new rules of patents in the Trade Related Aspects of Intellectual Property Rights agreement, which introduced radical rules of intellectual property rights protection.

24   *See* Buckman, *supra* note 5, at 49.

25   *See* Buckman, *supra* note 5, at 8.

or putting a more "humane face" on globalization, in order to insure sustainable development of the world economy.[26]

There has also been increasing resistance to globalization. The past decade saw increasing protests made not only by developing countries but also by ordinary people, academics, environmental activists and human rights activists in developed countries. In 1999, Seattle saw a huge demonstration against the WTO. In the following years, anti-globalization protests broke out in Davos, Washington, Windsor, Ontario, Los Angeles, Nice, Melbourne, and Trieste. While moderate protestors call for sustainable globalization including introducing fairer trading rules and reforming the WTO and the Bretton Woods institutions, radical anti-globalization activists campaign for winding back globalization or de-globalization.[27]

Making Globalization Work

Paul Samuelson, a Nobel Prize winner in economics, claimed in his record selling textbook *Economics*: "In economics, we say that an economy is producing efficiently when it cannot make anyone economically better off without making someone else worse off".[28] Unfortunately, this represents exactly the picture of the current globalization. Opponents of globalization proclaim that the current globalization driven by transnational corporations and the G-7 does not offer sustainable development and will lead the world to inequality and deflation.[29] Indeed, globalization has been facing the crisis of legitimacy since the late 1990s. It has been criticized for being responsible for the third world debt crisis, the Asian Meltdown, and increasing inequities of distribution of income among the industrial countries.

What will be the apogee of globalization driven by transnational corporations? Will the momentum of globalization be contained? Are there alternatives? Will the world be able to choose a better alternative instead of a bad one? These are the concerns of many people.

---

26 *See generally* Joseph E. Stiglitz, Making Globalization Work (New York: W.W. Norton & Company, 2006). *See generally* Brian Barrett-Lennard, *supra* note 4. *See generally* Caroline Lucas and Colin Hines, Time to Replace Globalisation: A Green Localist Manifesto for the World Trade Organisation Ministerial (London: The Greens/European Free Alliance, 2001).

27 The IMF and IBRD were formed at the Bretton Woods Conference held at Bretton Woods, New Hampshire, in July 1944. They have been known as the Bretton Woods Institutions since.

28 *See* Paul A. Samuelson and William D. Nordhaus, Economics 4 (18th edition, New York: McGraw Hill, 2005).

29 *See* Walden Bello, Deglobalization: Ideas for a New World Economy 6–9, 15–16 (London: Zed Books Ltd, 2002).

To many developing countries, the most attractive part of globalization has been the promise of fast economic growth generated by increased exportation of their products and the inflow of international investments.[30] This also means acceleration of industrialization and modernization in these countries. To people of both developed and developing countries, globalization should offer easy and rapid access to new technology and more business opportunities. Based on such anticipation, ordinary people accepted the notion sold to them by globalization institutions and agents that the main driving force of globalization should be transnational corporations for the reason that these transnationals possess the superior ability to most efficiently coordinate land, labor, capital, and technology.[31] Countries have been constantly told to accommodate these transnational corporations through deregulation and removing trade and currency control. The underlying irrationality of this approach is that it leaves private companies unchecked in the international business arena. Any sustainable system is built on equilibrium of powers and interests, and globalization can make no exceptions. For globalization to operate effectively, corporate powers must be subject to a reasonable degree of regulation and control, and governments must retain the capacity to safeguard their own countries' financial safety.

Some point out that globalization has victimized most poor countries as well as many people in developed countries. They hold the view that the only effective remedy is to bring globalization to a halt by promoting national and regional centered economies.[32] Consequently countries need to have the object of developing an economy of self-reliance. The priority is to protect local industries and domestic investors. Necessary preferential treatments should be given to local investors, and trade tariffs and quotas need to be introduced.[33] Transnational corporations should be subject to enhanced regulation and control. Accordingly, fundamental changes need to be made to the current globalization institutions. It is necessary to replace the WTO with a less powerful, but more democratic and transparent international organization, or with several regional organizations.[34] The new organization or organizations will focus on facilitating local trades instead of international trade. Meanwhile, new international monetary bodies will replace the IMF and the World Bank. The new monetary bodies will not gain the policy powers as those possessed by the IMF and the World Bank. Their role will be accommodating local development and economic stability.[35]

Is this reform plan realistic? It seems that the possibility of implementing such changes is remote. Firstly, there is no candidate capable of initiating and carrying

---

30 *See* Stiglitz, *supra* note 3, at 4.

31 *See* Bello, *supra* note 31, at 2.

32 *See* Colin Hines, Localization: A Global Manifesto 64 (London: Earthscan, 2000).

33 *Ibid*, 65.

34 *Ibid*, 260.

35 *Ibid*, 144.

out such radical reforms. Who is going to dismantle the WTO, the IMF and the World Bank? Will these bodies be dissolved or devolved by agreements between their member countries? Currently, there is no sign of such changes. Perhaps, with the development of anti-globalization movements, some countries may take the initiative in shaping a new world trade order in the future.

The moderate anti-globalization activists suggest a set of fairer trading rules to be formulated within the framework of the current world trade order. They emphasize that globalization needs to focus on battling poverty. The main strategies suggested include easing rich country protectionism, giving poor countries favorable treatments, cancelling third world debts, and increasing regulation on transnational corporations.[36] The deficiency of this approach is that it does not address the issue of how to guarantee that all countries will have equal power in shaping global trade rules.[37] Currently, the rule-making powers in the WTO and other world trade organizations are concentrated in the hands of a few world powers, namely the G-7. Poor countries have no say in the international rule-making process. Within the current international trade framework, it is a remote hope that a set of fair-trade rules are going to be produced based on all countries' true consent. Moreover, there is no way to ensure that the new rules are truly fair. Indeed, anti-globalization activists succeeded in speaking for victims of globalization. However, they have not formed a set of viable policies that will convey a world economic system of self-reliance and localization.

The term "globalization" has fascinated people worldwide. People expected that globalization would accelerate the dissemination of new technologies and improve the freedom of choice in goods, services, employment and movement. This was anticipated that this would further encourage democracy and human rights movements. Developing countries hastily aligned themselves with proponents of globalization in the hope that it would assist their efforts of industrialization and modernization. They hoped that globalization could offer more export opportunities and direct much needed capital into their countries. Despite all the delusions and disappointment, the magical power of globalization has not entirely faded away in ordinary people's minds. People still trust that globalization can work for good causes in the future.

The task faced by all countries is to determine how a global market can be built, in which the benefits of globalization can be shared by the greatest number of people. The current anti-globalization movements in both developed and developing countries have begun to generate positive outcomes in bringing people's attention to the issues including sustainable development, environment protection and capital control. There have been growing calls for fair trade by

---

36 *See* Mark Curtis, Trade for Life 10 (London: Christian Aid, 2001). *See* also William F. Fisher and Thomas Ponniah, Another World Is Possible 44 (London: Zed Books, 2003). *See* also Susan George, The Debt Boomerang: How Third World Debt Harms Us All 171 (London: Pluto Press, 1992).

37 *See* Buckman, *supra* note 4, at 181.

developing countries within the WTO and other world organizations. It is hopeful that the problems including growing poverty, deterioration of environment, and degeneration of welfare may be deterred in a reasonable period of time, and the world will come together to work out a scheme of democratizing globalization, as Stiglitz put it.[38]

Conclusions

Historically, globalization was marked by various forms of unfair trade including colonization and occupation. In the past two decades there has been a new campaign for economic globalization by some leading economies, international institutions and transnational corporations. In many respects, the current economic globalization assumes an unfair trade pattern. The 1990s saw devastating consequences of exploitation of people and environment in the name of globalization. This has exacerbated poverty and economic stagnation. Failure to deliver on the promise of leading to economic growth and benefitting all has rendered the globalization campaign unfavorable. It is time for the international community to re-consider the ideology and approaches of globalization. Before a new regime of globalization is shaped, countries susceptible to financial crisis will have to learn to manage globalization, bearing in mind that globalization poses a "double-edged sword". They must continue to develop, but also simultaneously safeguard their economic safety.

---

38   *See* Stiglitz, *supra* note 26, at 269–92.

Chapter 11

Securities Market in the Context
of Globalization

The twentieth century witnessed two worldwide economic crises. The first economic crisis came by the end of the 1920s and haunted the world until the early 1930s. It broke out in industrialized countries and soon spread to the whole world. Many countries suffered economic recession for about a decade. It has since been known as the Great Depression. The second economic crisis occurred towards the end of the century. It hit hard many emerging economies including those Asian miracles, Mexico and Argentina, and eventually threatened the stability of the world economy. It is known as the Asian Meltdown. The difference between the two crises lies in that the first economic crisis was triggered by recession in industries and the second was caused by financial market meltdown in the affected countries. The economies of the affected countries were basically sound right before the Asian Meltdown.[1] The troubles in these countries started from currency speculation and collapses of banks and stock markets. The Asian crisis, therefore, was the crisis of the financial system.[2] The Asian Meltdown serves as a lesson for emerging economies, that speculation in currencies and securities could tumble banks and securities markets and threaten the entire economy.

Struggles in Securities Markets

The driving force of the current globalization is international capital flow. Capital flow depends on two essential factors: currency and banks.[3] Capital inflow means attraction of foreign investment into a country. Theoretically, this will greatly help the country's economy, since the capital will go to industries, and subsequently enhance the nation's productivity and create more jobs. However, if the capital is not absorbed in the process of production, it does not necessarily contribute to the country's healthy economic growth. Peter Brian summarized six conditions for sustainable economic growth. They are: (1) supply of profitable investment opportunities at acceptable risks to domestic investors; (2) import and export

---

1 Right before the crisis, the IMF forecast strong growth in these economies. *See* Joseph E. Stiglitz, Globalization and Its Discontent 90 (New York: Norton, 2002).

2 *Ibid*, at 113.

3 *See* Greg Buckman, Globalisation: Tame It or Scrap It? Mapping the Alternatives of the Anti-globalization Movement (New York: St Martin's Press, 2004).

balance; (3) enterprise finance balance; (4) equality between demand for and supply of goods and services; (5) industry-structure balance for avoiding capacity bottlenecks; and (6) human capital balance for ensuring that the educational standard of the workforce matches the technologies driving the economic growth.[4] It is only when all these six conditions are simultaneously met, that an economy is able to enjoy sustainable growth. When capital or foreign investments are directed to assist the country to achieve the above conditions, they contribute to the country's economic development. Otherwise, the inflow of short-term hot money has little to do with a country's sustainable development, but generates speculative spree and create social and economic instability.

The success of the Asian emerging economies owed much to their policies for sustainable economic development. The governments of these countries made great efforts to nurture local industries, encourage export, reduce poverty, limit inequality, and improve education.[5] They could have continued to progress had they adhered to the policies. However, the IMF, the World Bank, and the big players of the world economy had been relentlessly advocating capital market liberalization, extensive privatization, and free fluctuation of exchange rates before the Asian crisis. These countries eventually accelerated the pace of liberalizing their financial markets and freed exchange rates. This made these countries exposed to international speculative money.[6] Consequently, an onslaught on their currencies and then their securities markets began.

The Asian Meltdown started in July 1997. First, the Thai Baht, Indonesia Rupiah, Malaysian Ringgit and Philippine Peso devalued dramatically,[7] largely as a result of speculative attacks.[8] In October 1997, speculators targeted the Hong Kong currency. In November, South Korea ran into economic difficulties. In the meantime, Japan was in financial turmoil. By January 1998, currencies and securities markets of some South-East Asian countries fell to another historical low. This was triggered by the combination of several factors. For instance, some of these countries were experiencing a debt crisis. The Indonesia Rupiah further devalued about 50 percent. In addition, a few large companies in Hong Kong declared insolvency.[9] These factors resulted in turmoil in the securities markets of these countries. The financial turmoil lasted until January 1998. Since then, these economies have been in the process of recovery.

The Asian Meltdown also had an impact on developing countries. Ordinary investors were at the receiving end of the aftermath. The wealth of Wall Street

---

4   *See* Peter Brain, Beyond Meltdown: The Global Battle for Sustained Growth 25–32 (Melbourne: Scribe Publications, 1999).

5   *See* Stiglitz, *supra* note 1, at 92.

6   *Ibid*, at 99–104.

7   *See* China News, *The Four Phases of the Asian Crisis*, available at <http://www. china.com.cn/news/txt/2007-07/02/content_8466890.htm>.

8   *See* Stiglitz, *supra* note 1, at 89, 94–5.

9   *See* China News, *supra* note 7.

investors shrank about $4.6 trillion in the late 1990s.[10] The amount of loss was half of the US GDP and four times the wealth lost in the 1987 securities market crash.[11]

The experience of the Asian Meltdown once again speaks the truth that capital is likely to flow into a country during a boom and flow out during a recession.[12] When capital flows in during a boom, it exacerbates inflation pressure.[13] It flows out of a country usually at a time when it is most needed, thus triggers or worsens an economic recession and further weakens the economy. Moreover, speculative capital only does harm rather than good. They aim at speculating a country's real property market and securities market, and thus create economic bubbles. When the bubbles burst, the economy goes into recession, followed by social and political instability. It is true to say that appropriate financial policies and a healthy capital market are matters of a country's economic safety. The following part of this chapter will discuss the stories about losing out and survival in capital markets.

Intervention or Not

Joseph E. Stiglitz, in *Globalization and Its Discontent*, recounted the economic transition in Russia since the end of the 1980s. After the fall of the Berlin Wall, Russia whole-heartedly embraced the free market ideology. With the support of economic advisers from western countries, Russia tried to take a shortcut to the market economy. Without necessary institutions, welfare systems, laws and regulations in place, the country privatized all enterprises, freed all prices, and liberalized its financial system. Rapid privatization without careful guidance and supervision from the government resulted in asset stripping. The state assets were snatched by a few oligarchs and taken out of the country. The government ended up being heavily indebted to the IMF. The result was: Russia's GDP fell 45 percent during the period from 1990 to 1998.[14] The Russian people and government did not benefit from the privatization.

Speculation on the ruble and Russian securities in 1998 threw the country into further crises. By then, a number of foreign banks and financial institutions operating in Russia had attracted huge amounts of domestic savings. They had also found ways to borrow large amounts of rubles from Russia banks. In the meantime, these institutions widely purchased bonds from Russian citizens, which were distributed to workers at the beginning of privatization. They eventually had accumulated sufficient rubles and bonds for speculation. By June of 1998, because

---

10   *See* Walden Bello, Deglobalization: Ideas for a New World Economy 14 (London: Zed Books Ltd, 2002).
11   *See* the Editor, *When Wealth is Blown Away*, Business Week 33 (26 March 2001).
12   *See* Stiglitz, *supra* note 1, at 100.
13   *Ibid.*
14   *Ibid*, 143.

of the fall of the price of crude oil, Russia's economy fell further. However, the Russian government resisted devaluation of the ruble against the US dollar. As a result, US dollars were traded in black markets many times higher than the official exchange rate. Eventually confidence in the ruble eroded. The speculators subsequently had little risk to bet on the ruble's crash.[15] The government had opportunities to intervene on a few occasions, but let them slip. It is therefore justified to say that the Russian financial crisis in 1998 was mainly a result of the lack of regulation and control over the securities market and financial sector.

At the same time, the Hong Kong stock market was facing enormous pressure. International speculators had fixed their eyes on the Hong Kong Stock Exchange. Before 1998, the Hong Kong government tried to control speculation in the securities market by increasing the Hong Kong dollar interest rate. However, the increase in the interest rate resulted in the securities market and property market plummeting, causing economic stagnation.[16] This time, the speculators carefully planned their speculative strategies. Firstly, they would borrow the Hong Kong currency at a fixed interest rate and then convert the loans into floating interest rate loans. In doing so, they could make profits when the interest rate rose. Secondly, they would accumulate a substantial amount of shares and bonds on credit. If the rise of the interest rate resulted in a plummet of share prices, they could profit by repaying the debts at the fallen prices. Thirdly, they would profit by short selling when the Hang Seng Index fell. Fourthly, they would profit from repaying the principal at a low price when the Hong Kong currency was devalued. Lastly, they could make a fortune by closing out options when share prices fell.[17] With this perfect plan, the speculators were surer than ever that Hong Kong's capital market was their oyster.

Since early 1998, speculators began to accumulate put options. On 13 August 1998, the Hang Seng Index fell to a historical low over five years. The market was close to crisis. The Hong Kong government eventually decided to defend the Hong Kong currency and securities market. From 14 August, to stablize the exchange rate and the share prices, the Hong Kong government used US dollars in reserve to buy Hong Kong dollars and then use the Hong Kong dollars to purchase important shares on the securities market.[18] The battle intensified on 27 August. The trading value within the last 15 minutes before closing time reached HK $8 billion. The Hong Kong government ultimately maintained the stability of the Hong Kong capital market. However, the cost of doing so was high. Within 14 days, it purchased HK $120 billion worth of shares.[19] The remaining task was to dispose of the purchased shares and assure the public that Hong Kong would not

---

15   *Ibid*, 147.

16   *See* Xiaofeng He, Capital Markets and Investment Banks 61 (Beijing: Beijing University Press, 2005).

17   *Ibid*, at 62.

18   *Ibid*.

19   *Ibid*.

change its free market principle and that the government would only intervene into the market in extreme circumstances.

It is clear that like every system, the free market system is also subject to abuse. The capital market is particularly susceptible to abuse. The consequence of the abuse can be catastrophic to an economy, especially an emerging economy. It is thus essential for countries to carefully design their financial and currency policies, as well as to introduce an efficient regulatory regime for the securities business and capital market. Past experiences have proven that excessive direct governmental intervention into the economic life does more harm than good. It is therefore desirable that the role of the government in a free market economy is limited to providing economic policies and guidance, making rules for regulating markets and market participants, and adjusting tax, exchange rate and interest rate policies in order to constrain bubbles in the economy. However, rules and policies are always behind financial practice. An economy may bump into unprecedented challenges. When it happens the government has to decide whether or not to exercise justified intervention in an emergency.

Conclusions

Both intervention and non-intervention are double-edged swords. The collapse of the planned economies showed that too much direct governmental intervention could result in economic stagnation. On the other hand, the Asian Meltdown and the Russian experience have demonstrated the vulnerability of a small or transitional economy when encountering the attack of giant speculators in a free market. In such a circumstance, the result of financial speculation could be devastating. Millions of lives may be affected. When this happens, public opinions about governmental intervention into economic life are likely to be divided. Due to self-interest, people's arguments can be widely divergent. The polarity between different economic groups and countries could trigger trade wars between nations in the future. The international community will have to come up with policies to regulate the movement of short-term speculative capital and encourage genuine foreign investments, particularly in developing countries.

Chapter 12

Manage to Survive and Thrive in Globalization: A Challenge to China

Although having produced impressive GDP growth rates, China, in every respect, is still a third world developing country. Its securities market is in its infant stage and Chinese investors are immature. After ending its isolation, China sees the opportunity of integrating itself into the global market. It has been gradually but steadfastly opening up its financial market and loosening the Renminbi exchange rate control. However, the speculators cannot wait any longer for another feast of speculation. While these international sharks demand other countries to adhere to the free market principles and eliminate governmental intervention, they are not hesitant in asking their own governments to push their agenda.[1] It seems today as though the US regards liberalization of China's currency control and financial market as an issue of its national interest. The Renminbi has been under enormous pressure to increase its value against the US dollar.[2]

Since the beginning of the new century, international hot money has been manipulating China's securities market and property market.[3] By the end of 2007, China has opened its financial market to the world in fulfilling its WTO commitment. Now foreign banks, financial institutions, and investment funds are able to surge into China's financial market and acquire its resources. The country now faces the most crucial time in history. Will China survive?

Good and Bad: Life after the Economic Reforms

Since the economic reforms in 1978, China's GDP growth rate has scored an average of more than 9 percent in the past 30 years. The number of people living in extreme poverty has reduced from 250 million in 1978 to 30 million in 2000.[4]

---

1   *See* Joseph E. Stiglitz, Globalization and Its Discontent 102 (New York: Norton, 2002).

2   *See* the Editor, *A Review on Renminbi Exchange Rate Reforms*, available at <http://news.china.com/zh_cn/-focus/rmb/index.html>.

3   *See* Zhongli Yen, *Hot Money Attacks China*, available at <http://news.sina.com.cn/c/2005-12-31/11348743853.shtml>. *See* also Tian Tain, *Hot Money Hits the Capital Market*, available at <http://finance.news.tom.com/1001/1002/20031112-29011.html>.

4   *See* Dale Wen, China Copes with Globalization: A Mixed Review 2 (A Report by the International Forum on Globalization, 2006), available at <www.ifg.org>.

China has also enjoyed a favorable balance of trade with its major trade partners. It entered into the WTO in 2001 and has committed to open more economic sectors to foreign investment and trade since. Today, China's transformation from a planned economy into a free market economy appears to be successful. The long queues outside shops during the time of the planned economy have been forgotten. Today, Chinese shops and markets exhibit a seemingly endless array of goods.

However, beneath the success, worrying factors emerge. Firstly, China has not seen fundamental progress in some sectors concerning the people's livelihood and sustainable economic development. Some sectors have even degraded. For example, education and health in China have not substantially improved. Primary and high school education in rural areas has degenerated. The number of youths finishing high school education in rural areas decreased by 60 percent by the late 1990s.[5] Before the economic reforms, China had a state-funded health care system. Under this system, China made impressive improvements. Not only did it take the lead in low income countries but also outperformed some middle income countries. Life expectancy increased from 35 to 67 years and infant mortality dropped from 200 per 1,000 to 42 per 1,000.[6] However, medical services, particularly in rural areas, have declined since the 1980s, due to the market-oriented reforms in the health care systems, which resulted in dramatic increase of medical fees.[7] During the era of the economic reforms, China's progress in health care was below both the world average and that of low income countries.[8] Expensive medication and hospitalization costs have impoverished many families. In some areas, epidemics such as tuberculosis and HIV/AIDS spread rapidly.

Secondly, China's environment has deteriorated. China has suffered severe air, water and soil pollution since the economic reforms. According to the State Environmental Protection Administration, about 60 percent of China's major rivers are classified as being unsuitable for human contact.[9] Desert areas have grown to about 2.67 million square kilometers.[10]

Thirdly, China's economic reforms have resulted in acute polarization and inequality. In the beginning of the economic reforms, the government promised the Chinese people that the economic reforms would deliver common enrichment. With the acceleration of privatization and erosion of public welfare since the 1990s,

---

5   *See* Dongping Han, *Professional Bias and Its Impact on China's Rural Education: Re-examining the Two Models of Rural Education and Their Impact on Rural Development in China*, available at <http://chinastudygroup.org/-article/2/>.

6   *See* the World Bank, WDI-CDROM 2003.

7   *See* Minqi Li and Andong Zhu, China's Public Services Privatization and Poverty Reduction: Health Care and Education Reform (Privatization) in China and the Impact on Poverty, UNDP Policy Brief (Beijing 2004).

8   *See* Wen, *supra* note 4, at 25.

9   *Ibid*, at 3. *See also* the State Environmental Protection Administration, *2004 China's Environmental Situation Brief.*

10   *See* the Editor, *Desert Areas Growth in China*, People's Daily (25 February 2002) available at <http://english.people.com.con/200202/25/eng20020225_90962.shtml>.

millions of workers and farmers have lost out. Corporatization and privatization of the state-owned enterprises have resulted in massive layoffs. More than 40 millions jobs in state-owned enterprises were cut between 1995 and 2002.[11] Worst of all, increased unemployment comes together with diminished welfare and workers protection, extended working hours, and a marginalized social status for workers. This results in an increase of poverty and inequity. With rapid elimination of trade barriers to accommodate the WTO rules, poverty in rural areas has been exacerbated. For instance, between 2000 and 2002, nearly half of Chinese farmers experienced decreased income in absolute terms due to an influx of imported agricultural products.[12]

Fourthly, foreign investments have both advantages and disadvantages. The obvious advantage is that foreign investments, including joint ventures and foreign-owned enterprises, bring in capital and technology, increase export opportunities, and create jobs. The corresponding disadvantage is that some foreign investments only sought to create sweatshops. Adding to the problem, foreign-owned enterprises enjoy tax advantages in China. They pay two to three times less tax than that paid by a state-owned or collectively-owned enterprise.[13] Nevertheless, they seek to avoid paying any tax by concealing profits. Alarmingly, it has been reported that more than half of wholly foreign-owned enterprises claimed to be making a loss in 2003 alone.[14] Furthermore, foreign-owned enterprises are not required to contribute to education, health care and insurance for employees.

The economic reforms have created a rich class in China. The wealth of the richest 10 percent of the population expanded rapidly from 20 percent of the national income in the 1980s to 45 percent in 2005.[15] The gap between the rich and the poor has widened dramatically. It is widely concerned in China that the market economy and the economic globalization has only benefited and will continue to only benefit a few at the expense of many.

Strategies of the Chinese Government for Coping with Globalization

China has been one of the few destinations of international capital flow in the developing world. For some time, China, together with Brazil, Mexico, Argentina,

---

11   *See* Wen, *supra* note 4, at 17.

12   *See* George Gilboy and Eric Heginbotham, *The Latin Americanization of China?* 256–61 Current History (September 2004).

13   *See* Wen, *supra* note 4, at 9.

14   *See* the Editor, *Claiming Loss to Evade Taxes: 70 per cent of Foreign Enterprises in Suzhou Make Loss Intentionally*, Xinhua Net (16 September 2005), available at <http://news.xinhuanet.com/fortune/2005-09/16/content_3497540.htm>.

15   *See* the Editor, *Six Large Gaps Regarding Income: The Top 20% Has 45% of the Wealth*, XinHua Net (17 June 2005), available at <http://news.xinhuanet.com/fortune/2005-06/17/content/200411/6-1.htm>.

Thailand, and Indonesia, have absorbed around 60 percent of all foreign investment in developing countries.[16] The Chinese have regarded this as good fortune for China. In the meantime, China observed the third world debt crisis and learnt lessons from it. The Chinese government has been very aware of the importance of maintaining capital control and the balance of international payment. It has introduced mechanisms of controlling capital flows and defining borrowing limits.

To ease its foreign capital shortages, China has endeavored to attract foreign investments. The preference has been given to direct foreign investments. The Chinese government believes that direct foreign investment will not cause the problem of debt service.[17] To attract foreign capital to direct foreign investments, China offers a range of incentives in taxation and other areas to foreign investments. At the same time, a legal framework supporting direct foreign investments has been built rapidly. Today, about 90 percent of foreign capital legally inflowing into China takes the form of direct foreign investments.[18] In the meantime, the government closely supervises the activities of direct foreign investments. A registration and approval system was introduced to serve the purpose. All direct foreign investments must be registered subject to the approval of relevant government departments. After registration, foreign investors may open foreign exchange capital accounts at designated banks and engage in foreign exchange activities. Conversion of foreign currencies into Renminbi has to be approved by the State Administration of Foreign Exchange or its branches.[19]

In addition, the government has carefully designed the strategy of developing China's securities market investment and limited the risk of excessive speculation by international hot money. Shares of Chinese companies listed on domestic stock exchanges are divided into A shares and B shares. Before 2003, A shares could only be purchased by Chinese investors in Renminbi, while B shares were offered to foreign investors to be purchased in foreign currencies. These controlling measures helped China to escape the catastrophic speculation of "swallow money", which swept the whole East and South-East Asia at the end of the twentieth century.

China has effective control over foreign debts. As a result, it enjoys a comfortable position in foreign borrowing and external debt levers. Before the reforms, China strictly applied a policy on foreign debt control. Import expenditures were financed by export earnings. China started its economic reforms with virtually no foreign debt burden.[20] Since the start of China's economic reform program,

---

16   *See* Ankie Hoogvelt, Globalization and the Post Colonial World: The New Political Economy of Development 84 (London: Zed Books, 2001).

17   *See* Yongding Yu, *China: The Case for Capital Control*, in Walden Bello, Nicola Bullard and Kamal Malhotra (*eds*) Global Finance: New Thinking on Regulating Speculative Capital Markets 177 (London and New York: Zed Books, 2002).

18   *Ibid*.

19   *Ibid*.

20   *See* the World Bank, China, Reform and the Role of the Plan in the 1990s 36 (Washington D.C.: The World Bank, 1992).

foreign borrowing has increased rapidly. However, with the increasing capacity of its exports, it is still modestly indebted.[21] This enables China to continually access foreign credits and make sufficient use of them.

Foreign loans are under tight governmental control. The Ministry of Foreign Trade and Economic Cooperation is the only institution that can borrow from foreign governments.[22] It also assumes the tasks of negotiating loans with foreign governments for local governments. The People's Bank of China is the only institution handling loans from the IMF and the Asian Development Bank.[23] The Ministry of Finance handles loans from the World Bank. Chinese financial institutions and industrial and commercial enterprises may borrow from foreign banks and financial institutions with the authorization and approval of the State Administration of Foreign Exchange.[24] Borrowing by Chinese citizens is also subject to the approval of relevant government departments.

The above policies have allowed China to efficiently utilize foreign capital, maintain the stability of the Renminbi, and sustain a low interest rate to stimulate domestic consumption and the economy. However, the above mechanisms of capital control are under severe erosion and challenge in recent years. Today, China's financial safety is under the most serious threat. It is not an exaggeration to say that China has never been so vulnerable financially since the economic reforms.

The first challenge or erosive element is internal. There exist serious irregularities in capital flows, resulting in evasion of capital control. The perpetrators include Sino-foreign joint ventures, wholly foreign-owned enterprises, transnationals, and Chinese enterprises and citizens. The forms of evasion are many. For instance, some foreign enterprises use domestic collateral to borrow Renminbi.[25] It has become more prevalent that foreign investors use Chinese citizens as agents to buy A shares. Transfer of price by transnationals is not a rare incident. Corruption inside Chinese financial institutions and enterprises has exposed China's financial safety to further risks. Many Chinese enterprises invest abroad without authorization. Many forge documents to obtain foreign exchange as advances for non-existing imports.[26] There are also increased reports on cases where individuals falsify certificates or commercial documents to purchase foreign exchange.

China's fledgling market system and legal regime are experiencing growing difficulties in exercising capital control. Its securities market and property market face more frequent and unbridled speculation. The high property price has been

---

21 *See* Nicholas R. Lardy, *The Role of Foreign Trade and Investment in China's Economic Transformation*, in Andrew G. Walder (*ed.*) China's Transitional Economy 117 (London: Oxford University Press, 1996).

22 *See* Yu, *supra* note 17, at 181.

23 *Ibid.*

24 *Ibid.*

25 *See* Linghua Zhao, *An Analysis of the Forms of Irregular Capital Flows in China,* International Economic Review 3–4 (1999).

26 *Ibid.*

engulfing Chinese citizens' wealth often accumulated by nearly two generations. To many, the benefits of the economic reforms are diminishing.[27] The securities market is excessively speculated and manipulated. Ordinary investors are exploited. Though being able to successfully rely on administrative intervention into the capital and property markets in the early years, the government now acutely feels the difficulty in making swift intervention. For instance, the government has determined to control the property price. Regulations and methods are introduced. However, it appears that developers and speculators have reached a tacit consent to defeat the government's scheme.

The second challenge is from the WTO and the US. China has been cautious in developing financial markets and liberalizing its capital account. The Chinese government has made great efforts to maintain a fixed Renminbi exchange rate and to control its financial market.[28] After the Asian financial crisis, it has become even more aware of the importance of shelving capital liberalization. The Chinese discovered that the countries most affected in the Asian crisis, each possessed the following shared characteristics: firstly, these countries all adopted a catch-up economic policy facilitating accelerated economic development. Secondly, these countries' financial systems were still in a stage of development and not ready for free trade. Thirdly, because they loosened capital control too early, their currencies were exposed to speculation and resulted in currency crisis. The currency crisis then triggered large scale financial crises. Fourthly, the ratio of external debt to equity was too high in these countries. Finally, their currencies and financial markets all encountered speculation of international capital. Once their currencies and financial markets were under stress, external debts also pressed on them.[29]

Knowing China's financial system has similar problems, the Chinese government is keen to take a gradual step in freeing up the Renminbi exchange rate and the financial market. Some Chinese commentators even urge the government to find ways to reduce China's balance of payment surplus, in order to appease some major trading partners such as the US and Japan and allow China to slowly increase the value of the Renminbi against the US dollar.[30]

However, time is running out. The US, Japan and interested groups have put mounting pressure on the Chinese government to free up its exchange rate and increase the Reminbi value against the US dollar. In July 2005, China announced

---

27   *See* Tong Nie, *Professor Xianping Lang Claims that the Property Market is Hurting Ordinary People*, Inner Mongolia Morning Edition (13 April 2007), available at <http://bj.house.sina.com.cn/scan/2007-04-13/1725185462.html>.

28   *See* Yunliang Chen, *National and International Regulation of the Renminbi*, in Zhipan Wu (*ed.*), Jurists in Economic Law 273 (Beijing: Beijing University Press, 2003).

29   *See* the Editor, *Should Not Forget the Lessons of the Asian Financial Crisis*, China Net, available at <http://www.china.com.cn/news/txt/2007-07/02/content_8465918.htm>.

30   *See* the Editor, *China Reflects the Asian Financial Crisis and Enhances the Reforms of Its Financial Sectors*, China Net, available at <http://www.china.com.cn/news/txt/2007-07/02/content_8465918.htm>.

that the exchange rate between the US dollar and the Renminbi would be reduced to 1:8.11. Soon, the value of the Renminbi against the US dollar was pushed up again. Since May 2007, the floating range of the exchange rate of the Renminbi has increased from 0.3 percent to 0.5 percent.[31] It means that within a single trading day, the Renminbi value could increase 0.5 percent against the US dollar. It also means that China's savings over the past few decades could shrink dramatically.

China's banking sector is also under pressure to further open up. Since the end of 2007, foreign banks and financial institutions are allowed to carry on financial business in China. They are able to compete with Chinese banks on equal terms. This, in fact, puts Chinese banks in a disadvantageous position, since China's banking sector is still in the process of transition from a banking system designed for facilitating the planned economy to a banking system working in the market economy. Compared with big banks in some mature markets, they are less experienced in handling complex banking business in a market economy. Like a beginner swimming in the rough sea, Chinese banks are forced to jump into fierce competition before they are ready. It is crucial for China's banking sector to survive the competition, since the banking sector is the cornerstone of a country's financial arch. An economic crisis could become a real threat, when China's capital market and banking sector are under stress at the same time.

Some Recommendations

Many Chinese people, including many Chinese economists, have whole heartedly embraced the neo-liberal economic theories. They believe that for the purpose of improving the economic efficiency of firms, massive layoffs are necessary, or at least understandable. They did not endeavor to think of alternative strategies accommodating both the need of improving the economic performance of Chinese firms and the need of orientating firms' productive activities to achieve the objects of attaining sustainable development and improving the life quality of the population. A significant amount of discussions on corporate governance single-mindedly focuses on the agency theory and assumes that Chinese managers are rational beings identical to those described in the neoclassical economic theory, without paying sufficient attention to the cultural, social and economic variables.

A typical example is the designation of the internal structure for Chinese corporations. Originally, Chinese company law acknowledged the merits of having a permanent monitoring organ exercising close supervision over management and thus adopted the German two-tier board system. However, since the state-owned and state-dominated companies had insider control problems, most supervisory boards did not function effectively.[32] In such companies, the state continued to be

---

31   *Ibid.*

32   *See* Yuwa Wei, *Directors' Duties under Chinese Law – A Comparative Review*, 3(1) University of New England Law Journal 38 (2006).

the owner of the new corporatized enterprises. Relevant government departments continued to appoint the directors and supervisors in these enterprises. Compared with a state-owned enterprise in the planned economy, the only difference was that the corporatized state-owned or dominated enterprises were given much more autonomy and could directly organize their business activities according to the market needs. Consequently, the management seized greater powers without being effectively monitored. As a result, the supervisors and directors in these enterprises share common interests and are likely to collaborate to advance their personal interests and undertake reciprocal concealment of misconduct and breaches.[33] To restrain the insider control problem, the amended company law requires companies to appoint independent directors in addition to the supervisory board. While such an arrangement has definitely increased supervisory costs, its effectiveness remains to be seen. The lesson for the Chinese in this regard is that imported corporate governance mechanisms will work only when comparable social, economical, cultural, and legal environments and infrastructures are present.

In traditional China, a contention for prerogative penetrated the bureaucratic hierarchy and took root in the Chinese culture. These cultural factors have had a strong impact on China's economic life. Before means of effectively controlling favoritism and prerogative are put forward, privatization and management freedom in the name of a free market could only foster unbridled corruption and flagrant appropriating public property.

Some people's expectation of the securities market is based on the same fallacy. They believed that the operation of the securities market will assist listed companies to develop sound corporate governance and Chinese investors will face no trouble in making rational business decisions. The reality has cruelly suggested the opposite. Many companies regard the capital market as the place of raising easy money. It has become evident that in China, issuing shares on the stock exchange is much cheaper than asking loans from banks, since banks will require the companies to return the principal and pay interests, whereas investors cannot require the repayment of the principal and the companies do not necessarily distribute dividends on a frequent basis. Hence, companies aim to present themselves as successful operations either by right or dubious means. Even such efforts can be avoided if the market is manipulated and stock investors are in some forms of investment mania. Furthermore, the violent volatility on the securities market demonstrates that Chinese investors usually do not make rational business decisions, rather, they are easily manipulated. Developing a securities market without introducing a practical monitoring regime in China's current social, economic and cultural environment leaves many regulatory pitfalls and results in many irregularities in the capital market.

The most dangerous move made by China was entirely opening the securities market to international investment funds and allowing international banks and financial institutions to enter into its financial sector at such an early stage.

---

33   *Ibid.*

China's capital market is small in size. Huge investments funds may find ways to manipulate the market for speculative profits. Under speculation, the market will go from boom to recession. During recession, if investors and Chinese citizens lose their confidence in Chinese securities, currency, and banks, they would hastily sell their shares, bonds, other financial products, and Reminbi. The market would fall further and banks would be under more pressure. When this happens financial crisis would become a real threat.

Today, it is of utmost importance for China to introduce workable policies and laws that promote economic efficiency of its capital market and financial sector on the one hand, and effectively safeguard its economic safety on the other. This is particularly true in the financial market, banking sector and currency regime since the modern history of economic crises suggests that these are sensitive areas of economic meltdown.

The Securities Market

In modern China, two markets are under relentless speculation: the property market and the securities market. At the time when economic crises broke out in other Asian financial markets at the turn of the last century, China's capital market remained unaffected. This was mainly attributed to the fact that China's capital market was insulated due to its domestic A share market being unavailable to foreign investors. For a while, international speculative money only had access to the property market. As a result, housing prices soared in major Chinese cities. Since the enactment of the *Provisional Administrative Regulations for Qualified Foreign Institutional Investors* in December 2002, foreign institutional investors are now permitted to invest in A shares, treasury bonds and other financial instruments in Chinese domestic stock exchanges.[34] By 2003, the CSRC had approved seven foreign financial institutions to be qualified foreign institutional investors (QFIIs).[35] Since then, China's capital market is no longer insulated. The purpose of introducing QFIIs was to attract investment capital, introduce rational investment ideology, and accelerate the integration of China's securities market into the world economy.[36] Due to the inflow of large amounts of capital, since 2006 China's capital market has fluctuated drastically, while share prices have maintained a momentum of constant increase. The securities administrative authority has made some efforts to alleviate the investment propulsion. However,

---

34 *See* China Securities Regulatory Commission and People's Bank of China, the *Provisional Measures on Administration of Domestic Securities Investments of Qualified Foreign Institutional* Investors (2002), sec. 18.

35 *See* Run Chen and Qiang Zhu, *The Risk and Regulation of QFII in China's Securities Market*, in Zhipan Wu, Jurists in Economic Law 354 (Beijing: Beijing University Press, 2005).

36 *Ibid*, 354.

the speculative money in action is substantial enough to continue to manipulate the market in climbing to new heights.

Research shows that institutional investors are important forces of stabilizing capital markets.[37] However, this does not suggest that a country can excessively rely on foreign institutional investors. This is because foreign institutional investors will eventually remit their profits abroad and may withdraw their investments at any time, particularly at a time when the investments are mostly needed in the host countries. In order to maintain a sustainable securities market, it is essential for China to establish a significant number of domestic investment funds. However, the development of investment funds in China has been slow. By 2003, China had established 59 securities investment funds.[38] Their total capital merely reached RMB 102,100,000,000, with an average amount of RMB 1,730,000,000 per investment fund.[39] On the other hand, the investment capital of a QFII may reach RMB 6,600,000,000.[40] Relying on abundant capital and rich experience, QFIIs are likely to gain the upper hand in the competition with Chinese domestic investment funds. If the situation does not change reasonably quickly, China's capital market will soon fall into the hands of QFIIs. The concern is that QFIIs may transfer their capital overseas, particularly at the time when China's capital market is under pressure, resulting in crises in China's capital market. Therefore China must hasten the process of developing its own investment funds.

Furthermore, China needs to establish a practicable regulatory system governing the securities business. The current Chinese securities laws and regulatory framework closely follow the US model and practice. However, the investment environment and market participants in China are much different from that of the US. For a long time, in the US, commercial banks were forbidden from directly investing in industrial companies.[41] As a result, shareholdings in listed US companies are dispersed. The lack of dominant shareholders results in professional management firmly grasping the controlling powers in large public companies. Small and dispersed shareholders usually invest in shares for short term benefits. It is therefore crucial for the US to have a highly developed securities market for companies to raise capital and for investors to make frequent transactions. Consequently, to maintain a prosperous securities market, the US law has a focus on protecting minority shareholders.[42]

In China, most large and middle-sized listed companies are state-dominated companies with the state being the controlling shareholder. Small-sized companies are usually family controlled businesses, with a family being the dominant

---

37 *Ibid*, at 358.
38 *Ibid*, at 359.
39 *Ibid*.
40 *Ibid*.
41 The law changed since 1999.
42 *See* Yurun Zhang, *Rationality and Mechanisms of Securities Regulation*, in Zhipan Wu (*ed.*), Jurists in Economic Law 340–41 (Beijing: Beijing University Press, 2003).

shareholder.[43] Therefore, significant shareholders in Chinese companies are likely to be stable shareholders, particularly in state-dominated companies since state shares are not freely transferable. The development of the corporate economy suggests that corporate systems with large, stable shareholders in their large public companies usually possess a comparatively less developed securities market. Germany, Japan, France and Italy are examples. The shareholding structure in Chinese listed companies is concentrated, like that in the German, Japanese and French systems. However, the difference of shareholding structure in listed companies seems not to be a problem to China in its endeavor to develop a securities market as advanced and prosperous as its US counterpart. The Chinese securities law adopts the US approach of emphasizing the protection of general investors.[44] However, the effect is not the same. Reports suggest that the Chinese securities regulatory system does not work as efficiently as expected in constraining market manipulation, insider trading and fraudulent disclosure by listed companies. Public investors are not effectively protected either.

This reveals that China has not yet developed a model of securities regulation specifically for its own characteristics and being able to work effectively with its own social, economic, and cultural environment. In the process of building up its own securities regulatory system, China may transplant technical mechanisms from the developed countries since these technical regulatory mechanisms are generally applicable. However, China may not directly import some practices developed in some other countries within their unique social, political, economic and cultural environments. For instance, some Chinese commentators have been urging reduction of state shares in listed companies with the state as the dominant shareholder. It is the author's view that to ensure the scale of economy and the survival of Chinese companies in international competition, it is highly necessary for China to have a significant number of state-controlled large companies and corporate groups. Establishing a prosperous securities market does not necessarily require dismantling concentrated shareholding in large Chinese companies.

Most importantly, China must establish a regulatory system with its own characteristics. It may have a focus of effectively restraining large shareholders from abuse of their majority voting power, and in the meantime provide sufficient protection for minority shareholders. Currently, it is necessary to enhance the regulatory strength in the areas of civil remedies against misconduct in the securities market.

The Banking Sector

Since the Asian financial turmoil, the Chinese government has attached great importance to the safety of its banking sector. A functioning banking system is

---

43   *See* Yujun Zhang, *Expanding the Channels of Direct Investment*, China Securities Daily (23 July 2002) at 10.
44   *See* Zhang, *supra* note 42, at 341.

fundamental to dealing with speculation on the financial market and weathering financial crises.[45] In 1993, China initiated the banking sector reforms, aimed at establishing a banking system that could better facilitate a market economy.[46]

The first step taken was to establish a central bank in China. Under the planned economy, China had a single bank system. It was the People's Bank of China (PBOC). The PBOC functioned as the treasury, the central bank, as well as the commercial bank in China. Although commercial banks emerged after the economic reforms, the PBOC has remained as the central bank.

Today, The PBOC makes and implements monetary policy and oversees the State Administration of Foreign Exchange (SAFE) which formulates foreign-exchange policies.[47] The China Banking Regulatory Commission (CBRC) is responsible for the regulation and supervision of banks, asset management companies, trust and investment companies, as well as other deposit-taking financial institutions, in order to maintain a safe and sound banking system in China.[48] Beneath the above regulatory and supervisory bodies are the so called "big four" – the four state-owned commercial banks. They are the Bank of China (BOC), the China Construction Bank (CCB), the Agricultural Bank of China (ABC), and the Industrial and Commercial Bank of China (ICBC). The government-directed spending functions are exercised by three policy banks including the Agricultural Development Bank of China (ADBC), China Development Bank (CDB), and the Export-Import Bank of China (Chexim). They are responsible for financing economic and trade development and state-invested projects. Beneath the "big four" are smaller state-owned commercial banks including the Bank of Communication, CITIC Industrial Bank, China Everbright Bank, Hua Xia Bank, China Minsheng Bank, Guangdong Development Bank, Shenzhen Development Bank, China Merchants Bank, Shanghai Pudong Development Bank, and Fujian Industrial Bank.

The second step of reforming the banking sector was to increase the liquidity and capital adequacy of the commercial banks. After the Asian financial crisis, China has accelerated the pace of its financial reforms. In 1998, the Ministry of Finance issued 2,700 billion worth of treasury bonds and the income was injected into the "big four" banks to improve their capital adequacy. Years of government-directed lending has resulted in the big four banks having large amounts of non-performing loans. According to the PBOC report, non-performing loans account

---

45   *See* Baoshu Wang, The Theory of Economic Law 276 (Beijing: Social Sciences Documentation Publishing House, 2004).

46   *See* Shan Ye, *An Analysis on Policies relating to Disposing Bad Loans, the Restrictions, and Perfecting the Relevant Laws*, in Zhipan Wu (*ed.*), Jurists in Economic Law 274 (Beijing: Beijing University Press, 2003).

47   *See* the PBOC, The Functions of the PBOC, in Introduction to the PBOC, available at <http://www.pbc.gov.cn/-renhangjianjie/zhineng.asp>.

48   *See* the State Council, the *Administrative Law of the Banking Sector*, sec. 2 (2003).

for 21.4 percent to 26.1 percent of total lending of China's four big banks in 2002.[49] The figure is well beyond the ceiling set up in the New Basel Capital Accord. In 1999, four asset management companies were established to transfer the non-performing assets from the banks and to deal with these assets. About RMB 14,000 billion non-performing loans were acquired by the four asset management companies.[50] After the transfer, the bad loan rate in the four banks was reduced to around 10 percent.

The third step was to adopt the international practice and corporatize the four commercial banks. At present, three of the four commercial banks have completed their transformation from wholly state-owned banks to bank corporations.[51] Their shares are listed on China's two national stock exchanges and the Hong Kong Stock Exchange.

The above strategies illustrate that China is determined to integrate into the global world economy. It has taken steps to reform its enterprises and banks for the purpose of facilitating a market system. Until the task is completed, China prefers close governmental supervision over the process, in order to make sure that its progress towards transition into a market system will not be interrupted by unexpected financial and economic turmoil that may thwart its efforts for prosperity. Having regard to the Chinese banking law, one can clearly perceive that the top priority of the law is to ensure the financial safety of the banking sector.

Some suggest that China has achieved close control over its banking sector at the expense of the banks' competitive strength.[52] They believe that China's banking sector is overly controlled. As a result, valuable business opportunities and significant amounts of commercial profits have been lost.[53] Some hold contrary views. They believe that retaining effective governmental control over the banking sector is necessary.[54] It is harmful to frequently change policies and laws safeguarding the nation's financial safety for mere economic benefits. They warn the Chinese people not to be short sighted.[55]

Globalization brings opportunities, and in the meantime, also brings enormous risks, especially to developing countries. Countries are exposed to unprecedented financial risks. Assuring financial safety is a top priority of every country. The

---

49 *See* Baozhong Gao, Institutional Analysis of Asset Securitization in China 155 (Beijing: Social Science Academic Press, 2005).

50 *See* Yanrong Hong, Studies of Legal Issues concerning Asset Backed Securitization 223 (Beijing: Beijing University Press, 2004).

51 The only bank that has not yet been corporatized is the ADBC.

52 *See* Xin Wang and Xiangpin Bian, *The Goals and Efficiency of the Banking Law and Regulating Banking Competition*, in Zhipan Wu (*ed.*), Jurists in Economic Law 263 (Beijing: Beijing University Press, 2003).

53 *Ibid*, at 264.

54 *See* Shiyuan Zhang and Cheng Liu, *Economic Safety Issues from an Economic Law Perspective*, in Zhipan Wu (*ed.*), Jurists in Economic Law 171 (Beijing: Beijing University Press, 2003).

55 *Ibid.*

foundation of a country's financial safety is the security of its banking system. In the case of China, state-owned banks have no choice but to shoulder the task of defending the country's financial safety when circumstances require. Hence, the fall of a state-owned bank during economic turmoil would be fatal. Therefore, important work faced by the Chinese and the Chinese government is to establish a regulatory framework that guarantees sound operation of the state banks and in the meantime promotes the banks' economic efficiency. It is important for the policy-makers to have the following objects in mind when designing the regulatory framework:

Firstly, the state-owned banks need to endeavor to reduce their non-performing loans and maintain reasonable liquidity and adequate reserve capital. This reduces the risks of insolvency of the banks during times when the financial system is under stress.

Secondly, it is important to give the Chinese people the assurance that the government has policies and strategies in place to warranty that state-owned banks or "big banks" are too big to fail. This will enhance the Chinese investors' confidence and ensures the effectiveness of governmental intervention through banks during troubled times.

Thirdly, encourage state banks to engage in market competition in order to improve state banks' economic efficiency and bring market mechanisms into the management of the banks. Only then, will the state-owned banks be able to improve their profitability, as well as develop their capacity of handling financial matters in a market economy.

Renminbi Exchange Rate

China has made the Renminbi enter into the floating exchange rate regime since 1994. This is also part of its commitment to the WTO requirements.[56] The government retains final control over the exchange rate. Since 1994, the Chinese currency has been constantly increasing its value against the US dollar. The decision to increase the value of the Renminbi was made under political pressure from some super powers including the US and Japan, which are also China's important trading partners. It was estimated that when the Renminbi increases 0.1 percent, China's GDP drops one point.[57] Consequently, in recent years, the inflation rate in China has rocketed. Inflation in turn causes a decrease of domestic purchase power. This could bring China's economy into a vicious circle.

Furthermore, China's economy relies heavily on export. With a strong Renminbi exchange rate, international demands for Chinese products will decline significantly. A diminished international market plus a flat domestic market will

---

56   *See* Chen, *supra* note 28, at 272.

57   *See* Cheng Chen, *Increase of Renimbi Value = GDP Decrease by One Point*, China Management (17 January 2005) available at <http://biz.163.com/50117/7/1AAKGBMI000213LR.html>.

destabilize China's economic development. To ensure the sustainable development of China's economy, the Chinese government has a right and a duty to maintain a stable Renminbi exchange rate.[58] Furthermore, no international convention, agreement, or organization including the WTO imposes restrictions on signatories or member states from exercising control over their exchange rates.

At this time, it is unrealistic to hope that the Renminbi exchange rate will go down. What the Chinese people can do is to closely watch the development and be cautious in allowing further increase.

In the meantime, China needs to prepare to allow the Renminbi exchange rate to further float in the future in order to meet the true demands of the international currency market. This can only be done when mechanisms of preventing potential currency crises are in place.

Conclusions

In the past three decades China's economy has delivered some stunning performances. The Chinese people's living standards have improved dramatically. The country has accumulated sizeable hard currency in reserve. However, all this can melt away very quickly if there is instability in financial markets, causing investors and citizens to lose their confidence in China's currency and financial products. Opening China's capital market to international investors and removing currency control have exposed China's banking sector, currency and listed companies to fierce international competition and have increased risks of financial crisis and economic slowdown. Despite the unprecedented challenges, the Chinese government is determined to continue the open door policy and accelerate China's integration into the global economy.

China has taken a proactive approach in resisting financial crises. It has endeavored to commit to the WTO agreements in relation to opening up the domestic market to internal companies and financial institutions. At the same time, China has been vigorously reforming its banking sector, developing its securities regulatory system, and improving corporate governance practices in large public companies. In the past few years, China enacted a series of laws regulating financial institutions and the capital market. In 2004 alone, more than 60 securities laws and regulations were promulgated.[59] The new laws have introduced more mechanisms of protecting general public investors. For instance, decisions concerning important matters of a company must be approved by a majority at a meeting of public investors. The pilot project of paying debts by transferring shares to the creditor has been launched. In a case where majority shareholders unlawfully expropriate minority shareholders' proprietary interests, the majority

---

58   *See* Chen, *supra* note 28, at 278.
59   *See* Yang Li, Financial Regulation in China 42 (Beijing: China Finance Press, 2003).

shareholders are required to compensate minority shareholders by transferring their shareholding to the minority shareholders. The purpose of this practice is to restrain majority shareholders from abusing their powers.

All of these suggest that China is actively searching for its own path of integrating in the world economy and developing strategies and mechanisms to weather potential economic crises. It is in our interest to see how successful China will be in achieving this goal.

Conclusion

In 1904, the first Chinese company law was enacted. Since then, corporate legislation was gradually developed. The first securities law was enacted ten years later. However, the first half of the twentieth century saw China occupied with both world and civil wars, and the country was unable to provide a supportive environment for businesses. During that time, the securities market was basically treated as a casino by the Chinese with securities dealing more akin to a gambling game rather than being an investment activity.[1] There were many dramatic events occurring on the securities market. Nevertheless, before 1949, China had the largest stock market in Asia: the Shanghai Stock Exchange. After the establishment of the People's Republic of China in 1949, the country introduced the planned economy of the Soviet model and promoted state ownership. As a result, all companies were gradually converted into state-owned enterprises. By the end of the 1950s, all securities activities were eliminated, together with companies.[2] The planned economy dominated China's economic landscape for the following 20 years.

Under the planned economy, private ownership was subject to nationalization. This social project was described as "socialist reforms". It took China ten years to complete the socialist reforms. The aim of the reforms was to transform all privately-owned enterprises into state-owned or public-owned enterprises. By 1958, the socialist reforms were basically completed, with most enterprises reformed into state-owned or collectively-owned entities. In the following 20 years, the concepts of stocks and capital markets had disappeared from Chinese people's daily lives. In this planned economy, the market played a very limited role, since public-owned enterprises operated according to state plans. The state was responsible for determining the number of products needed, the amount of materials to be used, and how the final products would be distributed.

Today, it is no longer debated whether the planned economy has supremacy over the market economy, or vice versa. With the collapse of the former Soviet Union and economic reforms being carried out in most former socialist countries, it appears to be evident that the planned economic model failed to meet its ultimate targets – achieving maximum material abundance for the majority of the population.

---

1   *See* Zhong Chen, Wind and Cloud on The Securities Market in China 3–4 (Shanghai: Shanghai Transportation University Press, 2000).
2   *See* Changjiang Li, The History and Development of China's Securities Market 28 (Beijing: China Wuzi Publishing House, 1998).

In contrast, only a couple of decades ago, the issue divided the world into two ideological camps. At some stages, the fact that the planned economy worked in some countries for a certain period inspired much discussion on which economic model was better amongst commentators and researchers. Statistics show that the economic performance of the Soviet Union from the 1920s to the end of the 1960s was stronger than that of the US.[3] Apart from the World War II period, the GDP growth rate of the Soviet Union was constantly higher than that of the US.[4] In China, the planned economy performed reasonably well during the 1950s. China's economy recovered rapidly in the post war period and the country's GDP grew impressively for about two decades.

The planned economy model eventually became stagnant in nearly all economies practicing it around the 1970s. Economists tried to interpret the phenomenon. Some pointed out the governance deficiencies in the planned economy. Some simply labeled it as a utopian model. Peter Brain in *Beyond Meltdown* argued that the economic stagnation in the former socialist countries was essentially caused by the development in technology. According to Brain, the planned economy had the physical capacity for the age of mechanization – the technology used up to the 1950s. However, when the world came into an era of technological innovation and wide application of information technology, the planned economy lost its competitive advantage.[5] Furthermore, the planned economy was unable to switch from import replacement to export expansion.[6] The conclusion is that the collapse of the soviet-style planned economy was unavoidable.

China initiated its economic reforms in 1979. It was the first socialist country carrying out fundamental economic reforms to effect a transformation from the planned economy to a market economy. The reason that China launched its economic reforms earlier than other planned economies was that the country encountered economic difficulties at an early stage. Between the end of the 1950s and the end of the 1960s, China's economy was distressed by a combination of political and economic mis-management, namely the Great Leap Forward and the Cultural Revolution. The Chinese government was under pressure to seek a new path of economic development in order to bring the nation's economy out of stress. This might well explain why countries like the Soviet Union, Romania, and East Germany lagged behind China in undertaking their economic reforms.

To gain an understanding of China's financial market and regulation, it is crucial to first obtain a background overview of China's economic reforms. This is because in China the introduction of any market mechanism is for the chief purpose of accommodating the economic reforms, and is a side product of the economic reforms. Hence, any discussion on the development of China's securities market

---

3   *See* Paul Samuelson, Economics 829–30 (New York: McGraw-Hill, 1961).

4   *See* A. Maddison, Monitoring the World Economy: 1920–1992 (Paris: OECD, 1995).

5   *See* Peter Brain, Beyond Meltdown: The Global Battle for Sustained Growth 83–4 (Melbourne: Scribe Publications, 1999).

6   *Ibid.*

and regulation would be incomplete without giving at least a brief review of the economic reforms in the country.

In the beginning of the economic reforms, a securities market was not considered by the policy makers. In fact, nobody was certain which path China should take in achieving the goals of the economic reforms. The Chinese were undertaking an unprecedented social project – reforming the planned economy into a market economy. There was no existing theory on which to reply and no successful model to follow. China was the first country to make such an attempt. With a great degree of caution, the Chinese policy-makers were determined to adopt the approach of "gradualism". This gradualist approach was expressed in a Chinese saying "cross the river by feeling the stones under feet". Underlying this comedic metaphor were the values of determination, sadness and heroism, which guided the reforms.

At the time when the economic reform project had just been launched, a leading Chinese economist attended a conference in the US and informed the audience about China's economic reforms. He caused great laughter upon informing the audience that China's fundamental policy for the economic reforms would be "cross the river by feeling stones under feet". Indeed, the statement sounded unconventional and too instinctive. The Chinese economist was not amused, and he asked in retort: "If the Chinese cross the river without stepping on stones and sink, will the US rescue us?"[7]

Under the gradualist approach, in the initial stage of the reforms, the Chinese government had the goal of retaining public ownership in most economic sectors. The government had sensed the danger of massive privatization. In a country where state-owned enterprises employed two-thirds of all industrial employees and also provided social welfare to these employees, retirees and their families, rapid privatization meant the potential emergence of social inequality and instability. A less draconian reform strategy was thus necessary.

At first, the Chinese government attempted to reform the enterprise without changing the public ownership. Strategies aimed at introducing market mechanisms and incentives into the enterprise system without challenging the public ownership status of these enterprises were introduced. These strategies included increasing the operational autonomy of enterprise managers and the contract responsibility system. However, such strategies did not improve the economic performance of state-owned enterprises satisfactorily.[8] Ten years later, a considerable number of state-owned enterprises continued to trade a loss. Moreover, without the installation of controlling mechanisms, these enterprises could drag the state banks to the verge of insolvency.

---

7   *See* Shangqing Sun, *Market Economy and Development of Productivity*, 6 Economic Studies (Jing Ji Yan Jiu) 4–5 (1996).

8   *See* Yuwa Wei, Comparative Corporate Governance: A Chinese Perspective 98–100 (London: Kluwer Law International, 2003).

Eventually, the Chinese government responded with the decision of furthering the enterprise reforms by corporatizing the state-owned enterprises. It was expected that corporatization would introduce modern managerial mechanisms into Chinese enterprises and consequently improve the economic efficiency of these enterprises. Furthermore, by introducing restructure and exit mechanisms including insolvency, merge and acquisition, the government was able to limit financial risks.[9] Consequently, most state-owned enterprises were transformed into state-owned or state-dominated companies.

However, the improvement of the managerial efficiency in the newly corporatized enterprises was not as significant as expected. The enterprises suffered from new problems. The most alarming was the problem of insider control. Insider control referred to the situation where the management and the supervisory board of state-owned or state-dominated companies collaborate to entrench their personal interest at the expense of the company. It was caused by a control vacuum existing in state-owned or dominated companies. In these companies, the state as the sole or dominant shareholder had to rely on agents to exercise the owner's rights, and had to rely on agents to appoint directors and supervisors. As a result, a control vacuum existed in these companies and there was no effective supervision over the management.

In an attempt to curtail the insider control problem, it was necessary to introduce external supervision into these companies. In addition, there was the need to provide a new channel for companies to raise funds so that state-banks would not be further encumbered. It was against such a background that the Chinese government decided to establish a capital market in China. State-owned and state-dominated companies were encouraged to become listed on domestic or international stock exchanges. In doing so, the government expected that these companies would be disciplined by the securities markets because they had to comply with the listing rules of the stock exchanges. In the meantime, by issuing shares to the general public, the listed companies would create a certain number of outside shareholders. These external shareholders would play a positive role in monitoring the management of these companies. This would mitigate the insider control problem. From this, it can be seen that in China, the development of the securities market was part of the broader efforts to achieve the goal of the economic reforms.

However, as discussed throughout this book, irregularities exist in China's capital market. As a result, the purpose of promoting good corporate governance by placing companies under market control has not been well served. This poses a serious threat to the long-term prosperity of China's securities market. The Chinese authority has attached great importance to the regulation of the securities. Laws and regulations were passed to curtail market misconduct. Again the effect was not satisfactory.

---

9   *Ibid*, at 101–8.

The evidence suggests that the external governance mechanism is not the solution for the failure of internal corporate governance. Rather, they interact and interdepend on each other. When fraud becomes common, the control function of the capital market is substantially undermined. To avoid the failure of market control, it is necessary to enhance regulatory intervention into the operation of the market, and in the meantime to introduce workable mechanisms to improve the efficiency of corporate internal control. Mechanisms of improving internal corporate control include practicable strategies of holding the supervisory board, the independent directors, and internal and external auditors accountable, promoting shareholder activism, and implementing an efficient board structure. When designing internal control strategies, elements such as culture, economic and political environment, and legal infrastructure must be taken into consideration.[10]

The regulatory framework for market control in China is in need of further improvement. The current securities laws have defects. The major code Securities Law leaves gaps to fill. For instance, it does not provide sufficient remedies to compensate securities investors, nor sufficient regulation over securities companies and intermediaries. It also fails to provide adequate mechanisms to control market misconduct such as non-disclosure, misleading disclosure, insider trading, and market manipulation. The Chinese law makers have been working on perfecting laws regulating companies and the securities market. Amendments were made to the *Company Code* and the *Securities Law*. There is no doubt that the regulatory framework for the capital market will be constantly improving. However, how to effectively implement the laws is another challenge faced by the Chinese.

In sum, China's financial market and many Chinese enterprises are facing mounting pressure from international competitors and foreign investment funds in the post-WTO entry era. The country's economic reforms are in a crucial time. Past experience suggests that the persistence of corporate inefficiency and market misconduct could trigger financial crises and eventually cause economic recession. If measures of improving corporate efficiency and market transparency are not implemented as soon as possible, the progress of the economic reforms could be severely jeopardized.

I would like to conclude this book by hoping that China will be able to feel more stones beneath the water and continue to tread on them in its course of crossing the river.

---

10   A comprehensive discussion on internal corporate governance in China is outside the scope of this book. For detailed treatment of this subject, please read my earlier book – Comparative Corporate Governance: A Chinese Perspective (Kluwer Law International, 2003).

Bibliography

Books and Articles

Adams, Edward S., "Corporate Governance After Enron and Global Crossing: Comparative Lessons for Cross-National Improvement", 78 *Indiana Law Review* (2003).

Anderson, Daniel M., "Taking Stock in China: Company Disclosure and Information in China's Stock Markets", 88 *Georgetown Law Journal* (June 2000), available at http://www.findarticles.com/-p/articles/mi_qa3805/is_200006/ai_n8889116.

Augustyn, Francene M., "A Primer for Incorporating Under the Income Tax Laws of France, Germany, or the United Kingdom", 7 *Northwestern Journal of International Law and Business* (1985).

Australian Securities and Investment Commission (ASIC), "ASIC at a Glance", available at <http://www.asc.gov.au>.

Australian Securities and Investment Commission (ASIC), "The Laws", *ASIC Administers*, available at <http://www.asc.gov.au>.

Baldwin, Robert and Martin Cave, *Understanding Regulation: Theory, Strategy, and Practice* (New York: Oxford, 1999).

Barrett-Lennard, Brian, *Anti-Globalisation* (Mornington: Beach Box Books, 2001).

Baumol, William J. and Alan Blinder, *Economics, Principles and Policy* (New York: Harcourt Brace College Publishers, 1988).

Bello, Walden, *Deglobalization: Ideas for a New World Economy* (London: Zed Books Ltd, 2002).

Black, Bernard and Reinier Kraakman, *Russian Privatization and Corporate Governance: What Went Wrong?* (Stanford Law School John M. Olin Program in Law and Economics Working Paper No. 178, 1999), available at <http://papers.ssrn.com/paper.taf?abstract_id=181348>.

Black, Bernard, Reinier Kraakman and Anna Tarassova, *Russian Privatization and Corporate Governance: What Went Wrong?* (Stanford Law School, Working Paper No. 178, 2000).

Blair, Margret M., *Ownership and Control: Rethinking Corporate Governance for the Twenty-First Century* (Washington, D.C.: The Brookings Institution, 1995).

Blake, David, *Financial Market Analysis* (New York: John Wiley & Sons, 2000).

Brain, Peter, *Beyond Meltdown: The Global Battle for Sustained Growth* (Melbourne: Scribe Publications, 1999).

Brandeis, Louis D., *Other People's Money and How the Bankers Use It* (New York: A.M. Kelley, 1971).

Brickley, James A. and Christopher M. James, "The Takeover Market, Corporate Board Composition, and Ownership Structure: The Case of Banking", 30(1) *Journal of Law and Economics* (1987).

Briston, R.J., *The Stock Exchange and Investment Analysis* (London: George Allen and Unwin Ltd, 1973).

Buckman, Greg, *Globalisation: Tame It or Scrap It? Mapping the Alternatives of the Anti-globalization Movement* (New York: St Martin's Press, 2004).

Cai, Wenhai, "Private Securities Litigation in China: Of Prominence and Problems", 13 *Columbia Journal of Asian Law* (1999).

Caskey, John P., *The Evolution of the Philadelphia Stock Exchange: 1964–2002* (Research Department, the Federal Reserve Bank of Philadelphia, Working Paper No. 03-21, 2003).

Cha, Laura M., "Speech at Video and Telephone Conference on Inspection on the Governance of Listed Companies", available at <http://www.cnstock.com/shzqb/shiwuban/200205130056.htm>.

Cha, Laura M., "The Future of China's Capital Markets and the Role of Corporate Governance" (Luncheon Speech at China Business Summit, 18 April 2001), available at <http://www.csrc.gov.cn/en/jsp/detail.jsp?infoid=1061948105100 andtype=CMS.STD>.

Chandler, Alfred D. Jr., *Scale and Scope: The Dynamics of Industrial Capitalism* (Massachusetts: The Belknap Press of Harvard University Press, 1990).

Charkham, Jonathan, *Keeping Good Company* (New York: Oxford University Press, 1995).

Cheffins, Brian R., "Mergers and Corporate Ownership Structure: The United States and Germany at the Turn of the 20th Century", 51 *American Journal of Comparative Law* (2003).

Chen, Cheng, "Increase of Renimbi Value = GDP Decrease by One Point, China Management" (17 January 2005), available at <http://biz.163.com/50117/7/1AAKGBMI000213LR.html>.

Chen, Gong, Shengye Zhou and Xiaoqiu Wu, *Securities Issuance and Transaction* (Zhengquan Faxin Yu Chengxiao, Beijing: the People's University of China, 1996).

Chen, Mingwu, "Remarks", in Wenmin Zhang et al. (eds), *The Great Economic Debate in China* (Zhongguo Jingji Da Lunzhan, Beijing: Economic Management Press, 1997).

Chen, Qingbo, *Securities English* (Zhengquan Yingyu, Beijing: China Machine Press, 2003).

Chen, Run and Qiang Zhu, *The Risk and Regulation of QFII in China's Securities Market*, in Zhipan Wu, *Jurists in Economic Law* (Jingji Fa Xuejia, Beijing: Beijing University Press, 2005).

Chen, Su, *Special Research on Securities Law* (Zhengquan Fa Zhuanti Yanjiu, Beijing: Tertiary Education Press, 2006).

Chen, Ting, "The Institutional Defects in China's Securities Market", in Baisan Xie (ed.), *International Comparison of Securities Markets* 647 (Zhengquan Shichang De Guoji Bijiao, Volume 2, Beijing: Qinghua University Press, 2003).

Chen, Xiaohong, "Chinese and Japanese Enterprise System: Some Descriptions and Analyses", in Liming Li (ed.), *The Comparison of Chinese and Japanese Enterprise Systems* (Zhong Ri Qiyi Falü Zhidu Bijiao, Beijing: Law Publishing House, 1998).

Chen, Yiehua, *Theories of Securities Self-Regulation and China's Practice* (Zhengquan Ye Zilü Guanli Lilun Yu Zhongguo De Shijian, Beijing: China Financial Press, 2006).

Chen, Yunliang, "National and International Regulation of the Renminbi", in Zhipan Wu (ed.), *Jurists in Economic Law* (Jingji Fa Xuejia, Beijing: Beijing University Press, 2003).

Chen, Zhengao, *The Historical Materials of Present Chinese Industries* (Zhongguo Jindai Gongye Shi Ziliao, Volume 4, Beijing: Living, Reading and New Acknowledge Three Joint Publishing House, 1961).

Chen, Zhengrong, "What is Share Split? Daily Economy News", available at <http://finance.sina.com.cn/stock/t/20050531/02561638152.shtml>.

Chen, Zhiwu, "Class Action Is an Effective Means of Protecting Securities Investors, New Fortune" (11 April 2005), available at <http://www.p5w.net/scoop/xcfwz/200504/t307823.htm>.

Chen, Zhong, *Wind and Cloud on The Securities Markets in China* (Zhongguo Gushi Fengyun Lu, Shanghai: Shanghai Transportation University Press, 2000).

China News, "The Four Phases of the Asian Crisis", available at <http://www.china.com.cn/-news/txt/2007-07/02/content_8466890.htm>.

China Securities Association, *Securities Investment Analysis* (Gupiao Touzi Fenxi, Beijing: China Finance and Economics Press, 2004).

China Securities Regulatory Commission, *About Us*, available at <http://www.csrc.gov.cn/-en/homepage/about_en.jsp>.

China Securities Regulatory Commission, *Report on the Development of China's Securities Industry* (Zhongguo Zhengquan Ye Fazhan Baogao, Beijing: China Finance and Economy Press, 2004).

China Securities Regulatory Commission, "China's Securities and Futures Markets" (April 2004), available at <http://www.csrc.gov.cn/cms/uploadFiles/introduction2004edition.1087888443500.-doc>.

Choi, Stephen J. and Adam C. Pritchard, "Behavioral Economics and the SEC", 56 *Stanford Law Review* (2003).

Claessens, Stijn, Simeon Djankov and Gerhard Pohl, *Ownership and Corporate Governance: Evidence from the Czech Republic* (World Bank, Policy Research Working Paper Series, No. 1737, 1997), available at <http://www.worldbank.org/html/dec/Publications/Workpapers/WPS1700series/-wps1737/wps1737.pdf>.

Coase, Ronald, "The Nature of the Firm", in Ronald Coase, *The Firm, the Market and the Law* (Chicago: The University of Chicago Press, 1988).

Coffee, John C. Jr., "Regulating the Market for Corporate Control: A Critical Assessment of the Tender Offer's Role in Corporate Governance', 84 *Columbia Law Review* (1984).

Coffee, John C. Jr., "Inventing a Corporate Monitor in Transitional Economies: The Uncertain Lessons from the Czech and Polish Experience', in Klaus Hopt et al. (eds), *Comparative Corporate Governance: The State of Emerging Research* (Oxford: Clarendon Press, 1998).

Coffee, John C. Jr., *Privatization and Corporate Governance: The Lesson from Securities Market Failure* (Columbia Law School Center for Law and Economics Studies, Working Paper No. 158, 1999), available at <http://papers.ssvn.com/paper.taf?abstract_id=190568>.

Coffee, John C. Jr., "The Rise of Dispersed Ownership: The Role of Law in the Separation of Ownership and Control" (Annual Raben Lecture, Yale Law School, January 2001), available at <http://papers.ssrn.com/paper.taf?abstractid=254097>.

Cohen, David, *Fear, Greed and Panic: The Psychology of the Stock Market* (New York: John Wiley & Sons Inc., 2001).

Commentator, "The Market on the Two Stock Exchanges Continues to Fall, and the Index Dives More Than 21 Points", available at <http://finance.people.com.cn/GB/67815/68059/5480901.html>.

Conard, Alfred F., *Corporations in Perspective* (New York: The Foundation Press, 1976).

Coram, Paul, Colin Ferguson and Robyn Moroney, "The Value of Internal Audit in Fraud Detection", available at <http://www.afaanz.org/research/AFAANZ%200642.pdf>.

Covel, Michael, "Technical Analysis v. Fundamental Analysis: Difference?" available at <http://www.turtletrader.com/technical-fundamental.html>.

Cox, James D., Robert W. Hillman and Donald C. Langevoort, *Securities Regulation Cases and Materials* (New York: Aspen Law and Business, 2001).

Cull, Robert, Jana Matesova and Mary Shirley, "Ownership and the Temptation to Loot: Evidence from Privatized Firms in the Czech Republic", 30(1) *Journal of Comparative Economics* (2002).

Curtis, Mark, *Trade for Life* (London: Christian Aid, 2001).

Dallago, Bruno, "Corporate Governance in Transformation Economies", in Bruno Dallago and Ichiro Iwasaki (eds), *Corporate Restructuring and Governance in Transition Economies* (New York: Palgrave Macmillan, 2007).

Davies, K.G., "Joint-Stock Investment in the Later Seventeenth Century", 4 *The Economic History Review* (1951–52).

Deng, Yiwen, *Cross Swords: Great Debate on State Ownership Reforms* (Feichang JiaoFeng: Guoqi Chanquan Gaige Da Taolun, Beijing: Ocean Press, 2005).

Department of Foreign Affairs and Trade (Australia), *Australia – China Free Trade Agreement Joint Feasibility Study* (2003), available at <www.dfat.gov. au/geo/china/fta>.

Dickson, Peter George Muir, *The Financial Revolution in England* (London: Macmillan, 1967).

Dimsdale, Nicholas and Martha Prevezer (eds), *Capital Markets and Corporate Governance* (Oxford: Clarendon Press, 1994).

DiPiazza, Samuel A. and Robert G. Eccles, *Building Public Trust: The Future of Corporate Reporting* (New York: John Wiley & Sons, 2002).

Dou, Jianmin, *Research on the History of Corporate Ideology in China* (Zhongguo Gongsi Zhi Sixiang Yanjiu, Shanghai: Publishing House of Shanghai University of Finance and Economics, 1999).

Du, Shuming, "The Development of Securities Investment Funds: A Great Leap in Ten Years' Time" (Yinhe Securities, 9 September 2007), available at <http://www.p5w.net/stock/lzft/jjyj/200709/-t1229655.htm>.

Duflo, Esther and Emmanuel Saez, "Participation and Investment Decisions in a Retirement Plan: The Influence of Colleagues' Choices", 85 *Journal of Public Economics* (2002).

Dunlop, Alex, *Corporate Governance and Control* (London: Kogan Page, 1998).

Easterbrook, Frank H. and Daniel R. Fischel, "The Proper Role of a Target's Management in Responding to a Tender Offer", 94 *Harvard Law Review* (1981).

Easterbrook, Frank H. and Daniel R. Fischel, "Corporate Control Transactions", 91 *Yale Law Journal* (1982).

Easterbrook, Frank H. and Daniel R. Fischel, *The Economic Structure of Corporate Law* (Massachusetts: Harvard University Press, 1991).

Economist Intelligence Unit, Country Commerce Germany § 9.1 (2004), available at 2004 WLNR 13986210.

Edesess, Robert, "The End of Innocence: An Actual Knowledge Threshold for Intermediaries Holding Fiduciaries/Clients' Assets", 2 *DePaul Business and Commercial Law Journal* (2004).

Editor of Stock Exchange Secrets, "London Stock Exchange Listing Requirements", available at <http://www.stockexchangesecrets.com/london-stock-exchange-listing-requirements.html>.

Editor, "A Brief History of the Japanese Stock Market", available at <http://thejapanese-stockmarket.com>.

Editor, "A Review on Renminbi Exchange Rate Reforms", available at <http://news.china.com/-zh_cn/focus/rmb/index.html>.

Editor, About Us (the Federal Financial Market Service website), available at http://www.fcsm.ru/eng/.

Editor, "China Fund Industry Report 2006–2007", available at <http://www.okokok.com.cn/Abroad/-Class126/Class106/200701/115045.html>.

Editor, "China Reflects the Asian Financial Crisis and Enhances the Reforms of Its Financial Sectors", *China Net*, available at <http://www.china.com.cn/news/txt/2007-07/02/content_8465918.htm>.

Editor, "Claiming Loss to Evade Taxes: 70 per cent of Foreign Enterprises in Suzhou Make Loss Intentionally", *Xinhua Net* (16 September 2005), available at <http://news.xinhuanet.com/-fortune/2005-09/16/content_3497540.htm>.

Editor, "Desert Areas Growth in China", *People's Daily* (25 February 2002) available at <http://english.people.com.con/200202/25/eng20020225_90962.shtml>.

Editor, "Encyclopaedia of American History", available at <http://www.answers.com/topic/market-1>.

Editor, "Experts Forecast China's Capital Market: The Economy Needs a Stable Securities Market" (Liaowang News Weekly, 16 April 2007), available at <http://news.xinhuanet.com/fortune/2007-04/16/content_5982891.htm>.

Editor, "History/Competence", available at <http://www.fcsm.ru/catalog.asp?ob_no=1438>.

Editor, "Indices List" (the Shenzhen Stock Exchange website), available at <http://www.szse.cn/-main/en/marketdata/Indiceslist/>.

Editor, "Investopedia", available at <http://www.investopedia.com/terms/s/speculation.asp>.

Editor, "Let's Know about Japanese Stock Market", available at <http://www.japanese-stockmarket-now.com>.

Editor, "MMM" (pyramid), available at <http://en.wikipedia.org/wiki/MMM_(pyramid)>.

Editor, "Notice to Members" (The Shanghai Stock Exchange website), available at <http://www.sse.com.cn/sseportal/en_us/ps/member/nm.shtml>.

Editor, "Share Glossary", available at <http://www.denguang.com/html/98/6098-9048.html>.

Editor, "Share Slip: Capital Looks at Valuable Opportunities" (Zhongying Investment website), available at <http://www.zysg.net/Article_1735.aspx>.

Editor, "Should Not Forget the Lessons of the Asian Financial Crisis, China Net", available at <http://www.china.com.cn/news/txt/2007-07/02/content_8465918.htm>.

Editor, "Six Large Gaps Regarding Income: The Top 20% Has 45% of the Wealth" (Xinhua Net, 17 June 2005), available at <http://news.xinhuanet.com/fortune/2005-06/17/content/200411/6-1.htm>.

Editor, "SSE Index, the Shanghai Stock Exchange website", available at <http://www.sse.com.cn/-sseportal/en_us/ps/sczn/zstx_home.shtml> and <http://www.sse.com.cn/sseportal/en_us/ps/sczn/-zstx.jsp>.

Editor, "Stock Market Crash", available at <http://www.stock-market-crash.net/1929.htm>.

Editor, "The Facts in 2.19 B Share Policy Divulgence Incident", available at <http://stock.163.com/-edito/010221/010221_36369.html>.

Editor, "The Forum of Electricity and Gas, Electricity and Gas Net", available at <http://bbs.chinaaba.com/archiver/showtopic-6591.aspx>.

Editor, "The History", at the SEEC homepage, available at <http://www.cei.gov.cn/doc/lhcjjg/-seec/doc01.htm>.

Editor, "The History of Stock Exchange and Trust Companies in Old China, China Net of Finance and Securities", available at <http://www.zj365.cn/zj4.htm>.

Editor, "The History of the Stock Market", *The New Enlightenment*, available at <http://www.hermes-press.com/wshist1.htm>.

Editor, "The Legal Framework of the Credibility of Listed Companies", available at <http://www.xingzhi.org/law/civillaw/6538_3.html>.

Editor, "When Wealth is Blown Away", *Business Week* (26 March 2001).

Editor, Wikipedia, available at <http://en.wikipedia.org/wiki/Behavioral_Finance>.

Editor, Wikipedia, available at <http://en.wikipedia.org/wiki/Financial_analyst>.

Editor, Wikipedia, available at <http://en.wikipedia.org/wiki/Financial_markets#Definition>.

Editor, Wikipedia, available at <http://en.wikipedia.org/wiki/Robber_baron_(industrialist)>.

Editor, Wikipedia, available at <http://en.wikipedia.org/wiki/Securities_market>.

Editor, Wikipedia, available at <http://en.wikipedia.org/wiki/Sarbanes-Oxley_Act>.

Editor, Wikipedia, available at <http://en.wikipedia.org/wiki/Stock_market#History>.

Editor, Wikipedia, available at <http://en.wikipedia.org/wiki/Speculation>.

Editor, Wikipedia, available at <http://www.stockmarketinvestinginfo.com/smi_history.html>.

Eisenstadt, Peter, "How the Buttonwood Tree Grew: The Making of a New York Stock Exchange Legend", 19 *Prospects: An Annual of American Cultural Studies* (1994).

Eu, David, "Financial Reforms and Corporate Governance in China", 34 *Columbia Journal of Transnational Law* (1996).

Fama, Eugene, Lawrence Fisher, Michael Jensen and Richard Roll, "The Adjustment of Stock Prices to New Information", 10 *International Economic Review* (1969).

Fama, Eugene F., "Efficient Capital Markets: A Review of Theory and Empirical Works", 25 *Journal of Finance* (1970).

Fama, Eugene F. and Michael C. Jensen, "Separation of Ownership and Control", 26 *Journal of Law and Economics* (1983).

Fama, Eugene F., "Efficiency Survives the Attack of the Anomalies", *GSB Chicago Alumni Magazine* (1998).

Fang, Fuqian, *The Theory of Public Choices* (Gonggong Xuanze Lilun)(Beijing: People's University of China, 2000).

Farrar, John, *Corporate Governance: Theories, Principles, and Practice* (Melbourne: Oxford University Press, 2005).

Fernald, John and John H. Rogers, "Puzzles in the Chinese Stock Market", 84(3) *The Review of Economics and Statistics* (2002).

Fisch, Jill E., "Regulatory Responses to Investor Irrationality: The Case of the Research Analyst", 10 *Lewis and Clark Law Review* (2006).

Fischel, Daniel R., "Efficient Capital Market Theory, the Market for Corporate Control, and the Regulation of Cash Tender Offers", 57 *Texas Law Review* (1980).

Fisher, William F. and Thomas Ponniah, *Another World Is Possible* (London: Zed Books, 2003).

Fohlin, Caroline, "Regulation, Taxation, and the Development of the German Universal Banking System", 6 *European Review of Economic History* (2002).

Franks, Julian and Colin Mayer, "Ownership and Control of German Corporations", 14(4) *Review of Financial Studies* (2001).

Frydman, Roman, Marek Hessel and Andrej Rapaczynski, *Why Ownership Matters?: Politicization and Entrepreneurship in the Restructuring of the Enterprises in Central Europe* (C.V. Starr Center, Working Paper No. 98-14, April 1998).

FSA, *FSA, History* (FSA website), available at <http://www.fsa.gov.uk/Pages/About/Who/-History/index.shtml>.

Fu, Qilin, *Well-Known Cases relating to China's Securities Market in the Past Ten Years* (Zhongguo Zhengquan Shichang Shinian Zhuming Anli Pingxi, Beijing: Publishing House of China University of Political Science and Law, 2002).

Gan, Peizhong, *The Law of Enterprises and Companies* (Qiye Yu Gongsi Fa, Beijing: Beijing University Publishing House, 1998).

Gao, Baozhong, *Institutional Analysis of Asset Securitization in China* (Zhongguo Zichan Zhengquan Hua De Zhidu Fenxi, Beijing: Social Science Academic Press, 2005).

Gao, Xiqing, "Some Regulatory Issues of the PRC Securities Market", in *China 2000: Emerging Investment, Funding and Advisory Opportunities for a New China, OnlineBooks*, available at <http://www.asialaw.com/bookstore/china2000/chapter01.htm>.

Geng, Xiao, "China's Securities Market Development: Lessons from Hong Kong and Other Asian Markets" (15 January 2003), available at <www.econ.hku.hk/~xiaogeng/research/Paper/Securities%20market%20development%20in%20China-English.pdf>.

George, Susan, *The Debt Boomerang: How Third World Debt Harms Us All* (London: Pluto Press, 1992).

Gerschenkron, Alexander, *Economic Backwardness in Historical Perspective* (Cambridge: Harvard University Press, 1962).

Gilboy, George and Eric Heginbotham, "The Latin Americanization of China?" *Current History* (September 2004).

Gilligan, George, "Expecting Too Much? Enforcement Limitations in the Regulation of Financial Markets" (conference paper at Conflicting Interests: Evaluating Regulation, Ethics and Accountability in Capital Markets Governance, Australian National University, Canberra, 14–15 March 2007), available at <http://cbe.anu.edu.au/capitalmarkets/papers/GILLIGAN-CAPITAL-MARKETS.pdf>.

Gilson, Ronald and Curtis J. Milhaupt, *Choices as Regulatory Reform: The Case of Japanese Corporate Governance* (Columbia University Law School, Center for Law Economic Studies Working Paper No 251; Stanford Law School, John M. Olin Program in Law and Economics, Working Paper No. 281; and European Corporate Governance Institute, Law Working Paper No. 22/2004), available at <http://ssrn.com/abstract=537843>.

Glaese, Edward, Simon Johnson and Andrei Shleifer, "Coase Versus the Coasians", 116(3) *The Quarterly Journal of Economics* (2001).

Global Policy Forum, "Defining Globalization", available at <http://www.globalpolicy.org/globaliz/-define/index.htm>.

Goldsmith, Raymond William, *Capital Market Analysis and the Financial Accounts of the Nation* (New Jersey: General Learning Press, 1972).

Gower, L.C.B., *Review of Investor Protection: A Discussion Document* (HMSO, January 1982).

Gower, L.C.B., *Review of Investor Protection: Final Report* (Cmnd, 1984).

Graham, Benjamin and David Dodd, *Security Analysis: The Classic 1934 Edition* (New York: McGraw-Hill Companies, Inc., 1934).

Graham, Benjamin and David Dodd, *Security Analysis* (New York: McGraw-Hill Book Company, 1940).

Graham, Benjamin and Jason Zweig, *The Intelligent Investor: The Definitive Book on Value Investing* (New York: HarperCollins, 2003).

Gray, Cheryl, *In Search of Owners: Lessons of Experience with Privatization and Corporate Governance in Transition Economies* (World Bank Policy Research Working Paper No. 1595, 1996).

Green, Stephen, "Something Old, Something New", 18 *China Review* (2001), available at <http://www.cmagic.co.uk/home-fp01/g/b/www.gbcc.org.uk/crcon.htm>.

Gu, Lei and Baojie Wang, *Crimes and Irregularities on the Securities market and Legal Control* (Zhengquan Shichang Weigui Fanzui Toushi Yu Falü Ezhi, China Prosecution Press, 2004).

Guo, Feng, "A Research on the Establishment of Good Faith Principle in Chinese Securities Market", 2 *Securities Law Review* (Zhengquan Falü Pinglun, 2002).

Hall, Art Alcausin, "International Banking Regulation into the 21st Century: Flirting with Revolution", 21 *New York Law School Journal of International and Comparative Law* (2001).

Han, Anna M., "China's Company Law: Practicing Capitalism in a Transitional Economy", 5 *Pacific Rim Law and Policy Journal* (1996).

Han, Dongping, "Professional Bias and Its Impact on China's Rural Education: Re-examining the Two Models of Rural Education and Their Impact on Rural Development in China", available at <http://chinastudygroup.org/article/2/>.

Han, Zhiguo, "The Mechanisms of Development and Innovation of China's Corporate Economy", 1 *Securities Law Review* (Zhengjuan Falü Pinglun, 2001).

Hang, Xing and Hunran Pan, "A Comparative Analysis of the Efficiency of US, Japanese and German Securities Markets and What Inspiration China Can Get From It", in Baisan Xie (ed.), *International Comparison of Securities Markets* (Zhengquan Shichang De Guoji Bijiao, Volume 1, Beijing: Qinghua University Press, 2003).

Hanousek, Jan and Randall K. Filer, "Lange and Hayke Revisited: Lessons from Czech Voucher Privatization", 21(3) *Cato Journal* (2002).

Hansmann, Henry and Reinier Kraakman, *The End of History for Corporate Law* (Harvard Law School, John M. Olin Center for Law, Economics, and Business Working Paper No. 280, 2000).

Hayek, Friedrich A., *Constitution of Liberty* (Chicago: University of Chicago, 1960).

Hazen, Thomas Lee, "The Short-Term/Long-Term Dichotomy and Investment Theory: Implications for Securities Market Regulation and for Corporate Law", 70 *North Carolina Law Review* (1991).

Hazen, Thomas Lee, *The Law of Securities Regulation* (St. Paul, Minnesota: West Group, 1996).

He, Peihua and Minzhang Wu, "Issues Concerning Takeovers by Foreign Investors and Citizenship Treatment After China's Entrance Into the WTO", in Ping Jiang and Zhenshan Yang (eds), *Civil and Commercial Law Review* (Minshang Falü Pinglun, Beijing: China Fangzheng Press, 2004).

He, Xiaofeng, *Capital Markets and Investment Banks* (Ziben Shichang Yu Touzi Yinhang, Beijing: Beijing University Press, 2005).

Heakal, Reem, *What Was The Glass-Steagall Act?* available at <http://www.investopedia.com/-articles/03/071603.asp>.

Heilbroner, Robert L. and Lester C. Thurow, *Economics Explained* (New Jersey: Prentice Hall, 1982).

Heilbroner, Robert and Lester C. Thurow, *Economics Explained* (New York: Touchstone, 1998).

Hines, Colin, *Localization: A Global Manifesto* 64 (London: Earthscan, 2000).

Hogarth, Robin M. and Melvin W. Reder (eds), *Rational Choice: The Contrast Between Economics and Psychology* (Chicago: The University of Chicago Press, 1987).

Hogarth, Robin M. and Melvin W. Reder, "Introduction", in Robin M. Hogarth and Melvin W. Reder (eds), *Rational Choice: The Contrast between Economics and Psychology* (Chicago: The University of Chicago Press, 1987).

Hong, Harrison, Jeffrey D. Kubik and Jeremy C. Stein, "Social Interaction and Stock-Market Participation", 59(1) *The Journal of Finance* (2004).

Hong, Yanrong, *Studies of Legal Issues concerning Asset Backed Securitization* (Beijing: Beijing University Press, 2004).

Hopt, Klaus et al. (eds), *Comparative Corporate Governance: The State of Emerging Research* (Oxford: Clarendon Press, 1998).

Hopt, Klaus J. (ed.), *Comparative Corporate Governance, Essays and Materials* (Berlin: Walter de Gruyer, 1997).

Hoogvelt, Ankie, *Globalization and the Post Colonial World: The New Political Economy of Development* (London: Zed Books, 2001).

Hoover, Herbert, *Memoirs: The Cabinet and the Presidency* (New York: Macmillan, 1952).

Hoshi, Takeo, "The Economic Role of Corporate Grouping and the Main Bank System", in M. Aoki and R. Dore (eds), *The Japanese Firm: The Sources of Competitive Strength* (New York: Oxford University Press, 1994).

Hu, Bei, "China Urged to Adopt Class Action Suits", *South China Morning Post* (Nan Zhongguo Chenbao, 21 November 2002).

Hu, Xiaoke, *Preliminary Study on the Prohibition System of Securities Fraud* (Zhengquan Qizha Jinzhi Zhidu Chulun, Beijing: Economic Science Press, 2004).

Huang, Sujian, *Companies* (Gong Si Fa, Beijing: People's University Publishing House, 1989).

Huang, Zhenzhong, *Civil Liability and Civil Litigation in US Securities Law* (Meiguo Zhengquna Fa Shang De Minshi Zeren Yu Minshi Susong, Beijing: Law Press, 2003).

Hurt, Christine, "Regulating Public Morals And Private Markets: Online Securities Trading, Internet Gambling, And The Speculation Paradox", 86 *B.U. L. Rev.* 371 (2006).

Hutchens, Walter, "Major Revision to PRC Company Law Moving Forward", *Walter Hutchens' Blog* (25 February 2005), available at <http://www.rhsmith. umd.edu/faculty/whutchens/2005/02/major-revision-to-prc-company-law. html>.

Institution of Internal Audit, *Definition of Internal Auditing* (Altamonte Springs, 1999).

International Finance Corporation and US Department of Commerce, "The Importance of Good Corporate Governance for Russia, The Russia Corporate Governance Manual" (2004), available at <http://trade.gov/goodgovernance/ adobe/CGMEnPart_1/p1_importance_of.pdf>.

Jacobs, Michael, *Short-Term America: The Causes and Cures of Our Business Myopia* (Boston: Harvard Business School Press, 1991).

Jaffee, Dwight and Bertrand Renaud, *Strategies to Develop Mortgage Markets in Transition Economies* (World Bank Policy Research, Working Paper No. 1697, 1996).

Jandik, Tomas and Graig G. Rennie, *The Evolution of Corporate Governance and Firm Performance in Emerging Markets: The Case of Sellier and Bellot* (European Corporate Governance Institute Finance Working Paper No. 59/2004, 2005), available at <http://www.fma.org/Chicago/Papers/-jandik_ rennie_fmae05.pdf>.

Jenkins, Alan, *The Stock Exchange Story* (London: Heinemann, 1973).

Jensen, Michael C. and William H. Meckling, "Theory of the Firm: Managerial Behavior, Agency Costs and Ownership Structure", 3 *The Journal of Financial Economics* (1976).

Jia, Baoli, "Looking Back the Past Ten Years", *Shanghai Securities Newspaper* (10 September 2007), available at <http://www.p5w.net/fund/fxpl/200709/t1204772.htm>.

Jin, Dehuan, *A Study of Volatility of the Chinese Securities Market and Control* (Zhongguo Zhengquan Shichang Bodong Yu Kongzhi Yanjiu, Shanghai: Shanghai University of Finance and Commerce Press, 2003).

Johnson, Simon, Peter Boone, Alasdair Breach and Eric Friedman, *Corporate Governance in the Asian Financial Crisis* (Rutgers University Department of Economics, Working Paper No. 279, 1999).

Johnson, Simon, Rafael La Porta, Florencio Lopez-de-Silanes and Andrei Shleifer, "Tunneling", 90 *American Economic Review* (2000).

Kahneman, Daniel and Amos Tversky, "Prospect Theory: An Analysis of Decision under Risk", *XLVII Econometrica* 263–91 (1979).

Kanda, Hideki, "Trends in Japanese Corporate Governance", in Klaus J. Hopt (ed.), *Comparative Corporate Governance, Essays and Materials* (Walter de Gruyer, Berlin, 1997).

Kanda, Hideki, "Disclosure and Corporate Governance: A Japanese Perspective" (Paper at A Conference on Corporate Governance in Asia: A Comparative Perspective, Seoul, 3–5 March 1999).

Katona, George, "Contribution of Psychological Data to Economic Analysis", 42 (239) *Journal of the American Statistical Association* (September 1947)

Kelleher, Brian, "Foreign Banks Target China", *Australian Banking and Finance* (17 November 2004).

Keynes, John Maynard, *The General Theory of Employment, Interest and Money* (London: Macmillan Cambridge University Press, 1936).

Kindleberger, Charles P. and Robert Z. Aliber, *Manias, Panics and Crashes: A History of Financial Crises* (Basingstoke: Palgrave Macmillan, 2005).

Kirby, William C., "China Unincorporated: Company Law and Business Enterprise in Twentieth-Century China", 54 *The Journal of Asian Studies* (1995).

Kitch, Edmund W., *Regulation of the Securities Market* (University of Virginia Law School, Working Paper No. 5660, 1999).

Kochetygova, Julia and Oleg Shvyrkov, "Corporate Governance Practices in Russia and the Implementation of the Corporate Governance Code", available at <http://www.ebrd.com/pubs/-legal/lit061j.pdf>.

Koliandre, Alexander, "A Decade of Economic Reform", *BBC News* (24 December 2001), available at <http://news.bbc.co.uk/1/hi/business/1727305.stm>.

Kuhn, Robert Lawrence, *Investment Banking: The Art and Science of High Stakes Dealmaking* (London: Longman, 1990).

Lai, Chi-kong, "The Qing State and Merchant Enterprise: The China Merchants' Company 1872–1902", in R. Ampalavanar Brown (ed.), *Chinese Business Enterprise* (Volume 6, London: Routledge, 1999).

Lardy, Nicholas R., "The Role of Foreign Trade and Investment in China's Economic Transformation", in Andrew G. Walder (ed.), *China's Transitional Economy* (London: Oxford University Press, 1996).

Lardy, Nicholas R., *China's Unfinished Economic Revolution* (Washington D.C.: Brookings Institution Press, 1998).

Lawrence, Susan V., "Ally of the People", *Far East Economic Review* (9 May 2002).

Legal Dictionary (defining tippee as person who receives tip), available at <http://www.answers.com/-library/Legal%20Dictionary;jsessionid=315obodddmmog-cid-447479963-sbid-lc01a>.

Leung, Erika, Lily Liu, Lu Shen, Kevin Taback and Leo Wang, "Financial Reform and Corporate Governance in China", *MIT Sloan School of Management 50th Anniversary Proceedings* (Cambridge Massachusetts, June 2002).

Li, Buyun and Ping Jiang, *WTO and China's Legal Development* (Beijing: China Fanzhen Press, 2001) WTO Yu Zhong Guo De Fa Lu Fa Zhan.

Li, Changjiang, *The History and Development of China's Securities Markets* (Beijing: China Wuzi Publishing House, 1998); See also I.A. Tokley and Tina Ravn, *Company and Securities Law in China* 62 (Hong Kong: Sweet and Maxwell Asia, 1998).

Li, Guangyuan, in Wenmin Zhang et al. (eds), *The Great Economic Debate in China* (Beijing: Economic Management Press: 1997).

Li, Minliang, *Studies of Hotly Debated Legal Issues concerning Securities Market* (Beijing: Commerce Press, 2004) ZhengQuan ShiChang ReDian Falü WenTi YanJiu.

Li, Minqi and Andong Zhu, "China's Public Services Privatization and Poverty Reduction: Health Care and Education Reform (Privatization) in China and the Impact on Poverty", *UNDP Policy Brief* (Beijing 2004).

Li, Qiang and Liang Han, *Cases and Important Issues of Securities Law* (Zhengquan Fa Qianyan Wenti Anli Yanjiu, Beijing: China Economy Press, 2001).

Li, Qiaoning, "The Regulatory Framework of Issue of Securities Has Been Built Following the Publication of Five Supplementary Documents", *Securities Times* (2 September 2003), available at <http://www.china.com.cn/chinese/2003/Sep/396047.htm>.

Li, Shiping, *Case Studies of Essential Issues Concerning the Securities Law* (Zhengquan Fa Qianyan Wenti Anli Yanjiu, Beijing: China Economics Press, 2001).

Li, Yang, *Financial Regulation in China* (Zhongguo Jinrong Fazhi, Beijing: China Finance Press, 2003).

Li, Zhijun, *Government Regulation of the Securities Market* (Zhengquan Shichang Zhengfu Jianguan Lun, Changchun: Jilin People's Press, 2005).

Liang, Wen, "Some Legal Problems of Reforming the State Owned Enterprises into Limited Companies", in Hua Chen and Jingwei Jiu (eds), *Research on the State Owned Enterprise Reform and Corporate Law* (Guoyou Qiye Gaige Yu Gongsi Falü Wenti Yanjiu, Xiamen: Publishing House of Xiamen University, 1997).

Licht, Amir, "David's Dilemma: A Case Study of Securities Regulation in a Small Open Market", 2 *Theoretical Inquiries Law* (2001).

Liddell, Locke and Sapp L.L.P., "Corporate Governance Alert: SEC Adopts Reforms to Executive Compensation Disclosure Rules" (3 August 2006), available at <http://attorneys.lockeliddell.com/-files/Publication/c66a8233-3273-4634-bb65-07e4d7e7d2fc/Presentation/PublicationAttachment/-4c6737a2-4bf4-417a-bc1d-0ad29136324d/Corporate%20Governance%20Ale rt%20-%20August%202006.pdf>.

Lin, Yie, *Securities Law* (Zhengquan Fa, Beijing: People's University Press, 2000).

Liu, Yipeng, Guilong Zhang and Chi Meng (eds), *Complete Works on the Company Law of the People's Republic of China for Practice* (Harbin: Harbin Publishing House, 1994).

Liu, Zhiying, "A Review of Chinese Stock Exchanges in Old China", 15 *Modern Bankers* (2006), available at <http://www.modernbankers.com/modernbankers/jrws/200609/20060926153010.-shtml>.

Liu, Zhunhai, "The Important Issues Relating to Corporate Law Reforms", in Liming Wang (ed.), *Forum of Civil and Commercial Laws* (Minshang Fa Qianyan Luntan, Volume 3, Beijing: People's Court Press, 2004).

Lockwood, William W., *The Economic Development of Japan: Growth and Structural Change, 1868-1938* (Princeton: Princeton University Press, 1954).

London Stock Exchange, *Our History* (London Stock Exchange webpage), available at <http://www.londonstockexchange.com/en-gb/about/cooverview/history.htm>.

Loss, Louis and Joel Seligman, *Fundamentals of Securities Regulation* (New York: Aspen Publishers, 2004).

Lu, Jing, "Institutional Defects that Hampering the Development of China's Securities Market", available at <http://www.china-review.com>.

Lu, Tong, "Corporate Governance in China" (China Center for Corporate Governance), available at <http://www.iwep.org.cn/cccg/pdf/Corporate%20G overnance%20in%20China%20%20Prof.pdf>.

Lucas, Caroline and Colin Hines, *Time to Replace Globalisation: A Green Localist Manifesto for the World Trade Organisation Ministerial* (London: The Greens/European Free Alliance, 2001).

Ma, Qingquan, The History of China's Securities Market (Zhongguo Zhengquan Shi, Beijing: CITIC Publishing House, 2003).

Ma, Shiling and Zhongfu Yao, "The Case of Lu Jiahao (Former Independent Director of Zheng Bai Wen) Versus the CSRC Will Be Heard Next Thursday", in Baisan Xie (ed.), *International Comparison of Securities Markets* (Zhengquan

Shichang De Guoji Bijiao, Volume 2, Beijing: Qinghua University Press, 2003).

Maddison, A., *Monitoring the World Economy: 1920–1992* (Paris: OECD, 1995).

Mahoney, Paul, "Is There a Cure for 'Excessive' Trading?", 81 *Virginia Law Review* (1995).

Mahoney, Paul G., "The Exchange as Regulator", 83 *Virginia Law Review* (1997).

Mahoney, Paul, "The Origins of the Blue Sky Laws: A Test of Competing Hypotheses", 46 *Journal of Law and Economics* (2003).

Manglik, Gauri, "Countering Over-confidence and Over-optimism by Creating Awareness and Experiential Learning amongst Stock Market Players", *Program for the European Association of Law and Economics 24th Annual Conference* (13–15 September 2007).

Manne, Henry G., "Mergers and Market for Corporate Control", 71(1) *Journal of Political Economics* (1965).

Manne, Henry G., "Our Two Corporation Systems: Law and Economics", 53 *Virginia Law Review* (1967).

Mao, Zedong, *Selected Works of Mao Zedong* (Beijing: Mao Zedong Xuanji, Foreign Languages Press, 1965).

Mao, Zedong, "The Chinese Revolution and the Chinese Communist Party" (1939), in Zedong Mao, *Selected Works of Mao Zedong* (Beijing: Mao Zedong Xuanji, Foreign Languages Press, 1965).

Mao, Zedong, "New Democratic Economy" (1940), in Zedong Mao, *Selected Works of Mao Zedong* (Beijing: Mao Zedong Xuanji, Foreign Languages Press, 1965).

Mao, Zedong, "The Coalition Government" (1945), in Zedong Mao, *Selected Works of Mao Zedong* (Beijing: Mao Zedong Xuanji, Foreign Languages Press, 1965).

Mao, Zedong, "The Current Situation and Our Duties" (1947), in Zedong Mao, *Selected Works of Mao Zedong* (Beijing: Mao Zedong Xuanji, Foreign Languages Press, 1965).

Marris, Robin, *The Economic Theory of "Managerial Capitalism"* (London: Macmillan, 1964).

Marsh, Paul, "Market Assessment of Company Performance", in Nicholas Dimsdale and Martha Prevezer (eds), *Capital Markets and Corporate Governance* (Oxford: Clarendon Press, 1994).

Mayer, Colin, "Stock-markets, Financial Institutions, and Corporate Performance", in Nicholas Dimsdale and Martha Prevezer (eds), *Capital Markets and Corporate Governance* (Oxford: Clarendon Press, 1994).

McArdle, Wayne P.J., "Russian Financial Crisis", available at <http://library.findlaw.com/1998/Sep/1/-128169.html>.

McEwin, R. Ian, "Law and Economics as an Approach to Corporate Law Research", 3 *Canberra Law Review* (1996).

Mei, Shenshi, *Research on the Structure of Modern Corporate Organs' Power: A Legal Analysis of Corporate Governance* (Xiandai Gongsi Quanli Gouzhao Lun: Gongsi Zhili Jiegou de Falü Fenxi, Beijing: Publishing House of China University of Political Science and Law, 1996).

Melville, Lewis, *The South Sea Bubble* (Boston: Small, Maynard & Co., 1921).

Michie, Ranald, *The London Stock Exchange: A History* (Oxford: Oxford University Press, 1999).

Midgley, Kenneth and Ronald Burns, *The Capital Market: Its Nature and Significance* (London: Macmillian, 1977).

Miyagawa, Shigeyoshi and Yoji Morita, *Lessons from Japan's Prolonged Recession* (Working Paper 44, Department of Economics and Accounting, University of Tampere, Finland, 2005).

Moley, Raymond, *The First New Deal* (New York: Harcourt, Brace and World, 1966).

Monks, Robert A.G. and Neil Minow, *Corporate Governance* (Massachusetts: Blackwell Business, 1995).

Morgan, E. Victor and W.A. Thomas, *The Stock Exchange: Its History and Functions* (London: Elek Books Limited, 1969).

Murphy, John J., *Technical Analysis of the Financial Markets: A Comprehensive Guide to Trading Methods and Applications* (New York: New York Institute of Finance, 1999).

Myant, Martin, *Transforming Socialist Economies* (Aldershot: Edward Elgar Publishing Limited, 1993).

Naidu, Anupama J., "Was Its Bite Worse Than Its Bark? The Costs Sarbanes-Oxley Imposes on German Issuers May Translate into Costs to the United States", 18 *Emory International Law Review* (2004).

Neill, Humphrey, *The Art of Contrary Thinking* (Caldwell: Caxton Printers, 1980).

Nie, Tong, "Professor Xianping Lang Claims that the Property Market is Hurting Ordinary People", *Inner Mongolia Morning Edition* (13 April 2007), available at <http://bj.house.sina.com.cn/scan/2007-04-13/1725185462.html>.

Niederhoffer, Victor, "The Speculator as Hero", *The Wall Street Journal* (10 February 1989).

Niederhoffer, Victor and Laurel Kenner, *Practical Speculation* (New Jersey: John Wiley & Sons, 2003).

Nishimura, Yoshiaki, "Economic Policy for Transition to Market Economy: Overview" (2001), available at <http://www.esri.go.jp/en/tie/russia/russia1-e.pdf>.

Nofsinger, John R., *The Psychology of Investing* (New Jersey: Prentice Hall, 2005).

Oesterle, Dale Arthur, "Securities Markets Regulation: Time to Move to a Market Based Approach", available at <http://www.cato.org/publs/pas/pa374.pdf>.

O'Hara, Maureen, "Searching for a New Centre: US Securities Markets in Transition", Q4 *the Federal Reserve Bank of Atlanta Economic Review* (2004).

O'Sullivan, Pauline, "Governance by Exit: An Analysis of the Market for Corporate Control", in Kevin Keasey et al. (eds), *Corporate Governance: Economic and Financial Issues* (London: Oxford University Press, 1997).

Olsson, Mikael, *Corporate Governance in Economies of Transition – The Case of the Slovak Republic* (Uppsala Papers in Financial History, Report No. 5, Department of Economic History, 1995), available at <http://www.diva-portal.org/diva/getDocument?urn_nbn_se_uu_diva-2357-1__fulltext.pdf>.

Opper, Sonja et al., *The Power Structure in China's Listed Companies: The Company Law and its Enforcement* (H.K. Institute of Economics and Business, Strategy Working Paper No. 1039, 2002).

Osaki, Sadakazu, "Reforming Japan's Capital Markets", 1(1) *Public Policy Review* (2005).

Osterland, Andrew, "Board Games", *CFO Magazine* (1 November 2002), available at <http://www.cfo.com/article.cfm/3007026?f=search>.

Overholt, William H., "The Lessons of the Asian and Latin American Financial Crises for Chinese Bond Markets" (2004), available at <http://www.rand.org/pubs/occassional_papers/2005/-RAND_OP117.pdf>.

Pan, Pan, "Legal Restrictions on the Right of Commercial Banks in Making Securities Investments", in Zhipan Wu and Jianjun Bai (eds), *Law and Practice of Securities Transaction* (Zhengquan Shichang Yu Falü, Beijing: China University of Political Science and Law, 2000).

Paredes, Troy, "Blinded by the Lights: Information Overload and Its Consequences for Securities Regulation", 81 *Washington University Law Quarterly* (2003).

Paredes, Troy, "The Importance of Corporate Law: Some Thoughts on Developing Equity Markets in Developing Economies", Speech at the Symposium on Judicial Independence and Legal Infrastructure at the University of the Pacific, McGeorge School of Law (October 2005).

Patrikis, Ernest T., "Japan's Big Bang Financial Reforms" (1998), available at <http://www.newyork-fed.org/newsevents/speeches/1998/ep980427.html>.

People's Bank of China, "The Functions of the PBOC", in *Introduction to the PBOC*, available at <http://www.pbc.gov.cn/renhangjianjie/zhineng.asp>.

Penrose, Edith T., *The Theory of The Growth of the Firm* (New York: Oxford University Press, 1959).

Peyrard, Josette, *La Bourse* (Paris: Librairie Vuibert, 1998).

Pinto, Arthur R., "The United States", in Arthur R. Pinto and Gustavo Visentini (eds), *The Legal Basis of Corporate Governance in Publicly Held Corporations: A Comparative Approach* (London: Kluwer Law International, 1998).

Pirrong, Stephen Craig, "The Self-Regulation of Commodity Exchanges: The Case of Market Manipulation", 38 *Journal of Law and Economics* (1995).

Pistor, Katharina and Chenggang Xu, *Governing Stock Markets in Transition Economies Lessons from China* (Center for Law and Economics Studies, Columbia Law School, Working Paper No. 262, 2004).

Porter, Michael, *Capital Choices: Changing the Way America Invests in Industry* (Washington D.C.: Council on Competitiveness and Harvard Business School, 1992).

Pring, Martin J., *Investment Psychology Explained: Classic Strategies to Beat the Markets* (New York: John Wiley & Sons, 1992).

Pritchard, Adam C., *Self-Regulation and Securities Markets* (John M. Olin Center for Law and Economics, Working Paper No. 03-004, 2003), available at <http://www.law.umich.edu/-centerandprograms/olin/papers.htm>.

Pyland, James, "Free-market Activists Distort Original Message of Adam Smith's 'invisible hand'", *Online Journal* (11 February 2006), available at <http://www.onlinejournal.com/artman/-publish/article_499.shtml>.

Qi, Shaozhou, *The Integration of EU Securities Market* (Oumeng Zhengquan Shichang Yiti Hua, Wuhan: Wuhan University Press, 2002).

Rankin, Clyde E. III, "United States Corporate Governance: Implications for Foreign Issuers", in Dennis Campbell and Susan Woodley (ed.), *Trends and Developments in Corporate Governance: The Comparative Law Yearbook of International Business Special Issue* (London: Kluwer Law International, 2003).

Ratner, David L. and Thomas Lee Hazen, *Securities Regulation in a Nutshell* 34 (St. Paul, Minnesota: West Group, 2002).

Redmond, Paul, *Companies and Securities Law: Commentary and Materials* (Sydney: LBC Information Service, 2005).

Richards, Lori, "Self-Regulation in the New Era", available at <http://www.sec.gov/news/-speech/spch398.htm>.

Samuelson, Paul, *Economics* (5th edition, New York: McGraw-Hill, 1961).

Samuelson, Paul A. and William D. Nordhaus, *Economics* (18th edtion, New York: McGraw Hill, 2005).

Secretariats of the United Nations Conference on Trade and Development and the United Nations Economic Commission for Europe, "The Russian Crisis of 1998" (Geneva, October 1998), available at <http://www.twnside.org.sg/title/1998-cn.htm>.

Securities and Exchange Commission, "Final Rule: Selective Disclosure and Insider Trading", available at <http://www.sec.gov/rules/final/33-7881.htm>.

Securities and Exchange Commission, "The Investor's Advocate: How the SEC Protects Investors, Maintains Market Integrity, and Facilitates Capital Formation", available at <http://www.sec.gov/about/whatwedo.shtml>.

Securities and Exchange Commission, "The Laws that Govern the Securities Industry", available at <http://www.sec.gov/about/laws.shtml>.

Seligman, Joel, *The Transformation of Wall Street: A History of the Securities and Exchange Commission and Modern Corporate Finance* (New York: Aspen, 2003).

Shang, Fulin (ed.), *Securities Market Regulatory Regimes: A Comparative Study* (Zhengquan Shichang Jianguan Tizhi Bijiao Yanjiu, Beijing: China Finance Press, 2006).

Shaw, Alan and Paul von Nessen, "The Legal Role of the Australian Securities Commission and the Australian Stock Exchange", in Gordon Walker (ed.), *Securities Regulation in Australia and New Zealand* (Sydney: LBC, 1998).

Shefrin, Hersh, *Beyond Greed and Fear: Understanding Behavioral Finance and the Psychology of Investing* (Boston: Harvard Business School Press, 2000).

Shen, Linying, "The Great Acceleration of the Banking Reform in 2005: From Separation Fragmented Banking to Universal Banking", *Securities Daily* (21 December 2005), available at <http://news.xinhuanet.com/fortune/2005-12/31/content_3991701.htm>.

Shen, Wenying, "MBO in the U.S. and European Countries and Trouble Caused by the Practice of MBO in China", in Baisan Xie (ed.), *International Comparison of Securities Markets* (Zhengquan Shichang De Guoji Bijiao, Volume 1, Beijing: Qinghua University Press, 2003).

Shen, Yan, "Panic Penetrates: Investors Are Confused by the Drastic Fluctuation on the Securities Market", *Shanghai Hot News Online* (24 January 2008), available at <http://news.online.sh.cn/-news/gb/content/2008-01/24/content_2207433.htm>.

Sheng, Xuejun, *Research on Disclosure System in Securities Business* (Zhengjuan Gongkai Guizhi Yanjiu, Beijing: Law Press, 2004).

Shi, Meilun, Vice-Chairperson, China Securities Regulatory Commission, "Speech at the Conference on Supervising Investment Funds" (28 November 2001), available at <http://www.csrc.org.cn/en/jsp/-detail.jsp?infoid=1059880761100&type=CMS.STD>.

Shleifer, Andrei, *Inefficient Markets: An Introduction to Behavioral Finance* (New York: University Press, 1999).

Shleifer, Andrei and Robert W. Vishny, "A Survey of Corporate Governance", 52 *The Journal of Finance* (1997).

Shui, Pi, *Who is Victimizing China's Stock Market?* (Shuizai Yurou Zhongguo Gushi, Beijing: China Economics Press, 2005).

Simon, Herbert A., "Rationality in Psychology and Economics", in Robin M. Hogarth and Melvin W. Reder (eds), *Rational Choice: The Contrast between Economics and Psychology* (Chicago: The University of Chicago Press, 1986).

Smith, Adam, *The Wealth of Nations* (Oxford: Clarendon Press, 1976).

Smith, Adam, *An Inquiry into the Nature and Causes of the Wealth of Nations* (New York: Modern Library, 1994).

Sobel, Robert, *The Money Manias: The Eras of Great Speculation in America, 1770–1970* (New York: Weybright and Talley, 1974).

Soderquist, Larry D., *Understanding the Securities Laws* (translated by Xuanzhi Ju and Yunhui Zhang, Beijing: Law Press, 2004).

Staines, Paul, *The Benefits of Speculation: A Bond Market Vigilante Replies to Will Hutton's The State We're in* 1 (article written for Libertarian Alliance, 1996), available at <http://libertarian.co.uk/-lapubs/econn/econn069.pdf>.

State Environmental Protection Administration, *2004 China's Environmental Situation Brief.*

State of Wisconsin Department of Financial Institutions, "A Brief History of Securities Regulation", available at <http://www.wdfi.org/fi/securities/regexemp/history.htm>.

Steinberg, Marc I., *Understanding Securities Law* (USA: Lexis Nexis Matthew Bender, 1996).

Stigler, George J., "Public Regulation of the Securities Markets", 37(2) *The Journal of Business* (1964).

Stiglitz, Joseph E., *Globalization and Its Discontent* (New York: Norton, 2002).

Stiglitz, Joseph E., "Globalization and Growth in Emerging Markets and the New Economy", 25 *Journal of Policy Modeling* (2003).

Stiglitz, Joseph E., *The Roaring Nineties, Why We're Paying the Price for the Greediest Decade in History* (London: Penguin Books, 2003).

Stiglitz Joseph E., "Social Justice and Global Trade", 169(2) *Far Eastern Economic Review* 18 (2006).

Stiglitz, Joseph E., *Making Globalization Work* (New York: W.W. Norton and Company, 2006).

Stiglitz, Joseph E. and Thea Lee et al., "Taming Global Capitalism Anew", *The Nation* (17 April 2006 issue), available at <http://www.thenation.com/doc/2006417/forum>.

Stout, Lynn, "Are Stock Markets Costly Casinos? Disagreement, Market Failure, and Securities Regulation", 81 *Virginia Law Review* (1995).

Stringham, Edward, "The Emergence of the London Stock Exchange as a Self-Policing Club", 17(2) *Journal of Private Enterprise* (2002).

Sun, Shangqing, "The Dominance of Public Ownership is the Foundation of Fairness", *Economic Reference* (*Jing Ji Can Kao Bao*, 24 September 1994).

Sun, Shangqing, "Market Economy and Development of Productivity", 6 *Economic Studies* (*Jing Ji Yan Jiu*, 1996).

Sun, Zheng, Zhe Juan and Yongqing Hu, *Innovations and Regulatory Studies of Emerging Capital Markets* (Xinxing Ziben Shichang De Zhidu Chuangxin He Guifan Yanjiu, Shanghai: Shanghai Economics and Finance University Press: 2005).

Sutherland, Peter, Chairman, Goldman Sachs International and Chairman, Overseas Development Council, *The 1998 Per Jacobsson Lecture: Managing the International Economy in an Age of Globalisation* (21 October 1998), available at <www.imf.org/external/am/1998/perj.htm>.

Tafara, Ethiopis, "Speech by SEC Staff: U.S. Perspective on Accountancy Regulation and Reforms", available at <http://www.sec.gov/news/speech/spch070803et.htm>.

Tamaki, Norio, *Japanese Banking: A History: 1859–1959* (London: Cambridge University Press, 1995).

Teng, Tai, *Value Creation and the Growth of Securities Companies* (Jiazhi Chuangzao Yu Zhengquang Gongsi De Chengzhang, Shanghai: Shanghai University of Finance and Economy, 2003).

Thomas, Stephen C. and Chen Ji, "Privatizing China: The Stock Markets and Their Role in Corporate Reform", 58 *China Business Review* (1 July 2004).

Thurlow, Bradbury K., *Rediscovering the Wheel: Contrary Think and Investment Strategy* (New York: Fraser Publishing Company, 1981).

Tian Tain, "Hot Money Hits the Capital Market" available at <http://finance.news.tom.com/1001/-1002/20031112-29011.html>.

Tong, Daochi, "Securities Market Reform in China: Advancing Corporate Governance", at *Asia Perspective Seminar: Advancing Corporate Governance Reform in Asia* (28 February 2002).

Tong, Daochi, "Building Up a Clean Corporate Culture in an Era of Economic Growth and Development: the Role of Corporate Governance", China Securities Regulatory Commission Luncheon Speech, at *2005 Leadership Forum: Successes Through Ethical Governance.*

Unknown Grass, "'A Hundred Years' History of China's Capital Market", *East Blog*, <http://blog2.eastmoney.com/wswzfy123,528407.html>.

US Securities and Exchange Commission (SEC), "The Investor's Advocate: How the SEC Protects Investors and Maintains Market Integrity", available at <http://www.sec.gov/about/-whatwedo.shtml>.

Vasiliev, D., "Capital Market Development in Russia", available at <http://siteresources.worldbank.org/-ECAEXT/Resources/VassilievPaper.pdf>.

Vasilyev, D.V., "Corporate Governance in Russia: Is There Any Chance of Improvement?", available at <http://www.imf.org/external/pubs/ft/seminar/2000/invest/pdf/vasil2.pdf>.

Venys, Ladislav, *The Political Economy of Privatization in Czechoslovakia* (Carnegie Council/DRT International Privatization Project, 1991), available at <http://www.cceia.org/resources/-publications/privatization_project/0002.html/_res/id=sa_File1/2_Ladislav_Venys.pdf>.

Vitols, Sigurt, *The Transition from Banks to Markets in the German and Japanese Financial Systems* 10 (Working Group on Insts., States, and Mkts., Discussion Paper No. P 02-901, 2002).

Walter, Carl E. and Fraser J.T. Howie, *Privatizing China: The Stock Markets and Their Role in Corporate Reform* (Singapore: John Wiley & Son (Asia) Pty. Ltd, 2003).

Wang, Baoshu, *The Theory of Economic Law* (Jing Ji Fa Yuan Li, Beijing: Social Sciences Documentation Publishing House, 2004).

Wang, Baoshu and Qinzhi Cui, *The Theory of the Chinese Company Law* (Zhongguo Gongsi Fa Yuanli, Beijing: Social Science Literature Publishing House, 1998).

Wang, Chao, "Redesigning China's Regulatory System over Securities Business in Law", Wu, Zhipan and Jianjun Bai (eds), *Law and Practice of Securities Transaction* (Beijing: China University of Political Science and Law Press, 2000).

Wang, Jiangyu, "China's Securities Experiment: The Challenge of Globalization", available at <http://www.eastlaw.net/research/securities/securities-no1.htm>.

Wang, Jing and Biyan Teng, *Comparative Study of Securities Law* (ZhengQuan Fa BiJiao Yan Jiu, Beijing: China University of People's Public Securities Press, 2004).

Wang, Xin and Xiangpin Bian, "The Goals and Efficiency of the Banking Law and Regulating Banking Competition", in Zhipan Wu (ed.), *Jurists in Economic Law* (Jingji Fa Xuejia, Beijing: Beijing University Press, 2003).

Wang, Yuling, "Wang Lianzhou: the Amendments to Securities Investment Fund Law", *Xinhua News Net* (10 January 2008), available at <http://news.xinhuanet.com/newscenter/2008-01/10/content_-7400682.htm>.

Watkins, Kevin et al, *Rigged Rules and Double Standards: Trade, Globalisation and the Fight Against Poverty* (Washington D.C.: Oxfam International, 2002).

Wei, Yuwa, *Investing in China: Law and Practices of Joint Ventures* (Sydney: Federation Press, 2000).

Wei, Yuwa, "The Historical Development of the Corporation and Corporate Law in China", 14 *Australian Journal of Corporate Law* (2002).

Wei, Yuwa, "Seeking a Practicable Chinese Model of Corporate Governance", 10 *Michigan State University-DCL Journal of International Law* (2002).

Wei, Yuwa, *Comparative Corporate Governance: A Chinese Perspective* (Alphen aan den Rijn: Kluwer Law International, 2003).

Wei, Yuwa, "The Development of the Securities Market and Regulation in China", 27(3) *Loyola of Los Angeles International and Comparative Law Review* (2005).

Wei, Yuwa, "Securities Regulation and Corporate Governance in China", in *Enhancing Corporate Accountability Prospects and Challenges: Conference Proceedings* (Corporate Accountability Conference, Monash University, Melbourne, Australia 8–9 February 2006).

Wei, Yuwa, "Directors' Duties under Chinese Law – A Comparative Review", 3(1) *University of New England Law Journal* (2006).

Wei, Yuwa, "Volatility of China's Securities Market and Corporate Governance", 29(2) *Suffolk Transnational Law Review* (2006).

Wei, Yuwa, "Maximising the External Governance Function of the Securities Market: A Chinese Experience", 3 *International Company and Commercial Law Review* (London: Sweet & Maxwell, 2008).

Wen, Dale, "China Copes with Globalization: A Mixed Review" (A Report by the International Forum on Globalization, 2006), available at <www.ifg.org>.

White, Richard, "The Review of Investor Protection – Gower Report", 47 *The Modern Law Review* (1984), available at <http://www.jstor.org/view/00267961/ap030246/03a00030/0>.

Williams, Frank J, *If you Must Speculate Learn the Rules* (New York: Fraser Publishing Company, 1981).

Wincott, Harold, *The Stock Exchange* (London: Sampson Low, Marston & Co., 1946).

Wood, Arnold S., "Fatal Attractions for Money Managers", *Financial Analysts Journal* (1989).

Wood, Arnold S., "Behavioral Risk: Anecdotes and Disturbing Evidence", *The Journal of Investing* (1997).

World Bank, *China, Reform and the Role of the Plan in the 1990s* (Washington D.C.: The World Bank, 1992).

World Bank, *China's Management of Enterprise Assets: The State as Shareholder* (Report No. 16265-CHA, June 5, 1997).

World Bank, *Transition, the First Ten Years: Analysis and Lessons for Eastern Europe and the Former Soviet Union* (Washington D.C., 2002), available at <http://siteresources.worldbank.org/-ECAEXT/Resources/complete.pdf>.

World Bank, *WDI-CDROM* 2003.

Wu, Amy, "PRC's Commercial Banking System: Is Universal Banking a Better Model?", 37 *Columbia Journal of Transnational Law* (1999).

Wu, Hong and Wei Hu, *Market Regulation Law – Basic Theory and System of Market Regulation Law* (Shichang Jianguan Fa Lun – Shichang Jianguan Fa De Jichu Lilun Yu Jiben Zhidu, Beijing: Peking University Press, 2006).

Wu, Jinglian, *Where to Seek Great Wisdom* (Hechu Xunqiu Da Zhihui, Beijing: Sanlian Press, 1997).

Wu, Xiaobing, Wenjun Liu and Ye Chen, "Who Pulled the Trigger?", available at <http://zhoukan.hexun.com/Magazine/ShowArticle.aspx?ArticleId=11963>.

Wu, Zhipan (ed.), *Jurists in Economic Law* (Jingji Fa Xuejia, Beijing: Beijing University Press, 2003).

Wu, Zhipan and Jianjun Bai (eds), *Law and Practice of Securities Transaction* (Beijing: China University of Political Science and Law Press, 2000).

Xie, Baisan, "China Needs not to Go with the Tide on the US Securities Market", available at <http://cn.biz.yahoo.com/070317/16/l9c6.html>.

Xie, Baisan, *China's Securities Market* (Zhongguo Zhengquan Shichang, Guangzhou: Guangdong Economics Press, 2002).

Xie, Baisan (ed.), *International Comparison of Securities Markets* (Zhengquan Shichang De Guoji Bijiao, Volume 1, Beijing: Qinghua University Press, 2003).

Xie, Baisan (ed.), *International Comparison of Securities Markets* (Zhengquan Shichang De Guoji Bijiao, Volume 2, Beijing: Qinghua University Press, 2003).

Xie, Baisan, "Huge Deficits of Shen Kang Jia Reveal the Serious Problem in the Company's Share Issue", in Baisan Xie (ed.), *International Comparison of*

Securities Markets (Zhengquan Shichang De Guoji Bijiao, Volume 1, Qinghua University Press, 2003).

Xie, Baisan and Meiting Lu, "The Pricing Approaches of IPO in Some Other Countries and the Arduous Reforms of Issuance of New Shares in China", in Baisan Xie, *International Comparison of Securities Market* (Zhengquan Shichang De Guoji Bijiao, Volume 1, Beijing: China University of Political Science and Law Press, 2003).

Xie, Baisan, Xuelai Dai and Lan Xu, "A Comparative Study of Chinese and US Securities Markets", in Baisan Xie (ed.), *International Comparison of Securities Markets* (Zhengquan Shichang De Guoji Bijiao, Volume 1, Beijing: Qinghua University Press, 2003).

Xie, Shujiang, *China's Capital Market: An Analysis Based on the Theory of Competition* (Zhongguo De Ziben Shichang: Jiyu Jingzheng Lilun De Fenxi, Beijing: China Finance and Economy Press, 2004).

Xie, Zengyi, Conflicts of Interest in Demutualized Stock Exchanges (Gongsi Zhi Zhengquan Jiaoyi Sou De Liyi Chongtu, Beijing: Social Sciences Academic Press, 2007).

Xinhua News Agency, "The Companies that Received Penalties from CSRC for Making Misleading Disclosure", in *Zhe Jiang Daily* (18 January, 2002).

Xinhua Press, "China Selects Firms for Experiments to Tackle Major Problem Facing Sluggish", available at <http://english.people.com.cn/200505/10/eng20050510_184242.html>.

Xinhua Press, "Chinese Stock Market Witnesses Unexpected Bear Period", available at <http://english.people.com.cn/200406/16/eng20040616_146483.html>.

Xinhua Press, "Poor Governance Blamed for Securities Market", available at <http://english.people-.com.cn/200504/03/eng20050403_179230.html>.

Xu, Jiansheng, "Commercial Laws and Enterprise Development in the Republican China", *China History Education Net*, available at <http://hist.cersp.com/kczy/sxdt/200705/6394_2.html>.

Xu, Yi, *The History of Debts Borrowing by the Qing Government* (Qingdai Waizhai Shi Lun, Beijing: China Press of Finance and Economy, 1996).

Yakovlev, Andrei, "Evolution of Corporate Governance in Russia: Government Policy Vs. Real Incentives of Economic Agents", 16(4) *Post-Communist Economies* (2004).

Yan, Bin and Xia Wang, "The Study of the Fee Rate of Open-ended Securities Investment Funds in China", in China Securities Association, *The Research on Innovative Topics concerning the Development of China's Securities Market* (Zhongguo Zhengquan Shichang Fazhan Qianyan Weiti Yanjiu, Beijing: China Press of Finance and Economy, 2005).

Yang, Liang, *A Comparison of the Regulatory Systems of the Capital Adequacy of Securities Companies*, in Zhipan Wu and Jianjun Bai, *Law and Practice of Securities Transaction* (Beijing: China University of Political Science and Law, 2000).

Yang, Xinying et al, "The Report on Performance Evaluation of Sino-Foreign Securities Investment Funds", in China Securities Association, *The Research on Innovative Topics concerning the Development of China's Securities Market* (Beijing: China Press of Finance and Economy, 2005).

Yang, Zhihua, *A Study of Securities Regulatory System* (Zhengquan Jianguan Xitong Yanjiu, Beijing, China University of Political Science and Law, 1995).

Yao, Chengxi, *Stock Market and Futures Market in the People's Republic of China* (New York: Oxford University Press, 1998).

Ye, Shan, "An Analysis on Policies relating to Disposing Bad Loans, the Restrictions, and Perfecting the Relevant Laws", in Zhipan Wu (ed.), *Jurists in Economic Law* (Jingji Fa Xuejia, Beijing: Beijing University Press, 2003).

Yen, Zhongli, "Hot Money Attacks China", available at <http://news.sina.com. cn/c/2005-12-31/11348743853.shtml>.

Yiannaki, Simona, "Redefining Approaches of Globalization for Today's Corporate and State Governance", available at <http:papers.ssrn.com/so13/papers. cfm?abstract_id=980961>.

Yu, Yongding, "China: The Case for Capital Control", in Walden Bello, Nicola Bullard and Kamal Malhotra (eds) *Global Finance: New Thinking on Regulating Speculative Capital Markets* (London and New York: Zed Books, 2002).

Zeng, Xianyi, *Securities Law* (Zhengquan Fa, Beijing: the Publishing House of the People's University, 2000).

Zhang, Chunting, "A Brief History of China's Securities Market: Before the Economic Reforms", *The Forum of China's Economic History*, available at <http://economy.guoxue.com/article.php/73>.

Zhang, Chunting, "A Brief History of China's Securities Market: The Late Qing Period", *The Forum of China's Economic History*, available at <http://economy. guoxue.com/article.php/71>.

Zhang, Chunting, "A Brief History of China's Securities Market: The Republican Period (1)", *The Forum of China's Economic History*, available at <http:// www.zlunwen.com/financial/stock/4079.htm>.

Zhang, Chunting, "A Brief History of China's Securities Market: The Republican Period (2)", *The Forum of China's Economic History*, available at <http:// economy.guoxue.com/article.php/71>.

Zhang, Ning, *Study of Allfinanz Model* (Quan Jinrong Moshi Yanjiu, Beijing: China Social Science Press, 2006).

Zhang, Shiyuan and Cheng Liu, "Economic Safety Issues from an Economic Law Perspective", in Zhipan Wu (ed.), *Jurists in Economic Law* (Jingji Fa Xuejia, Beijing: Beijing University Press, 2003).

Zhang, Wenkui, "The Role of China's Securities Market in SOE Reform and Private Sector Development", available at <http://www.tcf.or.jp/data/20020307-08_ Wengkui_Zhang.pdf>.

Zhang, Wenmin et al (eds), *The Great Economic Debate in China* (Zhongguo Jingji Da Lunzhan, Beijing: Economic Management Press: 1997).

Zhang, Xudong, "How to Evaluate the Effect of the Share Reform", *Xinhua News Net* (15 May 2005), available at <http://news.xinhuanet.com/stock/2005-05/15/content_2961394.htm>.

Zhang, Yong, "Shanghai Stock Exchange 1990", *Economic Observation Daily* (5 August 2007), available at <http://www.p5w.net/stock/news/zonghe/200708/t1131816.htm>.

Zhang, Yujun, "Expanding the Channels of Direct Investment", *China Securities Daily* (23 July 2002, at page 10).

Zhang, Yurun, "Rationality and Mechanisms of Securities Regulation", in Zhipan Wu (ed.), *Jurists in Economic Law* (Jingji Fa Xuejia, Beijing: Beijing University Press, 2003).

Zhao, Di, "What Are Securities Investments Funds?", available at <http://book.jrj.com.cn/book/-TextBookDetail/12467.htm>.

Zhao, Linghua, "An Analysis of the Forms of Irregular Capital Flows in China", *International Economic Review* (1999).

Zheng, Shunyan, "The Legal Analysis of Fund Raising by China's Securities Company", in Zhipan Wu and Jianjun Bai, *Law and Practice of Securities Transaction* (Zhengqua Shichang Yu Falü, Beijing: China University of Political Science and Law, 2000).

Zhou, Daojong, "The Securities Market is Facing Good Opportunities" *Securities Daily* (19 November 2007), available at <http://stock.jrj.com.cn/news/2007-11-19/000002940708.html>.

Zhu, Jinqing, *Securities Law* (Zhengquan Fa, Beijing, Beijing University Press, 2007).

Zhu, Kemin, *Theoretical Analysis on Share Structure in China's Securities Companies* (Woguo Zhengquan Gongsi Guquan Jiegou Lilun Fenxi, Shanghai: Shanghai University of Finance and Economy Press, 2006).

Zhu, Sanzhu, *Securities Regulation in China* (New York: Brill, 2001).

Legislation, Reports and Guidelines

China Securities Regulatory Commission, *Code of Corporate Governance*, available at <http://www.csrc.gov.cn/en>.

China Securities Regulatory Commission and State Economic and Trade Commission, *Code of Corporate Governance for Listed Companies in China* (7 January 2001), available at <http://www.csrc.gov.cn/en/jsp/detail.jsp?infoid=1061968722100&type=CMS.STD>.

China Securities Regulatory Commission, *Implementing Procedure on Listing Suspension and Termination of Listed Companies Operating at Loss*, available at <http://www.csrc.gov.cn/en/jsp/detail.jsp?infoid=1061948161100&type=CMS.STD>.

China Securities Regulatory Commission, *the Opinions about Standardizing Shareholders' Meetings* (1998).

China Securities Regulatory Commission, *the Guidelines for Listed Companies* (1998).

China Securities Regulatory Commission, the 1999 *Some Opinions about Further Strengthening the Administration over Securities Companies.*

China Securities Regulatory Commission, *Suggestions on Regulating the General Meetings of Listed Companies* (2000).

China Securities Regulatory Commission, the 2001 *Revised Measures Concerning Suspension and Termination the Listing of the Shares of Lose Making Listed Companies.*

China Securities Regulatory Commission, *the Provisional Methods of Administrating the Securities of Securities Companies*, available at <http://www.jincao.com/fa/law09.50.htm>.

China Securities Regulatory Commission, the People's Bank of China and State Administration of Foreign Currency, the 2006 *Measures of Administrating Investments in Chinese Securities by Qualified Foreign Institutional Investors.*

China Securities Regulatory Commission and People's Bank of China, *the Provisional Measures on Administration of Domestic Securities Investments of Qualified Foreign Institutional Investors* (2002).

China Securities Regulatory Commission and China Economy and Trade Commission, *Announcement of Carrying Out Inspection on the Governance of Listed Companies* (13 May 2002), available at <http://www.csrc.gov.cn/en>.

Commission of the European Communities, *Modernising Company Law and Enhancing Corporate Governance in the European Union – A Plan to Move Forward* (2003).

Commonwealth of Australia, *Financial System Inquiry Final Report* (1997).

Financial Services and Markets Act 2000 (UK).

Glass-Steagal Act (US).

People's Bank of China, the 1990 *Provisional Measures of Administering Securities Companies.*

People's Bank of China, the 1991 *Announcement about Strengthening the Administration over the Examination and Approval of Securities Investment Funds in China.*

People's Bank of China, the 1993 *Emergency Announcement about Prohibiting the Activities of Irregularly Issuing Shares of Investment Funds and Trust Units.*

People's Congress, the 1993 *Company Law of the People's Republic of China.*

People's Congress, the 1995 *Commercial Banking Law of the People's Republic of China.*

People's Congress, the 1998 *Securities Law of the People's Republic of China* (revised in 2005).

People's Congress, the 2003 *Law of Securities Investment Funds of the People's Republic of China.*

Sarbanes-Oxley Act of 2002 (US).

Securities Commission of the State Council (China), the 1997 *Provisional Administrative Measures on Securities Investment Funds.*

State Council (China), the 1950 *Interim Regulations for Joint State-Private Enterprises.*

State Council (China), the 1956 *Provisional Regulations for Fix Interest in Joint State-Private Enterprises.*

State Council (China), the 1981 *Regulations of the People's Republic of China on Government Bonds.*

State Council (China), the 1993 *Shares Regulations.*

State Council (China), the 1993 *Antifraud Regulations.*

State Council (China), the 2001 *Measures of Administering Stock Exchanges.*

State Council (China), *the Administrative Law of the Banking Sector* (2003).

Supreme Court (China), *Some Rules about Hearing False Statements on the Securities Market* (2003).

Index

For Product Safety Concerns and Information please contact our EU
representative GPSR@taylorandfrancis.com
Taylor & Francis Verlag GmbH, Kaufingerstraße 24, 80331 München, Germany

www.ingramcontent.com/pod-product-compliance
Ingram Content Group UK Ltd.
Pitfield, Milton Keynes, MK11 3LW, UK
UKHW021013180425
457613UK00020B/931